JOURNAL FOR THE STUDY OF THE OLD TESTAMENT
SUPPLEMENT SERIES
20

Editors
David J A Clines
Philip R Davies
David M Gunn

Department of Biblical Studies
The University of Sheffield
Sheffield S10 2TN
England

THE PSALMS
OF THE
SONS OF KORAH

MICHAEL D. GOULDER

Journal for the Study of the Old Testament
Supplement Series, 20

Copyright © 1982 JSOT Press
ISSN 0309-0787
ISBN 0 905774 40 X (cloth)
ISBN 0 905774 41 8 (paper)

Published by
JSOT Press
Department of Biblical Studies
The University of Sheffield
Sheffield S10 2TN
England

Printed and bound in Great Britain at
The Camelot Press Ltd, Southampton

British Library Cataloguing in Publication Data

Goulder, M.D.
      The psalms of the Sons of Korah.— (Journal for
      the Study of the Old Testament. Supplement
      Series, ISSN 0309-0787; 20)
      I. Title   II. Series
      223'.206   BS1430.2

      ISBN 0-905774 40 X
      ISBN 0-905774 41 8 PbK

CONTENTS

ILLUSTRATIONS

Plates

Figures

Plates I, II, III, and IV, and Figs. 3 and 4 are copyright Tel Dan Excavations. Reproduced by kind permission of Professor A. Biran.

Plate V was first published in *IEJ* 19 (1959) by Y. Yadin. Reproduced with permission.

PREFACE

Disagreements on the interpretation of the Psalms, of which there are many, arise in large part from their apparent lack of context. For most of this century they have been treated as so many independent units, flotsam washed up by the tides of the late centuries before our era. Fame and acclaim have attended those who could convincingly group these scattered units into lots of similar form, and who could infer from the evidence of such groups the setting they once held in Israelite life. But one man's selection and interpretation have often seemed as good as another's, and the permutations in exegesis have turned out to be large. I have tried a different approach, by treating more seriously the context given to the psalms in the Psalter; that is, the collections in which they are gathered, the order in which they stand, and the technical notes—Maskil, Selah, על־ששנים, etc.—in the text. These matters are, of course, noted in all standard works, and a few authors, like John Peters and Gunther Wanke, have treated them as important; but I think that mine is the first attempt to offer a comprehensive theory of the psalms in which these contextual matters are determinative. I have begun with one of the earliest and most interesting collections, the psalms of the Sons of Korah, to which, for reasons to be explained, I have added Ps. 89; and I might suitably have appended a sub-title, A Study in the Psalter, to stress the importance of the given context in my exposition. It will not surprise the reader to find that a new exegetical principle yields an overall view of the psalms markedly different from those currently on offer.

The first problem facing all interpreters of the Psalms is the text; historically the widest differences of attitude have obtained, and still do. One scholar may reflect that all texts are liable to scribal corruption; that we have ample evidence of the inadequacies of the Massoretic Text in I Samuel; that the vocalisation can be held to be authoritative only for the text of AD 900; that we have a duty to make sense of the psalm; and that we shall sometimes therefore be led to desert the Hebrew, both in vowels and consonants, with or without the support of the Versions or Targums. Another may consider that there has been preserved to us only a fraction of the living classical Hebrew; that our psalms are poetic, and perhaps from an early period and away from Jerusalem; and that in such a situation one cannot expect always to supply exact parallels to any usage; that many of the psalms were originally in liturgical use, and are likely to have been preserved because they continued to be in liturgical use; that under such conditions oral tradition of vowels is far from valueless; and that in all variant readings the harder text should be preferred. While it can never be held that the first view is wrong, it is clear that we can never have confidence in an interpretation which requires conjectures, or the preference of easier readings; and especially will this be true when (as in 49) the rate of alterations to the MT, even in a committee translation like NEB, approaches one per verse, or where (as in 87) the order of the verses has been drastically changed. My contextual interpretation has this to commend it: it claims *always* to make sense of the MT. I do not of course think that the MT always represents the composition of the original author; but I think it does so much more often than is generally allowed, and that when it does not, it is the adaptation of an original of which traces survive, made for reasons which are readily understandable.

When reading the work of others, I have sometimes found it a difficulty to be sure what reading was being followed, and when somewhat unusual translations were being adopted. I have therefore made it a practice to print the Revised Version margin translation (1881) at the head of each section of commentary. Words not in the Hebrew, italicised in RV, are shown in brackets. All changes to the translation are shown by putting the Hebrew word in parenthesis. Words which I take to be added to the original by the MT are indicated by square brackets; in the rare cases where I take a word to have been removed in the tradition, I have said so in the comments. The scholarship and integrity of the RV translators give much cause for admiration, and I hope that my work may appear on the centenary of theirs as a small tribute. I hope also that in this way my book will be usable not only by specialists but also by students with only a basic knowledge of Hebrew. The use of the RV entails the English numbering, so those using the Hebrew Bible will have to make an adjustment, usually the adding of one to the verse number in the Psalter.

When so much has been written on the Psalms, it is necessary to be sparing in discussion of the opinions of others. I have usually given the line of interpretation of a psalm taken by a selection of commentators: Delitzsch, Duhm and Kirkpatrick from the pre-form-critical period; Gunkel and Mowinckel, and J.P. Peters, from the towering '20s; Kraus, Weiser, Eaton and Dahood from the '50s and '60s; Anderson, Rogerson and McKay, and Jacquet from the present decade. Their names, and those of others cited occasionally, refer to their commentaries as specified in the Bibliography, *ad loc*. I have avoided discussions of proposals for emending the text, and for idiosyncratic philological suggestions, except in particular *cruces*, as these are readily available elsewhere, e.g. in Anderson or Kraus (5th edn.).

I am grateful to my colleague John Eaton, who with characteristic generosity has read the typescript, and given me much valued advice; I am sorry to note that sometimes I have disagreed with details in his excellent writings, but his influence has been profound. David Cook has also kindly read Chapter 3, and commented helpfully. I am grateful to the British Academy, who provided for me to visit Dan and other sites from its Small Grants Research Fund in the Humanities; to Prof. A. Biran for kindly permitting me to use his photographs and drawings; to Allen Parker, my head of Department, for his constant support; and to my adult students, who have often asked me common-sense questions which I had missed, and improved the book beyond measure.

December, 1980   Michael Goulder

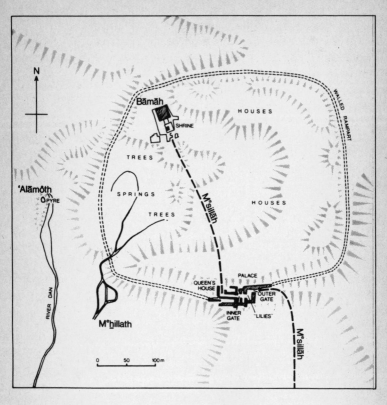

Fig. 1 DAN IN THE TIME OF AMOS

Natural features, and those shaded, from A. Biran, *Biblical Archeologist* 43
(1980), p. 170. For the names, see text. The course of the road, and of the
south-west part of the rampart and wall, is approximate.

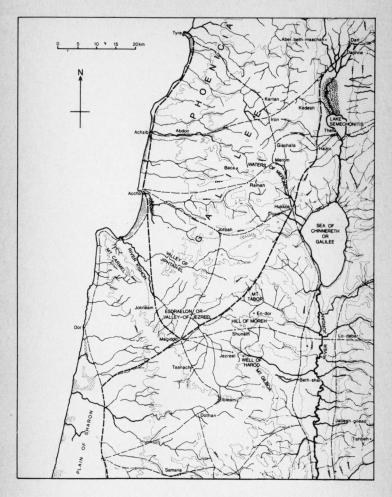

Fig. 2 THE ROADS IN (NORTHERN) ISRAEL

The roads follow Y. Aharoni, *The Land of the Bible*, ch. 3, and especially the
map on p. 44. The main roads are in bold type.

xiii

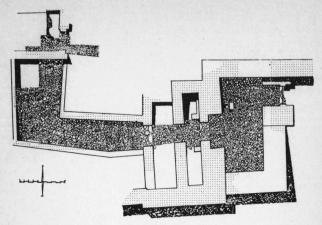

Fig. 3 THE NINTH-CENTURY GATE COMPLEX AT DAN

Plan from A. Biran, 'Dan, Tel,' in M. Avi-Yonah (ed.), *Encyclopaedia of Archaeological Excavations in the Holy Land*. The site of the throne is opposite the outer gate.

Fig. 4 RECONSTRUCTION OF THE BAMAH AT DAN

The platform is almost sixty feet square, and was built to this size in the time of Ahab. It lies to the north side of the city, with the steps on the city side. There was a wall on the east and west sides, and temple buildings on the south side, enclosing a *temenos*. The rising slopes of Hermon form a natural amphitheatre from which tens of thousands of Israelites could watch and participate in the ritual.

I

A SEQUENCE OF FESTAL PSALMS

The oldest commentary on the meaning of the psalms is the manner of their arrangement in the Psalter: that is, the collections in which they are grouped, the technical and historical notes they carry, and the order in which they stand. Some of these data (many of the historical notes, for instance) are certainly irrelevant, and it might be that all such commentary were merely trivial. The collections might be just a handful of laments, hymns, etc., that happened to be in the repertoire of fourth century Levites; and the order might be no more significant than the alphabetical order in which church hymns may be arranged. But it cannot be sensible to *assume* that this is so, as is often done; I do not know a commentary, of those written in the last fifty years, which treats the existence of the Korah collection seriously.

An examination of these ancient indicators may seem to be more urgent in view of the impasse in which psalm criticism has been for the last half-century, and in which it shows limited signs of progress. The great debate between Hermann Gunkel and Sigmund Mowinckel, which fills the incomparable pages of the latter's *Psalmenstudien* (1921-4) and the former's *Einleitung in die Psalmen* (1933),[1] has degenerated into a discussion reminiscent of the book of Job, in which both sides repeat their positions and the argument never advances. Books on the Psalms tend to follow either Gunkel, as do Edward Kissane (1953), Hans-Joachim Kraus (1960, 5th edn, 1978), Claus Westermann (ET 1966) and Louis Jacquet (1976-8); or Mowinckel, as do Aubrey Johnson (1955, 1979), Artur Weiser (ET 1962), John Eaton (1967, 1976) and most Scandinavians. A. A. Anderson (1972), John Rogerson and John McKay (1977) and others tread a rather uncomfortable middle ground. Anything that would help resolve this blockage should be welcome, and here at least is a possible means of advance. My hope is that it will carry us a long way towards a new general theory of the Psalter.

I. THE PSALMS OF THE SONS OF KORAH

I have chosen to begin with the Korah psalms because of their great
interest, and because they display with comparative clarity features
which underlie several of the other collections; and in addition they
have a number of distinctive linguistic features, so that the collection
can be seen not to be adventitious. They form a manageable unit. The
heading לבני קרה, 'of the sons of Korah,' stands before eleven psalms:
42, 44-49, 84-85, 87-88. There is, however, so much in common
between 42 and 43 that almost all commentaries bracket the two
together, and the absence of the heading in 43 is often explained by
their being substantially one psalm.[2] The Korah psalms themselves
may thus be said to comprise two broken sequences: 42-49, with the
(?accidental) omission of 43; and 84-88, less the interpolated 'David'
psalm 86.[3] But there are reasons for treating 89 along with the Korah
psalms, despite its lacking the heading. It is headed 'Maskil of Ethan
the Ezrahite,' and the heading of 88 ends 'Maskil of Heman the
Ezrahite,' phrases which are peculiar to these two psalms in the
Psalter. In addition, it is placed as the last psalm in Book III, and thus
follows the second Korah sequence 84-88 (less 86), and completes it, so
to speak. These seem to be two indications that whoever arranged
Book III understood 89 to have an association with the Korah psalms;
and there is a third indication, which I shall set out shortly, in that
some of the phrases in the plea of 88 seem to be strongly echoed in the
opening assertions of 89. I have therefore extended the study of this
book to include thirteen psalms: twelve Korah psalms, 42-49, 84-85
and 87-88, and one associated Ethan psalm, 89. 89 is not a member of
the Korah collection, but it is associated; it has, as we shall see,
important differences as well as important similarities with the Korah
group.

The title presents little difficulty. ל is so commonly found on
artefacts[4] with the meaning 'belonging to,' that this forms a natural
interpretation here. The psalms belonged to a group called the sons of
Korah, probably the Korah family; we cannot be more specific and
press the ל to mean 'composed by the sons of Korah' (ל *auctoris*),
although ultimately the one might imply the other. The identity of the
sons of Korah is discussed in Chapter 3.

A more immediate question is the status of the collection. Was there
in fact a single collection, or were there two, one 42-49, where the
name of God is predominantly Elohim, and one 84-85, 87-88, preferring the name Yahweh? And are they (an) adventitious collection(s)

in that the sons of Korah collected them in a late period, as children collect stones on the beach; or are they (an) ancient collection(s), really belonging together, like the Vermeers in the Rijksmuseum at Amsterdam? Gunther Wanke pointed to the presence of the technical terms מזמור, שיר, משכיל, which stand at the head of all the Korah psalms (but 43), both the first sequence and the second, in contradistinction from the Asaph psalms, 50, 73-83, where they are in every case missing; and concluded that the two Korah sequences belonged together.[5] But to establish that the collection is meaningful, it is necessary to look at the content.

The group is held together first by a number of expressions found in it exclusively or predominantly. (i) אל־חי 'the living God,' occurs twice in the Psalter, both times in the Korah psalms, 42:2 and 84:2. It comes twice elsewhere in the OT, Hos. 1:10 (Heb. 2:1) and Josh. 3:10. (ii) אֶרְאֶה פְּנֵי אֱלֹהִים, 42:2, and אֵרָאֶה אֶל־אֱלֹהִים, 84:7, are both almost universally understood as alterations of reverence for the Qal, 'see God.' The expression is not uncommon elsewhere, mainly for attendance at the festivals (Exod. 23:15; 34:24; Deut. 16:16; 31:11; Isa. 1:12); but is found only here in the Psalter. (iii) לחץ, 'oppression,' comes in the Psalter only at 42:9; 43:2; 44:24. (iv) משכנות(יך), '(thy) tabernacles,' for a shrine, comes in the OT in Pss. 43:3; 84:1; 87:2 ('shrines'), 132:5, and משכני in Ps. 46:4, Ezek. 37:27. (v) God's people is referred to as 'Jacob' throughout the Korah sequence: at 44:4; 85:2, not to mention the ambiguous phrase 'the God of Jacob.' It is never spoken of as 'Israel,' which does not occur; 'the Holy One of Israel' comes in 89:18. I cannot think of another unit in the OT where the people is always called Jacob and never Israel. (vi) עיר אלהים, 'city of God,' occurs at 46:4; 48:1, cf. v. 8; עיר האלהים at 87:3. These phrases do not come outside the Korah psalms, though עיר יהוה occurs at 101:8 and Isa. 60:14. (vii) יהוה צבאות 'LORD of hosts,' occurs at 24:10; 46:7, 11; 48:8; 69:7; 84:1, 3, 12 in the Psalter; יהוה אלהים(ם) צבאות, 'LORD God of hosts,' at 59:6; 80:4, 19 (cf. 7, 14); 84:8; 89:8.[6] The shorter form is thus preponderant in the Korah psalms, with six usages out of eight. The two forms come almost entirely in Books II and III. 'LORD (God) of hosts' is parallel to 'God of Jacob' at 46:7, 11 and 84:8 only. (viii) מגן, 'shield,' is used for 'king' at 47:9; 84:9, and 89:18. The only similar use outside the Psalter is at Hos. 4:18. (ix) Mercy and truth, righteousness and peace, are four quasi-angelic powers in 85:10-13, with righteousness going before Yahweh's face. In 89:14 righteousness and judgement are the foundation of Yahweh's throne, mercy and truth go before his face. Graces as the foundation of the divine throne recur at 97:2, cf. 96:6. Most of these expressions are part of the religious vocabulary of the community, and so are especially significant. It may be noted that none of them occurs in 45, 49 or 88; but the subject-matter of these psalms is distinctive.

It is noticeable, secondly, that at least the greater part of the Korah collection are public psalms, often with an element of ritual. 44 is a national lament, with a day of bowing and grovelling (v. 25). 45 marks the blessing and marriage of the king, with a ride, anointing, presenting of gifts, and the escort of the queen to her marriage-bed. 46 is a people's hymn of confidence. 47 is their celebration of Yahweh's kingship, with ritual shouting, trumpets, and procession of his symbolic presence. 48 is their celebration of God's city, with a liturgy in the Temple (v. 9) and a circumambulation (vv. 12f). 49, although lacking any evident ritual, is addressed to 'all ye peoples.' 85 is a second public lament; 87 a second national celebration of God's city, with singing and dancing (v. 7); 89 a hymn to Yahweh's power in creation and providence, with a march and acclamation (v. 15). Thus far there might be general agreement.[7] Of the remainder, 42-43 are associated with ritual, in that the speaker 'goes mourning' and will go up to the altar with music; and 84 seems to presuppose a public ritual in that the speaker prays for the king as 'our shield,' and describes the journey of the pilgrims to the sanctuary at the time of the early rains. It is however disputed whether 42-43 and 84 were originally public or private psalms, and I postpone the discussion of them, and of 88, to a later point. Nevertheless it can be said that the greater part of our psalms are national songs. Wanke's conclusion is open to dispute, that they were an assortment, with one or two psalms carefully selected from each of Gunkel's major groups.[8]

But although the two sequences of Korah psalms are thus largely united in a certain common vocabulary, and a design for public use with ritual (perhaps with some exceptions), they are usually thought to be divided by their customary name for God. In the first sequence the name Yahweh is used 5 times absolutely and 3 times in combination, while Elohim occurs 34 times;[9] the second sequence (excluding 89 now) has Yahweh 12 times absolutely and 5 times in combination, while Elohim occurs 4 times. This is part of a larger phenomenon. In Book I Yahweh occurs 278 times and Elohim 15; in Books IV and V Yahweh comes 339 times and Elohim 9; but in Books

II and III, if we except 84-89, Yahweh comes 44 times and Elohim 200.[10] For this reason 42-83 have come to be known as the Elohist psalter, with the first Korah series giving the two names in due proportion, while the second group is bracketed with the Yahwist psalms.

The standard explanation for this state of affairs is that 42-83 were collected and edited by the 'Elohist redactor,' who went through changing the name Yahweh to Elohim; and we find Kraus, for example, going through the collection changing Elohim back to Yahweh. The case for an Elohist redactor is not usually argued in detail in modern commentaries, but I give the reasons cited by Alexander Kirkpatrick.[11] (i) Phrases with Elohim in 42-83 sometimes occur elsewhere in the OT with Yahweh, e.g. 50:7, Exod. 20:2, 'I am God thy God/the LORD thy God'; and the Elohim form is awkward. (ii) 14, 40:13-17 and 108 are virtual duplicates of 53, 70 and 57:7-11 + 60:5-12. Elohim occurs regularly in the Elohist version, except that Yahweh comes twice in 70 unaltered. Kirkpatrick is lost for a reason for the redaction, dismissing late avoidance of the Sacred Name (since some of the psalms in Book V are very late); nor can he accept as reasons a missionary desire to avoid the exclusive 'Yahweh,' or the effect of the exile. Gunkel suggests that we have evidence from the Chronicler's work that in the worship of the time Elohim was preferred to Yahweh.[12]

It is difficult to know what Gunkel is thinking of, as he gives no references. In the worship passages in I Chron. 16 (the coming of the ark to Jerusalem), 29 (David's dedication of the Temple material), II Chron. 6 (Solomon's prayer), 20 (Jehoshaphat's prayers), Ezra 9 and Neh. 9, Yahweh is used quite freely, and the absolute Elohim hardly at all. I Chron. 16 seems to be an acid test of his hypothesis, and a decisive rebuttal of it, for here we have parts of three Yahwist psalms (105, 96, 106), and Yahweh is retained throughout. We have thus no parallel for the supposed procedure of the Elohist redactor. Furthermore, we not only are unable to provide a motive for him, but we cannot make him a credible editor either. Lady Bracknell said that to lose two parents seemed like carelessness; to overlook forty-four uses of Yahweh seems like negligence so great as to be unbelievable!

When we examine the duplicate psalms in detail, it is clear that in each case the Book II version is earlier. 108 has clearly been put together from the two pieces of 57 and 60, becauses it contains six of the nine instances of Elohim in Books IV-V, and it has turned the difficult 'Philistia, shout thou...' of 60:8 into the easier 'Over

Philistia will I shout' (v. 9). The two uses of Yahweh in 70 are required for variation: '(Make haste), O God, to deliver me; Make haste to help me, O LORD . . . Make haste unto me, O God: . . . O LORD, make no tarrying' (vv. 1, 5). The parallel to 70:1 in 40:13 has Yahweh twice, which looks like a weak avoidance of Elohim. At 40:17 there is no Yahweh for 70 supposedly to copy; but, *per contra*, the Yahwist of 40 has Elohim like 70:5—the carry-over is from 70 to 40, with fatigue at the end of the psalm. Similarly 53 has Elohim six times, in every case, while 14 has Yahweh four times and Elohim twice (vv. 2, 5). It is 14 which has carried over twice from 53 the to him slightly unnatural Elohim. As for the 'awkwardness' of phrases like 'God, my/thy God' compared with 'Yahweh my/thy God,' this seems to be the inevitable consequence of the normal use of Elohim, which we know to have obtained for the Elohist community that produced the E-traditions in the Pentateuch. Of course 'I am God, thy God' may have involved substituting Elohim for Yahweh in Ps. 50, and there are several instances of the same thing in 68; but there is nothing to show that these substitutions did not take place in a community which used Elohim naturally, when the psalm was composed, rather than at the hands of a redactor in a later period. The priority of the Elohist duplicate psalms in Book II, and the absence of a credible motive and setting for the redactor, and his supposed overlooking of 44 instances of Yahweh, all tell in favour of Elohim being part of the original form of 42-83.

How then are we to account for the phenomena? First, it is an error to make a division between the two Korah series. 84, in the second series, has Yahweh alone twice (vv. 2, 11), Elohim alone twice (vv. 7, 9), Yahweh Elohim once (v. 11) and Yahweh (Elohim) Zebaot four times (vv. 1, 3, 8, 12). Delitzsch wrote, 'the characteristics of the Elohistic type of psalm are quite patent. Not only does the poet use אלהים twice, and that too in one instance (v. 7), where a non-Elohimic Psalm must have said יהוה; but he delights also in composite divine names'; we have already noted how Yahweh-of-hosts, so far from dividing 84 from the first Korah series, is actually an impressive link with it. So 84 belongs with the first Korah series, and the fact that it uses Yahweh absolutely twice in no way goes against this; exactly the same is true of 47. With 84 goes the neat cleavage, 42-49 Elohistic, 84-85, 87-88 Yahwistic. Furthermore the bracketing of psalms together, in the way that commentaries do on this question, has the effect of blurring the issue. It is not helpful to speak of 84-89 together as 'the

Yahwistic appendix'; 86 and 89 are not Korah psalms, and cannot be included with them. 87 has Yahweh twice and Elohim once, and such figures cannot justify calling it Yahwistic; especially when it is so closely linked with the Elohist 48, which begins 'Great is Yahweh.' The only two psalms in the Korah collection which definitely prefer Yahweh are 85 and 88 (four times each); and rather than positing an unexplained and capricious redactor, it may seem wise to ask whether there may be some special reason for the difference. I will suggest below two other reasons for thinking that the psalms in the second sequence are older than most of those in the first; and it could be, for example, that Yahweh was more used in the Korah community in the early period, but eschewed later.

I conclude, therefore, that (i) the Korah psalms are on the whole held together by their vocabulary, and by their general public and ritual content. There may be exceptions to this, especially 88; but the two sequences are not significantly divided by their use of divine names. (ii) The Korah group, the Asaph group (50, 73-83), and the second David group (51-72) all show a preference for Elohim, while using Yahweh not infrequently. This contrasts with Book I and Books IV and V, and suggests that Books II and III came either from different communities from those which produced I, IV and V, or from a different period, or both.

II. THE ORDER OF THE PSALMS

The order in which the psalms stand was a matter of concern to earlier commentators. Franz Delitzsch, perhaps the greatest nineteenth century writer on the Psalter, sought links of thought from one psalm to the next: sometimes genuine thematic links as between 50 and 51, sometimes more adventitiously, as when the word 'angel' links 34 and 35, or 'dove' 55 and 56. The same is true of Kirkpatrick. However, it is clear that only a minority of the psalms can be linked in this way, and that suggestions may often be subjective. Gunkel's classifications of psalms similarly corresponded only very partially to the order in which they stand, and he recognized that his classifications could in no way be supposed to explain that order.[13] Gunkel did not feel this to be a scandal; but he wrote words (in another sense of 'context') which properly express the situation: 'Now it is an unbreakable principle of scientific investigation that nothing can be understood without its context. *The proper task of Psalm criticism will therefore be to rediscover the connections between individual psalms.*'[14] The stress is

Gunkel's own; if we take him at his word, we are reminded of Ernst Käsemann's humble introduction to his *Testament of Jesus*, 'I would like to begin this study with the unusual confession that I shall be discussing a subject which, in the last analysis, I do not understand.'[15]

Gunkel's method in practice treated the order of the Psalms as nugatory. The key to understanding a psalm was to classify it; what shed light on 47 was not its relation to 46 or 48 as its neighbouring psalms in the tradition, but to 93, 97 and 99 as fellow songs of Yahweh's throne-ascent. Almost all writing on the psalms since Gunkel has followed this method, and it has been fruitful. An author shows his mastery of the subject by moving at ease from 110 to 2, and thence to 132; to Exod. 15 and I Sam. 2 and Jon. 2. The dazzled student soon suppresses as naive his instinct that it is proper to study 1 before 2, and that there is something curious in beginning a book on the Psalter with the 110th, or 89th psalm. In time the student suppressing his instincts becomes a professor, teaching what he does understand, and ignoring what he does not. Sporadic attempts to maintain that the order of the Psalms is significant have seemed either quixotic,[16] or too vague to carry conviction.[17]

The instinct that the order of the psalms may be important is not however naive, and is far from irrational. On the general level, the notion of *assorted* collections seems to be more modern than ancient. The modern parish clergyman expects an assorted collection, say *Hymns Ancient and Modern*, from which to select suitable material for a coming service. But *The Book of Common Prayer* does not give him the luxury of choosing; it directs what he shall read in church, the psalms following a set monthly order, the collects, epistles and gospels following a set annual order. Before the Prayer Book there were breviaries and lectionaries and books of hours, and they also pre-scribed what was to be read in order. Jewish practice in public reading of the Law, as far back as we can trace it—that is, at least to the Mishnah[18]—was not to choose, but to follow a *lectio continua* from week to week. Earlier still, there are Babylonian tablets prescribing liturgies for the days of a festival taken in order.[19] So it is entirely proper to begin the study of the Psalter with the expectation that it will be an ordered and not an assorted collection; or, at the very least, that it will contain elements that were rationally ordered.

This general expectation is at least partially confirmed by a review of the particular collection of psalms which are the subject of this study. It is not necessary to argue for the association of 43 with 42; the refrain at the end of the two psalms (and at 42:5), as well as a number of other common phrases set out below (Chapter 2), have made that accepted. But the links of 42-43 with 44 are also described by Delitzsch as 'numerous,' and are extended by Kirkpatrick. At 44:4 God is prayed to 'command ישועות,' as he was to command his lovingkindness at 42:8, and he was looked to for ישועות at 42:5, 11; 43:5. 'Thou hast cast us off' (44:9), 'cast (us) not off for ever' (v. 23), take up the plea of 43:2, 'why hast thou cast me off?' The long passage 44:13-16, 'Thou makest us a reproach to our neighbours . . . All the day long is my dishonour before me . . . For the voice of him that reproacheth and blasphemeth . . .' echoes the complaint of 42:3, 'they say unto me all the day, Where is thy God?,' repeated in 42:10; in the latter it is said, 'mine adversaries reproach me.' The term לחץ, oppression, occurs only three times in the Psalter, at 44:24; 42:9 and 43:2. The expression, 'our soul is bowed down to the dust' (44:25, שחה), recalls the refrain, 'Why art thou cast down, O my soul?' (42:5, 11; 43:5, תשתוחחי, root שחח). There is an appeal to God's lovingkindness in 44:26 as in 42:8, and the intention of 'confessing' (נודה) his name is expressed in 44:8 as in 42:5, 11; 43:5. There are thus strong associations of content in 42-44 which justify Delitzsch's conclusion that the order is intentional.

It is often suggested that 45 has been placed after 44 as being a משכיל (as 42 is also). It is doubtful, however, if this is a very helpful comment, since there is no agreement on the significance of the term משכיל, and it is hard to think of any category shared by 44 and 45; I shall propose an interpretation of a different kind for the term below. Nor is it the case, as is suggested by Wanke,[20] that the collection has gathered all the maskil's together at the beginning, for 88 is said to be a maskil also. 45 has therefore to be left for the moment as without signs of connection with 44.

There are widely recognised common themes between 46, 47 and 48; and these extend, to a lesser degree, to 45 also. The last ends with the expectation of children 'Whom thou shalt make princes in *all the earth*,' and that '*the peoples* shall give thee thanks for ever and ever' (vv. 16f). The subjugation of the Gentiles, and their participating in Israel's worship, are repeated themes of 46-48. 'I will be exalted among *the nations*, I will be exalted in the earth' (46:10); 'O clap your hands, *all ye peoples* . . . He subdueth *the peoples* under us, And *the nations* under our feet . . . For God is the King of *all the earth* . . . God reigneth over *the nations* . . . The princes of *the peoples* are gathered together (To be) the people of the God of Abraham: For the shields of *the earth* belong to our God' (47:1, 3, 7ff); the city of God is 'the joy of *the whole earth . . .* As is thy name, O God, So is thy praise unto *the ends of the earth*' (48:2, 10). The 'subduing' (47:3) is depicted at length in 46:6-9, 'The nations raged, the kingdoms were moved; He uttered his voice, the earth melted . . . He maketh wars to cease unto the end of the earth. He breaketh the bow . . .,' and in 48:4-6, 'For lo, the kings assembled themselves, They passed by together. They saw it, then were they amazed; They were dismayed, they were stricken with terror . . .' We find the same theme, albeit with the stress on the king's military power under God, in 45:2-5, 'God hath blessed thee for ever. Gird thy sword upon thy thigh, O mighty one . . . Thine arrows are sharp; The peoples fall under thee; (They are) in the heart of the king's enemies.'

46 and 48 have in common a stress on the inviolability of God's city, under attack from his enemies, human and demonic. Though the infernal waters roar and the mountains shake, the city of God will be glad, 'The holy place of the tabernacles of the Most High. God is in the midst of her; she shall not be moved . . .' (48:1f, 8). God is a high tower for his people there (46:7, 11; 48:3). 48 closes with reference to a procession round the holy city, glorying in its towers, bulwarks and fortifications, which are to be the confidence of generations to come (vv. 12f). God is called 'the LORD of hosts' in 48:8 as in 46:7, 11, and 'the great king' in 48:2 as in 47:2 (cf. vv. 6, 7). He is (greatly) exalted[21] and praised in 46:10; 47:9; 48:1. He takes up his reign on his holy throne in 47:8, recalling the eternal throne below where his divine one reigns in 45:6. There is thus a strong common content to the triumphal hymns 46, 47 and 48; and enough common content to 45 with its three successors to give *prima facie* justification to a conscious ordering of the collection.

49 opens, 'Hear this, all ye peoples,' as 47 opened, 'O clap your hands, all ye peoples'; so that there is a link of a formal kind at least between 49 and its predecessors. The sense of inspiration in the opening verses, 'the meditation of my heart . . . I will incline my ear' (vv. 3f), also recalls the poet's sense of inspiration at the beginning of 45, 'Mine heart overfloweth . . .,' like a cauldron bubbling over the divine flame. But a full discussion of 49 must be postponed, for the connections with 45-48 seem to me to be of a far more extensive kind than can be allowed by the received 'Wisdom-Poem' interpretation.

When we turn to the second Korah series in the 80's, our sense of a purposeful ordering of the collection is confirmed. 84 is widely recognised as the closest pair in the Psalter to 42, with the speaker's soul longing and fainting/panting and thirsting for the 'tabernacles' and altar(s) of the living God. Many details of language and structure are common to the two psalms (see below, Chapter 2); so that the two Korah series begin on the same note. Even when, as with Kraus, the psalms are categorised differently, the extensive common matter brackets them together.

84 is followed by 85, which is best interpreted, with Kraus, as a *Volksklagelied*. First the community recalls Yahweh's favour to 'Jacob' in time past, and then prays him to cause his present indignation to cease. In the second half of the psalm a more confident note is struck: the God Yahweh will speak peace to his people, his covenanted ones, and will give הטוב, that is all kinds of plenty; glory will dwell in the land, with mercy and truth, righteousness and peace joining in the divine blessing. There is some link with 84, which ended, 'The LORD will give grace and glory: No good thing (טוב) will he withhold from them that walk uprightly. O LORD of hosts, Blessed is the man that trusteth in thee' (vv. 11f). The glory and the 'good' are verbally the same: in meaning, grace is not different from mercy, truth, etc., nor God's people, his covenanted ones, from those who walk uprightly and trust in him. But much more important is the link with 44. We have here two National Laments, each opening with an appeal to Yahweh's favour (רצית(ם), 44:3; 85:1) to Jacob (44:4; 85:1) in time past (44:1-8; 85:1-3). The second section in both is a plea for the remission of divine anger. In 44 God has cast his people off, made them turn back from the enemy, given them like sheep, scattered them, etc.; in 85 he is prayed more generally, to turn us, cause his indignation to cease, quicken us, show us his favour. In both cases what is needed is salvation (44:3, 4, 6, 7; 85:7, 9). In the last section of both psalms, the community puts its trust in the covenant (44:17-26; 85:8-13). The Hebrew words used are ברית at 44:17 and חסד at 44:26; חסד at 85:8 and צדק in 85:10, 11, 13. There are obvious differences on tone between the two psalms, in that 85 is more confident than 44, which verges on desperation; and in that the salvation looked for in 85 is envisaged in terms of plenty while 44 is concerned with military survival. But this should not conceal from us the closeness of the general structure, and of the thought and language between them.

After 85 comes 87, usually classified as a *Zionslied*, like 46 and 48. Indeed the similarities are inescapable: the phrase 'city of God' (87:3; 46:4; 48:1; cf. v. 8), founded on the holy mountain(s) (v. 1; 48:1), where all nations are to acknowledge Yahweh (vv. 4-6; 46:10; 48:2, 10), to be 'established' by God for ever (v. 5; 48:8), the source of 'all my' fountains/gladdening streams (v. 7; 46:4). It can hardly escape our notice, then, that the Korah 'supplement' seems to be following the same general order as the main sequence:

42-43	84	Psalm of longing for Yahweh's 'tabernacles'
44	85	National Lament
46-48	87	'Song of Zion.'

45 and 47 have no counterpart in the 80's, but the parallel ordering of the remaining psalms can hardly be accidental.

There is no obvious connection between 87 and 88, but there seems to be some connection between 88 and 89. 88:11f asks, 'Shall *thy lovingkindness* be declared in the grave? Or *thy faithfulness* in Abaddon? Shall *thy wonders* be *known* in the dark? And *thy righteousness* in the land of forgetfulness?' 89:1, 2, 5 seem to echo this cry: 'I will sing of the *lovingkindness* of the LORD for ever: With my mouth will I make *known thy faithfulness* to all generations. For I have said, *Lovingkindness* shall be built up for ever; *Thy faithfulness* shalt thou establish in the very heavens ... And the heavens shall praise *thy wonders*, O LORD; *Thy faithfulness* also in the assembly of the holy ones.' Yahweh's faithfulness recurs in 89:8, and his righteousness in v. 16.

There are certainly gaps in the ordering of which I have now set out a *prima facie* claim. 42, 43 and 44 seem to be securely linked together, and 46, 47 and 48. There are some connections between 45 and 46-48, and of 49 with 47, but not of a compelling kind. We have no connection between the sad psalms 42-44 and the happy ones 45-48. The first three psalms in the second sequence, 84, 85 and 87, are strongly connected to 42-3, 44 and 46-48 in the first sequence, and follow the same order: the order begins with the beginning of the two sequences, but does not extend to 45 and 47. 88 and 89 exhibit some links between themselves, but are not related to the other members of the group. All in all, the indications of intentional order seem to be considerable, though not as yet satisfying. Their pursuit will be a key feature in my argument.

III. ORIGIN AND DATE

The only modern study of the Korah collection is Gunther Wanke's *Die Zionstheologie der Korachiten* (1966), and, as the title implies, Wanke took the collection to stem from Jerusalem. Earlier, John

Peters, in his postumous *The Psalms as Liturgies* (1922), had treated all the collections as units, and had concluded that the Korah collection came from Dan, in Northern Israel. Wanke's examination of the texts led him to believe that the bulk of the Korah psalms was composed in the fourth century, while Peters gave a date in the eighth or ninth centuries. The questions of provenance and of date are only partly connected; most commentators side with Wanke in placing most of the collection at Jerusalem, and with Peters in giving most of them an early date. Such disparate results rest upon different readings of contradictory evidence.

It must be said that Wanke overstates his case when he says that 42-43, 46, 48, 84 and 87 'show a striking interest in Zion-Jerusalem.'[22] Neither Zion nor Jerusalem is mentioned in 42, 43 or 46. Zion is referred to three times in 48 (par. 'the daughters of Judah' in v. 11), once in 84 and twice in 87; the name Jerusalem does not occur in the whole series. Nevertheless, the inference may not be unfair; if the Korah psalms are a unit, and three psalms give a central place to Zion, it seems reasonable to think that other references to 'the city of God,' etc., will mean Jerusalem. In favour of Peters' theory, it may be argued that 42 says, 'I remember thee from the land of Jordan, And the Hermons, from the little mountain' (v. 6); and that although 48:2 specifies mount Zion, the syntax is difficult, and the description, 'Fair in height, the recesses of the north,' is quite unsuited to Zion. The latter is not impressive in height at all, being surrounded by higher hills (125:2), and it is difficult to make sense of the phrase 'the recesses of the north' either geographically or mythically; whereas Mount Hermon is 9,100 ft high, three times the height of any other hill in Palestine, and really is in the extreme north of the country. If we allow the association of 89, 'Tabor and Hermon rejoice in thy name' (v. 12) make a Jerusalem setting difficult, since the northern sanctuaries were there held to be abominations.

Other geographical indications of a northern origin are advanced. 84 mentions Zion, but it also mentions the early rains, which hardly ever fall in time for the seventh month festival at Jerusalem, but would usually be in time for the northern, eighth month celebration. Jerusalem has two springs, Gihon and En-Rogel, and a brook, the Kidron. Dan is built by the main source of the Jordan, where the river issues from the side of Hermon, already twelve feet wide and three feet deep, running steeply down to a confluence with the river from Baneas. The Korah series contains several references which read as though the water available were plentiful. 42:7 is the difficult 'Deep calleth unto deep at the noise of thy cataracts: All thy waves and thy billows are gone over me'; the previous verse is the Jordan-Hermons-Mizar reference cited above. 46 says that the waters roar and are troubled, but are 'a river, the streams whereof make glad the city of God' (v. 4). 87 ends, 'All my fountains are in thee.' There are numerous springs inside the rampart at Tel-Dan. Even 88 contains the phrase, 'Thou hast afflicted me with all thy waves' (v. 7), though this is usually taken as a metaphor only. Now it is true that in the prophetic imagination of Ezekiel (47:1-12), Joel (3:18) and Zechariah (14:8), the Kidron became a mighty river running down to the Dead Sea; so that it is possible to read the psalm-texts as similarly visionary. But a more natural reading of 42, 46 and 87 seems to envisage a considerable river present to the eyes; and if these psalms were early, and came to be used at Jerusalem, they could have assisted in the development of the Temple river theme in Ezekiel and his successors.

Secondly, historical points are proposed on both sides, carrying various degrees of conviction. In favour of a northern origin, it is said of 45 that the king has princesses among his 'honourable women' (that is, his seraglio), and that mention is made of 'the daughter of Tyre,' who may be the bride. Tyrian relations would be more natural for Israel than Judah, and the kings of Judah usually married the daughters of Judaean noblemen. The ivory palaces (v. 8) have often been connected with Ahab, though Solomon also imported ivory. 47:9 seems to envisage the princes of the peoples being incorporated into the people of the God of Abraham; it is possible to imagine the neighbouring countries sending their kings as representatives to Israel's festival in the high days of Jeroboam I and II, and of Ahab, but it is difficult to think that Judah ever possessed such hegemony after Solomon. On the other hand 49 is almost universally believed to be a late Wisdom poem, perhaps with an incipient belief in the hereafter, and on this understanding must belong in the south. 85 has often been interpreted as implying the return from exile in 'Thou hast brought back the captivity of Jacob' (v. 1), though the translation is questioned. 89 in its present form has been taken to presuppose the fall of the Davidic monarchy; but the psalm is also open to a liturgical interpretation, and Gunkel and others have divided it into an early hymn and an extended Judaean lament.

Thirdly, our psalms contain a number of mythological elements, which have seemed to be early, and perhaps northern; though the link is insecure, and southern poetry, such as the book of Job, may contain elements of semi-digested Canaanite myth at quite a late stage. I merely note therefore the main points, without suggesting that they have any probative value. 46:2f reflects a belief in the subterranean waters as chaotic powers intent on 'shaking' God's ordered universe. In 47 'God goes up with a shout,' which, in the context, must imply some enthronement ceremony, as Gunkel saw; though whether the ark is implied, or some other symbol of divine presence, is not clear. In 48:2 'the recesses of Zaphon' may be a reference to the mythical Mt Zaphon, in whose recesses Baal had his palace in the tablets at Ugarit. The four 'virtues' in 85, meeting, kissing, springing, looking down, going before Yahweh's face, have a kind of semi-autonomous being which seems rather primitive; and two of them carry the names of Canaanite gods. 88 has been found to contain several phrases in common with passages in the Ugaritic tablets, where Baal and his messengers go down into the underworld, to the house of 'separation,' and are 'counted with them that go down into the earth.' 89 describes a scene in the 'assembly of the holy ones,' where Yahweh terrorises 'the sons of the gods,' a passage which also has parallels at Ugarit; and it further associates the creation of the world with the breaking of Rahab in pieces, a myth which no longer finds its place in Genesis, though it is to be seen from early texts like Ps. 74 through II Isaiah to Job.

Finally, there are a number of linguistic details which have been presented as arguments for northern as against Jerusalem origin. There is a long tradition in scholarship associating the name Elohim with northern traditions, and although this has been much disputed, the argument may still have some weight. We should not need the (anyhow implausible) form of the theory that Elohim was always and only used in the north, but the weaker form, that Elohim was normal, with Yahweh and other names used on occasion; rather as the Book of Common Prayer normally addresses the Collects to 'Almighty (and everlasting) God,' but quite often 'Lord,' and even once to Christ. Stronger arguments can be drawn from other names. אל־חי, 'the living God' only occurs in two northern texts and twice in the Korah Psalms; and may be related to the slogan 'Thy God, O Dan, liveth' (Amos 8:14). Yahweh-of-hosts comes eight times in the Psalter, six of which are Korah uses, one the Elohistic 69:7 and one the ancient 24:10; Yahweh-God-of-hosts comes five times in the Psalter, all in Elohistic psalms. The titles are often associated with the northern sanctuary at Shiloh. The phrase 'to see God,' which is peculiar to our psalms, is certainly primitive, and may imply the presence of an image, whether of Yahweh or of Baal; such would be more likely in northern sanctuaries. Perhaps the name Jacob for the people, and the phrase 'God of Jacob,' are linked with the Jacob shrines at Shechem and Bethel; we find both in the Asaph psalms, which have some northern associations. Sometimes individual turns of phrase in the collection have seemed to Hebraists to be evidence of northern provenance: ענוה, מני and שגל, for example, seemed to Delitzsch to suggest a northern origin for 45.

I have not attempted to make this catalogue of points exhaustive, or to indicate other than generally the way in which they have been supported and countered. Almost all of them are controversial, and they, and other arguments, will be discussed in the analysis of the individual psalms in the chapters ahead. My aim here has been to show the extent of the problem. How are we to reconcile the conclusions that the Korah (-Ethan) psalms are a coherent collection, seemingly arranged in some purposeful order, largely in connection with public ritual worship, with the apparent evidence of both northern and southern, both ancient and post-exilic provenance?

IV. A DAN HYPOTHESIS

The basic conviction from which I begin is that things must have come into this situation somehow, and that it should not be beyond our wits to piece together a hypothesis that will account for it. But it will call for a bold hypothesis, and in this I hope not to disappoint my reader.

First, it seems to me that enough evidence has been proposed in the last section to justify both Peters' and Wanke's main theories; and that reconciling them is not difficult. All our psalms, indeed all our Old Testament, has been funnelled through the Jerusalem community. If there are northern psalms surviving in the Canon, it is because they were accepted in the south; and it is not likely that anything was accepted without being used. So inevitably, any mention of a northern sanctuary, and sometimes mentions of northern mountains, would have been required to be changed to Jerusalem or Zion; and it is not surprising that we find only the shorter of these two options in the collection. Nor is it surprising that we find Zion alongside phrases inapposite to its geographical features. The northern tradents had to amend their sanctuary's texts; and no doubt they would do so with a good heart, seeing the real fulfilment of the divine promises in Jerusalem. But the Korah psalms have been little amended. Only 89 has been greatly changed, from a primitive northern hymn, vv. 1-2, 5-18, which I refer to as 89A, by the addition of the massive sixth-century lament, vv. 3-4, 19-51. This conclusion was already reached by Gunkel. So Wanke is right that the Korah psalms represent a theology of Zion as they were used in Jerusalem from the seventh century on. But Peters is more right in seeing that they were composed in the north in a much earlier period, and he is also right in identifying their shrine of origin as Dan.

Peters did not merely see the collection as coming from Dan: he saw that the corollary of this was that the psalms were a part of the Tabernacles liturgy there—for Dan was, with Bethel, the locus of the Northern Kingdom's Tabernacles celebration, a pilgrim feast attended by 'all Israel' (I Kings 12:29f).[23] So we are able to account not only for the many northern features suggested above, but also for the fact that most of the psalms are national ritual psalms. It seems to me that in fact all the psalms are national and ritual. Of the three psalms which Gunkel denied to be liturgical, 42-43 and 88 are already matters of dispute. For 49 I shall propose a new interpretation, seeing it also as a national festal psalm; though here also Peters has been in part before me. Only so is it possible to follow the Massoretic Hebrew. The standard, 'Wisdom-Poem,' view is in practice maintained only by considerable, sometimes large-scale, alterations to that text: preferring the easier text of the versions, conjecturing different vowels and different consonants, shuffling the verses, aporias, and other expedients. So the second part of my hypothesis is that all our psalms are public, and all are part of the Dan Tabernacles liturgy.

I have, however, a more important proposal to make that goes beyond the work of Peters; for I need to account for the elements of order on which I have commented, as well as for the coherence and public ritual character of the collection. The first striking feature of the order noted is that 42-43 and 84 are a pair, and that each comes first in its respective sequence. Now 84 is the psalm of pilgrims arriving at the sanctuary; and once 42-43 is divorced from its supposed yearning for Zion, it can be seen to have the same setting, and specifically at the Jordan/Hermons/Mizar. So we would seem to have two sequences of Dan Tabernacles psalms, each beginning with a song of the pilgrims on arrival; and this suggests that the order is a liturgical order, one psalm being sung each evening, following a day of ritual (42:8). 44 and 85, two national laments, will then follow as the prayers preceding the festival. 45 will mark the close of the opening day, 15th Bul, which has been taken up with the procession, enthronement, anointing and new marriage of the King. 46 will close the second day, 16th, which has celebrated the victory of Yahweh over his enemies, both below and upon the earth. 47 will belong to the third day, 17th, with its triumphal procession of the symbol of Yahweh's presence up to the bamah. 48 will complete the fourth day, the 18th, with its ceremonies in the Temple and with a march around the walls. 49 will end the fifth day, 19th, with its dire warnings to all powerful enemies who contemplate the invasion of Israel. All these psalms, except 49, require a full day for the carrying out of the rituals which they imply, and the rituals are in each case different. So we require in any case a hypothesis of an extended national festival, with a different theme for each day; all I am doing is accepting the evidence of order, and supposing that the order of the psalms as they stand corresponds to the order of the ritual, day by day, in eighth century Dan.

Ritual is conservative, but its verbal expression may vary, and will tend to vary with changing conditions. The Northern Kingdom lasted two centuries. In the first, especially under the strong kings, Jeroboam I, Omri and Ahab, Israel often prospered. In the second century, except in Jeroboam II's long reign, when there was a respite, things were less good; and after 750 national affairs went down to disaster. This changing political situation will account for the second Korah sequence, as a 'supplement' of older, ousted hymns. The Dan festival had opened with the old, happy, confident, 84 and 85 in the ninth century, and the almost boastful 87 had been the celebration of Dan as the city of God. After Jeroboam II's death Israel felt the need to go humbly with its God, and the more chastened, more political, more anxious, 42-43, 44 and 48 were composed to replace them. 84, 85 and 87 were remembered, and retained in their old order, and stand as evidence that the hypothesis of an ordered ritual sequence is correct.[24] In this way we have an explanation both for the relative common order, and for the Elohim/Yahweh phenomenon. Elohim is dominant in the later, substituting psalms, 42-43 (Elohim 10 / Yahweh 1), 44 (4/0), 48 (4/1). Yahweh is less uncommon in the earlier psalms, both the ousted ones in the 80's, and the ones for which no substitute was composed: 46 (Elohim 5 / Yahweh 3), 47 (7/2), 84 (4/7), 85 (0/4) and 88 (0/4). 45 (2/0), 49 (2/0) and 87 (1/2) have too few uses to be significant.

88 and 89 have been ousted too, but in Jerusalem, not in Dan. 88 was the psalm for the sixth day of the feast, 20th Bul, and it reflects the

ritual of a human scapegoat driven from the community for a day. It stands in conscious contrast to 89, whose links with it I have already noted. 89:12, 'Tabor and Hermon rejoice in thy name,' suggests that 89A came not from Dan but from the near-by, and much smaller, sanctuary at Tabor. Perhaps the Danite priests moved down to Tabor after the loss of Dan and Naphtali in the 730's and took the hymn into their collection then. It is a splendid climax to the week's celebrations, and was welcomed and expanded in Jerusalem. But after the exile, hope for the restoration of the Davidic kingdom ebbed; and human scapegoats no doubt seemed a barbarism. So 88 and 89 were relegated to join the supplement; and in their place a cycle of psalms was added to 42-49, psalms believed to have been written by David in his times of trouble, from the Bathsheba incident (51) to his final triumph in the accession of Solomon (72)[25] These twenty-two psalms took the full day from the evening of 20th to the evening of 21st—'evening and morning and noonday,' as is said in 55:17. But their exposition must await another occasion; I am only concerned now to show that my supposed Dan festal sequence of the ninth and eighth centuries could actually have finished as a real unit in our present Psalter, Book II.

There, then, is my hypothesis in outline; the rest of the book is an argument for its truth. It builds, of course, on the insight of Mowinckel and others that the psalms in many cases had their original setting in the autumn festival liturgy; but it does not accept such views uncritically, and it draws in new evidence to their support. The general case for the primacy of the autumn festival in the monarchy is stated by Eaton with cogency and restraint in ch. III of *Kingship and the Psalms* (1976), and does not need to be repeated here. He concludes, 'before recourse is made to the psalms at all, it is clear enough that the dominant festival under the Jerusalem monarchy was the autumn pilgrimage, and that this would be the context for the society to renew its foundations, purifying and re-sanctifying men and institutions, re-experiencing the divine salvation which had created its world and life and hope' (p. 104). The same will be equally true of the northern monarchy, whose only recorded festival is that in the autumn (I Kgs. 12:32f; Hos. 9:5).

The centrality and outline of the autumn festival had already been perceived by Julius Wellhausen in his *Prolegomena to the History of Israel* (ET 1885, 92ff) and Paul Volz in *Das Neujahrsfest Jahwes* (1912). It was Mowinckel who saw that the psalms celebrating Yahweh's kingship must have been composed for use at this festival, in his *Psalmenstudien* II (1922). The psalms which suggested this to him—and also, independently and less definitely to Gunkel (*Einleitung*, pp. 94-116)—were 47, 93 and 95-100. It was the path along which psalm-criticism was to advance that psalms of similar form and content should thus be classed together; but such abstraction, in almost total disregard of the collections and order in which these psalms are set in the Psalter, inevitably resulted in a one-sided emphasis. Mowinckel added further psalms to his picture of the festival: 24, 29, 46, 48, 76, 81, 82, 84, 118 and 149. But it was the original nucleus that gave to the festival his name of *Thronbesteigungsfeier Jahwes*, that was both so illuminating and so fertile of misunderstanding, rejection and theological polemic. From the perspective of this book it seems extraordinary that Gunkel and Mowinckel should have paid no serious attention to the fact that whole sequences of psalms, standing together in our Psalter, 46-48, 93 and 95-100 (and later 101), were being invoked, without considering other psalms alongside them, like 94 and the remaining psalms of Book IV. It also seems surprising that all the collections were so easily assumed to stem from Jerusalem without differentiation, Korah, Asaph, David and Book IV psalms alike.

The festival of Yahweh, as the Israelites called it (Hos. 9:5; Jg. 21:19; Lev. 23:39), or 'the festival' *tout court* (I Kgs. 8:2, 65; 12:32), or 'Ingathering' (Exod. 23:16; 34:22), had a ritual of Yahweh's ascent to his throne as a single feature, and it is not at all suitable to foist on it a modern name that stresses the part rather than the whole. Nor is Volz's 'New Year Festival' a very good name. The feast took place at the 'revolution of the year' (Exod. 34:22), at the 'going out' of the year (Exod. 23:16); and although the last phrase can be rendered 'the going forth' of the year,[26] this translation must be wrong because in the lists of festivals, Ingathering/Tabernacles is always placed last (Exod. 23:16; 34:22; Deut. 16:1-7; Lev. 23; Num. 28:16–29:40). Being at the turning point of the year, it contains many themes looking forward to the new year, but not these alone. The same applies to Weiser's 'covenant festival,' a theme which bulks large in the Asaph psalms, and occurs in other collections, but it is not omnivalent. The festival had agricultural roots, but the name 'Ingathering' was dropped in time as being inadequate. In this book it is spoken of by the neutral term 'the autumn festival,' or sometimes as Tabernacles. All Israel, that is all the able-bodied adult males of a total population that must be computed in hundreds of thousands, went to the national sanctuary for a week or more in the autumn, and built themselves temporary homes there (cf. II Sam. 11:11; I Kgs. 20:12, 16); and in the course of time the feast came to be called after them, Tabernacles (Deut. 16:13, rationalised in Lev. 23:43).[27]

A similar criticism will apply to the work of Aubrey Johnson, Ivan Engnell, John Eaton and others in extending Mowinckel's picture of the festival to include the ideas of humiliation and reconsecration of the king. In *Sacral Kingship in Ancient Israel* (1955) Johnson uses 72, 132, 89, 18, 118, 2, 110, 101 and 21, and many further psalms are added by Engnell and Eaton. Much light has been shed in this way on the theology of kingship in Jerusalem. But the picture contains, from the perspective I am using, embarrassing lacunae. None of Johnson's psalms comes from either the Korah or the Asaph collection; and I have already indicated that I should resist the use of 89 in this way, since 89A is an early hymn of triumph from Tabor, and the long addition is most simply explained in terms of the historical disasters which befell the line of David in the sixth century. So there is no plain evidence of the humiliation of the king in the northern traditions; though his reconsecration is amply witnessed in our collection by 45. Eaton proposes Korah psalms 42-43, 44 and 84 as having 'royal content'[28]; but it remains an interesting point of discussion whether the מנצח, the 'director' who is given by most headings as the speaker of the Korah psalms, is really the king, or some other national leader, perhaps one of the sanctuary priests. The king is expressly excluded from being the speaker in 45, 84 and 89A.

The advantage of my hypothesis over all those which I have just mentioned is that they are selecting their evidence, albeit often on sound criteria, while I am accepting a given ancient unit. Their picture of the autumn festival depends by definition on their own criteria and interests; mine emerges from what was put together by the sons of Korah. Yet although I am claiming to understand more than they, I am profoundly conscious of my debt to them, and many others to whom I shall refer. Of the scholar's gifts, they all excel me in Old Testament learning; and to the thoroughness, imagination and judgement of Gunkel, Mowinckel and Eaton I am indebted for insights without which I could never have proposed a theory of my own.

The praise of Gunkel and Mowinckel is common to many books on the Psalms. I should like to add a line in praise of Peters, whose work I did not read until after I had formulated my ideas. Peters had a doctorate in science, and he was for years pastor to a congregation in

New York. He was professor in New Testament in the University of the South, an institution not widely known in Europe. His *The Psalms as Liturgies* came out in 1922, when Mowinckel's *Psalmenstudien* were the talk of OT scholarship, and when Gunkel was in his heyday. He delivered the book as the Paddock Lectures in 1920, in about his eightieth year, and was dead before they were published. Beside the great German and Norwegian his commentary often seems slight, and his suggestions not well supported. He was followed by Stacey Waddy in *Homes of the Psalms* (1928), but has not otherwise been much regarded. But he saw three things which subsequent scholars have neglected to their loss: first, that the collections of psalms are ancient and significant; second, that the Korah collection came from Dan; and third, that it comprised liturgical psalms used there at the feast of Tabernacles. In the last resort, there is no substitute for being right; and I hope perhaps that through my own work the stone which the builders rejected may yet become the headstone in the corner.

II

THE PSALMS OF PILGRIMAGE (Psalms 42, 43, 84)

The close association of 42 with 43 is not controversial. 42:9, 'Why hast thou forgotten me? Why go I (אלך) mourning while the enemy oppresseth?'; 43:2, 'Why hast thou cast me off? Why go I (אתהלך) mourning while the enemy oppresseth?' 43 closes with the verse, 'Why art thou cast down, O my soul? And why art thou disquieted within me? Hope thou in God: for I shall yet praise him, The help of my countenance and my God'; 42 closes with the identical verse, and almost the same words form 42:5. The two psalms are in the same 3:2 (Qinah) metre. So it looks as if they belonged so closely together that they did not require a second heading. 42 has more the nature of a lament, 43 of a prayer; perhaps they belonged together at the beginning and end of some liturgy,[1] or by a similar link.

The situation underlying 42-43, however, has been a problem, and various proposals have been made to explain it. The features requiring explanation are principally the following:

(i) Is the speaker a national or a private person? He uses a number of bold expressions: God is his God (42:6; 43:4), the God of his life (42:8), his rock (42:9), the salvations of his face and his God (42:11; 43:5), the God of his strength (43:2). Such language is testified of the king (I Kgs. 3:7; 8:28; I Chron. 17:25; 21:17; 29:17; II Chron. 6:19, 40; Ps. 18:2, 6, 21, 28; 89:26), the national leader (Ezra 9:6; Neh. 5:19; 6:14; 13:14, 22, 29, 31), and prophets (Isa. 25:1; Jer. 31:18; Hos. 2:25; 8:2; Joel 1:13; Jon. 2:7; Hab. 1:12; Zech. 3:9; Dan. 9:18, 19); but it also occurs in the Psalter not infrequently, usually in 'David' psalms, where it may or may not have originated in the mouth of a private individual.[2] Other phrases incline the balance somewhat in favour of a national leader. The taunt, 'Where is thy God?' (42:3, 10), occurs elsewhere in the Psalter addressed to Israel as a people (79:10; 115:2). 'Oppression' is usually the oppression of Israel (Exod. 3:9; Deut. 26:7; II Kgs. 13:4; Ps. 44:24; more generally, Job 36:15, I Kgs. 22:27; Isa. 30:20); here the enemy oppressing is 'an ungodly nation' (43:1). The speaker looks forward to going to the hill shrine under divine escort (43:3),

presumably to make sacrifice, amid joyful cultic music (43:4), and to
see the face of God (42:2). He is either spoken of as leading (RV, RSV;
cf. late uses in Jastrow) or as participating in (RVmg, NEB; cf. Isa.
38:15) the festival pilgrimage procession (42:4). It is probably rather
easier to see him as a national leader taking part in the cult.[3]

(ii) There is some constraint upon the speaker. He asks, 'When shall
I come and see the face of God?' (42:2). He weeps continually while the
enemy demands, 'Where is thy God?' (42:3, 10). He grovels and moans
(42:5, 11; 43:5). God has forgotten him (42:9) and cast him off (43:2);
his enemies oppress him, and have their sword in his bones (42:9f;
43:2); he wears mourning (ibid.).

(iii) Nevertheless he expects to surmount this constraint. 'The
LORD will command his lovingkindness in the daytime, And in the
night his song shall be with me' (42:8). He sees himself as being
escorted to God's holy hill, to his tabernacles, and going up to God's
altar (43:3f).

(iv) The psalm is associated with a definite site: 'Therefore will I/do
I remember thee (אזכרך) from the land of Jordan, and the Hermons,
from the hill Mizar/little mountain' (42:6). The imperfect could refer
to either present or intended action. It is the precise location which is
the distinctive and most puzzling feature of the psalm.

(v) The speaker appears to be on the move. Twice he asks, 'Why go I
mourning?' (42:9; 43:2). He prays God to send his light and truth to
lead him and bring him to his holy hill (43:3), which, in the context of
the preceding verse, looks like a continuation of the present 'going.'

(vi) There is the mysterious 42:7, 'Deep calleth unto deep at the
noise of thy cataracts: All thy waves and thy billows are gone over me.'

The proposals to explain these features vary widely. Earlier
commentators cast about for possible historical situations. Ewald
thought of Jehoiachin en route for Babylon, and is followed by Briggs
and Barnes. Hitzig conjectured Onias III in 198 BC, as did Duhm.
Exiled Levites have been favoured: by Delitzsch at Mahanaim during
Absalom's rebellion; by Jacquet during the monarchy; by Norman
Snaith in the time of Nehemiah.[4] *Gattung*-critics have been less
specific. The man is a faithful Israelite in dire sickness, according to
Gunkel and Kraus, in prison according to Schmidt, in exile according
to Kissane and Weiser; either in the land of Jordan, or far from it
(מארץ) in Babylon (Kissane). Writers who stress the festival connections of the Psalter see the speaker as the Davidic king. Mowinckel
thinks he is on his way to give an account of himself to his overlord,

accompanied by Levites praying for his safe return; Eaton that he is on campaign, with Levites in a field cult.[5]

Most of these suggestions may seem to be catching at a straw, but are not perhaps to be blamed for that; there is not much to catch at. Gunkel and Kraus are at their weakest, for they overlook the signs of a national situation; and Kraus himself hesitates over the repeated taunts of the heathen if the man is just a good Israelite at death's door away from home.[6] The Israelites did not treat the sick Naaman like that. Further, it is a cardinal feature of Gunkel's theory that the individual laments lack personal details, and for this reason could be assimilated into the Temple hymn-book at Jerusalem; but 42-43 contain some extremely specific personal details of a geographical kind, and it is evident that they did not originate in Jerusalem. So it becomes problematic how they ever came to be incorporated in a collection for general use at the Temple.

There is, however, a much more serious objection, which none of these theories answers: for none of them is able to give an account of the sequence of thought in 42:6-8. Here the speaker first assuages his depression by the thought of worship at Mt Hermon ('my soul is cast down . . . Therefore I do remember thee . . .'); then follows directly 'Deep calleth unto deep . . .,' interpreted variously, but always as indicative of the speaker's troubles; then, again directly, comes the confident sentence, 'Yahweh will command his lovingkindness in the daytime . . .' Commentators given to emendation, like Gunkel and Dahood, emend the text; even the Revisers are driven to insert a 'Yet' before v. 8.

There are two options over the deeps/cataracts/waves of v. 7. Earlier writers took these to be real waterfalls, such as there are near the source of the Jordan on the slopes of Hermon; and this has the advantage that the waterfall references follow on directly from the Hermon/Jordan references in v. 6. Anderson, for example, sees the great virtue of reading the two verses together. Kirkpatrick then gives these real waters a metaphorical force: 'God is sending upon him one trouble after another. He is overwhelmed by a flood of misfortunes. The metaphorical language is derived from the surrounding scenery.' Such a view is now generally supplanted by Gunkel's proposal, that the deeps should be understood as the subterranean waters of death, a poetic way of saying that the speaker is as good as dead. There are many texts to support the view of waters as demonic powers hostile to Yahweh, and in particular the same clause, 'All thy waves and billows are gone over me,' recurs in Jon. 2:4.

Neither of these options answers the difficulty that v. 7, taken as a lament over a flood of misfortunes, over being as good as dead, is then immediately followed by the confident 'Yahweh will command . . .' of v. 8. But, for all its wide following, Gunkel's theory is open to several further objections. The call of deep to deep as a 'grauenvolle Gesang' over a human death seems a very strong poetic expression, for which we have no parallel; nor does the text say that it is what the deeps cry. Underwater cataracts and waterfalls are also otherwise unknown. Jon. 2:4 is not a very helpful parallel, because it is a much later text than 42:7, and the phrase may have been, as Gunkel says, copied from the one passage into the other.[7] But above all, the basis of the theory is that the waves and depths of Sheol are the powers of chaos and Yahweh's opponents. How then are we to account for '*thy* cataracts,' '*thy* waves,' '*thy* billows'? Gunkel sees the difficulty and emends the text.

An even more serious problem arises from the threefold specific detail of the geographical setting in the previous verse. Why the great emphasis that arises from saying that God is (to be) remembered from the land of Jordan, and the Hermons, from the little hill? Because it is such a pathetic place, say Gunkel and Kraus, an obscure knoll in a remote place outside Israel, far from the festal joys of Zion. I do not find this very convincing in itself; but it is surely wrong because it denies the force of 'Therefore.' The speaker's soul is cast down; therefore he (will) offer(s) worship from the land of Jordan, etc. The thought comforts him, as his hope in God does in the previous verse. Even more curious is Kissane's suggestion that he is in exile far from Palestine; if what he wants is to worship in Jerusalem, why does he grieve that he is far from the Jordan and Mt Hermon? Dahood, followed by Anderson, takes all three references to be symbolic of death, and thus provides a link with v. 7; but the ingenuity of rewriting the text, and the doubtfulness of the Ugaritic parallels, make his reconstruction very speculative.

The most natural reading of v. 6 would seem to be that the speaker *wants* to worship in the land of Jordan, etc., and that the threefold geographical detail is significant of this. We may see this from a modern parallel. My friend might say to me, 'I shall be praying for you in Ashby de la Zouch,' and this would mean that he happens to be going to Ashby de la Zouch, but there is nothing very significant about the place. He would hardly say, 'I shall be praying for you in Ashby de la Zouch, in the main square by the clock-tower.' But suppose he said,

'I shall be praying for you by the de Pau river, in the Pyrenees, in the grotto,' the detail would at once suggest that the location was significant: he is going on a pilgrimage to Lourdes. Would it be possible to read v. 6 then as similarly significant of a well-known place of prayer? Indeed it would; as Gunkel says, one may think of the great shrine at Dan. Dan stands at the main source of the Jordan on the slopes of Mt Hermon, and the site has now been excavated. The ancient town was on a knoll, so that all three details agree with its situation.[8] The Jordan is mentioned because Dan was at the Jordan's source. The Hermons are in the plural because the enormous pile of Hermon has several peaks (cf. 68:15f, 'a mountain of summits is . . . the mountain of Bashan'); and it dominates the whole north-east of Israel. The hill Mizar gives the precise location: this is where the city and shrine are, on the 'high place.' It is spoken of in 43:3 as 'thy holy hill,' 'thy tabernacles.'

The Jordan has four sources. There are two smaller streams which run down the west side of Hermon, but the major streams are the Nahr Leddan, the heaviest but shortest of the four, and the Nahr Banias, rising about two miles north-east, at the ancient Paneas/Caesarea Philippi; both of the latter flow from the south side of Hermon, in Israelite territory. George Adam Smith writes,[9] 'Travellers usually arrive first at the source of the Leddan, a mound, perhaps a hundred yards long, and rising some sixty feet above the plain before the plain rises to Hermon. Draped by trees and bush, it is plumed and crested by a grove of oaks. On the west side, through huge boulders, whose lower half its rush has worn bare, a stream, about twelve feet broad by three deep, breaks from the bowels of the earth; while another, more shallow and quiet, appears higher in the jungle of reeds and bushes. This opulent mound is called Tell-el-Kadi, and Kadi means the same as Dan. It is therefore supposed to be the site of Laish or Leshem, which the Danites took for their city.' The Arabs often translated ancient names into their own language, and the equation Kadi = judge = Dan has now been shown by archaeology to be a correct indication that this is the site of the ancient shrine. So the 'opulent mound,' Tel Dan, could very well be the hill Mizar, the little hill. It was a holy place from time immemorial, being the source of the one great river in the country.[10]

If this is so, it is easy to see the connection with the two following verses. Dan stands at the headwaters of the Jordan, and deep can be heard calling to deep as the thundering waters pour down the hillside. תהום does not by any means always mean the sinister subterranean ocean. In Ezek. 31:4 it stands for the nourishing, fructifying force of the Nile, and Deut. 8:7 says, 'For the LORD thy God bringeth thee into a good land, a land of brooks of waters, of fountains and depths (תהומות), springing forth in valleys and hills.' This is exactly the sense here, as one 'depth' calls to another in the roar of the waterfalls.[11] The waters are not a metaphor for misfortunes, or a poetic expression for the powers of death. On the contrary, the speaker is panting as the hind pants for the water-brooks; his soul thirsts. Water is the means of life to him, and he is nothing but comforted to remember the God of his life at Dan, where the new-born river can be seen as 'thy cataracts,' 'thy waves,' 'thy billows.' So of course confidence follows on unbroken in v. 8, 'Yahweh will command his lovingkindness'; the thread of thought of all three verses is confident. Nor should we translate עלי עברו 'are gone over me'; עבר על often means to pass by. This good significance of water is not confined to 42 among the Korah psalms. In 46, although the waters shake the mountains, yet they are a river which makes glad the city of God (v. 4), and in 87 all mankind's fresh springs are in the city of God; the contexts fit Dan rather than Jerusalem in both cases.

The difficulties of 42-43 disappear if we accept the obvious indications that the speaker is not wishing to worship at Jerusalem but at Dan.[12] As a national leader—whether the king, or a leading priest, or one speaking in the king's name—he is going to the national shrine. He is on the move because he is leading the people in the annual pilgrimage-festival. He goes mourning, moaning, weeping, because the past year has not been blessed. Perhaps no year was thought of as fully blessed—campaigns and harvests might always have gone better; but 42 seems to echo military reverses, with enemies gloating and deriding and oppressing, and it is most likely these which constrain the speaker. He yearns to see God's face, and to approach his altar with singing, now that, weary and thirsty, he has reached the end of his pilgrimage; he 'remembers' God as the 'deeps call' and the waters flow beside him.

42   For the Chief Musician; Maschil of the sons of Korah.

1   As the hind panteth (תערג) after the water-brooks,
       So panteth my soul after thee, O God.

2   My soul thirsteth for God, for the living God:
       When shall I come and see [point וְאֶרְאֶה] the face of (פני)
         God?'

The psalm allows no decision on the identity of the מנצח; kings and priests alike represent Israel in intercession and sacrifice, and may call the God of the sanctuary their God. But later psalms in the group, such as 45 and 84, which also carry this heading-note, cannot have been chanted by the king, and the balance of evidence seems to favour one of the Dan priests— see below, on Ps. 84. For Maschil see pp. 88-91.

The imagery of the opening verses, as of much of the Korah psalmody, is concrete, and not only metaphorical. The speaker has been actually panting and actually thirsty over the hundred and ten miles of stone road since the party left the palace at Samaria, walking (42:9; 43:2) all the way, in part over drought-stricken hills. It is November, and even if the first rain has begun (84:6), the parched countryside absorbs all that falls after five months of clear skies and heat. The physical panting and thirsting mirror the inward panting and thirsting; his whole self, his soul, is involved. The drought drives the wild creatures away from western Palestine, as the water-holes dry up, and even the Kishon is reduced to a trickle; the deer must go to the streams that do not dry up (אפיקי מים), and can be seen by the pilgrims as they also make their way to the source of life at the head waters of the Jordan. Worship at Dan during the northern monarchy is testified not only by the Deuteronomistic (D) historian, who tells of the eighth month festival there (I Kgs. 12:29ff), but also in Amos 8:14, 'They that swear by the sin of Samaria, and say, (As) thy God, O Dan, liveth; and, (As) the way of Beersheba liveth; even they shall fall.' The prophet seems to say that the slogan of the worshippers at Dan was, חי אלהיך דן; which in turn appears to echo the psalmist's אל חי. The same expression comes only once elsewhere in the Psalter, at 84:2, another Korah psalm, and in Hos. 1:10 (Heb. 2:1) and Josh. 3:10. The last passage is also concerned with the Jordan, so perhaps the unceasing flow of life-giving water from the hill-side gave Dan the reputation of the shrine of the living God. Arrival at the city, at the end of the journey, intensifies the yearning to come (into the shrine, cf. 118:19) and see God's face. Almost all commentators accept the likelihood that MT has made a reverential repointing וְאֵרָאֶה 'and appear the face of God'—cf. below on 89:15, Chapter 9. No man, in later times, might see God and live. But in early days the whole people, all Israel, was required to see God's face at the major festivals (Exod. 23:17; 34:23; Deut. 16:16). Even the Syriac and Targum have 'see the face.'

42:3   My tears have been my meat day and night,
       While they say all the day unto me, Where is thy God?

4   These things shall I remember, and pour out [cohortatives]
       my soul upon me,
       When I pass over (כי אעבר) with the throng, and go in
       procession with them to the house of God,
       With the voice of joy and thanksgiving, a multitude on
       pilgrimage (חוגג).

5   Why art thou bowed down (תשתוחחי), O my soul?
       And (why) art thou disquieted within me?
       Hope thou in God: for I shall yet praise him (Who is) the
       help of my countenance, and my God [pc MS Aquila Syr.].

For perhaps ten days the speaker has been on the way, mourning
ritually as he went, both on the road by day and at the evening
encampment. With every step he can feel the gloating of Israel's
enemies over her discomfiture, 'all the day.' But even in days of
military success tears were probably normal, that God might send the
rain; just as we find pious Jews mourning in the eighth month in the
Mishnah when rain is delayed.[13] So do we find also priests and
ministers weeping between porch and altar in Joel 2:17, when the
trumpet has been blown (v. 15), that Yahweh may give the former rain
in righteousness (v. 23). Joel's verse ends, 'Wherefore should *they say*
among the peoples, *Where is* their *God*?'; and his prophecy is related to
the psalm in other ways, for it says, 'Yea, the beasts of the field *pant
unto thee*: for *the water brooks* are dried up' (1:20). The continued
drought must seem a sign of God's impotence, and such signs are
levers often used to prise favours from heaven—surely God will not
permit the heathen so plausible a blasphemy (Exod. 32:12; Deut.
32:27, etc.).

RV translates v. 4 'These things I remember and pour out my soul
upon me, How I went . . .'; but this is not too easy, as the 'how' clause is
separated from 'remember' by a considerable phrase, 'and pour out my
soul upon me,' which cannot govern it. In fact the main verbs are
cohortatives; the speaker reinforces his resolve to lay his nation's
troubles before God with full earnestness. The object of 'remember' is
'These things,' and no 'how' clause is required; the remembering is a
religious, liturgical remembering, as in v. 6, not the forlorn self-pity of
so many commentaries. כי will then mean 'when,' with a verb in the
future. He means to intercede for God's vindication of Israel as he
passes over (עבר) the last lap of his way to the house of God, the shrine

at Dan. סָךְ occurs here only, and we can either retain the Massoretic vowel and translate 'throng,' deriving from סכך II, to interweave; or point בְּסֹךְ with the versions, 'to/in the tabernacle.' But the versions also read אדרם for אֶדַּדֵּם, and seem to have been avoiding difficulty; nor can we take the one without the other, for the suffix ם on אדרם requires 'the throng' or something similar as a referent. So the MT is our best text.

The speaker is travelling in procession, then, with a 'throng'; which is now paralleled by המון חוגג, a host on pilgrimage: really a host, for at least at the autumn festival 'all Israel' went from early times to see God's face at the national sanctuary (Exod. 23:17; 34:23; I Kgs. 12:30,32). Reliable figures are hard to come by, but it is likely that the Northern kingdom mustered some sixty thousand men of substance by the eighth century,[14] and more than this total probably converged on the central shrine each year. The scene would have been in part reminiscent of the Gathering of the Clans to Charles Stuart at Glenfinnan in 1745; but the king himself is likely to have travelled through many of the main centres of population (see below), collecting the pilgrims as he went. Such processions went up to the sanctuary 'with joy and thanksgiving' as 43:4 will testify shortly, even if the time before the festival was given to fasting and mourning (cf. Joel 2:15-27).

With v. 5 the speaker reassures himself. The end of the mourning road has been reached, and he need no longer prostrate himself with his face in the dust. As before, the language should be taken literally: the bowing down is a physical bowing down, and the 'disquieting' (תהמי) is a vocal disquieting, or moaning. The shrine is now in sight, and he will yet adore the God who has undertaken to bless him, the source of all 'salvations' for him. We can take the Massoretic word division, '(For) the help of his countenance. My God . . .,' or the Versions' division (= 11; 43:5), 'The help of my countenance and my God,' without much affecting the meaning. It can be said in MT's favour that the refrain in 49:12, 20 is varied, and that God's 'countenance' is significant in v. 2; 44:3; 89:15; but it would be easy to understand a scribe taking 'the salvations of his face' as the cause of praise, instead of the Versions' more difficult '(who is) the salvation of my face.' So for once the MT seems less attractive; and this gives an easier rhythm in v. 6 also.

42:6 My soul is bowed down upon me (עלי):
Therefore will I remember thee (אזכרך) from the land of

Jordan,
And the Hermons, from the hill Mizar [RV text].
7 Deep calleth unto deep at the noise of thy cataracts:
   All thy waves and thy billows are gone by me (עלי).
8 The LORD will command his loving kindness in the
   daytime,
   And in the night his song will be with me,
   (Even) a prayer unto the God of my life.
9 I will say unto God my rock, why hast thou forgotten me?
   Why go I mourning while the enemy oppresseth?

The speaker's distress, expressed in such prostrations, will now lead
him on to prayer: '*Therefore* will I remember thee...' Israel has
reached the source of the Jordan issuing from the side of the vast
Hermon range, at 'Judge's Mound,' the hill Mizar. The long dreamed-
of water tumbles down the hillside before them; here are God's
cataracts, as the fast-flowing river rushes over the rapids in headlong
career, God's waves and billows which pass them by, signs of divine
life-giving power. עבר על means 'pass by' rather than 'over,' cf.
'Everyone who passes by it (עובר עליה) is horrified' (Jer. 18:16). BDB
refers to sixteen other cases of the phrase with this meaning. עבר is
used of water flowing at Hab. 3:10 and Job 11:16.[15] עלי precedes the
verb as in vv. 5a, 7a. The thought carries straight on in v. 8; we do not
need RV's inserted 'Yet.' The coming worship at Dan ('I will
remember thee...') will have a double focus. Day by day (יומם)
through the feast God will command, that is, bid his angels (43:3)
renew, his blessing upon Israel according to his covenant promise
(חסדו)—blessing upon the king (45) and upon the people and upon
Dan his holy city (46-48). The ritual in connection with this blessing,
with the large number of participants, will occupy most of each day. In
the evening (בלילה) the nation will respond with a series of songs, the
Korah psalm-cycle, all of which are implicitly, and 44 and 88
explicitly, prayers; prayers to the living God of Dan, 'the God of my
life.' Death is a real threat (v. 10; 44:19; 48:14; 88), and it is life that is
desired for speaker and community. Such songs in the evenings of the
festival week were established customs in Jerusalem also; Isaiah says,
'Ye shall have a song, as in the night when the feast (חג) is hallowed'
(30:29). The image, 'God my rock'[16] is perhaps due to the soaring rock
of Hermon from which the river bursts, in the same way that the sight
of the immovable city in 46 leads to the invocation of 'God our
refuge... our high tower.' Surely Yahweh is a God on whom one may

depend; he sees the long pilgrimage march (אלך), the dust-covered face and mourning dress of the leader (קדר); he will hear the prayer and remember his people, and drive back their invading oppressors. The noun לחץ, oppression, is peculiar to the Korah psalms within the Psalter, recurring in 43:2 and 44:24; it is used for the Syrian ascendancy over Israel in II Kgs. 13:4.

> 42:10 As with a death stroke (רצח) in my bones, my adversaries reproach me;
> While they continually say unto me, Where is thy God?
> 11 Why art thou bowed down (תשתוחחי), O my soul?
> And why art thou disquieted within me?
> Hope thou in God: for I shall yet praise him,
> (Who is) the help of my countenance, and my God.

The thought of the oppression brings back the air of menace that has hung over the march, the powerful feeling, no doubt justified, that in other autumn festivals in the shrines of enemy peoples, prophets are at work cursing and deriding Israel and its God: 'Where are the gods of Hamath and Arpad? Can they deliver Samaria out of my hand? . . . With these thou shalt gore the Israelites, till thou hast destroyed them.' Such taunts and curses sow the seeds of disaster in the soul of Israel's leader, powerful jinxes that are death-strokes (Eaton) in his bones.[17] He turns and takes up the refrain of hope with which he closed the first part of his lament: in God there is yet hope, praise will yet be offered him, salvation will yet descend from him.

42:8 suggests that Yahweh's song is normally chanted at night, and we might suppose that 42 itself was in consequence an evening psalm. The caravan has completed its final day's march, and arrived outside the sacred city. Footsore and depressed, it raises its lament, and hopes for better things. 42 is divided from 43, never mind how close the rhythm, wording, ideas and refrain may be, and we need an explanation for this division. 43:3 suggests just such an explanation: 'O send out thy *light* and thy truth; let them lead me'; 43 is chanted before dawn the following morning. The great host is astir in the morning twilight, and the royal cortege leads the worship in a brief reprise, before the sun comes up and the pilgrimage reaches its conclusion, with the morning sacrifice at the altar at Dan.

> 43:1 Judge me, O God, and plead my cause against an ungodly nation:

O deliver me from the deceitful and unjust man.

2 For thou art the God of my strength; why hast thou cast me off?

Why go I mourning while the enemy oppresseth?

Israel's leader's hope is in God's covenant. When God judges him, he will be vindicated, since Israel has been faithful (44:17ff); God will cease to cast him off from his covenanted sonship (44:9, 23), and will condemn his foreign enemy, a man outside the covenant (לא־חסיד), full of double-dealing and ill-will. The theme of the previous evening, the march in ritual mourning, is repeated; but the mourning clothes are now to be put away—they are not suited to the joy of communion with God.

43:3 O send out thy light and thy truth; let them lead me:
      Let them bring me unto thy holy hill, and to thy tabernacles.

  4 Then will I go unto the altar of God, unto God the gladness of my joy:
      And upon the harp will I praise thee, O God my God.

  5 Why art thou bowed down (תשתוחחי), O my soul?
      And why art thou disquieted within me?
      Hope thou in God for I shall yet praise him,
      (Who is) the help of my countenance and my God.

God's light and truth are thought of as his angels of escort, angels which have their effect through natural phenomena (85:10-13; cf. 104:4). His light is the sun which will soon guide Israel to their journey's end; his 'truth' is associated with harvest growth in 85:11, and may indicate the rain. God's holy hill is the Hill Mizar, but the particular goal of this final procession is the rising slope on the north side of the city, where the high place was, 'thy tabernacles.' This במה was excavated by Professor A. Biran in a series of campaigns from 1966 on,[18] and is the largest to be discovered in Palestine. It consists of a central platform of large stones laid on top of each other, probably erected by Jeroboam I in the tenth century, and extended in the reign of Ahab to its present 18.7 × 18.2m. The fine headers and stretchers are of the classic Israelite masonry pattern. It was further extended with a broad flight of steps, 8m wide, probably by Jeroboam II. This platform was surrounded on the west, south and east by a courtyard with a floor of crushed yellow limestone, 7m wide on the sides and 14m to the south, the whole forming a *temenos* bounded by walls. The open side to the north, where the city wall is quite close, probably formed an open area from which ordinary Israelites could watch the sacrifices and other rituals which were to form the substance of the festival. There were temple buildings in the side courtyards, but the shrine itself was to the south of the whole complex. It has been usual to explain 'thy tabernacles' as a plural of majesty,[19] but it may be that it should rather be thought of as referring to the sacred complex; it is found in 46:4 and 84:1 in the Korah cycle, as well as in 132:5 and Ezek. 37:27. In the centre of the high place will have been 'the altar of God,' destroyed by the Assyrians; but we hear also of 'thy altars' — see below, p. 42. The contrast between the present sadness and the expected transport of joy, with music and sacrifice in God's presence, could hardly be more powerfully drawn; and the refrain which broke and ended 42 restates the speaker's rising hope once more.

It seems therefore that the whole of 42-43 can be accounted for without recourse to empty accounts of their particular features, the Jordan–Hermon–Mizar–cataracts–waves elements, or 'symbolic' explanations, or emendations of the text; once we allow the hypothesis that the setting has nothing to do with worship at Jerusalem, but is a national pilgrimage to Dan. This view is confirmed by the further, more general point, indicated in Chapter 1: the use of Elohim for God, apart from Yahweh in 42:8, throughout the two psalms, and predominantly through the Korah group. A long line of exegetes[20] have associated the name Elohim in the Pentateuch with the traditions of the Northern Kingdom; and the main outline of the Joseph story, glorifying the eponym of the central tribes, does the same. A corollary of such a view must be that Elohim traditions were handed down in the Northern sanctuaries, and that means especially Bethel and Dan. We do not need the extreme and unlikely hypothesis that God was invariably called Elohim there, and never Yahweh; just that Elohim was usual, in the same way that evangelical Christians more commonly speak of Jesus, and catholic Christians of Christ. This would correspond to the balance of names in 42-49; and we should need to suppose that Yahweh had been much more commonly used in the earlier period when 84-88 were composed, as was suggested in the last chapter. I will later give reasons for thinking that the Asaph psalms, 50 and 73-83, are the product of Bethel in the eighth century, and show a preference for Elohim over Yahweh similar to that in 42-49. It cannot but be helpful to our understanding of the psalms if we can find so straightforward an explanation of the predominance of Elohim in the Korah and Asaph collections, and of Yahweh in Books I, IV and V.[21]

The Korah and Asaph psalms originated in the northern sanctuaries, where it seems that in the eighth century God was called Elohim in the Pentateuchal traditions also; I, IV and V were always Jerusalem psalms, and the Jerusalem Pentateuch traditions also called God Yahweh.

One further matter arises from the consideration of 42-43 as psalms of pilgrimage to Dan. Jeroboam made his capital at Shechem (I Kgs. 12:25), or Tirzah close by (14:17), and Omri made his palace at Samaria, about ten miles west. From either of these towns it would be more than a hundred miles to Dan, and it is not to be thought that an army of pilgrims on foot, mustering tens of thousands, some with tents carried on pack-animals (Hos. 12:9), some driving tithe-cattle to be eaten on arrival (Deut. 14:22-27), could cover more than ten or twelve miles a day.[22] It would be necessary therefore to allow nearly a fortnight for the journey. Besides, the ancient Jewish calendar was lunisolar, with twelve moons to the normal year; but under this arrangement the calendar was constantly falling behind by eleven days a year, and the feast of Ingathering could only be kept as a harvest festival by the insertion of a thirteenth month every so often. In the first century AD this was done by *ad hoc* decree,[23] and this is sure to have been the system earlier; so the king would have had to decide when the festal month had come, and to announce it. These two necessities will account for the practice of 'blowing up the trumpet in the new moon' (81:3).[24] The trumpet announced to all at the capital and in the surrounding villages that the king was about to set out on the pilgrimage, and they should join him. The sound of the shofar would be taken up from town to town, like the Armada beacons, so that all Israel knew and made ready. We should expect the route of the pilgrimage to follow the line of the main centres of population, and there is some indication in the second pilgrimage psalm, 84, that this was in fact the case. This would take the throng north to Ibleam, and down the Kishon through Taanach, Megiddo and Jokneam to Accho; and thence over the hills to Dan. The procession would snowball as it went, and was bound to be difficult to manage. It was therefore desirable to arrive at Dan a day or two early, so that there should not be any anxiety over readiness for the full moon, when the festival must begin. Furthermore, tents were heavy and cumbrous to bring, and most Israelites preferred to cut boughs from the trees, and to build themselves temporary shacks (סכות, Lev. 23:40-42) on arrival, and time must be allowed for this.

In this way we have a plausible explanation of the origin of the later calendar, which has always been something of a mystery.[25] The H-law in Lev. 23 provides for a memorial of blowing trumpets on the first day of the seventh month (Tishri), and for the 'afflicting of your souls' on the tenth, the Day of Atonement. Traditionally, Judaism keeps the whole of the ten days as a period of penitence in preparation for the feast,[26] and this would seem to stand in neat succession to the ritual which I have inferred from Pss. 42-43. Sephardic Judaism still uses 42-43 for the eve of Tabernacles—a remarkable survival of a lament in a festival of joy.[27] The festal month began, then, with the blowing of trumpets, and for (about) ten days Israel 'went mourning' on the road to Dan, the pilgrimage closing with a ritual climax of bowing down and moaning with the chanting of 42. Then there was a brief pause before the feast began. In exile, and in the tiny Judaean community of the fifth century, there was no processing. The trumpet-blowing, the ten days of penitence and the climax on Yom Kippur were the ritualised fossils of a once living pilgrimage, bound by the inexorable factors of distance and terrain. Of course, the *ten* days of procession is only an estimate, and has no Biblical evidence; but it is a likely estimate none the less.

The Korah group includes a second pilgrimage psalm, 84, whose basic character is less controversial, though some matters are in dispute.

(i) The speaker longs, faints and cries out for the tabernacles and courts of the living God, just as in 42:1f. They are lovely to him (v. 1), and he sees as blessed those who live there (v. 4), and even the birds nesting round the altars (v. 3). Blessed too are those 'in whose heart are highways' (v. 5), who pass through the Balsam Valley to see God (vv. 6f). The situation presupposed is evidently that of a pilgrim arriving at the national shrine. The pilgrimage is for the feast of Tabernacles, as may be inferred from the mention of the early rain in v. 6; and perhaps also from the prayer for the king in v. 9.[28]

(ii) The speaker uses the same privileged expressions for his relation to God, 'my God' (vv. 3, 10), as occurred in 42:5, 11; 43:5, but he is clearly not the king, as he intercedes for the king as 'our shield' and 'thine anointed' (v. 9). The prayer for the king makes best sense as a public intercession, in which the speaker prays both in his own name ('hear my prayer'), and also in that of his fellow-pilgrims ('our shield'). The same sense of pastoral responsibility seems to underlie v. 7, 'They go from strength to strength, Every one of them seeth God.' He should therefore be an accepted liturgical figure, perhaps the high priest of the sanctuary, who has accompanied the pilgrimage, or his deputy. There is no reason to think that he is any different from the speaker in 42-43, who will therefore not be the king either. Both psalms carry the heading למנצח which probably means 'For the Director' (I Chron. 23:4; Ezra 3:8). No doubt at the time of putting the Psalter together the expression referred to the musical director, or senior Levite; but it may mask a reference to an earlier, liturgical director, whose priestly office was no longer respectable. The presence of this title in all the Korah psalms except 43, 48 and 87, together with the fact that 45 and 84 are dissociated from the king, suggests that none of the Korah psalms was spoken by the king, or directly in his name.[29] But most of them also presuppose a public figure speaking on behalf of the whole community, so it seems proper to take the speaker for the moment to be the high priest, or similar figure; I shall refer to him as the priest.[30]

(iii) 84 has much in common with 42-43. It is mainly in 3:2, Qinah rhythm. 'Thy tabernacles' (v. 1) came in 43:3. 'The living God' occurs only at v. 2 and 42:2 in the psalter. V. 7 and 42:2 both look forward to 'seeing God('s face).' The pilgrims have been 'going,' on the move, in v. 7 as in 42:9; 43:2. The speaker's soul longing, fainting and crying out (v. 2) is close to the speaker's soul panting and thirsting in 42:1f, and there is crying out (רנה) in 42:4c. The comparison of the worshipper to nesting birds in 84:3 recalls the comparison to the thirsting hind at 42:1. 'They will yet (עוד) praise thee' (v. 4) is like the refrain 'For I shall yet confess him' in 42:5, 11; 43:5.

The similarities of 84 and 42-43 extend to a detailed triple structure (Kirkpatrick). 84 is in three equal parts, vv. 1-4, 5-8, and 9-12, broken formally by Selahs after v. 4 and v. 8; just as 42-43 is formally broken by the refrains into three almost equal sections. The first in each case describes the speaker's longing for God's house, like the animals, and his looking forward to the renewed praise of God; the second speaks of the trials of the way (42:9; 84:5f; the Balsam valley and the highways) in contrast with the joys of arrival (42:6f; 84:7); the third is a prayer, for the king (84:9) and people (84:11f; 43:1ff), in expectation that God will bless them with light and truth (43:3)/grace and glory (84:11).

(iv) Like all other psalms in the Psalter, 84 was in the end used at the Jerusalem Temple. This is in the text, 'Every one of them seeth God in Zion' (v. 7); and it is probably implied in the heading על הגתית.[31] However, this leaves open the question whether the psalm was originally designed for use in Jerusalem, or whether these two features were added to adapt the psalm for worship in the south. Such a suggestion is against the common opinion, but it is suggested by the four points following.

(v) The divine names in the psalm, 'the living God,' 'Yahweh (God) of hosts,' and 'the God of Jacob' all have northern associations, as I have shown above on p.15—'the living God' (v. 2) with the Jordan, and perhaps even with Dan (Amos 8:14), 'Yahweh (God) of hosts' (vv. 1, 3, 8, 12) with Shiloh, 'the God of Jacob' (v. 8) with Shechem and Bethel. Elohim is used in v. 7 and v. 9, and Yahweh Elohim in v. 11a. Yahweh occurs on its own in v. 2 and v. 11b.

(vi) In vv. 5-7 the pilgrims are described en route to the sanctuary ('to Zion,' as v. 7 now stands). The MT (RVmg) gives for v. 6, 'Passing through the valley of the Balsam tree (הבכא), they make it a place of springs; yea, the early rain covereth it with blessings.' Although this is not immediately plain, it seems clear that the early rain falls on the pilgrims on their road to the festival. Now it is possible for us to make a comparison between the likelihood of this happening on the way to the Jerusalem and the Dan festivals; and what matters is the likelihood on a regular basis, since the psalm will have been preserved on the basis of regular use, and people do not wish to celebrate what does not usually happen. The Jerusalem festival was held in the seventh month, so that (if we exclude leap-years) the feast would begin on a date varying between mid-September and mid-October. The average rainfall in Jerusalem in modern times is 0.1 inches in September and 0.3 inches in October; and in both cases tends to fall towards the end of the month. The Dan festival was held in the eighth month (I Kgs. 12:32f), so the feast would usually begin between mid-October and mid-November. The average rainfall at Safad (the nearest weather-station to Dan) in modern times is 0.8 inches in October and 2.7 inches in November.[32] Indeed, texts like Joel 2:23 and Zech. 14:16ff show that the Jerusalem Tabernacles was in some measure a season of prayer for the renewal of the rains; and pious men in the time of the Mishnah used to fast and mourn when the rains had not begun in the eighth month.[33] It is thus extremely unlikely that Jerusalem pilgrims could expect the early rain to cover their route with blessings; whereas the northern festival had more the character of a thanksgiving for the rain, and the pilgrims could regularly expect a foretaste of God's blessings en route to the sanctuary.

(vii) Where then is 'the valley of the Balsam tree'? The phrase is sometimes taken to be an allusion to the valley of Rephaim, which may be either north or west of Jerusalem, in which there are said to have been balsam-trees in II Sam. 5:23f—the very context in which David is about to bring up the ark to the city. However, the valley is actually called the Valley of Rephaim, which seems to rule it out.

Josephus mentions a small town in Galilee called Βακα, and it is an attractive speculation that this is the area referred to.[34] Baca lies at the head of a dry valley running down to the sea at Accho; and it is precisely this region which would represent the most formidable part of the pilgrimage from Samaria to Dan (see map). The royal party leads a multitude on pilgrimage (42:4); and the multitude gathers to the advancing column at the sound of the shofar (81:3). There are two ways of going from Samaria to Dan. Either one can follow the course of the Kishon down through the populous cities of Ibleam, Taanach, Megiddo and Jokneam to the sea at Accho, and thence up via the Baca valley to the waters of Merom, and north through Gischala and Kedesh; or one can skirt Mt Tabor to the Sea of Galilee, and follow the Jordan to its source. The purpose of the pilgrimage would in itself indicate the former route: the aim was the mobilisation of Israel for worship and for holy war, and there would be no point in going the way where the people did not live. In particular the main centre of the national chariotry was Megiddo.[35] The party would thus be able to follow the main road (מסלה), 'cast up' to take a traffic of thousands, including horses, down the Kishon valley. There would be water for all in the eighth month, and established camping sites outside the towns, whose inhabitants would then join the procession the next day. At Accho the column would turn east and begin the climb to Baca; but there was perhaps no village there then, just הבכא, 'the balsam tree.'[36] Here for the first time water is a problem; the first rains would be entirely absorbed by the dried out soil. Just east of Baca, however, they would come to the Waters of Merom, whose force would have been renewed by the October rainfall: 'Passing through the Balsam-Tree Valley, they make it a place of springs; Yea, the early rain covereth it with blessings.'

Such a picture coheres so well with the data of the psalm that I do not think it an important objection that the name of the site was spelt בקע in rabbinic sources.[37] The corruption of place-names is a universal tendency, and none is more likely to be differently spelled than one named after a feature like a large balsam tree which dies and is gone. The tree is no more, but the valley (בקע) remains.

(viii) The phrasing of v. 5b, 'In whose heart are highways,' presents a problem. Most commentators find the phrase impossible, and many change the text. Gunkel and Kraus read כסלות for מסלות; but the plural 'confidences' is unparalleled and unlikely, and it is not easy to see a scribe changing it to 'highways.' RV puts 'In whose heart are the highways *to Zion*'; but '*to Zion*' can hardly be understood, and the same problem arises, how it came to be omitted. A simple explanation would be that the original Hebrew ran 'In whose heart are the highways to Dan,' the last word of which would be automatically cut out when the psalm came into use at Jerusalem. Similarly an original v. 7b, 'Every one of them seeth God in Dan/Hermon' would have to be emended, either by excising the last phrase, or by changing it to '. . . in Zion,' the present text.

So 84 looks increasingly like a Dan pilgrimage psalm, just like 42-43.

84   For the Chief Musician; at (על) the Gittite settlement (הגתית).
     A Psalm of the sons of Korah.
1   How lovely are thy tabernacles, O LORD of hosts!
2   My soul longeth, yea, even fainteth for the courts of the LORD;
     My heart and my flesh cry out [RV text] unto the living God. ·
3   Yea, the sparrow hath found her an house,
     And the swallow a nest for herself, where she may lay her young,
     By (את) thine altars, O LORD of hosts,
     My king, and my God.
4   Blessed are they that dwell in thy house:
     They will be continually (עוד) praising thee.   [Selah

Although על־הגתית has traditionally been understood as a musical direction, we have no evidence of a Gittite rhythm, and Mowinckel suggests a connection with the house of Obed-Edom the Gittite, from which David set out with the ark in II Sam. 6.[38] A public recital of the psalm in the Jerusalem liturgy preceding the Feast of Tabernacles would require the gathering of the pilgrims at some site short of the Temple itself; and it would be easy to imagine that the traditional Gittite point of departure for the last furlongs of the Temple pilgrimage still continued in use. The heading would have been added, then, after the psalm was domesticated in Judah. It occurs in 8 and 81 also, the latter being a traditional psalm for New Year.

Since we possess two psalms of pilgrimage in the same collection, with the same structure and a marked similarity of language, and apparently for use in the same sanctuary, we are in a position to combine them into a single background on the one hand, and to contrast them on the other. Both speak of God's 'tabernacles,' but 84 speaks of the shrine as having courts, and altars in the plural. The courts will be the walled areas excavated on three sides of the במה;[39] a similar surrounding walled area at Jerusalem is called 'the other court' (I Kgs. 7:8). In addition to the central altar (43:4), there seem to have been standing stones ('altars') in the outer court, and animal bones have been found.[40] A number of subsidiary altars would certainly be needed if the provisions of Deut. 12:5ff; 14:23ff were to be observed.

Both psalms are marked by the same yearning for the sanctuary, panting and thirsting in 42, longing, fainting and crying out here. It is easy to sympathise with the psalmists, for whom, even more than for us, the spiritual and the physical were so deeply interwoven. On the long march over the parched hills, fainting (כלתה) may often have happened, and the green meadows of Dan, with its trees and rushing cool water, still there today, have been a mirage of desire. The drought and weariness emphasize the need for God's power and blessing, which is to be felt all the more abundantly when the sanctuary is reached. How lovely is Dan after such a journey! Happy are the sacred birds nesting in the trees by the altars (Gunkel is surely right to translate את so); and happy too are the priests who live in so beautiful and holy a place, and sing God's praises round the year. The same adverb עוד, and similar verbs for praise, come in the refrain of 42-43; and the slightly different sense seems to confirm the conclusion that the speaker is himself a priest. In 42-43 the psalmist said to his soul, 'Hope thou in God: for I shall *yet* praise him'; he was looking forward to rejoining the *continual* praise of the priestly community to which he was privileged to belong. It would seem likely that the Danite priesthood would send a deputation to the capital to escort the royal party. The מנצח has had his fill of dust and heat; he knows the good life enjoyed by his colleagues amid praise and fruitfulness.

But the matter in common should not distract us from the marked differences between the two psalms. First, there is a clear difference of tone. 84 is a happy, confident psalm, and totally lacks the grim feeling of 42, whose speaker was hedged about with enemies taunting and deriding him. Enemies are a minor feature of 84, and are viewed with confidence (vv. 10f); the longing and fainting are only such as must be experienced by the pilgrim in heart and flesh. All that is in mind now is the delight in the sanctuary, its enclosures and altars and trees and birds, the strength and 'good' and glory and grace that Yahweh will bestow, on priests and people and king; even the hard road gives memories of springs and showers. The same is true of the names for God. Here, in common, in these two psalms alone in the Psalter comes 'the living God'; and we have Elohim twice in 84, and 'my God' in both, and Yahweh twice in 84 and once in 42. But we also have a completely new divine name, Yahweh (God) of hosts, which occurs four times in 84; and the combination Yahweh Elohim is new too. How are we to account for these sharp differentiations, when so much is in common? These clearly are not merely personal differences.

I offer a tentative hypothesis, for which I hope to supply further evidence as our study advances: 84 is an older psalm than 42-43. In the tenth and ninth centuries, broadly speaking, Israel was 'at peace'; that is, she was more powerful than her neighbours, and could contain, if not dominate them. 84 will come from this period, with no enemies worth mentioning. From the late ninth century onwards, however, the balance of power shifted, and first Syria and then Assyria dominated Israel. With this change, the need was felt to call more urgently upon God to fend off Israel's enemies; hence the composing of 42, and furthermore its gaining pride of place at the head of the main Korah sequence, and the relegation of 84 to an appendix. We could account for the divine names on the same basis. Yahweh is the normal name for God in all the 'relegated' Korah psalms in the 80's; it comes sometimes in the main sequence, but Elohim is preferred there, especially in the anxious 42-43 (10/1) and 44 (4/0), and in 48 (4/1), each of which has a more confident counterpart (84, 85, 87) in the second group (cf. p.18). The use of the more general term Elohim would be required to enable Yahwism to absorb the worship of Baal in just the way indicated and deplored by Hosea, who systematically sticks to Yahweh; so we can both evidence and account for a shift from Yahweh to Elohim between the tenth and eighth centuries in the north. Yahweh (God) of hosts similarly is an ancient title, associated with the ark (I Sam. 4; Ps. 24:10), still in use in 46 and 80, but obsolescent in the north. 'The Living God,' however, remains in use because of its association with Dan's living waters till the last years of the shrine (Amos 8:14). So the 'supplement' looks as if it were older than the main sequence on two grounds: it is more confident where it has counterparts, and it uses older divine names.

For Selah, see below, pp. 102ff.

84:5 Blessed is the man whose strength is in thee;
      In whose heart are the highways <? to Dan>.
   6 Passing through the valley of the balsam-tree (הבכא) they
        make it a place of springs;
      Yea, the early rain covereth it with blessings.
   7 They go from strength to strength,
      They see God [read יִרְאֶה אֱלֹהִים] [in Zion].
   8 O LORD God of hosts, hear my prayer:
      Give ear, O God of Jacob.   [Selah

The first section closed with the beatitude on the priesthood; the
second begins with the beatitude on the whole loyal people of Yahweh.
In their heart are the highways, the 'cast up,' or as we should say 'made
up,' roads that led from Samaria to Dan. We hear of such highways,
also in connection with the pilgrim road to Yahweh's festival, in Isa.
35:8; 40:3; 57:14; 62:10, etc., when he will lead Israel along them out of
Babylon. With tens of thousands of people tramping them, the normal
paths and cart-tracks would not do; and we find Ahaziah's chariot
driving full pelt along one from Ibleam to Megiddo on his last journey
(II Kgs. 9:27). As the word is not however limited to the pilgrimage
routes (e.g. Num. 20:19), it is difficult to give sense to v. 5b as it stands.
RV seems to feel the need to supply a destination, and adds 'to Zion.'
But then why should such a requisite phrase have dropped out of the
text? It would be easier to understand if a scandalous phrase stood
there, like אל־דן, which would automatically attract the censor's
pencil.

   Like the psalmist of 42:4 who 'passes' (עבר) with the throng, so does
the psalmist of 84 'pass' with the pilgrim host through the drought-
stricken balsam-tree valley up from the coast. Gunkel makes his own
difficulties, first translating עוז as 'refuge,' for which there is no
parallel, and then deriding the text of v. 6a, 'how could man do such a
miracle?' The point is that the great company's strength is in Yahweh,
and so their arrival miraculously causes the springs to bubble forth,
and the early rain to carpet the soil with green turf and bright
flowers.[41] The miracle will seem to the modern more indirect. At the
head of the valley up from Acre to Baca the pass leads over to 'the
waters of Merom'; here in modern times there is an annual rainfall of
35-40 inches a year, over this circumscribed area, against 20-25 inches
average for Northern Israel as a whole.[42] But there is a nil rainfall on
average at the nearby weather-station of Safad from June to September,
so that the springs dry up in some areas even here. Out of an annual

average of 29.1 inches at Safad, 0.8 fall in October and 2.7 in November, so the early rains will have fallen in significant amounts in most years by the time the procession passed this way in the second week of the eighth month. The resurgence of the springs, the rain and the verdure will have happened to coincide with the passing of the pilgrimage.

It is usual to interpret v. 7a by reference to Isa. 40:31, 'They that wait upon the LORD shall renew their strength'; but 'they go from strength to strength' sounds uncomfortably 'poetic,' taken so. The parallels offered by Kraus are in reality much more concrete: 'they proceed from evil to evil,' Jer. 9:3, i.e. from crime to crime; 'our garners are full, affording store from kind to kind,' Ps. 144:13. It is better to take the line concretely here too. חיל (a different word from 'strength' in v. 5a) is often used for Israel's armed strength. As the procession advances (ילכו) from town to town, it snowballs, it goes from strength to strength. After Merom it merges with other companies of Israelite pilgrims coming from Issachar and Naphtali, and from Reuben, Gad and Manasseh up the Jordan valley, up other מסלות (plural, v. 5). The sudden sight of the massed companies of their armed fellows streaming up the valley below, as they themselves come round the escarpment, strikes heart into the footsore company. How formidable a force is Israel's army! How goodly are thy tents, O Jacob; Like lign-aloes which the LORD has planted!

It is generally agreed that the text of v. 7b has been corrupted; the question is how much. It is very probable that אראה has been pointed as a niph'al, 'appear,' instead of an original qal, 'see,' for theological reasons, as in 42:2; it was later orthodoxy that no man might see God and live. LXX already takes the verb as a passive, but without avoiding the scandal: ὀφθήσεται ὁ θεὸς τῶν θεῶν. It is in fact a moot point whether there was an actual representation of God at Dan which Israel might see (cf. below Chapters 3 and 8). Secondly, MT points אֶל־ אֱלֹהִים, but the Greek and Syriac imply אֵל. The Massoretic pointing could be due to the need to supply a preposition after 'appear,' and thus be a conscious diplography. The Greek pointing is not likely to be right as this combination of two divine names does not occur elsewhere in the Korah psalms. A third difficulty is that we should have expected a plural verb, and many commentators have wished to replace the singular with a plural, in view of the distance from 'the man' in v. 5a; but the distance is not impossible (cf. 45:5), and MT gives a chiasmus. Finally, if the references to the early rain, and to the valley of Baca, and the general detailed similarity to 42-43, are sufficient to show that 84 was originally composed for the pilgrimage to Dan, then we should have to assume that 'in Zion' was an addition or an amendment when the psalm was taken over in Jerusalem. It would be easier to think that it replaced some offensive phrase, such as 'on Hermon,' than that it was inserted *de novo*.

The central section of the psalm now closes with the priest's petition for God to hear the prayer which will be voiced after the Selah. The impressive parallel of Yahweh God of Hosts//God of Jacob at the end of the section strongly echoes 46:7, 11, and is limited to these two Korah psalms. The petition is part of a public liturgy, it seems; the speaker can refer to 'my prayer' for the one termed 'our shield,' and the Selah could then mark an interval of corporate liturgical activity, of whatever kind, in the original context. I postpone a discussion of the precise force of the Selah to pp. 102ff.

> 84:9 Behold our shield, O God,
> And look upon the face of thine anointed.
> 10 For a feast-day blessing in thy courts (כי טוב־יום בחצריך)
> I had rather than a thousand (shekels) (מאלף בחרתי);
> To keep the threshold (הסתופף) in the house of my God
> Than to dwell in the tents of wickedness.

The prayer in v. 9 is straightforward, the intercession of the priest for the king, spoken of first as 'our shield,' as in 47:9 and 89:18 (both psalms in our collection); and then in parallel as 'thine anointed.' Everything seemed, and very many things were, dependent upon the king's success in ancient Israel; God's blessing upon him was therefore crucial.

The basis for the prayer (כי) however is not straightforward, and constitutes one of the Psalter's major sustained errors of translation.[43] The traditional version, 'For a day in thy courts is better than a thousand. I had rather stand at the threshold (*or* be a doorkeeper) in the house of my God, Than to dwell in the tents of wickedness,' is impossible for the following reasons: (i) It is an insult to say to anyone that a day in their courts is better than a thousand (days), and above all to God. No parallel is offered by any commentator for understanding 'than a thousand (days *elsewhere*),' and it is plainly impossible to understand such a crucial part of the contrast without expressing it. The supposed contrast also really requires '*one* day.' Gunkel says, 'Der Deutsche wurde "ein Tag" betonen'; and so will the Israelite. (ii) The traditional version gives no sense to כי. What is the connection of thought between a prayer for the king and an assertion that the faithful Israelite delights in the Temple courts? How can the first be said to lead on from the second ('For . . .')?[44] (iii) The Hebrew text joins טוב־יום with a maqqeph. The intimate link is trampled underfoot by the standard translation. (iv) The rhythm of v. 10a makes it natural to read בחרתי as the verb of the line; it is strained to place a stop before it, and to take it with v. 10b alone. (v) V. 10a and v. 10b look as if they were in parallel, preferring the courts/house of God to (elsewhere)/the tents of wickedness. But the latter two are not equivalent, and this leads to difficulties with the last phrase. Many, like Gunkel, emend the text. Kraus following Schmidt suggests that there was a temple gate liturgy in which the sheep (who 'walk uprightly') were divided from the goats (who were forbidden entry and had to 'dwell in the tents of wickedness'). But quite apart from the evidence that the speaker is an eminent national figure, this seems to imply that the unfortunate pilgrim had sweated all the way up the Baca valley only to remember his bad conscience on arrival!

The Hebrew makes excellent sense if we keep to the punctuation and natural rhythm. יום־טוב, 'a day of good,'[45] is a technical expression for a feast-day. David sent young men to Nabal to say, 'Let the young men find favour in thine eyes; for we come in a יום־טוב" (I Sam. 25:8)—perhaps a new moon or sabbath (II Kgs. 4:23), when petitions might be expected to be granted. At the end of Esther, 'the Jews had gladness and joy, a feast and a יום־טוב" (8:17; cf. 9:19, 22); the 'day of good' is here 14th Adar, the feast of Purim. In the Mishnah יום־טוב is the standard expression for one of the festival days. The expression טוב־יום, joined by a maqqeph, is therefore likely to mean 'good of a (festal) day,' or 'a feast-day blessing.'

But of course, as Kraus rightly says, Israel's festivals stressed the people's responsibilities of 'walking uprightly' as well as their privileges; and it was traditional to value God's covenant above money. Yahweh's judgements were 'more to be desired than gold, yea, than much fine gold' (19:10; cf. 119:127; Prov. 8:10f, 19); the law of his mouth was better to a later Psalmist 'than thousands of gold and silver' (119:72). 'Thousands' here naturally means thousands of *shekels* of gold and silver; and שקלים is frequently omitted with numerals in Hebrew,[46] just as 'thousands' means thousands of pounds in English. So the meaning of the line is quite easy, if somewhat banausic to the spiritual modern reader: 'For I prefer a feast-day blessing to a thousand shekels.' The similar phrase in 119:72 is not surprising, for the later psalmists had read and used the work of their predecessors. In one respect 119 has clarified the message of 84 by adding 'of gold and silver'; but it is interesting to note that the meaning of טוב־יום seems already to have become opaque. He opens his verse with טוב־לי, in the comparative sense, with the copula understood, 'is better than,' exactly like the traditional understanding of 84:10a.

The second half of the verse now repeats the message of the first, being governed by the same verb בחרתי. The only difficulty is the rarity of the two verbs in the infinitive. הסתופף is the hithpoʻel of a verb occurring only here. It is the denominative of סף, a threshold, and so must mean to frequent the temple threshold. The individual pilgrim theory meant that the speaker was reduced to being a beggar—like the blind man in Acts 3, comments Gunkel, or the beggars round the doors of Italian churches in his time. But we have seen the speaker as the Danite priest escorting the royal party, and so leading the nation, to his shrine, pronouncing his prayer to his God for the nation's shield, the king—notice here too 'the house of *my* God.' In ancient times the keeping of the temple threshold was among the highest of callings. Eli 'sat upon his seat by the door post of the temple of the LORD' at Shiloh (I Sam. 1:9). There were priests who kept the threshold and took Jehoash's collection in II Kgs. 12:9, and Josiah's in II Kgs. 22:4; and the five highest officers of the temple, whom Nebuzaradan brought to their execution at Riblah, were Seraiah the chief priest, and Zephaniah the second priest, and the three keepers of the threshold (II Kgs. 25:18). So our picture of the speaker becomes, at least potentially, more precise. Very likely the arrangements at Dan were much the same as at Jerusalem. The chief priest and deputy were no doubt normally old men who stayed at the shrine; the speaker, like a residentiary canon in a modern cathedral, is a younger man of sufficient strength for the two hundred mile journey, and sufficient dignity for the occasion, a Keeper of the Threshold.

Although דור in the qal occurs nowhere else in the Hebrew Bible, it means 'dwell' in rabbinic Hebrew, and at Ecclus. 50:26; so the traditional translation will do for v. 10b. The second half of the verse parallels the first: 'I had rather a (feast) day blessing in thy courts than a thousand (shekels): To keep the threshold in the house of my God than to dwell in the tents of wickedness.' The upright (v. 11), that is Israel, are celebrating the festival in the temple courts at Dan, or (in the case of the speaker) by the temple threshold. The wicked, that is the Syrians and such, may have their tents filled with ill-gotten shekels, but they miss the true blessing. Thus the כִּי link becomes clear: both v. 9 and v. 10 are concerned with the fortunes of the nation. The priest is able to pray for the king (v. 9) with confidence because (כִּי) his God's festal blessing is the most valued thing on earth. The connection is now expounded in the last two verses of the psalm.

> 84:11 For the LORD God is a battlement (שֶׁמֶשׁ) and a shield:
> The LORD will give grace and glory:
> No good thing will he withhold from them that walk uprightly.
> 12 O LORD of hosts,
> Blessed is the man that trusteth in thee.

The mention of 'wickedness' at the end of v. 10 is now clarified. The wicked are Israel's enemies, ever awake to raid (II Kgs. 5:2, 6, 8ff) and to invade (I Kgs. 20, etc.) and to despoil. Perhaps their 'tents' signify that they are thought of as campaigning (cf. II Sam. 11:11); and their 'thousands' may reflect the practice of bringing precious metals to battle (Jg. 8:21ff; II Kgs. 7:8; Ps. 68:12f; cf. below, pp.190f). But all this is in vain; for Yahweh is a shield, and will protect us. He will behold our shield, his anointed, and we shall win the battle. The bracketing of שֶׁמֶשׁ with מָגֵן seems to imply that the former should be understood in the sense of 'battlement,' as in Isa. 54:12—an interpretation which goes back as far as the Targum, and is followed by Gunkel, NEB and many. The crude statement that Yahweh is a 'sun' is unparalleled in the OT. The context of foreign invasion under other gods is perhaps responsible for the repeated naming of Israel's God as Yahweh here, as against the traditional Elohim in v. 7 and v. 9. He will give favour and honour to our army. Consecrated as we are to his law, and so walking in perfection, we shall be blessed with success, 'good,' the 'good of the feast-day' (v. 10), which Yahweh will bestow unstintingly. The military context which thus emerges from the third section of the psalm is likely to be responsible for the four occurrences of Yahweh (God) of hosts in 84. The other Korah psalm in which the name is repeated is 46, where the context is openly military (46:9); and the same is true of 48:8, following the abortive invasion pictured in 48:4-7. Yahweh is a fighting God, going to war with his ark, Yahweh of hosts, the succour of the hosts of Israel (44:9)—whatever the origin of the title, the military overtone was present in it, and seems to be taken up in many of the passages where it occurs. The psalm ends, as its first section ended, and its second section began, with a beatitude: blessed the Israelite with such a God to fight his battles.

We have, with the Dan hypothesis, been able to make sense of 42-43 and 84 in a way that available theories have found impossible. The impressive list of similarities in the two psalms is due to 42-43 being a pilgrimage sequence as 84 is. The Danite location accounts for the geographical details which have so long been surds: the land of Jordan, the Hermons and the Hill Mizar, the depths and waterfalls, waves and billows, in 42; the Balsam tree valley, the springs and the early rain in 84. The combination of personal and national elements in both psalms is resolved if the speaker is a Keeper of the Threshold, a member of the Danite hierarchy, who has led king and people to his shrine for the festival. The detailed wording of the two psalms has enabled us to trace a consistent picture of the route taken by the main festal procession, and of the mood and feelings of the participants. The contrasts between them, both in the far more plaintive tone of 42-43, and in the slighter, but noticeable, variation in the divine names, can be explained in terms of relative date, and the deteriorating political situation of the eighth century. Finally, since we have two, and only two, pilgrimage psalms in the Korah collection, and one comes at the beginning of the main sequence in the 40's and the other at the beginning of the subsidiary sequence in the 80's, we have the suggestion that the order of the collection is, as we have suspected, not an accident. Pilgrimages precede festivals, and we might expect pilgrimage psalms to precede festival sequences.

But before proceeding to the following psalms, 44 and 85, we must ask some more questions about the sons of Korah.

III

THE PRIESTHOOD AT DAN

i. *The Settlement*

For a reconstruction of the history of the priesthood at Dan, I have one resource not available to earlier scholars: the findings of the Israeli archaeological teams under the direction of Professor Avraham Biran, which have been excavating Tel Dan since 1966.[1] Apart from this slender advantage, I have to depend upon my own thread of Ariadne to lead me through the labyrinth of Biblical texts on the topic.

Tel Dan, or Tell el-Qadi, as it was known before 1948, covers the ancient city of Dan, a town of medium size—about fifty acres—as compared with Beth Shean, which was about two hundred acres, or Beersheba, which was about three acres. It stands on a small eminence, the hill Mizar (as I have argued), at one of the two main sources of the Jordan, the R. Dan, or Nahr Leddan; the main stream rises just to the west of the city, and there are numerous springs inside the ramparts, which combine to form a major tributary. The town has been fortified since the Early Bronze Age; its rampart now standing has a stone core 6.3m thick, with earth and debris on both sides of the core, dating from 1700 BC or earlier. Burials were made in the inner slope of the rampart in jars from this period, and a tomb has been found with Mycenaean pottery, including the painting of a charioteer from around 1300. The town, under its old Canaanite name of Laish, is mentioned in documents from Mari and in Egyptian texts from the eighteenth century. It was thus a place of some significance in the second millennium BC, and continued to be regarded as a sacred site down to Roman times, a sanctity due ultimately no doubt to its water, fertility and trees.

The town suffered two major destructions in this period, one in the fifteenth, one in the eleventh century. The first does not mark a major cultural upheaval, but the pottery above the level of the second fire is much more crude than that beneath, showing the new occupants to be less civilised than the old. This would correspond with the state of

affairs at Hazor, Megiddo and elsewhere, where the more advanced
Canaanites were displaced by the rougher Israelites at about the same
period, or a little earlier. The fit with the documentary evidence of the
Bible is, however, only partial. Jg. 18:27 says that the Danites 'smote
(the Laishites) with the edge of the sword, and burned the city with
fire'; but 18:31 says that Micah's image was at Dan 'all the time that
the house of God was at Shiloh.' Shiloh was taken by the Philistines in
the mid-eleventh century, as was Beth-Shean further north, and the
suggestion is therefore that the Philistine conquests extended as far as
Dan, which was then retaken by the Israelites under David. Such a
scenario might be seen as an attractive possibility. Philistine
pottery of the period has been found on the site, though this might
have been imported, or have belonged to an isolated Philistine family.
Certainly Israelite resistance to the Philistines centred on Benjamin
and Judah, and the Philistines may have made their way further north,
to the limit of Israelite possessions. We do not need to posit a major
destruction every time a town changes hands. Nonetheless, the
Philistine episode remains a conjecture. The Danites may just have
taken and burned the city in the eleventh century, and Israel held it till
the 730 period, with a short intermission of Syrian occupation early in
the ninth century.[2]

Our first Biblical text, then, is Jg. 17-18. Discussion has concentrated
on two questions in this connection: the debate whether the passage is
of a single original shape that has been heavily and repeatedly edited,
or whether two stories have been combined;[3] and the question of the
tendency of the present narrative, whether Deuteronomistic or going
back to the time of Jeroboam I. Modern opinion in general favours a
single source,[4] and I agree with this; two independent sources cannot
be shown to be necessary, and they would take the same poor view of
Dan; and it is difficult to suggest two different communities where
they could have been handed down. Martin Noth's proposal,[5] that the
harsh view of Dan is due to the activities of Jeroboam I, requires more
careful consideration.

Noth dismisses the earlier consensus that the anti-Dan, anti-Levite
tendency of the passage is in line with the thought of the D-historian.
In Jg. 17:6 and 18:1a it is said, 'In those days there was no king in
Israel,' and the former text adds, 'and every man did what was right in
his own eyes.' These sentences are remarkable, says Noth, in view of
the D-historian's general anti-monarchical bias. They should therefore
be viewed as part of the original northern tradition, which is here

glorifying Jeroboam as king of Israel. Jeroboam replaced Levitical priests with non-Levitical clergy of his own (I Kgs. 12:31f), the old silver statuette with his 'golden calf,' a tribal shrine with a national royal sanctuary. So our Jg. 17-18 is a heavily pejorative form of the original cult-legend, put about to discredit the old worship by the representatives of the new; and this has been taken over with minor elaborations as grist to the Deuteronomistic mill. Noth's arguments are not convincing. The same phrases about there being no king in Israel recur in the following complex, at 19:1 and 21:25; it is not surprising that they occur in Jg. 17-21 only, because Jg. 17-21 describe the only really serious scandals before the monarchy. Noth cites the perfectly satisfying judgement of Charles Hauret,[6] that David was an ideal king to the authors of the D-history, and that he and some of his loyal successors like Josiah saw that cultic matters were properly ordered. Noth's theory takes as history the highly tendentious passage in I Kgs. 12;[7] and even if matters were as he says, one is at a loss to account for the supposed onslaught on the older worship. One would have thought that an ancient and revered object like the silver statuette would be an asset to the extended sanctuary, in the same way as the brazen serpent was retained at Jerusalem. How, too, did the Levitical priesthood come to be assumed as normal later in the north, if it were reviled at both national shrines?

We are left then with the older, and fully adequate view, that Jg. 17-18 is the tatters of the original sanctuary legend at Dan, heavily overlaid with pejorative embellishment by its blackest enemies, the D-historians. The central thesis of their theology was that worship away from Jerusalem was apostasy from Yahweh, the apostasy that had brought about the fall of Samaria and the exile of Judah; and the two proudest centres of this perverted worship were Bethel and Dan. Nothing, in consequence, is spared in the project of disgracing the Danite cult: every detail that could be expected to disgust the hearer, and render the place odious to him, is supplied regardless of inconsistency. This does, however, have one simple and satisfactory corollary for the modern scholar: it is plain that anything told to the credit of Dan is mentioned because it stood in the original sanctuary-legend, and was too well-known to be suppressed. We are thus able to discern an outline of the original story, and even of the history.

The following distasteful details emerge from the final version. The centrepiece of worship at Dan was a graven image (18:30f), sometimes called a graven image and a molten image [8] (17:3, 4), a graven image and an ephod and teraphim and a molten image (18:14, 17, 18, 20, with slight variations), or just an ephod and teraphim (17:5). The silver out of which these abominations were made, eleven hundred shekels in weight, had originally belonged to the mother of a man called Micah, who had stolen it from her, and she had in consequence laid a curse upon it; but when he handed it back, she dedicated two hundred of the shekels to make the graven idol—rather a trivial amount, about six pounds in weight, the equivalent of some thirty modern silver tablespoons.[9] It is unclear what became of the remaining nine hundred shekels (17:1-4). Micah was a man without any kind of principle: he not only stole the money from his own mother, and then made an idol out of the silver which he knew to be cursed; he also made one of his sons his priest, despite his being an Ephraimite. Later, however, when a poor Levite passed by, he pushed out his own son, and hired the Levite for a pittance,[10] so expecting to manipulate Yahweh—'Now know I that the LORD will do me good, seeing I have a Levite to my priest' (17:7-13).

This was, however, but the beginning of iniquity. An advance party of Danites passing recognised the voice of the Levite, and prevailed on him to give them an oracle; and when the whole clan of six hundred migrated north, they in turn stole all the idols, and persuaded the priest to stand by in silence, and so double-cross his master. This he did gladly, in the expectation of increasing his income, since he would now be priest to a whole tribe instead of one household; in fact he purloined the idols himself (18:1-20). Micah went after them with his neighbours, but the Danites rebuffed him with insults, and held on to their ill-gotten gains by force majeure. They then proceeded to Laish, 'unto a people quiet and secure,' whom they murdered with impunity,[11] and set up the graven image to worship (18:21-30). The account ends, 'and Jonathan, the son of Gershom, the son of Moses, he and his sons were priests to the tribe of the Danites until the day of the captivity of the land. So they set them up Micah's graven image which he made, all the time that the house of God was in Shiloh' (18:30f).

It is obvious that this tale of multiple wickedness owes everything to the tendency of the writer and his tradition: small wonder if a cult of so evil a foundation brought its worshippers to final disaster. We can hardly hope with scissors and paste to reconstruct the foundation-legend of Dan which underlies it. But three points stand out by way of contrast as being to the credit of Dan, and it is precisely these which interest us in consequence.

(i) The founding priest of the shrine was not an anonymous waster, as the story had led us to expect, but a man called Jonathan, whose line continued to hold office there until the eighth century, when the northern provinces were enslaved by Tiglath-Pileser III (II Kgs. 15:29). This man, so far from being of disreputable background, was of the most unimpeachable family, being none other than the grandson of Moses himself, and that through his elder son, Gershom. This unpalatable fact, which has been preserved in the Greek and Latin and Harclean Syriac traditions, was too much for the Hebrew copyists, who have inserted a *nun* so as to make Jonathan the descendant of one of less virtuous name, Manasseh.[12] An unavoidable fact about the Danite priesthood was its Levitical descent, which comes out not only in so far as Moses was of the tribe of Levi, but even in the libels about Micah's household. Later on the author will tell us that Jeroboam made non-Levitical priests to serve at Dan, but the Judges account clearly gives this the lie.[13] He certainly would not have credited Dan with Levite priests if he could have avoided it.

(ii) The stress in the story of the cult-object falls on the graven image, that being the form of idol expressly forbidden in the Second Commandment; but there is also intermittent mention of the ephod and teraphim, and these are spoken of on their own at 17:5. Now 'the ephod' was a central part of the temple furniture at Nob (I Sam. 21:9), where it is uncriticised; Abiathar brought it with him in his flight (23:6), and David consulted it then and in I Sam. 30:7f, and perhaps II Sam. 5:19ff (cf. I Sam. 14:3, 18f [LXX], 36ff). Teraphim, similarly, are accepted in early traditions as being valid religious symbols (Gen. 31:19ff; I Sam. 19:13ff). It is true that the D-historians treat the ephod which Gideon set up at Ophrah (Jg. 8:27) as an idol like the Danite one, and couple teraphim with iniquity at I Sam. 15:23 (cf. II Kgs. 23:24; Ezek. 21:21; Zech. 10:2); but as late as Hosea, ephod and teraphim are treated as neutral northern institutions, like king, princes, sacrifice and pillar (Hos. 3:4). The ephod was not an idol, but was a kind of breastplate of precious metal carried before Yahweh,[14] comparable to the aegis worn by Zeus and Athena. Although the teraphim in Gen. 31 and I Sam. 19 are family images (of different sizes), teraphim are so often associated with the ephod (five times here, Hos. 3:4)[15] that they are probably the lots drawn from the ephod in these contexts. Ezek. 21:21 and Zech. 10:2 make them the means of divination (cf. I Sam. 15:23); they may of course have been shaped like images.

(iii) The Levite is said to have come from Bethlehem in Judah (17:7,

9). It is difficult to think of any reason why this detail should have been invented, if it were not traditional, especially as to the D-historians Bethlehem was a place of great honour, being David's home-town; and the Levite of Jg. 19-21 is also associated with Bethlehem. It seems a reasonable conjecture, therefore, that Gershom's family settled in the Bethlehem area at first, and that at least some of them migrated north quite soon. The Danites' road from Kiriath-Jearim through the hill-country of Ephraim (18:12f) is the main hill road from Bethel to Shechem. Bethel is not mentioned, but Micah's house cannot have been far away.

In this way we may glean the outline of the foundation-legend at Dan. The Danite priesthood was Levitical, descended from Jonathan the grandson of Moses, the archetypal priest of Israel.[17] Its cultic symbol was a silver ephod of no great weight and size, probably of immemorial antiquity; and this was understood to be a mysterious metallic robe, within which Yahweh's presence dwelt, and from which he showed his will by means of the teraphim lodged in its pocket. The Levites had at first settled in the Bethlehem area of Judah, as a secular group;[18] but they had specialised as priests, and migrated first to Ephraim and later to Dan.

A second early text which sheds light on the Levites is the genealogical fragment in Num. 26:58. The Priestly tradition established an 'orthodox' genealogy of Levi, with three sons, Gershon, Kohath and Merari (Gen. 46:11), and Aaron son of Amram son of Kohath as the high-priestly branch of the family (Exod. 6:16-27; Num. 3:17ff); a structure accepted by the Chronicler (I Chron. 6:1ff; and vv. 16ff, 31ff, with the spelling Gershom). This P tradition is found also in Num. 26:57, the last phrase of v. 58 and vv. 59ff; but in the main part of v. 58 there is found a heterodox genealogy, which has been widely accepted[19] as an older fragment. In the Hebrew this runs, 'These are the families of Levi: the family of the Libnites, the family of the Hebronites, the family of the Mahlites, the family of the Mushites, the family of the Korahites'; but the LXX omits the Mahlites, and as they are a standard pair with the Mushites as the 'orthodox' sons of Merari, Kurt Möhlenbrink has suggested that they have been glossed into the Hebrew tradition.[20] This would leave four 'families' of Levites, the Libnites, Hebronites, Mushites and Korahites. Two of these are names of towns in Judah, Libnah twenty-five miles west of Jerusalem, and Hebron twenty miles south-south-west of Jerusalem. No town is associated with the Mushites, who have been suspected of being downgraded Moses-ites.[21] Korah may similarly be a personal name, perhaps of Edomite origin (Gen. 36:5, 14, 18; I Chron. 1:35); but the Chronicler thinks of it also as the name of a village in the neighbourhood of Hebron, since Korah is one of the 'sons' of Hebron along with other local place-names in I Chron. 2:42f.

The Num. 26:58 fragment is usually taken to confirm the hint drawn from Jg. 17-18, that the Levites were at first a secular tribe who settled in the south, but who failed to establish themselves militarily, and became professional priests instead. It may be that Canaanite priests at Libnah and Hebron were adopted into the clan.[22] At all events it seems likely that the settlements in these two towns were permanent, for Hebron and Libnah are the first towns given to 'the children of Aaron' in Josh. 21:13, and Libni and Hebron are senior sons of Gershom, Kohath and Mahli in I Chron. 6:16ff. If so, then it was the Mushites and the Korahites who migrated north; and it will have been one or both of these two groups who became the priests at Dan. It would be a neat solution to identify the Mushites with the family of Jonathan the grandson of Moses, the priest of Dan. But this may be too good to be true. Perhaps the Jg. 17f story masks the historical settlement of the Gershom family in Ephraim, whence only Jonathan went on to Dan; in which case there were Moses-ites in two areas, and we should not know which group later became the Mushites. Or perhaps Jonathan was accompanied, or joined, by Levites from the family of Korah, in the same way that Eli was assisted by Samuel at Shiloh, and the Zadokites by other priests at Jerusalem in later times. All Num. 26:58 tells us is that the Levites at first settled in Judah, and that some of them, probably the 'Mushites' and Korahites, later moved north.

A third document from very early times is the story of Moses and the Levites embedded in Exod. 32—which in turn must be interpreted by the blessing of Levi in Deut. 33:8ff. Exod. 32 has a complex history, in which one basic story has been elaborated a number of times.[23] Eissfeldt suggested that the earliest ('L') component was the legend justifying the Levitical priesthood, that is, Exod. 24:14f; 32:17f, 25-9.[24] Moses and Joshua go up Sinai, leaving the people in charge of the elders, under Aaron and Hur. While they are away there is a riot—L did not include the Golden Calf—against Moses' authority, and hence Yahweh's; it is this that produces the shouting heard by Joshua on their descent. Moses issues the challenge that whoever is on Yahweh's side should execute the rebels, and 'all the sons of Levi' respond; as a result of which Moses bids them to 'fill their hand,' i.e. to consecrate themselves as priests. Although 'all the sons of Levi' are thus said to have stood by Yahweh, the story also says that they slew every man his son and his brother (v. 29, cp. v. 27), which makes it look as if the Levites had been on both sides, and that the Yahwist element had prevailed after internecine warfare. The tension between v. 29, 'Consecrate yourselves today to the LORD, for every man (hath been) against his son and against his brother,' and v. 27, 'slay every man his brother, and every man his companion, and every man his neighbour,' itself suggests that this part of Exod. 32 is older than its context; and that the companion and neighbour of v. 27 have been introduced to change the meaning of 'brother' from Levite to Israelite. A very similar picture emerges from Deut. 33:8f: Levi is he whom God loves, 'Whom thou didst prove at Massah, With whom thou didst strive at the waters of Meribah; Who said of his father, and of his mother, I have not seen him; Neither did he acknowledge his brethren, Nor knew he his own children: For they have observed thy word, And keep thy covenant.'[25] Exod. 32 does not take place, of course, at Massah/Meribah; but the northern tradition of Ps. 81 also refers to events now associated with Sinai (vv. 7b, 9, 10a) under the rubric, 'I proved thee at the waters of Meribah' (v. 7c).

While Eissfeldt may be wrong in some details, such as the exclusion of an element of idol-worship as the occasion for the riot, it seems clear that we do possess here an ancient aetiology for the Levitical priesthood, and that it stems, like Deut. 33 as a whole, from northern Israel. Now if we ask, 'Which sanctuary in northern Israel was concerned in the primitive period to legitimate the Levitical priesthood by reference to Moses?,' we are bound to think first of Dan. Of the priesthood at Shiloh, there is no plain evidence[26] that Eli was a Levite, and certainly Samuel was not, but an Ephraimite; and we are equally ignorant about Bethel, Jg. 20:27f being a late insertion.[27] But we do know from Jg. 18:30 that there was a Levitical priesthood at Dan, with Moses' own grandson as the sanctuary founder; and we know that the northern community, with its two main shrines at Bethel and Dan, persevered in honouring the legend right down to the eighth century (Deut. 33). As Bethel has no connection with Moses (as well as no known Levitical connection), it is at Dan that the Exod. 32:25-9/Deut. 33:8f legend is most likely to have had its home.

But if this is so, it tells us something further about the state of affairs at Dan. If the priesthood at Dan had been entirely of the family of

Moses' grandson Jonathan, then its legitimating legend would have justified the priesthood of Moses and his descendants. But this is not the case. The story presumes the priesthood of Moses, and legitimates the consecration of the Levites, who are represented as being other than Moses' family. It seems fair to conclude then that the priesthood at Dan mirrored the situation of the story, with a Mosaic ('Mushite') dynasty presiding, and a wider circle of non-'Mushite' priests assisting. On the basis of Num. 26:58, these must have been from one of the three remaining 'families': the Libnites, the Hebronites or the Korahites. We have seen that Libnah and Hebron are the names of towns in Judah, and that the implication is that the Levites belonging there settled there for a considerable time. So we have our first hint that there was an assistant Levitical priesthood at Dan, of the sons of Korah.

ii. Dan and Bethel

For the monarchical period, we are fortunate to have archaeological help again. Dan was rebuilt, with massive city-walls 3.6m thick at the base, rising to 12m in height above the plain, in the late tenth century; and the bamah was constructed of very large stones to about half its present size at about the same time, that is in the reign of Jeroboam I. The walls were breached at the city gate, and the bamah destroyed by fire at the end of the tenth century; thus confirming the Biblical account, 'And Ben-hadad hearkened unto King Asa, and sent the captains of his armies against the cities of Israel, and smote Ijon, and Dan, and Abel-beth-maacah, and all Chinneroth, with all the land of Naphtali' (I Kgs. 15:20). However, extensive rebuilding took place in the middle of the ninth century. The bamah was doubled in size to $18.7m \times 18.2m$, being constructed in the classic Israelite manner with headers and stretchers such as are to be found at Samaria; and an ornamental flight of steps was built to give access on the south side. These were improved a century later, and the present lower steps (see photograph, Pl. IV) date from this time, probably the reign of Jeroboam II (c.787-747). There are many signs of life in the city itself over the same period: three hundred small jugs, for example, have been recovered from a building over the gate, from the mid-eighth century, including one marked לעמץ, 'Amoz's.' The city was later occupied by the Assyrians, and continued to be inhabited through till Roman times.[28]

This framework is invaluable for the assessment of the notorious passage on Dan and Bethel in I Kgs. 12:25-33. Here Jeroboam I is said to fear that his subjects will go back to Rehoboam if they worship at Jerusalem: 'Whereupon the king took counsel, and made two calves of gold; and he said unto them, Ye have gone up long enough to Jerusalem; behold thy gods, O Israel, which brought thee up out of the land of Egypt. And he set the one in Beth-el, and the other put he in Dan. And this thing became a sin: for the people went (to worship) before the one (RV text)/each of them (mg) (לאחד), even unto Dan. And he made the house (את-בית) of high places, and made priests from among all the people, which were not of the sons of Levi. And Jeroboam ordained a feast in the eighth month, on the fifteenth day of the month, like unto the feast that is in Judah, and he offered upon the altar; so did he in Beth-el to sacrifice unto the calves that he had made . . .' (vv. 28-32). The account ends with Jeroboam settling his new-made priests in Bethel, sacrificing and burning incense himself at Bethel at his new-found eighth month festival.

Some of these details are as straightfordly libellous as the account in Jg. 17-18. J. Debus, in his *Die Sünde Jerobeams*, 40ff, has rebutted Noth's claim that the northerners would be likely to be drawn back to Jerusalem by the ark; Bethel and Dan were older Israelite shrines than Jerusalem, and they had managed without the ark for years enough. Similarly, 'Behold thy gods, O Israel, which brought thee up out of the land of Egypt' is a parody of the opening of the Ten Commandments; and Jeroboam's sacrifices, while intended to be scandalous, were probably normal for a king at the time. There are four questions, however, which are not quite so straightforward: (i) Leaving Bethel aside, did Jeroboam put non-Levitical priests in at Dan? (ii) What was the relation between the two national sanctuaries at Dan and Bethel? (iii) Why the eighth month feast? (iv) Was there a golden calf at Dan?

(i) Noth speaks of a national shrine at Dan alongside the old tribal shrine, and accepts the story of non-Levite priests.[29] It is difficult, however, to give credence to anything the D-historians say about Dan, since they have proved themselves so thoroughly tendentious. Here is a further statement which reads exactly like a damaging libel, in the light of the sixth century belief that all true priests are Levites; and furthermore it is contradicted by the note already observed in Jg. 18:30, that Jonathan's family were priests at Dan 'until the day of the captivity of the land' in the 730's. It is true that the phrase used is 'priests to the tribe of the Danites,' but this is written in the light of 18:19, and for the first century and more they served the Danites only.

(ii) The relationship between Dan and Bethel is unclear. In vv. 28f Jeroboam is said to have made two golden calves, one for Dan and the other for Bethel; but in v. 30 'the people went (to worship) before הָאֶחָד, even unto Dan.' אֶחָד can carry the meaning 'each' (BDB, *s.v.*, §2; RV mg), but the glossing phrase 'even unto Dan' seems to exclude it. The Lucianic text of LXX alone has 'and before the other, to Bethel' (so NEB), but this looks as if it has been added to solve the problem. V. 31 opens 'And he made אֶת־בֵּית־בָּמוֹת,' which confirms that the writer is speaking of a single sanctuary.[30] We should therefore understand vv. 31-32a as all referring to Dan—the house of high places, the non-Levitical priests, the eighth month festival and the king's sacrifices. The כֵּן with which v. 32b opens should then be taken as introducing parallel practice at Bethel: 'So did he in Beth-el'— sacrificing, new-made priests and high places, the eighth month festival, all being repeated, not vapidly, but as referring to Bethel. This seems to make sense of the text; our only hesitation is in v. 32b, 'So did he in Beth-el, to sacrifice unto the *calves* that he had made,' for in vv. 28f there were two calves, one in Dan and the other in Bethel. This quirk I postpone to (iv).

Most commentators suggest that Jeroboam chose two Israelite shrines for national worship, one in the extreme north, the other in the extreme south of the country. In this way all the inhabitants would be convenienced.[31] However, this proposal does not agree with the widespread, ancient and northern prescription that the autumn festival should be attended by 'all Israel,' 'all thy males' (Exod. 23:17; 34:23; Deut. 16:16) at a single sanctuary (Deut. 12; etc.); and it is implied in the passage that the king himself led the national worship. It seems therefore to be excluded that half the people went to Dan and half to Bethel. Nor is there any suggestion that the two sanctuaries took turn and turn about; and even if they did, the last motive Jeroboam could have had would be convenience, since sanctuaries in the extreme north and south would involve the maximum of travelling for everyone. Why not Shiloh, the recent cultic centre (I Kgs. 14)? Or Shechem, which he had rebuilt, and where he was crowned (I Kgs. 12)?

The answer seems to be given by the excavations. Jeroboam can only have had one national sanctuary, and the cultic building dug up and dated in his reign at Dan shows that Dan was his centre. We can only guess at the reasons: perhaps its position at the source of the

Jordan commended it; perhaps he had illusions of Solomonic grandeur, and thought it would be central for an empire stretching to the Euphrates. But any such ideas were soon humbled. Dan was captured and burned by the Syrians twenty years later, in the reign of Baasha (I Kgs. 15:20), and was in Syrian hands for a generation. Israel would then require another central sanctuary in safer lands further south, and Bethel was the choice. Perhaps Syrian incursions had begun in Jeroboam's last years, and the transfer was begun by him; or perhaps, as an Ephraimite, he honoured Bethel, and the transfer was actually made by Baasha after his death. But under the house of Omri Israel began to prosper again. Dan was rebuilt and magnificently extended, probably in Ahab's reign; and this presumably means that it was reinstated as the national sanctuary. Further extensions like the ornamental steps imply that it remained the central shrine down to the time of Jeroboam II, that is for more than a century until the devastation of Naphtali, Dan and Gilead in the 730's. Both Ahab and Jeroboam II had real pretensions to hegemony west of the Euphrates. Ahab's army was the backbone of the anti-Assyrian coalition at Qarqar in 853,[32] and Jeroboam II captured Hamath and Damascus (II Kgs. 14:28). After the loss of the northern provinces under his successors, Bethel resumed its place as the national centre. So the northern kingdom had two central sanctuaries, Dan and Bethel, as the D-historians say, but not two simultaneous central sanctuaries. Dan had the lion's share of the time, roughly 925-905, 880-732, and Bethel was merely a reserve, 'a royal house' (Am. 7:13). But it is Bethel which catches the edge of the prophets' tongues, because that was the central shrine when Amos and Hosea were prophesying, and it continued in operation of a kind for many years thereafter (II Kgs. 23:15ff; Zech. 7:2ff). Amos has an oracle against Dan (8:14), but he prophesied against Bethel as early as Jeroboam's time (7:10ff); and later, when Dan had fallen, against Bethel with Gilgal and Beersheba (5:4ff; cf. 4:4ff; 3:14).[33] Dan was lost when Hosea prophesied, and his words are centrally directed against 'Beth-aven' (4:15; 5:8; 10:5, 8). To the D-historians Dan is but a memory; Bethel is a recent menace, and is excoriated for the whole of I Kgs. 13.

(iii) This clarification of the relationship of Dan and Bethel seems to resolve the further problem of the eighth month feast.[34] The D-historian says that Jeroboam instituted such a feast as a novelty, and that its purpose was to prevent his subjects continuing to attend the feast at Jerusalem. But both these suggestions are generally rejected.

Jeroboam is likely to have gone back to old ways, not to have forced innovations; and in any case holding an eighth month feast would be a foolish way of trying to stop his people attending a seventh month feast elsewhere. So it looks as if Ingathering was celebrated in earlier times in Bul (November) rather than in Ethanim (October). In favour of this it is noted: (a) although Solomon dedicated the Temple in Ethanim (I Kgs. 8:2), he began it in Ziv ('the second month,' I Kgs. 6:1, 37) and completed it in Bul (v. 38); (b) provision is made for a second month Passover celebration (Num. 9:1-14), which could be a relic of an old use, with Ziv regarded as the spring month; (c) the name Bul means 'produce,' and would naturally be associated with the festival of Ingathering. But since Jerusalem use was to hold the feasts in Abib and Ethanim (the 'first' and 'seventh' months), celebrations in Ziv and Bul must have been northern, and due to climatic differences.

Against this it has been replied with effect that there is no important climatic difference. Gustav Dalman wrote, 'If climatic difference there be, Samaria is warmer than Judah,'[35] and Roland de Vaux, 'there is no difference in time of harvest between Bethel and Jerusalem.'[36] But such objections only apply on the standard assumption that the main sanctuary was Bethel. If the principal sanctuary was Dan, we have a very marked climatic difference, for Dan is not only a hundred and fifty miles north of Jerusalem, but also stands on a spur of Mt Hermon; it is cooler and wetter than Judaea, and the harvests come later. So it is only too likely that the Harvest Festival was kept there from time immemorial in the Harvest month, Bul; and that Jeroboam was compelled, rather to his inconvenience, to celebrate the feast at the time traditional to the sanctuary. Solomon's builders came from Tyre and Naphtali (I Kgs. 7:14), so this would explain their following a northern sacred calendar, while Solomon himself naturally observed the Jerusalem year. It is noticeable that when Hezekiah invited the northerners to participate in the Jerusalem Passover, the celebration was observed in 'the second month' (II Chron. 30), though the Chronicler is quick to prefer a cultic to a political motive for the changed date. So all the data can be explained on the basis of later grape and olive harvests at Dan than at Jerusalem. The difference is not so much as a month, and the practice of ad hoc intercalation of a thirteenth moon every two or three years would mean that in some years the feasts at the two centres coincided.[37]

(iv) It is usually taken that there was something like a golden calf at Dan, even if only a pedestal with golden bull(s) on it, with Yahweh enthroned invisibly above.[38] But our only evidence for this is I Kgs. 12, and there are three reasons for questioning that: first, its generally tendentious and hostile character; second, the way Dan has been made a golden replica of Bethel; and third, the detail already noted, that there were two calves mentioned in vv. 28f, and both seem to be present at Bethel in v. 32b. Now there is every reason to think that something like an empty throne with gold-plated cherub-bulls to either side was the focus of worship at Bethel. Hosea says, 'The inhabitants of Samaria shall be in terror for the calves of Beth-aven' (10:5).[39] Bethel is in Ephraim, and the Ephraim-Benjamin-Manasseh Ps. 80, in the Asaph collection, addresses God as 'sitting upon the Cherubim,' ישב הכרובים (80:1).

But the golden throne at Bethel was not the central sacred treasure of the author of Deut. 33, whose 'blessing of Moses' was composed in relatively happy times before 732, and includes Dan, Naphtali and Asher. To him the first thing to be said of Levi is, 'Thy Thummim and thy Urim are with him whom thou lovest' (v. 8). Now we know that Urim and Thummim were the lots kept in the ephod carried by Ahijah for Saul in I Sam. 14 (v. 41 LXX),[40] and that this ephod was taken by Abiathar to David (I Sam. 23:6ff; 30:7), and is never apparently heard of thereafter. It is not likely that other lots bore the same name,[41] and it seems a reasonable conjecture therefore to suppose that these are the same ephod and teraphim which were the sacral focus at Dan in the old cultic legend now parodied in Jg. 17f. As the principal national religious symbol, and means of discovering Yahweh's will, they had been brought south to be at the king's disposal during the Philistine wars—whether or not Dan fell to the Philistines for a period. They spent this troubled time first at Nob,[42] and then with David's entourage, and returned to their home sanctuary either when David preferred the ark, or at the time of Jeroboam's revolt.· Such a suggestion seems to be reflected in Hosea's prophecy, 'For the children of Israel shall abide many days without king, and without prince, and without sacrifice and without pillar, and without ephod and teraphim' (3:4). The central institutions which are to go down with the northern kingdom are king and prince(s), sacrifice and sacrificial stone, ephod and teraphim. The latter must have been the focus of the central sanctuary, even after the withdrawal from Dan when Hosea was preaching, when they were no doubt taken south a second time. The ephod was much too suspect to survive in eighth century Jerusalem, but it seems that the Urim and Thummim were received with honour, and finally set in the high-priest's robe, also called an ephod (Exod. 28:30; Lev. 8:8).[43]

In this way our evidence seems to suggest a continuity of both priesthood and cultic focus at Dan. The Israelite sanctuary was founded by a Mosaic priest, with Levite, probably Korahite assistants, and a silver ephod with teraphim: so much we have extracted from the travesty of Jg. 17f, the aetiological legend in Exod. 32:25-9, and the genealogical fragment of Num. 26:58. The Mosaic priesthood persevered until the 730's (Jg. 18:30). Ephod and teraphim (the latter now called Urim and Thummim) were withdrawn to Nob after the fall of Shiloh (Jg. 18:31; I Sam. 14:21), and were carried by survivors of the Nob priesthood, led by Abiathar, to David (I Sam. 23, 30). David made the ark the cultic focus at Jerusalem, and ephod, Urim and Thummim were in time restored to their earlier home in Dan. This is denied by the D-historians in I Kgs. 12, in favour of the slur that Dan had a golden calf exactly like Bethel; and this slur has led to the *suggestio - falsi* that the ephod remained there only 'all the time that the house of God was in Shiloh' (Jg. 18:31). But it is amply attested both by Deut. 33:8 ('Thy Thummim and thy Urim'), and by the implication of Hos. 3:4 ('ephod or teraphim').

We must be fair both to the Danites and to their Deuteronomistic critics. Yahweh was, to the Northerners, an invisible God who wore the ephod, and gave his people guidance by Urim and Thummim. But they did speak of 'seeing his face' (42:2; 84:7), and we shall find in 89 indications that Philo [44] was right in thinking that the Urim and Thummim were images. Both 85 and 89 suggest that the ephod was carried on a base with four animal figures representing the 'virtues.' Southern suspicions of 'calves' at Dan, and of precious metal images graven and molten, which were symbolic of 'the light of Yahweh's countenance,' were by no means unfounded.

iii. A Tale of Two Priesthoods

The clarification of the position at Dan enables us to find our way through the maze of later traditions, both legendary and genealogical.

The priesthood at Dan, the national shrine of the north, was Mosaic and Levitical; that in Jerusalem was neither. Zadok was a *novus homo* from the days of David's capture of Jerusalem. He first appears in II Sam. 8:17, 'Zadok the son of Ahitub, and Ahimelech the son of Abiathar were priests.' The genealogy is plainly not genuine; Abiathar, not Ahimelech, was the second priest, and he was son of Ahimelech the son of Ahitub.[45] Zadok and Abiathar are represented as co-priests in II Sam. 17:15; 19:11; 20:25, and the text has been disturbed at 15:24-9 to give Zadok priority.[46] It seems thus very likely that Zadok was not even an Israelite, but a Jebusite.[47] But in the crisis of succession at David's death, Abiathar unwisely supported Adonijah, and was exiled by Solomon to Anathoth (I Kgs. 2:6f); so Zadok, who anointed Solomon, became sole priest 'in the room of Abiathar' (v. 35).

The absence of Levitical ancestry did not cause the Zadokites to lose sleep; on the contrary, they gloried in it. Gen. 49, with its picture of a united twelve-tribe Israel presided over by Judah, probably comes from Solomon's court. Its attitude to Levi is contemptuous. Levi and Simeon are taken together, and deplored as violent and angry for their part in the foray at Shechem (Gen. 34): 'Cursed be their anger, for it was fierce; And their wrath, for it was cruel: I will divide them in Jacob, and scatter them in Israel' (vv. 5-7). Levi is not considered as a priestly tribe at all, but as an unsuccessful secular tribe which Yahweh has cursed, and which has in consequence no tribal land. This is not a cause of sorrow to the author, but of the greatest satisfaction, for it has enabled the Judahite house of David, although a later 'son of Jacob,' to take the throne, with evident and dramatic success. The priesthood was associated with Levi in the tenth century only in out-of-the-way places like Libnah, Hebron and Dan: Samuel had been an Ephraimite (I Sam. 1:1) and so had Micah's son, and Abinadab of Kiriath-Jearim had sanctified his son Eleazar as priest (I Sam. 7:1). The house of Zadok ruled Solomon's temple without anxiety.[48]

However, things could not go on like this for ever. The Deuteronomic laws, which were in process of development over the next two centuries in the north, steadily turned the priesthood there into a Levite monopoly. Even if there remains a shadow of doubt whether priests and Levites were identical, as seems to be implied by Deut. 18:1, 'The priests the Levites, all the tribe of Levi,'[49] it is clear from the repeated phrase 'the priests the Levites' that the priesthood was now limited to the single tribe. The influence of the Levite priesthood at the central sanctuary at Dan had made its mark throughout the community. Nor was Judah much isolated from its powerful neighbour. For some periods, as in Ahab's reign, Judah was a client state to Israel, and Jehoshaphat would have had ample opportunity to absorb northern religious norms (I Kgs. 22); and the story of Ahaz' visit to Damascus (II Kgs. 16:10ff) shows how impressionable the provincial southern kings were. So the desirability of a Levite ancestry began to appeal to the Zadokite priesthood also.

Danite claims rested upon two historical facts, the Mosaic ancestry of their chief priest, and the Levitical origin of all their priests, the latter being supported by the legend of Exod. 32:25ff. The southern priests had to counter both of these. In order to outflank the Mosaic claim, they needed to trace their own descent to an authority higher than Moses. In order to overrule the Levite claim, they needed to limit the priesthood to a single family of their own line. These two objects they achieved through the figure of Aaron.

It is a disputed question what traditions about Aaron were available at the time. He appears in what early sources remain to us as a colourless figure. According to Exod. 4:14 he was 'the Levite.' In 15:20 he is the brother of Miriam, Moses not being mentioned; and he and Miriam are linked again in Num. 12. He and Hur hold up Moses' hands during the battle against Amalek (Exod. 17:10-12), and he and Hur are left in charge of the people when Moses goes up Sinai (24:14). He leads the elders of Israel both to eat with Jethro and Moses before God in 18:12, and in the ascent of Sinai to the vision of God in 24:1f, 9-11, with Moses, Nadab and Abihu. Noth thinks that in the early sources he was not even Moses' brother, but that there was a richer tradition about him than now survives.[50] Eissfeldt thinks that he was just part of the scenery.[51]

What the P school—that is, the priestly community at Jerusalem, and later in exile from Jerusalem—has done over the years is to exalt Aaron into a figure transcending Moses. P never calls Moses a priest; the priesthood is vested in Aaron and Aaron's sons alone.[52] Aaron is not merely Moses' brother but his *elder* brother: a most significant move, and an augury of things to come. In the legend of Moses' birth it was implied that Moses was the first-born son: 'And there went a man of the house of Levi, and took to wife a daughter of Levi. And the woman conceived, and bare a son . . .' (Exod. 2:1f).[53] P glosses the story so as to make Miriam already born and grown up (vv. 4, 7f), and Aaron becomes the first-born son at Exod. 6:20; Num. 26:59, and all subsequent genealogies. At Exod. 7:7 Moses is made out by P to be eighty, while Aaron is eighty-three. Furthermore clumsy efforts are made to represent Aaron as outdoing Moses. Poor old Moses is unable to speak, so Aaron comes to meet him in Midian, and is to be his spokesman before the people (4:10-16, 27-30) and Pharaoh (6:28-7:2). He becomes Moses' shadow in 5:1, 4, 20; 7:8, 10, 20; 8:8, 12, 25; 9:8, 27;

10:3, 8, 16; 11:10 etc.; but his function as Moses' 'prophet' is soon forgotten, and Moses does almost all the speaking alone. Similarly Moses' rod (4:1, 17, 20) at first becomes Aaron's rod (7:9ff), with which the waters are made blood (vv. 19f; cf. vv. 15, 17), and the frogs (8:5) and the lice to swarm (8:16); but Moses remains the sole wonder-worker of the flies, murrain, boils, hail, locusts, darkness and first-born, that is, the last seven plagues. Almost all ritual activities are credited to Aaron and his sons. He is consecrated as the first priest of Israel, and his sons are the only lawful priests (Exod. 28-29); he intercedes for Israel and prevents the plague (Num. 16:41-50); his rod buds and blossoms miraculously as a token of his pre-eminence and faithfulness (Num. 17); the special laws for the priesthood, in both Leviticus and Numbers, are all committed to him; and he dies amid national mourning on Mt Hor, with the high priesthood ceremonially transferred to his son (Num. 20:22-29). Only the torah-giving (Exod. 18), the covenant sacrifice (Exod. 24), and the ordination of Aaron and his sons (Exod. 29; Lev. 8) remain to Moses. One cannot greatly admire P's handiwork as artistry; it is too careless, and his Aaron is a man of cardboard. But it fulfilled its political aim with dramatic success, by effrontery and constant repetition; it is no mean achievement to have edged Moses out of the position of Israel's first priest, which he had held historically, and was universally known for some four centuries to have held.

The line from Zadok to Aaron was variously traced (I Chron. 6:3-8, 50-53; cp. 9:11), but it began normally with Ahitub (II Sam. 8:17; I Chron. 6), and always ended with Phinehas, son of Eleazar, son of Aaron (from Exod. 6:23, 25 on). The choice of the last names is a further instance of P's effrontery. Requiring priestly names, he chose Eleazar, the name of the priest who had guarded the ark in I Sam. 7:1, and Phinehas, the name of the father of the priesthood at Nob in I Sam. 4. The latter had the additional advantage of annoying the posterity of the real Phinehas, eking out their poverty at Anathoth. In order to conform Eleazar to the standard Israelite pattern of the younger son succeeding (like Jacob, Judah and David), he took two Israelite leaders who had accompanied Aaron up Sinai, Nadab and Abihu (Exod. 24:1, 9), made them his elder sons, and killed them off (Lev. 10:1ff). So the Zadokites ended up with first class ancestry, which was to stand them in good stead.

The first direct evidence we have of this creative thinking in Jerusalem is Ps. 118, which is now widely thought to be a pre-exilic southern psalm:[54] 'Let the house of Aaron now say, That his mercy (endureth) for ever' (v. 3). But we have two pieces of indirect evidence that it is not later than the eighth century, in the Danite reactions to the sudden rise of Aaron, in Exod. 32 and Num. 12. The interpretation of Exod. 32 has been made difficult by the presence of two apparently opposite tendencies at work in the story. For on the one side there is an obvious relationship between Aaron's Golden Calf and Jeroboam's Golden Calves, which may lead us to think that the story is of southern origin and anti-Bethel (and anti-Dan); but on the other the villain of the story is Aaron, the hero of P, which suggests that the story is northern and anti-Zadokite. It is the first option which has been developed since R.H. Kennett in 1905;[55] but if this is taken, we are left with a double problem on our hands. Aaron has to become associated with the priesthood at Bethel; and then the priesthood at Bethel has in some way to become dominant at Jerusalem. Kennett tried to justify both these propositions, and many variants have been attempted since.[56] But the multiplicity of these theories itself raises doubts as to the viability of the first option; and these are reinforced by Noth's despair—'Unfortunately we can no longer ascertain the time or the circumstances of the addition of these [Aaron] passages.'[57]

Our picture of movements between Dan and Jerusalem in the ninth century suggests that there may be more hope in beginning with the second option. The news of Aaron's rise could hardly be received with acclaim at Dan; and it has called forth a characteristic rebuttal. Jerusalem impudence played straight into the hands of the confident Danites; for the southern hero Aaron was conveniently placed by the old tradition [58] as in charge of the people while Moses was up the mountain. The old tale of rebellion and idolatry, then, in which only the (pre-Danite) Levites were faithful, was waiting for some suitable elaboration. It thus becomes Aaron who organises the idolatrous project, calling for the contributions of ear-rings all round, and thus reversing the pious action of Jacob in Gen. 35:1-4 (vv. 2f). It is Aaron who personally accepts the tainted gold, and sets to with a graving tool (חרת), and fashions (ויצר) the image (v. 4a). (One cannot make a *molten* calf, מסכה, with a graving tool, so the Danites limited Aaron's image to a פסל, thought of as made of wood and plated with the gold.) It is Aaron who builds an altar before it, and proclaims a festival on the morrow, when sacrifices are offered to the idol, and are followed by scenes of unbridled sexual licence (vv. 5f; cf. Gen. 26:8). Moses, descending from the mount, comes upon such scenes with suitable wrath. He burns the image, grinds the gold to dust, and makes the people drink water mixed with it, a procedure guaranteed to find out the guilty (v. 20; cf. Num. 5). Yahweh, accordingly, smites the people, because of the image which Aaron made (v. 35—that the people made it, as well as Aaron—is a later exculpatory duplication). The Danites left in their old story of the Levites for obvious reasons, glossing it, 'for Aaron had let [the people] loose' (v. 25b), and making the Levites kill their brothers (i.e. fellow Israelites), companions and neighbours in v. 27, instead of their brothers and sons in v. 29. It is true that this means that they die both by the sword and by the curse-induced 'smiting' of Yahweh; but this is a small price to pay.

The northern vendetta against the usurping Aaron is continued in Num. 12. Here Aaron and his sister Miriam (Exod. 15:20) proudly demand whether Yahweh has spoken by Moses only, and not by them also. Yahweh hears, and suddenly summons the three of them from the tent of meeting; and when the pillar of cloud goes up, not only Miriam, as in the present story, but also Aaron was found smitten with leprosy. This is clear from Aaron's prayer to Moses in v. 11, 'O my lord, lay not, I pray thee, sin upon us, for that we have done foolishly, and for that we have sinned.'[59] The existence of these two anti-Aaronic stories shows that already before the fall of the northern kingdom the Zadokites were claiming Aaronic descent, and that this claim was not allowed to pass at Dan.

Of course Danite libels on Aaron would never have been allowed undiluted into the Jerusalem canon. That the stories were admitted at all is only partly due to the prestige enjoyed by northern traditions even after 722; the main reason is that while denigrating Aaron, they conceded that he was a figure alongside Moses, Moses' brother. But naturally they were admitted on Jerusalem terms. Miriam and Aaron—note the change of order—were quite right to speak against Moses, for he had married an Ethiopian woman (Num. 12:1); and only Miriam was smitten with leprosy—Aaron was not really to blame, and he interceded for his sister to good effect (v. 12). In Exod. 32 the blame is transferred, so far as is possible, from Aaron to the people (vv. 1, 7-14, 21-24, 30-34, 35); and, in a stroke of genius, the graven image becomes a molten calf, just like the ones which Jeroboam made at Bethel and Dan! The people echo Jeroboam's words down to the plural: 'These be thy gods, O Israel, which brought thee up out of the land of Egypt' (vv. 4, 8). Thus the impression is left with the hearer, and even with the modern scholar, even with Noth, that fundamentally the incident was a foreshadowing of northern sin at Bethel, committed by 'the people'; and that Aaron's involvement—since he was not killed either by the Levites or by Yahweh (nor was he punished with leprosy)—was a peccadillo. In the parallel account in Deuteronomy, the same process is carried even further (Deut. 9:8-21). Aaron is not mentioned at all until the penultimate verse, and the whole guilt is loaded on to the people. At 9:20 Yahweh's (apparently unmotivated) anger with Aaron is included, but is at once glossed away by Moses' intercession. So the Zadokites gained their main point, Aaron's parity with Moses, and had the last laugh on Bethel besides.

iv. From the Fall of Dan to the Exile

In the meantime the tide of history had turned against the once superior Levitical priesthood at Dan. In the late 730's Tiglath-Pileser took most of the towns in northern Israel and enslaved the people (II Kgs. 15:29); but Dan is not mentioned, nor are there signs of its destruction at this time in the excavations. Very likely its formidable defences withstood a siege (cf. pp.168f), and the priests and people moved south to safety. But within the decade the whole northern kingdom was swept away. Worship continued at Bethel (II Kgs. 17:24ff), until it was purged by Josiah (23:15ff), and on through the sixth century (Zech. 7:2).

Some at least of the Danite priests found a permanent home at Jerusalem. The D-historian does not mention such a move; but then the northern priests were anathema to him. The Chronicler, for what he is worth, mentions a considerable movement from the north, following letters from Hezekiah (II Chron. 30): there was proud refusal 'in Ephraim and Manasseh, even unto Zebulun,' but 'divers of Asher and Manasseh and of Zebulun humbled themselves and came to Jerusalem' (vv. 10f). He seems to discriminate between the central tribes who preserved their independence of spirit, and the northern tribes who were more amenable; and it is difficult to ascribe this distinction to any tendency.[60] But it is in any case certain that some of those responsible for handing on the old Dan and Bethel traditions found acceptance in Jerusalem—rather like Bucer and Peter Martyr in the England of Edward VI. For the whole code of northern laws in the middle chapters of Deuteronomy became canonical in Jerusalem before the century was up (II Kgs. 22f); the northern narrative traditions were taken over and assimilated into the Jerusalem corpus, in an only mildly edited form (including hostile northern narratives such as we have just considered); and the northern psalms of both the Asaph collection[61] and our own Korah collection became a valued part of the Jerusalem Psalter. Whether the northerners became acceptable through the reforming zeal of Hezekiah, or whether all Yahwists were driven to join hands during the oppression of Manasseh, accepted they certainly were.

Some time during the two following centuries a challenge was made to the Jerusalem priesthood—a challenge which was successfully rebutted, and which has left its scars in two further elaborations of the tradition, the stories of Phinehas and Korah. Both of these seem to have been added substantially earlier than 500, because both are referred to in Ps. 106, which apparently comes from that time.[62] 106:30 reads, 'Then stood up Phinehas and executed judgement . . .'; his deed, the staying of the plague, and his reward through all generations, here mentioned, correspond with the story in Num. 25:7-13. Ps. 106:16-18 reads, 'They envied Moses also in the camp, (And) Aaron the holy one of the LORD. The earth opened and swallowed up Dathan, And covered the company of Abiram. And the fire was kindled in their company; The flame burned up the wicked.' Korah is not mentioned by name here, but the psalmist shows his familiarity with the P Korah tradition. Dathan and Abiram rebelled against Moses only (Num. 16:1f, 12-15, 25-34); they were not Levites and did not envy Aaron; they were not burned but swallowed alive by the earth. Aaron, the issue of holiness, the repeated term 'company' (עדה) and the fire from heaven, all come in the P verses (vv. 3-7, 35). So the Korah expansion of the Dathan-Abiram story was already current by around 500, the name Korah being omitted by the psalmist, no doubt intentionally.[63] So we know who it was that challenged the Zadokites: it was the company of Korah.

But who were the company of Korah? We know plenty about the Korahites from later times, because they have left many marks on the Chronicler's work; but what we want to know about them is who they were before their disastrous quarrel with the house of Zadok. There is a variety of candidates available. They could be (i) the descendants of Abiathar at Anathoth; (ii) the priests of the towns and villages around Judah whom Josiah deprived of their shrines in II Kgs. 23, the so-called כמרים (vv. 5, 8f); (iii) the exiled priests of Dan; (iv) the exiled priests of Bethel; (v) the exiled priests of Tabor, Gilgal and other lesser northern tribes. We may strike out (v) at once, for if the priests of minor northern shrines could challenge the old Jerusalem priesthood, how much more the major northern shrines! Nor is the Bethelite priesthood (iv) a strong runner; according to II Kgs. 23:20 Josiah killed all the priests of Bethel, and even if this is an exaggeration, as it must be, worship continued at Bethel through the exile (Zech. 7:2), which would require Bethelite priests at Bethel. We may also eliminate (i), the descendants of Abiathar; they had been comfortably contained for 250 years, and traced their ancestry ultimately to Ithamar, not Korah.

So we are left with the priests of the Judah towns, and those from Dan. The local priests are less likely on three counts. First, II Kgs. 23:9 says they did not come up to Jerusalem at all: 'Nevertheless the priests of the high places came not to the altar of the LORD in Jerusalem, but they did eat unleavened bread among their brethen.' It is difficult to see therefore how they could have been felt to be a threat. Second, as we noted above, two of the four Levite groups of Num. 26:58 were called after the two Judahite towns of Libnah and Hebron, while two bore the names of people, Korah and Moses. It is likely therefore that the Judahite priests came from the two areas represented by the towns, Libnah to the west of Jerusalem and Hebron to the south, while the families of Moses and Korah spread over northern Israel. Thirdly, it is not easy to think that country priests, who had accepted the superiority of the Zadokites for centuries, would aspire to parity after their deprivation and disgrace; while it is easy to see how the proud Danites might. They had been Levites when Zadok's ancestors were pagans; they had presided over the national festival of a powerful empire under Ahab and Jeroboam II when Judah was a client ally; they had taught the Jerusalem bumpkins so much. Like Sir Robert Clive, they might well stand astonished at their own moderation.

It looks therefore as though the Korahites were the exiled priesthood of Dan; and this conclusion agrees with a number of features of the documents. The Phinehas story bears a marked similarity to the Danite priesthood legend in Exod. 32:25ff. There the Levites had been faithful when there was rebellion and idolatry in the camp; and so now the Zadokites have developed a similar story out of the J incident of Israel's faithlessness at Baal-Peor.[64] The tradition of eating the offerings of the dead (Ps. 106:28) has been dropped, and Aaron's grandson has been made the hero who took a spear and stopped the rot of idolatrous adultery with a single blow. Moses orders the slaughter of all the offenders (Num. 25:5) as in the Danite story, but he is made to stand by idle while the flagrant adultery takes place (v. 6). Phinehas then steps forward, and somewhat easily earns the covenant of an everlasting priesthood (vv. 7-12). So the descendants of Aaron–

Eleazar-Phinehas, and they alone (that is, the Zadokites), are the true priests in Jerusalem. Phinehas does the deed rather than Eleazar, who might have been theologically more suitable. But by this time Eleazar was presumably in his eighties. The present arrangement also commends itself in cutting out the descendants of Abiathar at Anathoth, who by this time were perhaps also linking themselves to Aaron via Ithamar, 'brother' of Eleazar. But Phinehas was Ithamar's nephew, so the covenant was with the house of Zadok alone.

The Korah story does what the Phinehas story leaves undone: it identifies and disposes of the opposition. The priestly author has to do a clumsy graft, for the story from which he works is the rebellion of two secular groups, Dathan and Abiram, against Moses; and it is this which has made plain the tendency of the story—to a happy unanimity among scholars.[65] Korah and his company were challenging (Moses and) Aaron for equality in 'holiness,' that is, in the priesthood; they aspired to offer incense, that is, the supreme priestly privilege.[66] But Yahweh said to Moses to bid the people withdraw from about them, and sent fire from heaven and devoured them all (16:23f, 27a, 35). The reality is all too easily transparent to the legend. It is one thing to welcome slightly heterodox refugees, and to take in their tradition as being more developed than one's own; it is quite another to accept their ministers as one's equals—a phenomenon not without parallel in the modern ecumenical movement. At some point between the reign of Hezekiah and the return from exile, the northern priests made a bid for parity with the Zadokites, a bid which was not a success with their hosts. Both stories narrow the priesthood to the Zadokites, but the Korah story effectively turns the tables on the immigrants. Once the Levitical priesthood was at Dan, and the Jerusalem priests had to work hard to obtain recognition; now the Zadokites alone are the Levitical priesthood, and the Korahite Danites are excluded. As the Deuteronomic paraenesis in Deut. 1-11 does not mention Phinehas in connection with Baal-Peor, nor Korah in connection with Dathan and Abiram (11:6), we should probably locate the Danite challenge in the sixth century, in the hour of greatest Zadokite weakness, the exile.

This conclusion is confirmed by two further texts, from Deut. 18 and Ezek. 44, which are usually interpreted of the country priests, but only for lack of an alternative. In Deut. 18:1-5 'the priests the Levites, all the tribe of Levi,' are provided for with income from the people's sacrifices, since they had no land. A short paragraph is appended: 'And if a Levite come from any of thy gates out of all Israel, where he sojourneth, and come with all the desire of his soul unto the place which the LORD shall choose; then he shall minister in the name of the LORD his God, as all his brethren the Levites do, which stand there before the LORD. They shall have like portions to eat, beside that which cometh of the sale of his patrimony' (vv. 6-8). John Emerton has argued forcibly that no distinction can be made between the Levite here and 'the priests the Levites' in 18:1.[67] In 18:1 'all the tribe of Levi' is in apposition to 'the priests the Levites,' and throughout Deuteronomy priests and Levites have the same duties: carrying the ark, teaching the law, ministering at the altar and blessing. So it is impossible to show the existence of two classes of Levites, one priestly by birth and the other not, in the thought of the Deuteronomic laws.[68]

Two features of the text suggest that the people under consideration are not country priests,[69] but exiled northern priests. First, in addition to Deuteronomy's standard 'the Levite within thy gates' (12:12, 18f; 14:27, 29; 16:11), we have here a second qualifying phrase, 'out of all Israel'. Why should this be added? The suggestion is that we are not concerned, as we usually are, with the poor priests of Judah, but with those from the northern kingdom as well. Second, since the poverty of the landless local priests is a presupposition of so much in Deuteronomy, commentators find the last phrase of v. 8 puzzling:[70] they have no land, so how can they have sold a patrimony? Matters would be quite different with national priests from Dan who could have laid up silver for the best part of two centuries, and would not be likely to leave it behind on their flight south. Although they are rich, yet they still need a current income. We may further add that the Deuteronomic laws come from northern Israel, and it would be surprising if their tradents did not gloss them in Jerusalem to provide for their own future; they have generously provided already for the Judah country priests from the alms of their fellow-townsmen. So there is evidence that in the seventh century the Danites claimed a share in the priestly office and revenue in Jerusalem, and even that they were accorded it. Incense-offering might be different, and the last straw.

The same situation seems to underlie Ezek. 44. Ezekiel had himself been a Jerusalem priest, and he is clear that in the restored Temple only 'the priests and Levites, the sons of Zadok' (40:46; 43:19; 44:15) shall minister at the altar. He wants no mistake, and he calls a son of Zadok a son of Zadok; indirect reference to Aaron is not the point here—who knows if some non-Zadokite might discover an ancestor among the sons of Phinehas? However, he wishes to make space for some who are not of Zadokite descent; and he adopts a proposal which was afterwards to be carried through. The menial tasks at the Temple had hitherto been performed by the old Canaanite slave-families, the Nethinim, and these he now bars as being uncircumcised in heart and flesh (Ezek. 44:6-9). In their place 'the Levites that went far astray from me, when Israel went astray, which went astray from me after their idols; they shall bear their iniquity. Yet they shall be ministers in my sanctuary, having oversight at the gates of the house, and ministering in the house: they shall slay the burnt offering and the sacrifice for the people, and they shall stand before them to minister unto them. Because they ministered unto them before their idols, and became a stumbling-block of iniquity unto the house of Israel . . . they shall bear their iniquity' (44:10-12). They may not act as priests, but as keepers of the charge of the house (vv. 13f).

Who then are these straying Levites? It is usually replied, the country clergy of II Kgs. 23:8f.[71] But 'idols' (גלולים) is a strong word. Manasseh is said to have set up idols in the Temple (II Kgs. 21:11, 21), and Josiah put away those who had familiar spirits, wizards, teraphim and idols in Judah and Jerusalem (23:24); but in the main account of the reformation the country priests are only said to have burned incense to Baal and the heavenly bodies in their places, which Josiah then defiled (23:5, 8). 'Idols' were characteristically served by the northerners (17:12), and were the cause of their downfall. Cody remarks that 'the exaggeratedly negative accusation of idolatry among the rival Levites can be discounted on the basis of the positive attitude . . . evident in Deuteronomy.'[72] But Ezekiel is not being exaggeratedly negative here; he is doing his best to fit the rival group into the Temple. How much easier if neither he nor the Deuteronomist is concerned with country priests at all! Ezekiel said that they went astray after their idols because it was well-known in Jerusalem that idols had been worshipped at Dan and Bethel; the Deuteronomist takes a 'positive attitude' because he is legislating in his own favour. If Ezekiel were hostile to these Levites, he would have no motive for including them in his ideal Temple; so he really thinks they had been idolaters, and that most easily implies Danites. Danites they were too in the opinion of later interpreters; for Ezek. 44:11 says that they should have oversight of the temple gates, a task primarily undertaken by the sons of Korah (I Chron. 26:1, 19); and 'they shall stand before them to minister unto them' is almost repeated in Moses' challenge to the Korahites in Num. 16:9, 'and stand before the congregation to minister unto them.'

So it seems that we can trace the Danite priesthood through its darkest days. They escaped the Assyrian disaster, and were received at Jerusalem, tactfully preferring to be known by their ancient patronymic, Korah, rather than Dan, their suspect city of origin. With their silver, their laws and narrative traditions, their psalms and their Urim and Thummim, they made themselves accepted in priestly circles, and tried, by glossing Deut. 18:6-8 on to vv. 1-5, to have themselves accorded parity. But this was to overplay their hand. The Zadokites rebutted their claim, first with the Phinehas, then with the Korah legend; and Ezekiel sealed their fate by providing them with the work and status hitherto enjoyed by the Nethinim. But this was by no means the end of them.

v. After the Exile

I cannot here give a full account of the struggles for power after the exile.[73] For the priesthood, the Zadokites were sufficiently weak that they allowed the descendants of Abiathar to participate: Abiathar's putative ancestor Ithamar was conceded to have been Eleazar's younger brother (Exod. 6:23; Num. 3:1-4; I Chron. 24). They retained the first sixteen priestly courses, and the last eight were taken over by remains of the house of Eli, who had waited half a millennium for the privilege.

The battle among the remaining priestly groups, now 'Levites' in the sense of second-class Temple personnel, was mainly fought by the composition of tendentious ancestries. We can see it settled in the fifth and fourth centuries in the genealogical table that is established in P and I Chron. 6; but busy hands have been at work redressing their clans' interests in many subsequent additions. The 'orthodox' genealogy, which is set out in Num. 3:17-20, and elaborated in I Chron. 6:16-29, is as follows:

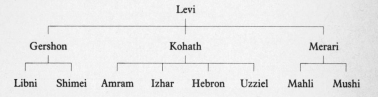

Now it is obvious that these eight 'grandsons' of Levi represent eight

groups which aspired to the Temple service in Jerusalem in the years
after the exile, and that the family-tree represents the settlement then
achieved. Libni stands for the Libnites, the country-priests from
Libnah. They come first because they had always been first, right back
in the twelfth century, when the tradition underlying Num. 26:58 gave
the order Libnites, Hebronites, Mushites, Korahites. Amram is the
oldest of the most prolific line, Kohath, because he is the father of
Aaron, and so of the established Jerusalem priesthood, both the
Zadokites through Eleazar and the house of Eli through Ithamar.
Izhar [74] is the father of Korah, and so of the main branch of the old
Danite priesthood, the subject of this book; the sons of Korah have
ended up second in the stakes that really matter. Hebron also goes
back to the old Num. 26:58 list, and represents the second group of
country-priests from Judah. It looks as if he was once the older son of
Kohath in a symmetrical 'three twos' genealogy, and has been pushed
down by the rise of the Aaronite and Korahite clans. Mushi is probably
the old Mosaic priesthood, also from Dan. Not so numerous, nor so
thrustful as the Korahites, but more dangerous because of the name
they carry, they have been made the lowest of the low, the junior son of
Merari, Levi's junior son.

This leaves us with three blank names, Shimei, Uzziel and Mahli;
and for these we must turn to the singers' genealogies, which follow in I
Chron. 6:33-47.[75] Here are given the ancestries of the three 'Davidic'
singers, Heman, Asaph and Ethan, in that order. Each line consisted
originally of fourteen names, but extensions have been made, to the
first line especially, in order to accommodate the family of Samuel.[76]
The names are given in reverse order, and yield the following family tree:

It is to be noticed where the orthodox genealogy (as in the previous
diagram) has been followed, and where not. The names in the first

line—Levi, Kohath, Izhar, Korah—are unchanged, and stand as in Num. 3, but the Kohath line has taken priority over the line of Gershom(n) [77] because the Korahites reckoned to be the senior singers. It is Heman whose name stands at the head of Ps. 88, the last of the psalms of the sons of Korah. The other two lines have suffered some alteration in the opening names. Gershom(n) had two sons in the earlier diagram, Libni and Shimei, and Shimei now appears as Gershom's grandson; similarly, Mahli and Mushi were Merari's two sons there, and Mahli is now Merari's grandson. Thus two of the missing (priestly) names turn up as coevals of Korah in the singers' families.

Of these, Ethan's name stands at the heading of 89, a psalm associated with the sanctuary at Tabor;[78] hence the Mahlites are likely to be the rump of the old Tabor priesthood, alongside the Mushites of Dan, two disreputable far northern groups who have somehow won their way to acceptance at the bottom of the league. The other line, of Asaph going back to Shimei, is associated with a whole group of psalms, as numerous as the Korah psalms and probably from Bethel;[79] so the Shimeites will be refugees from Bethel. If so they are likely to be latecomers at Jerusalem, since their old shrine was still an independent and respected force in the late sixth century (Zech. 7:2); and this would be borne out by the reference to them as distinct from the Levites in the (fourth century) prophecy of Zech. 12:13, 'the family of the house of Levi [shall mourn] apart, and their wives apart; the family of the Shimeites apart, and their wives apart.' Bethel is on the Ephraim-Benjamin frontier, and Shimei was an Benjaminite name earlier (II Sam. 16). We have no information about Uzziel; perhaps we may think of Gilgal as the most important outstanding sanctuary, but this is just a guess. For the rest we may say with varying degrees of confidence that the eight names of Levi's grandsons in the orthodox priestly genealogy represent the old pre-exilic priesthoods of the different sanctuaries: Libni that of Libnah, Shimei that of Bethel, Amram that of Jerusalem, Izhar that of the Korahites at Dan, Hebron that of Hebron, Mahli that of Tabor, and Mushi that of Moses himself, the Danite high-priesthood.

The Korahites had a head-start over the other priesthoods, having been in Jerusalem since the eighth century. They had lost the battle for equality at the altar, but they had won most of the other battles.[80] Some of these, like the right to bake the shewbread (I Chron. 9:31f), are not of great significance for our purposes. I shall conclude this sketch of their history with a brief comment on three battles that retain some significance, insofar as they are for continuations of positions they had held in happier times at Dan.

The first is the struggle to keep the Temple doors. According to passages which seem to be sources to the Chronicler [81] — Ezra 2:42, 70; Neh. 11:19; Ezra 7:24; 10:24 — the duty of watching the gates was performed in the fifth century by porters, the families of Akkub, Talmon and others, including perhaps Shallum, 172 in all. To the Chronicler himself, however, (if we may so speak) there were four thousand doorkeepers, and they were Levites (I Chron. 23:5). In a first expansion of this text (I Chron. 26:1-19) there are 93 (or 99) doorkeepers, in three groups: eighteen Korahites, the sons of (Me)Shelemiah, 62 or 68 of the family of Obed-Edom, and 13 Merarites, the sons of Hosah. The first and the last are of course Levites, and these are the only two mentioned in the recapitulation in v. 19. Obed-Edom is a Gittite to the Chronicler (I Chron. 13:13f), and it is unclear whether the later editor regarded him as a Korahite (Rudolph), an Asaphite (cf. the apparent disturbance of the text of 26:1), or a non-Israelite.[82] At all events, the Korahites keep the main door to the east with six men, and the north door with four. In a second expansion (I Chron. 9:17-24) a reconciliation has been attempted. Of the old porters, Shallum is now the chief, and is given the same ancestry as (Me)Shelemiah. He and his fellow-Korahites are over the work of service, keepers of the thresholds (הספים) of the tent on its four sides.[83]

It is not clear how the Korahites have contrived to take over the duty of keeping the Temple thresholds, but it is plain that this is what has happened in the course of the fourth and third centuries. In days of old the Korahite priest preferred to keep the thresholds of the courts of the shrine at Dan rather than to dwell in the tents of wickedness (Ps. 84:10). Perhaps they had risen to be keepers of the threshold at Jerusalem also by the end of the monarchy (II Kgs. 23:4; 25:18); perhaps not. But by the late fourth century, the humble porters who at first sufficed to watch the gates have either been adopted into or superseded by Levitical groups. I Chron. 26 gives half the work, including the two more important gates, to the Korahites. I Chron. 9 puts them in charge of it all, and restores something of the ancient dignity by calling them 'keepers of the thresholds.' It was not the dignity it had been in the days of Eli, Josiah and Zedekiah; but it was a place in the sun, not without power and income, and in the end the Korahites had it back.

It is the same with the singing. The Asaphites believed that they were the Temple singers par excellence. They had been the only singers to return from the exile (Ezra 2:41; Neh. 7:44); Asaph had ministered before the ark, and had led the music as it was brought into Jerusalem (I Chron. 16:5, 7, 37), while Heman of the line of Korah, and Jeduthun (Ethan) remained with the tabernacle of Yahweh at Gibeon (vv. 39ff); of the three singing 'guilds' set out in courses in I Chron. 25, the sons of Asaph come first. But the Korahites disputed this primacy, and successfully eroded it. In I Chron. 6:31-48 their singers' lineage is set out first, and includes Samuel the son of Elkanah; they stand in the middle, with Asaphites on their right, and Ethanites on their left; in 15:17ff the head Levites appoint singers and musicians at David's behest, in the order, Heman, Asaph, Ethan. Although Asaph is allowed first place in the musicians' courses in ch.25, he has only four sons and Jeduthun (= Ethan) six; while God gave to Heman fourteen sons and three daughters (like Job), so that the Korahites have fourteen of the twenty-four groups. In II Chron. 20:19 it is Korahites alone who support Jehoshaphat on campaign: 'And the Levites, of the children of the Kohathites, even (ו) of the children of the Korahites, stood up to praise the LORD, the God of Israel.'[84] Nor are the sons of Korah concerned merely to take the centre of the stage from the Asaphites. They exalt the function of music and singing far above its lowly place in Samuel-Kings. The musical accompaniment of the ark is now much the biggest feature of David's entry into Jerusalem. In I Chron. 25 the musicians do not merely celebrate, thank and praise the Lord (16:4): they prophesy with harps and psalteries and cymbals (v. 1), Asaph prophesies by order of the king (v. 2) as does Jeduthun (v. 3), and Heman is the king's seer in the words of God (v. 5). The old association of music and prophecy from the days of Miriam (Exod. 15:20) and Samuel (I Sam. 10:5) is still alive. In II Chron. 20:18ff, the function of the Korahites is crucial for the success of the battle. Their praise 'with an exceeding loud voice' (v. 19) is a prophecy (v. 20), and if the people believe them success will follow: they are appointed to chant a chorus, and when they begin to sing and praise, Yahweh turns the battle their way (vv. 21f).

The tendency of these passages is inescapable. The Korahites are constantly pushing the tiller in their own direction, not only at the expense of rival Levitical groups, but also at the expense of the priests—often and openly, for example in II Chron. 29f. It is no great puzzle that they have to make their way: their loss of the great challenge to the Zadokites in the sixth century brought about their discrediting in the Num. 16 expansion. But they remain numerous, able, influential and confident of their ancestral dignity; and slowly, step by step, they nudge their way back to the centre. Asaphites are easy meat, and can be allowed their share of the limelight; after all, they were fellow-northerners by origin, from the sister-sanctuary at Bethel. But far more important is the competition with the priests. The frequent pejorative references to the priests in Chronicles show that the old Danite aristocrats had not given heaven for lost. They would never be able to offer incense or handle sacrificial blood, tasks that any priest-peasant could perform. But they could preside with distinction over the offering of the heart in skilled music; and here surely was not merely the expression of Israel's true religion, but also the crucible in which new words of power could be forged. The same creative force that had stirred the heart of the poet of Ps. 45 or 49, bubbling over in meditations of divine potency, might stir afresh to gain God's blessing in harvest or battle. The Korahites were not content merely to chant their own treasured Danite repertoire. They appropriated other psalmodic traditions (II Chron. 20:21), and presided over the creation of the present psalter. They were the real leaders of worship rather than the sacrificing priests, and they had taken over the prophetic mantle also.

In tracing the evidence of the Korahites' growing ascendancy both in keeping the Temple and in its worship, we have uncovered a third and still more important field of their activity. They would never have been able to adjust the Chronicles account of Israel's history in detail after detail if they had not been both the authors of the book and its expositors. Korahite Levites retold the old Samuel-Kings stories and Korahite Levites wrote the new forms down; Korahite Levites, growing increasingly bolder, retold the stories more and more visibly in their own interest, and included the new forms in new versions of the text. Now and again they threw a sop to their Gershomite and Merarite brethren, yet they never give with one hand but that they take it back with the other. We can explain this consistent bias only on the supposition that it is Korahites who are the guardians of the tradition. The 'original' text of Chronicles bears less obvious marks of Korahite activity, but it bears manifest marks of Levitical authorship, and Korah is the hero even here, in such passages as I Chron. 6 and II Chron. 20; nor is it likely that the charge of the tradition would have changed hands. But this is true not only of Chronicles. The Pentateuch also has been preserved by the sons of Korah, and edited in their favour. We have noted the tendency in passages like Num. 3f and 7; but the same is true even in Exod. 6. Here the 'orthodox' genealogy of Levi is being set out for the first time, and Levi's eight grandsons are given as in the table above. But the editor has continued two of the lines for two generations further: not just Amram's sons, Aaron and Moses, and Aaron's four sons, as one might have expected; but Korah and his two brothers, the sons of Izhar, and Korah's three sons, Assir, Elkanah and Abiasaph. We could hardly ask for a plainer hint: R, the Redactor of the Pentateuch, was a Levite of the sons of Korah.

In happier times, at Dan, it was not thought that sacrificing was the priest's primary duty. 'Thy Thummim and thy Urim are with him whom thou lovest' (Deut. 33:8) had been the first thought of the author of Moses' blessing. Giving God's decisions was the priest's first privilege; and the second, 'They shall teach Jacob thy judgements, And Israel thy law' (v. 10a). Only third come the offering of incense and holocausts (v. 10b).[85] These priorities have remained with the Danite priesthood down the centuries, and we see them mirrored in the writings of Ben Sira. Urim and Thummim are no longer a part of living religion, but 'the law is faithful unto (a man of understanding) as when one asketh at the oracle' (Ecclus. 33:3). The priesthood and their offerings are a splendid thing (ch.50), but the essence of true religion is the law (ch. 24, and passim). So the Korahites felt. The Zadokite priesthood did fine work, but the backbone of Israelite religion was the Levites. They kept the Temple, they led the worship, and they were the guardians of the sacred tradition, both the national history and the Law itself. They no more grieved for sacrificial duties, nor envied those who performed them, than a modern Member of Parliament wishes he were a bishop. Bishops ruled the country as well as presiding over the liturgy in the Middle Ages; now they have the colourful, backwoods job, and the MP enjoys the everyday reality of power— well, perhaps. The Korahites had resigned showpiece altar-service to the house of Zadok, but no reader of Chronicles can doubt that they were content; the real threads of the national religious life were in their hands.

Perhaps the altar-service was let go the more easily because the sons of Korah had never presided fully at the altar, even at Dan. The Mosaic priests had done this, no doubt; the Korahites had composed and led the psalms, escorted the pilgrimage, recited the traditions and done most of the work even then. We cannot but admire them for their perseverance and determination; for their ability to survive repeated disaster—the Philistines, the Syrians, the Assyrians, the Zadokites; for their ability and devotion; and for their poetry and religious sense, some of the most moving in the Psalter. It must give us a certain satisfaction to reflect that the family has survived many further and more terrible disasters, and is alive and flourishing in England today. To name but one example, the firm of Corah, Ltd, is a major supplier to the retail business of Marks and Spencer; Corah and his company still do not get the publicity, but still they are busy behind the scenes, doing the work that matters, and thriving.

THE PRE-FESTAL LAMENT (Psalms 44, 85)

We have left priest and king and the host of Israel encamped before the city of Dan for long enough; it is time to leave our excursus and return to the Korah psalms, and in particular to 44, as following the pilgrimage-psalms 42-43, and to 85 as following 84. I have in fact already argued above that there is a close relationship between 42-43 and 44: God's 'casting off' of his people (43:2; 44:9, 23); the day-long reproaches of neighbours and adversaries (42:3, 10; 44:13-16); the enemy's oppression (42:9; 43:2; 44:24); the bowing/casting down of the speaker's soul (42:5, 11; 43:5; 44:25); the appeal to God's lovingkindness (42:8; 44:26) to command (42:8; 44:4) victories (42:5, 11; 43:5; 44:4).[1] There is a less obvious, but real connection between 84 and 85, in the glory (84:11; 85:9) and 'good' which Yahweh will give (84:11; 85:12) to those who walk uprightly/trust in him/fear him (84:11f; 85:9).[2] So we have already have some indication that we should regard 44 as the sequel to 42-43, and 85 as the sequel to 84.

The classification of 44 is not a problem: it is a national lament. The speaker varies between the dominant first person plural and the occasional 'I' ('my King,' v. 4; 'I will not trust in my bow . . . my sword,' v. 6; 'my dishonour . . . the shame of my face,' v. 15), and he clearly represents the people, as did the speaker in 84. Eaton thinks that he is the king; Kraus that he is not necessarily so, but still the national representative. We may think of him as the מנצח, the Korahite court-poet at Dan, the Keeper of the Threshold. The psalm breaks down into three sections. In the first (vv. 1-8, the end being marked by Selah), God's work in the days of old is remembered, and trust is expressed in the same transcendent power which brought blessing to 'our fathers.' In the second (vv. 9-16) a pitiful contrast is drawn: defeat in battle has been followed by spoliation, enslavement and dishonour. In the last portion (vv. 17-26) the people's loyalty to the covenant is protested, and God is summoned to arise and be faithful to his promise. The lament is clearly in face of a national military disaster, whether on a single occasion, or, in stylised form, being repeated year after year, to lay before God whatever defeats have been incurred.

Now 85 shows a strikingly similar structure to 44. In the first verses (vv. 1-3, broken by a Selah after v. 2), God's past grace is appealed to: 'LORD, thou wast favourable unto thy land . . . Thou didst forgive the iniquity of thy people . . . Thou didst take away all thy wrath' (see below, p. 101). But the present situation, envisaged in vv. 4-7, is in pathetic contrast: God is prayed to cause his indignation to cease, not to be angry for ever, but to quicken us again and grant us his salvation. As against 44, however, the contrast seems not to turn on any political or military occasion, for the blessings anticipated in the following verses are concerned only with fruitfulness. In the third section (vv. 8-13) the speaker expresses his confidence that God will speak peace to his people, that salvation is nigh, and that the land will yield her increase. In 85 as in 44 the first person plural predominates, but 'I' is present also—'I will hear what God the LORD will speak.' Delitzsch described 85 as a pendant to 44: 'Just as Pss. xlii.-xliii. and lxxxiv. form a couple, so also do Pss. xliv. and lxxxv. as being Korahite plaintive and precatory Psalms of national purport.'[3] As Kraus was to put it more crisply, 85 is a *Volksklagelied*.

It can hardly fail to strike us as singular that we have such a close tissue of interrelationships. 42-43 and 84 are both pilgrimage psalm-complexes, of similar language and three-part structure, marked by refrains or Selahs. Both stand at the beginning of a series of Korah psalms, the only two series we have. Both are succeeded by national laments, 44 and 85, which in turn have similar structures (clearly, though not formally marked); and there are connections of thought and language between 42-43 and 44, and between 84 and 85, extending to quite rare expressions. We shall certainly be better off if we can think of some explanation for so extensive a web of relatedness.

The hypothesis by which I propose to explain these and other features of the Korah collection is set out in outline at the end of Chapter 1: they are, in order, psalms for the celebration of the autumn festival at Dan in the eighth and ninth centuries before our era. 42-43 do not stand at the beginning of the first Korah sequence by accident; they are there because the first liturgical occasion in the rites of Tabernacles at Dan was the arrival of the festal procession a day or two before the feast. 44 stands second because it was the psalm for the second liturgical occasion of the feast, the national lament with which the festival opened as the sun went down on 14th Bul. The psalms for the feast were those finally fixed—that is, by 722—but they had won their way over competitors, in the same way that some modern hymn-books may contain two, or even three, competing metrical versions of Ps. 23. All the psalms from 42 to 49 were in the 722 edition of the Dan hymnal; but their ousted competitors were not forgotten. Of these 84 and 85 had been earlier opening psalms, for the pilgrimage and the lament respectively; and they with 87-89 formed the Korah (-Ethan) 'supplement,' with the old opening psalms still in the opening position in the supplement. 'Supplements' are a regular feature of hymn-book arrangements: the compilers of *Hymns Ancient and Modern* provide a primary selection of hymns for each Church festival, and amplify it with further suggestions from later in the book. 42-49 have to be viewed as the 'main Korah sequence,' and 84-89 (less 86) as the supplement, because 42-49 is the longer and prior series. Furthermore, it is easy to understand the ousting of the older, more confident 84 and 85, with their prayers for a plentiful harvest, and their use of both Yahweh and Elohim, by the anxious 42-43 and 44, which could well reflect Israel's military weakness in the northern kingdom's last years. I will suggest a new method by which these three psalms can in fact be dated in this period.

We do not need an argument for supposing that the arrival of the pilgrimage at Dan was the first event of the festival. But what reason is there for thinking that there was a national lament on 14th Bul? We have no account of the day-by-day festal ritual: it is this that I am trying to reconstruct. It is of course true that later Israelite use lays much stress on Yom Kippur as a day of afflicting the soul before Tabernacles (Lev. 23:9); but this is on the 10th, not the 14th. Our best available resource therefore is to broaden the hypothesis: if the Korah main sequence and the Korah supplement follow pilgrimage psalms with laments, perhaps there are other psalm-collections which might display similar patterns. For example, Book IV, with its many psalms on Gunkel's and Mowinckel's enthronement-psalm lists, seems to me to be, like the Korah psalms, the ordered psalmody for the celebration of Tabernacles;[4] and the Songs of Ascents another. Now both of these collections originated in Jerusalem, and one difference between Jerusalem and Dan is obvious: the king of Judah lived in Jerusalem, and, unlike the king of Israel, had no need to go on a pilgrimage to his national shrine. But in other ways we should expect the ritual of the two centres to be similar; and both Book IV and the Songs open with laments. 90 is a national lament built on the same pattern as 44 and 85.

First (vv. 1-4) Yahweh's reliability and permanence: 'Lord, thou hast been our dwelling place In all generations...' Then comes the community's present plight (vv. 5-12): 'For we are consumed in thine anger, And in thy wrath are we troubled...' Finally the people prays for better things (vv. 13-17): 'Return, O LORD; how long?...' 90 is later and grimmer and more conscience-wracked than 44 and 85; but it performs the same function of a pre-festal lament, praying 'that we may rejoice' (v. 14; 85:6). 120 is also a lament preceding a sequence of psalms of confidence, but is too short to have the three-theme structure of 44, 85 and 90; and it is Book IV which sustains most clearly the parallel of thought and action with the Korah collection, through to the end.

The text of 44 makes it clear that word and action are combined. Its chanting is accompanied by a ritual of humiliation and grovelling in which the whole community participates: 'For our soul is bowed down to the dust; our belly cleaveth unto the earth' (v. 25). This is not a brief prostration, but has occupied much of the day: 'All the day long is my dishonour before me, And the shame of my face hath covered me' (v. 15). Although the phrase is in part poetic (cf. vv. 8, 22 below), it is always unwise to exclude a literal meaning also. 42:8 said, 'And in the night his song shall be with me,' and Isaiah speaks of 'a song as in the night when a feast is hallowed' (30:29); so it is likely that 44 is an instance of an evening psalm at the close of a day of ritual. 90 is such another: 'O satisfy us *in the morning* with thy mercy, That we may rejoice and be glad all our days' (v. 14). The ritual of 14th Bul at Dan included more than mourning, as we shall see.

44 For the Chief Musician; (a Psalm) of the sons of Korah. Maschil.

There are five psalms in our group which bear the heading משכיל: 42, 44, 45, 88 and 89. I postponed consideration of this technical term when considering 42, but we must now grasp the nettle.

משכיל is a nettle because there is no satisfactory explanation of it on offer. Apart from our five psalms, the term heads four early David psalms in the second collection (52, 53, 54, 55), two Asaph psalms (74, 78), and two other psalms (32, 142). It also occurs in our group at 47:7, 'Sing ye praises משכיל.' The word is derived from the hiph'il of שכל, which means to look at, ponder, have insight, teach, act prudently, be successful; and in consequence three meanings have been proposed: (i) an instruction, or didactic poem, (ii) a skilful psalm, (iii) a psalm of inspired efficacy. The first, which is still maintained by E. Lipiński,[5] seems a frail hope; as Kissane says, only 32 and 78, of the maschils cited, could possibly be described as didactic poems. The best that could be said might be that the original meaning of the term was forgotten, and that 32 with its אשכילך (v. 8) was thought suitable to carry the now misunderstood heading. Kraus (pp. XXIIf) renders with 'Kunstlied,' and explains that it aims at exalting powerful expression suited to the object praised; but then, surely, all the psalms aim at this, and many not called Maschil are certainly artistic creations—119 for one. Mowinckel suggested the third option,[6] 'an efficacious song,' the outcome of supra-normal insight, and so full of active power. Eaton (p.16) accepts this, but observes, 'it is not clear how the thirteen psalms so headed differ from others.' In other words, the first proposal does not cover enough of the psalms in question, and the other two cover too many besides.

The second suggestion is supported by II Chron. 30:22, which speaks of the Levites as well-skilled (המשכילים שכל־טוב) in the service of the LORD; but the skill needs narrowing if it is to be meaningful. In this connection we may note the suggestion of H. Schmidt that 45, with its Tyrian princess and its ivory palaces, was the wedding-psalm of King Ahab; and the poet, who undertakes to make the king's name remembered in all generations, has included it by a kind of pun in v. 7, 'Thou hast loved (אהבת) righteousness.' The word-play is of a rough kind if so, but Israelite word-plays were rough; Pss. 9-10 and Nah. 1 are alphabetical poems, for example, which omit the play on several letters. Now 45 is a maschil, so maschil might mean a 'clever psalm' in which the name of the king or other protagonist had been included. In favour of such a suggestion is the importance given to the name by the Israelites: Solomon was a man of peace (I Chron. 22:9), Jehoshaphat a great institutor of judges (II Chron. 19:5ff), Uzziah a king of divine strength (II Chron. 26:5-16). There seems to be a play on the name Solomon in Ps. 72:7, 'and abundance of peace,' at least in the mind of whoever put 'of Solomon' at the head of the psalm. Other kinds of 'cleverness' with Hebrew poetry are the biblical alphabet psalms, and later *piyyutim* with the author's name formed as an acrostic of the initial letters.[7]

In order to test this idea we need to have at least a rough notion of the dates of some of the other maschils, in order to know what king's name to look for; and this is notoriously a lot to ask. Our best hopes will be 44 and 89. I have already given reasons for thinking that 44 comes from the end of the northern kingdom;[8] and the grim details implied in the middle verses—defeat (v. 9), spoliation (v. 10), slaughter (vv. 11, 22), deportation and enslavement (vv. 11f), relentless pursuit (v. 16), the obliteration of cities (v. 19)—suggest that matters have reached a desperate pass. In the first half of the eighth century Israel was ruled by strong kings, Joash and Jeroboam II. No disaster is recorded until II Kgs. 15:29f: 'In the days of Pekah king of Israel came Tiglath-Pileser, king of Assyria, and took Ijon, and Abel-beth-maacah, and Janoah, and Kedesh, and Hazor, and Gilead, and Galilee, all the land of Naphtali; and he carried them captive to Assyria. And Hoshea the son of Elah made a conspiracy against Pekah the son of Remaliah, and slew him, and reigned in his stead.' If this is correct, then the king whose name we are looking for is Hoshea; and four times in the first seven verses the psalmist uses the related verb ישׁע:

'Neither did their own arm save them (הוֹשִׁיעָה) ...' (v. 3)
'Command salvations (יְשׁוּעוֹת) for Jacob ...' (v. 4)
'Neither shall my sword save me (הוֹשִׁיעֵנִי)' (v. 6)
'But thou hast saved us (הוֹשַׁעְתָּנוּ) ...' (v. 7).

It would not be so surprising if the poet looked on the name of the new king הוֹשֵׁעַ as a hopeful omen of salvation, and worked it repeatedly into his text.

We are on safer ground dating 89. The king of the line of David has had his crown profaned to the ground (v. 39) and his throne similarly (v. 44); the days of his youth have been shortened. There is however still an anointed one (v. 51) to bear the reproaches of the peoples. It is common to think of the last years of the southern kingdom, either after the battle of Megiddo, when Jehoiakim became king, or after 597, when Jehoiachin/Jeconiah was deported. Now, as with 44, there are four uses of the root כון, to establish, in 89:

'Thy faithfulness shalt thou establish (תָּכִין) ...' (v. 2)
'Thy seed will I establish (אָכִין) ...' (v. 4)
'With whom my hand shall be established (תִּכּוֹן) ...' (v. 21)
'It shall be established (יִכּוֹן) for ever ...' (v. 37).

So again we might think that a king named Yahweh-will-establish might inspire a repeated appeal to Yahweh's promise to establish David. See further in Chapter 8.

For the other maschils even such indications of date are denied us. 42 evinces the same anxiety as 44, though not the desperation; I have given reasons for thinking that it also comes from the period after the death of Jeroboam II. The kings were called Zechariah, Shallum, Menahem, Pekahiah and Pekah. We do not find a key verb four times over in 42, but perhaps there is a surprising repetition of the verb זכר, to link the psalm with Zechariah:

'These things I remember (אזכרה) . . .' (v. 4)

'Therefore do I remember thee (אזכרך) . . .' (v. 6)

But Zechariah was king for only six months (II Kgs. 15:8); perhaps the 'salvations' (ישועות) in the repeated refrain (42:5, 11; 43:5) indicate rather a second instance of a Hoshea psalm. Although ישע is so common a verb in Hebrew its only occurrences in the Korah group are in 42-43 (3), 44 (4), 85 (2) and 88:1, 'O LORD, the God of my salvation.'

We do not have enough evidence to press the case, and it will not be helpful to add speculations on the maschils in other collections. Suffice it to say that the term must have had a defined meaning originally; that it is possible philologically to give it this meaning; that all five maschils in the collection can be plausibly dated within the reigns of corresponding kings; and that for the three psalms (44, 45, 89) where there is any confidence of dating, the wording seems to echo the king's name with some emphasis.

44:1　We have heard with our ears, O God, our fathers have told us,
　　　What thou didst in their days, thou, in the days of old, thy hand (אתה ידך).

　2　Thou didst drive out the nations, and plantedst them in;
　　　Thou didst afflict the peoples, and didst spread them abroad [RV text].

　3　For they gat not the land in possession by their own sword,
　　　Neither did their own arm save them:
　　　But thy right hand, and thine arm, and the light of thy countenance,
　　　Because thou hadst a favour unto them.

　4　Thou art my King, O God:
　　　Command victories for Jacob.

　5　Through thee will we push down our adversaries:
　　　Through thy name will we tread them under that rise up against us.

　6　For I will not trust in my bow,
　　　Neither shall my sword save me.

> 7 But thou hast saved us from our adversaries,
>   And hast put them to shame that hate us.
> 8 In God have we made our boast all the day long,
>   And we will give thanks unto thy name for ever.   [Selah

There are many references to the handing down of Israel's sacred tradition from father to son, sometimes in connection with Passover, sometimes more generally (Exod. 10:2; 12:26f; 13:8, 14f; Deut. 6:20ff; Ps. 78:3; etc.). In what context is this handing down being thought of here? Kraus says it is obviously not the main cultic recital, but family and clan traditions. Weiser says the conclusion which suggests itself most readily is that 'the action which the psalm immediately followed was the oral proclamation of the *Heilsgeschichte* as an integral part of the covenant cult (cf. v. 17).' Weiser seems to be nearer the truth. 44 is a lament of the whole nation, with whom God has made covenant (v. 17), and for whom, as 'Jacob,' he is prayed to command victories; national traditions of the Conquest are therefore to the point, not family traditions. The opening words are in so emphatic an order, 'God, with our ears we have heard . . . ,' that an immediate united experience is suggested, rather than the hearing of disparate traditions, each man in his father's house long ago. The same expression באזניהם is used of hearing the cultic recital at Deut. 31:11. This seems to be borne out by v. 8 also, for the people has been 'making its boast in' (הללנו) God, and giving thanks to his name all the day long—which presumably means continual cries of הללו יה. Such cries would be in place as responses to cultic recitals, such as Pss. 104, 105, 106. The combination of these verses with vv. 15, 25 gives an impressive picture of the day's ritual. A series of stories has been recited (ספרו) by the Levites and elders (Deut. 27:9; 31:9f)[9] through the day, recalling God's great works of the Conquest, and the people has responded with repeated cries of Hallelujah. But Israel has not only boasted in God all the day long; their dishonour has also been before them all the day long (v. 15). So the recitals will have been punctuated with prostrations, grovelling, the rending of clothes, the pouring of dust over the head, prayers of reproach, etc., such as are described in Josh. 7:6ff, Ezra 9:3ff, and are hinted at here in v. 25: 'our soul is bowed down to the dust: Our belly cleaveth unto the earth.' The festival was to be a time of joy and hope (Deut. 16:14); but its preamble is a time of weeping, and the contrasting of a great past with a harsh present.

Deut. 31:9ff preserves the tradition that every seven years the Levites and all the elders were to recite the תורה before all Israel 'in their ears' (באזניהם, v. 11); so it looks as if we have here at least a part of the context of that recital on the 14th Bul, the eve of 'the feast of tabernacles' (v. 10). The question of what traditions were in use, at which festivals and at which sanctuaries, has long been a matter of learned debate;[10] so it must be a cause of relief to us to have uncovered some new evidence on the matter. In Dan, in the eighth century, there was a recital of the Conquest traditions on the eve of the autumn festival. But does the language of 44 enable us to be any more specific in relating the Dan traditions to those preserved to us? In particular, could it be related to Josh. 24, a part of which (vv. 2b-13) was proposed by von Rad as an example of the primitive Israelite 'Credo' recited at festival gatherings[11]? While von Rad's thesis has been criticised in so far as it has been difficult to isolate pre-Deuteronomic language in the passage,[12] the latter does consist of an account of the Conquest (and some earlier traditions) which is recited to 'the people'; and in 44 we have a document much earlier than the D-history, and not likely to have influenced it. Hence we are in a position to make a comparison, and see if (in this respect) von Rad might be right.

Joshua begins, 'Your fathers dwelt . . .' (v. 2), and speaks of 'us and our fathers' (v. 17), just as 44 begins, 'Our fathers have told us' (v. 1). When he has finished the résumé of the patriarchs, he says, 'ye possessed (ותירשו) their land' (v. 8); cf. 'they gat the land in possession' (ירשו, 44:3). God 'drave the peoples out from before you' (v. 12a), 'not with thy sword, nor with thy bow' (v. 12b); cf. 'Thou didst drive out the nations . . . For they gat not the land in possession by their own sword . . . For I will not trust in my bow, Neither shall my sword save me' (44:2f, 6). Joshua warns, 'If ye forsake the LORD, and serve strange gods (אלהי נכר) . . . Now therefore put away the strange gods (אלהי הנכר) which are among you, and incline (והטו) your heart unto the LORD' (vv. 20, 23); 44 protests, 'Our heart is not turned back, Neither have our steps declined (ותט) from thy way . . . If we have forgotten the name of our God, Or spread forth our hands to any strange god (אל זר) . . . ' (vv. 18, 20). Joshua made a covenant with the people that day (v. 25) that Yahweh alone be their God; 44:17 says, 'Neither have we dealt falsely in thy covenant.' Finally we may note again the repetitions of the Yahweh-saves theme in 44:3-7, 'Neither did their own arm save them . . . Command salvations for Jacob . . . Neither shall my sword save me. But thou hast saved us . . .' Joshua's name was once Hoshea (Num. 13:16), and what could be more pointed than to compare the present Hoshea with his great forebear, through whom God indeed saved Israel in days of old?

While many of the phrases here are standard OT usage, not all are. In particular the use of sword//bow in battle occurs in the D-history only at Josh. 24:12, II Sam. 1:22 (David's Lament) and II Kgs. 6:22. אלהי נכר occurs only four times in the D-history, twice in this passage and in Jg. 10:16 and I Sam. 7:3, as against D's common 'other gods'; they come also in Gen. 35:2, 4, and the phrase is often thought to be typical of E. It seems to me therefore that the case is strong enough to bear the probable conclusion: the recital of the Conquest tradition at Dan culminated in the story of Joshua's making of the covenant with Israel, somewhat as told in Josh. 24:1-28. I do not need to stress that this is an important conclusion, and it is one to which I will return.

BHS recommends us to construe the words אתה ידך with v. 1, and to add the preposition ב before the latter. We should accept the first, which markedly improves the rhythm; and refuse the second, a baseless lectio facilior. Asyndeton is a minor feature of the Korah psalms (cf. 45:4b, 8a);[13] but more important, we find traces here of the view of God's hand as a semi-independent force, a view which becomes important in 89. It is 'thou, thy hand' which did the work in the days of old; 'thy right hand, and thine arm, and the light of thy countenance' which saved them (v. 3). In 89 Yahweh scattered his enemies//Rahab with the arm of his strength (v. 10): 'Thou hast a mighty arm: Strong is thy hand, and high is thy right hand' (v. 13). On the significance of this, and the association with 'the light of thy countenance' (44:3; 89:15), see below, pp. 226f. For the hand as semi-independent even with a human being, cf. 45:4, 'let thy right hand teach thee terrible things.'

For the rest, the passage raises few difficulties. In v. 2 ותשלחם could mean 'cast them forth' (RVmg), but most commentators prefer the balance given by 'spread them [viz. our fathers] abroad'; cf. the vine image developed in 80:8ff. Kraus says that the imperative 'Command victories' in v. 4 is impossible, and suggests taking the consonants with G as אלהי מצוה, 'my God who commandest,' as in 74:12 (so RSV, NEB). But 42:8 said that Yahweh would command his lovingkindness in the morning, and 43:3 prayed him to send out his minions to lead Israel to the sanctuary; it does not seem at all impossible that God should here be prayed to command Israel's victory from heaven (Delitzsch, Weiser). The imagery of such a victory in v. 5 seems traditionally northern. Jacob will be like a bull who gores (תנגח) his opponent, and tramples him (נבום) underfoot. In Deut. 33:17 it is said of Ephraim and Manasseh, 'With them he shall gore (ינגח) the peoples, all of them'; and it was at the gate of Samaria that the prophet made him horns of iron, and foretold to the northern king, 'With these thou shalt push (תנגח) the Syrians, until they be consumed' (I Kgs. 22:11). Bull imagery seems to belong to Joseph as the lion once symbolised Britain.[14]

The first person singular of vv. 4, 6 and 15 raises the question of what particular representative of the nation is here speaking. Modern interest in the ideology of kingship has promoted the candidature of the king, and in favour of this it is noted that v. 6 speaks of the representative's sword and bow, and that II Chron. 20 describes King Jehoshaphat as first leading the nation in prayer (vv. 6ff) and then in battle (so Eaton, and more cautiously Weiser and Anderson). While this may be so, the evidence is far from conclusive. The Chronicler may be writing half a millennium after the event, and certainly tends to idealise faithful Davidic kings. Israelite priests did not stand back from battle like the chaplains of a modern army; war was holy, and when necessary (I Macc.) they even commanded the host. 44 shares the heading למנצח with 45 and 84, which cannot be by kings, and it is probably, like them, composed by the priest-poet of Dan.

44:9 But now thou hast cast (us) off, and brought us to dishonour;
And goest not forth with our hosts.
10 Thou makest us to turn back from the adversary:
And they which hate us spoil for themselves.
11 Thou hast given us like sheep (appointed) for meat;
And hast scattered us among the nations.
12 Thou sellest thy people for nought,
And hast not increased (thy wealth) by their price.

The hint provided by the maschil enables us to see the reality underlying this pathetic appeal. Pekah would not have allowed a quarter of his kingdom, Gilead and Naphtali, to be ravaged without a fight, and no doubt he had lost repeated battles in the attempt to raise the sieges of Ijon, Kedesh, Hazor and the rest. God was not accompanying the army with his blessing: as they fled, the Assyrians were able to take the spoil of the army, and later the captured cities, butchering the soldiers and enslaving the inhabitants by the thousand. Yahweh of hosts (84:1, 3, 8, 12; 46:7, 11) had inexplicably cast off his hosts, sold his covenanted people for nothing, and not even been the richer for it. A coup had removed the leader who so manifestly lacked God's blessing, and the community appeals in stricken humility for his successor to be their saviour indeed.

44:13   Thou makest us a reproach to our neighbours,
            A scorn and a derision to them that are round about us.
     14   Thou makest us a byword among the nations,
            A shaking of the head among the peoples.
     15   All the day long is my dishonour before me,
            And the shame of my face hath covered me,
     16   For the voice of him that reproacheth and blasphemeth;
            By reason of the enemy and the avenger.

A clear distinction is drawn between the adversary in v. 10a, who is also the enemy and the avenger of v. 16b, that is the Assyrians, and the neighbours, the nations and the peoples round about, that is the Moabites, Edomites, Philistines and others, who reproach and blaspheme. Now the proud Israelites, who had dominated the smaller peoples for three centuries, were biting the dust before the pitilessly pursuing (מחנקם) Assyrians. To have enslaved or slaughtered the whole population of Naphtali bespeaks a good measure of inexorable cruelty. The glad news is told in Gath and published in the streets of Ashkelon: 'O daughter of Samaria, happy shall he be that rewardeth thee as thou hast served us. Happy shall he be that taketh and dasheth thy little ones against the rock.'

The II Kings 15 text does not imply that Tiglath-Pileser annexed the provinces of Naphtali and Gilead, merely that he took all the cities there, and deported their inhabitants into slavery. Nor did he have matters all his own way, for Dan was not taken, but its siege raised (see below, p.168). In his own account he says, 'The wide land of (Naphta)li, in its entire extent, I united with Assyria . . . Officers of mine I installed as governors upon them . . . All the inhabitants of Omri-land and their possessions I led to Assyria. They overthrew their king Pekah, and I placed Hoshea (A-u-si-') as king over them.'[15] The reality was probably marginally less flattering. 732 was a year of disaster for Israel, but by late summer the Assyrians had withdrawn with their spoil and their slaves, and left Dan in Israelite hands. Settlers and governors arrived in the following years, and Hoshea had to cede all claim to the northern third of the country, including his religious capital, and accept tributary status (cf. II Kgs. 17:3). As he led the national pilgrimage to Dan, perhaps for the first and last time, his way passed through the devastated areas of Naphtali; small wonder that he should cry repeatedly at the oppression of the enemy, and the reproach of those who said continually, 'Where is thy God?' (42:3, 10), and go mourning on his road (42:9; 43:2).

44:17 All this is come upon us; yet have we not forgotten thee,
Neither have we dealt falsely in thy covenant.
18 Our heart is not turned back,
Neither have our steps declined from thy way;
19 Though thou hast sore broken us into a place (במקום) of jackals,
And covered us with the shadow of death.
20 If we have forgotten the name of our God,
Or spread forth our hands to a strange god,
21 Shall not God search this out?
For he knoweth the secrets of the heart.
22 Yea, for thy sake are we killed all the day long;
We are counted as sheep for the slaughter.

The robust spirituality of these verses contrasts well with the grovelling self-abasement to which the post-exilic Israelites were reduced: contrast the more 'Christian' 90:8, 'Thou hast set our iniquities before thee, Our secret sins in the light of thy countenance,' and the protracted confessions in Lam., Ezra 9, Neh. 9 and Dan. 9. Generations of disaster were bound to issue in a saddened view of God, whose chastisement for even secret sins was to be seen in these trials. But in the eighth century a healthier spirit prevailed. God had made a covenant with Israel, and his major provision had been that there should be no idolatry, but his worship alone. This the community had kept (vv. 17b, 20f), and had been faithful to the 'way' (v. 18) he laid down. Why then, comes the humble but dignified reproach, has God not been true to his side of the covenant? The pitiful sight of one noble town after another ruined and without inhabitant, the habitation of jackals (Isa. 13:22; 34:13),[16] draws the brave thought that Israel has continued faithful although (כי) God has apparently failed them. The 'shadow of death' (צלמות) is all that is left behind by the retreating Assyrians. The same word is used in the famous prophecy of Isaiah, which is generally thought to refer to this occasion:[17] 'In the former time he brought into contempt the land of Zebulun and the land of Naphtali, but in the latter time he hath made it glorious, by the way of the sea, beyond Jordan, Galilee (*or* the district) of the nations. The people that walked in darkness have seen a great light: they that dwelt in the land of צלמות, upon them hath the light shined' (Isa. 9:1f). The prophet sees hope and light where the Danite priest can only pray in the darkness. The 730 context gives a vivid meaning to the controverted word צלמות: it is what the B 52 left behind at Hiroshima.

God knows the innocence of his people, for he sees to the heart (v. 21); indeed it is because of him (עליך, v. 22), because of his rejection of them and not for their fault, that these disasters are befallen. 44 was in fact the Korahites' swan-song. Assyrian settlers were on their way, and Hoshea had no alternative but to cede Dan, and transfer the festival to Bethel in the cheerful land of Ephraim; so did he earn the half-hearted approval of even the D-historian: 'he did what was evil in the sight of the LORD, yet not as the kings of Israel who were before him' (II Kgs. 17:2).[18]

44:23   Awake, why sleepest thou, O Lord?
        Arise, cast (us) not off for ever.
     24 Wherefore hidest thou thy face,
        And forgettest our affliction and oppression?
     25 For our soul is bowed down to the dust:
        Our belly cleaveth unto the earth.
     26 Rise up for our help,
        And redeem us for thy lovingkindness' sake.

The opening of the final appeal reminds us ironically of the prophets of Baal gashing themselves and calling on their god in the days of Elijah; and indeed it is not likely that the thought was very different. Nor was the event. It was the time of evening oblation then, and there was neither voice nor any to answer. It is evening now, and king and people may roll in the dust, and the Danite psalmist may compose the noblest of biblical laments; but the heavens are as brass, and the destruction of the nation is to come ineluctably within the decade. The psalm is a permanent monument to the dignity and stature of the Israelite people: the justification of their God's חסד (v. 26) is still a matter of dispute.

Although 85 has been widely understood since Gunkel—and even since Ewald—to be a *Volksklagelied*, it is by no means so straightforward a psalm as 44, and raises a number of interesting questions. The first is the strong contrast between vv. 1-3, God's past deliverance of his people, 'turning the turning of Jacob,' taking away his wrath and turning from the fierceness of his anger; and vv. 4-6, their present plight, in which he is prayed to turn and cease from his anger, wrath and indignation. This contrast is so strong that Duhm cannot be thought to exaggerate when he calls it a direct contradiction. There is a majority opinion which seeks to resolve this contradiction on the basis of a concrete historical situation, and there are two main dissenting proposals.

The mainstream solution is to understand the 'turning of Jacob' to mean the Return from Exile at the end of the sixth century, and so to date the psalm about 520. This is the traditional Jewish interpretation. The Ketib text of v. 1a reads שבות from שוב to turn; but the Qere' has שְׁבִית, from שבה to lead captive, and the Massoretes point with a hireq. So they understand the words to mean, 'Thou hast brought back the captivity of Jacob' (RV text); and they are followed by Delitzsch, Kirkpatrick, Schmidt, Kraus, Anderson and others. The phrase occurs fifteen times elsewhere in the OT, and the most common context, e.g. in Jer. 29:14; 30:3, 18; Deut. 30:3, is that of the Return from Exile. The tension between vv. 1-3 and vv. 4-6 is then explained on the basis of the continuing plight of the returned exiles: God's anger is still evident. In favour of the context at the Return it is argued: (i) the sense of Israel's past iniquities being pardoned agrees with Isa. 40:2, and other sixth century prophecies; (ii) the Return was a hard time, marked by shortages of food (Hag. 1:5-11; 2:15ff), and disillusionment (Zech. 1:12), which may be echoed by the hope that the land will yield her increase, and that Yahweh's indignation will at last cease; (iii) alternations of confidence and despair, such as come in vv. 1-6, are to be found in the nearly contemporary Trito-Isaiah (Kraus); (iv) v. 9b, 'that glory may dwell in our land,' can be associated with Ezekiel's vision of the departure of Yahweh's glory from the Temple in ch. 10, and the expectation of its return with the building of the new Temple (Hag. 2:9).

The weakness of this interpretation, like so many concrete datings of the psalms, is in part that the phrasing is too general, and the underlying situation is too common, to bear the weight of the conclusion. שוב שבות is found as early as Hos. 6:11, where it means 'the restoration of the wounded body politic' (Kraus[19]), without any thought of a return from captivity. There was probably no year in Israelite history but that either lost battles or spoiled harvests were ascribed to God's anger, or in which better times were not looked for, with peace and plenty. Hard times and hopes of better are the fibre of ancient life. Glory dwelt in the land whenever God acted to bring blessing and salvation, from early days (I Sam. 4:21f) to eschatological visions (Isa. 40:5), not just in connection with the rebuilding of the Temple; indeed the absolute use of כבוד (without 'his,' 'God's,' etc.) is limited to this verse and I Sam. 4.

There are however two more serious objections which seem to exclude this view. First it does not answer Duhm's point. In the first three verses the Hebrew has perfects, which are then followed by imperatives and rhetorical questions. A 520 context means that God's actions in vv. 1-3 are recent, and should be rendered by English perfects, as in RV: 'LORD, thou hast been favourable unto thy land: Thou hast brought back the captivity of Jacob . . . Thou hast taken away all thy wrath: Thou hast turned (thyself) from the fierceness of thine anger.' This is then followed without any break by the appeal, 'Turn us, O God of our salvation, And cause thine indignation towards us to cease. Wilt thou be angry with us for ever? Wilt thou draw out thine anger to all generations?' This is a direct contradiction in Hebrew as in English. If God has taken away all his wrath and turned from the fierceness of his anger, then he has already caused his indignation to cease, and is not drawing his anger out in perpetuity. We should require 'again,' 'once more,' or some such phrase to give the sense. Secondly, there is no evidence that any contemporary Israelite regarded the Return as a sign of Yahweh's forgiveness; indeed, there is the embarrassment that Ezra 1 may be nearer to fiction than to fact. Neither Haggai nor Zechariah has any consciousness of the 'Return' as a mighty act of Yahweh. On the contrary Zechariah says, 'O LORD of hosts, how long wilt thou not have mercy on Jerusalem and on the cities of Judah, against which thou hast had indignation these threescore and ten years?' (1:12). In 517 the history of the last seventy years looked like an unbroken sequence of divine anger; the prophet's message is to assure the people that all despite all appearance Yahweh is returned to Jerusalem with mercies (1:16; 8:3). Appeal to Ps. 126 is circular: there is nothing to date that psalm in the late sixth century, and its wording seems rather to associate it with Nehemiah (v. 2; Neh. 6:16). The 'Return' of 538 did not seem like the seal of Yahweh's forgiveness until the time of the Chronicler.

Two alternative possibilities have been proposed.[20] Gunkel correctly saw that vv. 1-3 cannot refer to some occasional deliverance, and suggested that the perfects are prophetic, and that they speak of the ultimate redemption of Israel already present to the prophet's thought.

But the latter proposal can hardly be right, for, as Mowinckel objected, there is no mention in the last verses of the overthrow of foreign oppressors, and other themes characteristic of Yahweh's ultimate redemption, but only truth springing out of the earth, and the land yielding its increase. Mowinckel therefore suggests a recurring use of the psalm at the autumn festival, when such harvest themes would be appropriate.[21] The first half of the psalm he explains on the basis of the extreme self-abasement of the Hebrew peasant: good harvests in earlier years mean that Yahweh had taken away his anger, and now he is prayed to do the same again. It is difficult to accept the latter part of Mowinckel's proposal, which trivialises the psalm, but his suggestion of an autumn festival use is attractive in itself, and is developed in a more useful direction by Weiser. Weiser thinks of the autumn feast as the festival of the covenant, and imagines the opening verses as a meditation on the *Heilsgeschichte*; in this he was anticipated by Peters, and followed by Eaton, and seems to me right, though insufficiently specific.

In Weiser's favour, 85 is often compared to 77 and 80; 80 especially is similar, being a national lament also, with a plea to God to 'turn us' (השיבנו, vv. 3, 7, 19), and 'quicken us' (v. 18; cf.85:6). Now 80 appeals to God's mighty acts in the past, the Exodus and Conquest; and 77 similarly is a national lament which refers to God's covenant-love, and his wonders of old at the Exodus. It is in this, and not in anything connected with Sheshbazzar and Zerubbabel, that Haggai puts his trust, 'the word that I covenanted with you when ye came out of Egypt' (2:5). We have evidence of the same later on in 85: 'he will speak peace unto his people, and to those of his covenant (חסידיו, v. 8); 'חסד and אמת are met together' (v. 10). This understanding will now enable us to resolve Duhm's contradiction, because we can put enough distance between vv. 1-3 and vv. 4ff to translate the Hebrew perfects by English preterites: 'LORD, thou wast favourable unto thy land: Thou didst turn the fortunes of Jacob ... Thou didst take away all thy wrath: Thou didst turn thyself from the fierceness of thine anger.' God did all this in the days of old, but now the cry is: 'Turn us, O God of our salvation, And cause thine indignation towards us to cease.' The pushing back of the context of the opening verses makes them the basis for the appeal which follows, and gives force to it. In this way 85 becomes even more like 44. Both psalms take their stand on the original turning of Jacob's fortunes and on God's favour (vv. 1-3; 44:1-8); both then contrast their present trials (vv. 4-7; 44:9-16) and close in reliance on God's faithfulness to the covenant (vv. 8-13; 44:17-26).

In the opening section of 44 the context was clear, God's grace in the Conquest; and was crystal-clear if in fact much of the day had been given to recitals of the Conquest tradition, culminating in a form of our Josh. 24. What seems unsatisfactory about Weiser's suggestion is its vagueness. Yahweh's favour to the land, and his turning the fortunes of Jacob, might again refer to the Conquest; but what is stressed is his forgiveness, his covering of all their sin, his removal of all his wrath and anger, and such phrases can hardly refer to the Conquest/Exodus. We require a more specific hypothesis.

85 For the Chief Musician. A Psalm of the sons of Korah.
1 LORD, thou wast favourable unto (רצית) thy land:
   Thou didst restore the fortunes (שבת שבות) of Jacob.
2 Thou didst forgive (נשאת) the iniquity of thy people,
   Thou didst cover (כסית) all their sin.   [Selah
3 Thou didst take away (אספת) all thy wrath:
   Thou didst turn (השיבות) from the fierceness of thine anger.

It is time for us to grasp a second nettle, the meaning of the interjection Selah (סלה). The word occurs 71 times in the Hebrew psalter (92 times in G) and three times in the Psalm of Habakkuk. The uses are spread over 39 psalms: 9 in Book I, 17 in Book II, 11 in Book III, none in Book IV, 2 in Book V. These include all our psalms except for 42-43 and 45; eighteen Selahs in 10 psalms, with two apiece in 84, 87 and 88, three in 46 and four in 89. LXX renders with διάψαλμα, and is usually followed by Symmachus and Theodotion; probably an instrumental interlude is intended—the Greek, unlike the Hebrew, never has Selah at the end of a psalm. Aquila renders ἀεί and the curious Massoretic pointing corresponds with that of נצח, 'eternity': it is likely that he understood Selah to stand for a doxology, such as 'Blessed be Yahweh for ever and ever!'

This difference in the ancient interpreters, and the fact that the term is almost missing from the last two Books of the Psalter, suggests that it is ancient, and that its meaning has been lost. It is not even clear what its etymology is. It is more usually derived from סלל, to raise, but B. D. Eerdmans connects it with an Aramaic root צלא, with a supposed Hebrew cognate סלה, to bend, or pray.[22] On the latter understanding, the word should be a call to the worshippers to prostrate themselves; and Kraus draws attention to certain Sumerian prayers in ten sections called *kirugu*, bowings, at the close of which each of the congregation kneels and bows. If the derivation is from סלל, the meaning could be 'lift up the voice,' as it is in Ps. 68:4. R. Gyllenberg takes this meaning, and suggests that whereas a psalm was normally sung by a cantor, Selah signifies that a choir, or even the whole people, was to join in; the Selah precedes the refrain in 59 for example, and often corresponds with refrains, so that choir or people would have something to sing.[23] Alternatively, says Kraus, they might just lift up their voices in a shout. Another possibility is that proposed by Robert Stieb, that it is the eyes which are to be lifted up on the text-sheet, and so the previous verse is to be repeated; Selah often follows a verse which is the heart of its psalm.[24] Or again, Norman Snaith notes the levitical practice of breaking psalm-singing at the daily offering with trumpet-blasts and prostrations; he suggests that Selah is an ancient signal for such a break, which he supposes to have taken place twice during and once after each psalm.[25]

So we have little common ground; nor are the theories I have mentioned very persuasive. We are better to derive the word from a Hebrew root we know rather than from one conjectured from Aramaic, and to take the meaning given in Ps. 68:4 'lift up the voice' if we can. Further, Stieb's 'lift up the eyes' involves the choir (and even the people) in the use of written texts, which, as Gyllenberg says, can hardly be assumed at so early a period; and it is difficult to think that all the verses followed by Selah are the heart of the respective psalm (84:8 and 87:3, for example). But Gyllenberg's choral theory involves more difficulties. He chooses between MT and LXX attestations at will, and frequently finds the Selah misplaced: for he takes it to indicate choral use of the following verse, as in 59, but often it follows the refrain, and sometimes, as in 49, bears no relation to the refrain. 49 is a test-case for Snaith too; and the text from the Mishnah, which is his starting-point, mTam. 7.3, makes no reference to psalms being sung in three sections, and includes 92 which has no Selah. This leaves us with Kraus's shout, a proposal so general that it is hard to fault; all one can note is that, if it is right, the shouting was sometimes triumphant, as at 46:7, 11, and sometimes in lament, as at 88:7, 10; sometimes at natural breaks, as in 46, sometimes in the middle of a section, as at 85:2, the text before us.

I do not think any of these proposals is satisfactory, and should like to make a new suggestion. We should derive Selah from סלל, and take it to mean 'lift up the voice,' as in Ps. 68:4; but give it the technical meaning of 'cantillation' or 'recitative,' that is, the cantillation of the

relevant section of the tradition. This might be a prayer,[26] but more
often would be a story. I have already argued that 44:1, 'We have heard
with our ears, O God, our fathers have told us,' refers to the recital of
the stories of the Conquest, which have been told during the day. The
opening section ends,

44:8 In God have we made our boast all the day long,
And we will give thanks unto thy name for ever.   [Selah
The Selah, or סֶלָה as it would perhaps have been originally, is the
indication that the psalm should be broken off here for the cantillation
of the Josh. 24 story, the climax of the Conquest tradition. The psalm
has been written in the light of this story, and references to 'driving out
the nations,' 'getting the land in possession,' and 'not trusting in my
bow,' lead up to this; after the recital, the story is echoed in the appeal
to the covenant, and the protestation that the people's heart has not
declined from God's way, nor have they worshipped strange gods. In
this way it is possible to explain the immediacy of the references, and at
the same time to provide a clear place for the recital within the autumn
festal liturgy, a place which Deut. 31:9ff shows it must have had.

There are two other instances of Selah in the Korah psalms where
the text seems to indicate the recital of some tradition. One is at 48:8f.

48:8 As we have heard, so we have seen
In the city of the LORD of hosts, in the city of our God:
God will establish it for ever.   [Selah
9 We have thought on thy lovingkindness, O God,
In the midst of thy temple.
'We have heard,' שמענו, is the same expression with which 44 opened;
but on this occasion 'we have heard' that God will establish his city for
ever. The implication is that there was, as part of the ritual, the recital
of the sanctuary-legend at Dan, including God's promise of the
inviolability of the city. The verse follows an imaginative description
of the kings assembling and invading Israel, but on seeing God's holy
mountain, fair in height, they are dismayed and flee away. So, the poet
concludes, what we have heard recited year after year we have seen to
be true: the city really is established for ever. The Selah, as the recital
of the legend, is thus introduced in the text of the preceding verse: 'As
we have heard . . .' leads on immediately to the ceremonial 'hearing'
once more. Furthermore, we then have an explanation for the ritual
reference in the following verse. God's 'lovingkindness' (חסד) is his
covenanted blessing, which he was to command day by day (42:8). I
give a fuller discussion of דמינו below (p.166), but there is better

evidence of the meaning in RV (cf. BDB 'imagine') than for proposals of some ritual representation or enactment. The meaning will then be given by the now completed recital of the legend: the poet recommences his psalm with a reference to what has been done—'we have pondered your gracious promise to us and our city, O God, in the midst of your temple-enclosure'—and then moves on to God's praise.

We have a similar indication in 87, which is a twin-psalm to 48, being also concerned with God's city, and containing the same promise, 'the Most High himself shall establish her.' So it would not surprise us if the same sanctuary-legend were recited in connection with 87 in the ninth century as in connection with 48 in the eighth; indeed, it might well be that the phrase 'God/the Most High shall establish her' was the climax of the legend. Now there is a Selah after v. 3:

> 87:3 Glorious things are spoken of thee,
>   O city of God.   [Selah

The poet does not mean that Israelites speak about Dan in the bazaars, or that Egyptians and Babylonians can scarce forebear to cheer. He means that God speaks its shining destiny; and there could not be a more suitable moment to have that destiny recited than following these introductory words. So no less than three of the eighteen Selahs in our psalms are accompanied by references in the text to 'hearing,' 'speaking' and 'thinking on' the relevant portion of the tradition.

We cannot expect such indications regularly; but in many other cases, including 85:2, this interpretation of Selah helps to solve the problem of the psalm. We have already seen that 85:1-3 is best understood with Weiser as referring to the *Heilsgeschichte*; but that we still have the difficulty that the events of the (Exodus and) Conquest cannot be plausibly connected with the repeated expressions for forgiveness and remission of wrath. But on our present hypothesis, Selah would be the indication of the recital of a part of the sacred history, and might well refer to some part in which Israel's sin evoked God's anger, which was then withdrawn in forgiveness. There is even perhaps an encouragement to take this seriously in the position of the Selah; for this is not placed after v. 3, at the end of the opening section, at the natural break where we might have expected corporate shouting, musical intervals, doxologies, etc., but after v. 2, in the middle of things. We should have a more satisfactory explanation of this position if Selah means 'recitative': the community first *refers to* God's forgiveness in the days of Moses (vv. 1f), then it *recites* the story in full (Selah), then it *recapitulates* the message (v. 3), and finally *prays* for similar forgiveness now on the strength of it (vv. 4-7).

The northern community may have had a number of traditions of Israel's sin and forgiveness, but one story which we have already seen to have been central at Dan is the story of apostasy, judgement and divine mercy which is now enshrined in Exod. 32-34. The core of this now extended passage was the Levites' consecration legend in Exod. 32:25-29, but this certainly cannot have stood on its own,[27] and our best way forward must be to compare the language of 85 with these chapters, and see how much, if anything, may be in common. Such linguistic evidence has priority over the uncertainties of documentary criticism, since we can have little confidence in excluding more than a small proportion of the material as unavailable in ninth century Dan. We do not know, for example, whether E or J traditions, or both, were to hand or not, or even whether Deuteronomic sections may be expansions of earlier outlines; indeed, if the present hypothesis should seem sound, we should be in a position to check and correct the hydra-like growth of documentary hypotheses. It might also be the case that some correspondences of language were due to the familiarity of the author of 85 with a part of the present Exod. 32-34 story, while other correspondences arose from later editors of Exod. 32-34 being familiar with the association with 85.

There are five phrases in common between the two passages. (i) When Moses learns of the people's idolatry, and God's intention to destroy them, he says, 'Turn from the fierceness of thine anger (שוב מחרון אפך, Exod. 32:12).' 'Thou didst turn (thyself) from the fierceness of thine anger (השיבות מחרון אפך),' says the psalmist (v. 3). The correspondence is the more striking because of the difficulty of the Hebrew indicated by RV's italicising of 'thyself.' Kimhi interpreted, 'Thou hast called back thy wrath from burning'; Duhm and others delete the ם; Gunkel emends הֵשַׁבְתָ. The intensive use of מן + השיב has a parallel in Ezek. 14:6 (Delitzsch), but the usage is rare and therefore impressive. (ii) After the Levites' heroic interposition, Moses prays, 'Yet now, if thou wilt forgive their sin—' (תשא חתאתם, Exod. 32:32). God promises to visit their sin on them, but later proclaims his name as merciful, 'forgiving iniquity (נסא עון) and transgression and sin' (34:7). So 85:2 runs, 'Thou didst forgive the iniquity of thy people (נסאת עון), Thou didst cover all their sin.' (iii) The proclamation of Yahweh's name in Exod. 34:6 begins, יהוה יהוה אל, 'Yahweh, Yahweh, a God ...' The use of אל here is uncommon, as a class of divine beings, one of whom is Yahweh (cf. 34:14; 15:11; Deut. 3:24; Dan. 11:36), and recalls 85:8, 'I will hear what the God Yahweh (האל יהוה) will speak.' האל יהוה does not occur elsewhere, and should be taken as like המלך דוד (Delitzsch). (iv) Exod. 34:6 continues '... plenteous in mercy and truth (חסד ואמת).' The same phrase comes at 85:10, 'Mercy and truth are met together.' (v) Moses was told to lead the people to the land, and was promised, 'behold, my angel shall go before thee' (ילך לפניך, Exod. 32:34). Eissfeldt suggested that the 'angel' was an expression for the ark,[28] but it may rather be a euphemism for one of the divine figures on the ephod's throne, which seem to be described in 85 (see below). 85:13 in particular says, 'Righteousness shall go before him' (לפניו יהלך).

Five points are not inconsiderable from a short psalm, and the concentration of parallels with Exod. 34:6f is noticeable. With such a recital covered by the Selah, we are in a position to explain both the language of vv. 1-3, and also, soon, the problematic v. 8a. The same situation is presupposed as with 44. Israel has gathered for a pre-festal lamentation on 14th Bul, expressing in ritual what is to be expressed in words in vv. 4-7. But in place of the political troubles which fill the horizon in the later 44, the anxiety here is with the age-old problem of the harvest. So the psalmist begins, 'LORD, thou wast favourable unto thy *land*,' and he ends in the confidence that 'our land shall yield her increase.' There is the same reliance on Yahweh's favour (רצית): our fathers took the land in 44:3 because Yahweh favoured them (רציתם). Probably some of the same Conquest traditions as are implied in 44:1-8 were recited in the course of the day including some stressing the fertility of the land (? the 'angel' passage in Exod. 23:20ff). But the impact of the Exod. 32ff story soon begins to make itself felt. Yahweh 'turned the turning of Jacob'; perhaps both in that he restored the fortunes of Jacob with harvest blessings and also in that he restored the people he had so justly punished (cf. Hos. 6:11). For he forgave the iniquity they had committed with their idolatry, and covered all their sin (v. 2). After the people had been smitten (Exod. 32:35), he took away his wrath, turned from his fierce anger and showed himself to be a God of mercy and truth (v. 3). Such graciousness gives the community hope that there may be mercy and truth awaiting them in the coming year, and salvation from hunger.

85:4 Turn us (שובנו), O God of our salvation,
      And cause thine indignation towards us to cease.

> 5 Wilt thou be angry with us for ever?
>   Wilt thou draw out thine anger to all generations?
> 6 Wilt thou not quicken us again:
>   That thy people may rejoice in thee?
> 7 Shew us thy mercy, O LORD,
>   And grant us thy salvation.

As Yahweh turned the fortunes of Jacob of old (v. 1), so he is prayed to turn his people to times of greater prosperity now. The phrasing of vv. 4-6 is echoed in the Asaph laments, 77, 79 and 80, each of which appeals to God's mighty acts in the Exodus and Desert; but, perhaps significantly, there is no reference to or hint of the Exodus in the Korah psalms. Especially close are 80:3f, 18f, 'Turn us again, O God . . . How long wilt thou smoke against the prayer of thy people? . . . Quicken thou us . . . Turn us again.' Vv. 6f recalls 90, the opening lament of the psalms in Book IV: 'O satisfy us in the morning with thy mercy; That we may rejoice . . .' (v. 14). The Danite priest prays to see the חסר which Yahweh promised in his covenant, the salvation of a bountiful crop next year (vv. 9ff); Tabernacles should be a feast of rejoicing, because the LORD 'shall bless thee in all thine increase' (Deut. 16:14f). The stress in v. 6a falls upon 'thou': it is Yahweh alone who can give these blessings which will quicken his people in new life (cf. 44:3-7).

> 85:8 I will hearken to what the God Yahweh speaks
>   (אשמע מה־ידבר האל יהוה)
>   For he speaks (ידבר) peace unto his people, and to his
>   covenanted ones (חסידיו);
>   But let them not turn again to folly.

The dramatic change of tone, and of person from the plural to the singular, is explained in modern commentaries by the hypothesis of the interposition of a cultic prophet. Gunkel says, 'Aus dem Kreise der Sänger erhebt sich ein Mann, um Jahves Antwort zu verkünden.' Anderson commends Weiser's imaginative reconstruction of the scene: 'From the midst of the praying congregation somebody (probably a prophet) steps forward and listens for what God will say in answer to the prayer. Suddenly he hears the mysterious voice of God speaking. It foretells salvation for the people. Filled with prophetic enthusiasm this seer then reveals to the multitude that listens to him in words full of splendour the promise of divine blessing.' The cultic prophet has become a major figure in the interpretation of the psalms, from Mowinckel's *Psalmenstudien III, Kultprophetie und Prophetische*

Psalmen (1923) to A. R. Johnson's *The Cultic Prophet in Israel's Psalmody* (1979); and Johnson can claim that 85 'contains internal evidence which goes far in support of (his) general theory' (p.200).

Mowinckel argues that priest and prophet were never far apart in Israel. Prophets were part of the cultic personnel, and in early times seers amd priests had sometimes been the same, e.g. Samuel. Priests delivered torah, sometimes by lot, and the prophets were expected to deliver oracles of a freer kind; though often the content, and even the words, might be governed by tradition and by non-religious factors. Such oracles would provide explanations for the sudden change of tone in many psalms, 12 and 60, for example, where the move to a confident tone coincides with words of Yahweh. Yahweh's 'decrees' or promises are set out at length in such psalms as 2, 89 and 132. It may be that the prophet was assisted by omens (5:4; 27:4 being possible instances), or other 'tokens,' but often the inspiration seems to come direct. In this connection, two psalms are particularly significant, 81 and 85, because there the prophet introduces his visionary message. Mowinckel renders:

> 81:5c I hear a voice that I know not.
> 6 'I took the burden from thy back . . . ,'

and comments, 'What will the mystic have heard that the others cannot hear? Suddenly he knows. The unknown voice becomes clear words; these form sentences—and now he tells the people what he has heard' (pp. 38f, my translation).

> 85:8 I will listen to what God speaks through me:
> certainly, Yahweh is speaking welfare
> to his people, to his faithful devoted,
> and hope to those who turn to him (*PIW*, 61).

The argument, both for Mowinckel and for Johnson, is a cumulative one, with numerous psalms invoked as evidence of the cultic prophet's activity in the psalmody.

I do not wish to contest the importance of cultic prophets in Israel, and any disputes over individual psalms must be undertaken in their place; but 81 and 85 are crucial to the argument. First, it must be noted that Mowinckel is not really translating the Hebrew. In 81:6 the text has been twice emended, 'thy back . . . thy hands' being substituted for 'his . . . his . . .' In 85:8a 'through me' has been added, following G [ἐν ἐμοί; in v. 8b Yahweh, which has been separated from האל, has been placed after כי instead of before; in v. 8c 'to those who turn to him' partly follows G, while omitting G's καρδίαν;[29] and כסלה has been rendered 'hope', for which there is no parallel. So much alteration of the text is not necessary to the theory, for Johnson's translation of 85 is close to the Hebrew; but for 81 he writes,

> 81:5c I can hear the speech of one whom I know not,
>   10c 'Open thy mouth wide that I may fill it!'

'The psalmist . . . is thus summoned to surrender to the [Spirit] as a vehicle for the divine message' (p.8). The fact is that although the text can carry the oracle interpretation, it does so more convincingly if one emends the text, transposes the verses, prefers the Greek in part, etc. Oracles can hardly open with third person references ('his back . . . his hands'). 'The God Yahweh' is, as we have noted, unparalleled elsewhere; and the oracle of 85 is supposed to be one of 'welfare'; it is not therefore very suitable to begin it with a warning, 'But let them not again turn to folly.' This is why Mowinckel and Johnson (and many other exegetes using the oracle hypothesis) treat the text so roughly; but it does not commend their theory.

Secondly, the oracle view implies a quite implausible procedure. Even if we allow some such scene as Mowinckel and Weiser have imagined, how are we to suppose that the psalm was first used? Was an interval left every time the prayer had been completed to allow the same prophet to come forward and repeat his message? Did he preface it with his 'words of inspiration' each time? Or did the priestly choir take over the words of inspiration, even though they were now meaningless? Kraus boldly calls the original speaker a *shalom*-prophet, but excuses him from Jeremiah's attacks on the ground that after Deutero-Isaiah messages of peace were genuine revelations of God's intentions. But were the Israelites really such simpletons, that they could go on repeating, as if they were a prophecy, words that must frequently have been falsified? Mowinckel writes, 'Now here perhaps the pious Bible-reader would object, "This idea makes it the duty of the cult-prophet to produce inspired, and yet in substance pre-composed prophecies. But that would be a profanation of the Psalms; indeed it would come down to an almost conscious hypocrisy for the poet in question. Such we should not attribute to the holy men of holy scripture"' (p. 8). I fully agree with Mowinckel's pious Bible-reader, and am not at all persuaded by his reply that the repetition of the prophecy is like the liturgical assurance of Christ's forgiveness.

We are better if we can manage without the oracle hypothesis; and surely we can. 81:5c should be translated, 'I will hearken to a voice I did not know'; the voice being the voice of Yahweh whose words are about to be recited in the Selah at the end of v. 7. The psalm harps upon the crucial importance of hearkening to what Yahweh said at Meribah:

'Hear, O my people . . . if thou wouldest hearken unto me' (v. 8), 'But my people hearkened not to my voice' (v. 11), 'O that my people would hearken unto me' (v. 13). It also stresses Israel's failure to 'know' that voice in the past: Israel would none of God, and was let go in the stubbornness of their heart to walk in their counsels (vv. 11f). The content of the Selah is clearly the covenant revelation (vv. 4f, 7, 9). The oracle theory only causes unnecessary trouble, because 'his shoulder . . . his hands' (v. 6) refers naturally to Joseph in Egypt in v 5ab; which makes perfect sense provided there is no change of speaker. It is the intrusive prophet who requires either emendations or a transposition.

It is the same with the present passage. The change of speaker is to be explained in 85 in just the same way as in 44, 84, 81 and other osalms. The psalm is 'for the מנצח,' the priest who leads the music, and he speaks on behalf of the nation. Usually therefore he uses the first person plural—'us,' 'our fathers,' 'our shield,' etc.—while sometimes, as the people's representative, he drops into the first person singular—'I will not trust in my bow . . . ,' 'hear my prayer,' 'I will hearken.' We find the same alternation in Solomon's prayer in I Kgs. 8. The boldest use of 'I' is in 81:5, 'I will hearken to a voice I have not known,' for while the first 'I' expresses the speaker's intention, representing and leading the people, the second speaks for Israel over the generations, and verges on the now suspect 'corporate personality' concept. Here the use is more simple. The priest-poet leads the assembly in hearkening to, laying to heart, what the God Yahweh speaks: for in the passage just recited at the Selah, the Danite version of Exod. 32-34, Yahweh proclaimed his name, 'Yahweh, Yahweh, an אל full of compassion and gracious . . .' (Exod. 34:6f), and promised Israel the land of the Amorites in the covenant (Exod. 34:11, 24), and his angel to go before them (Exod. 32:34). So we do not require 'the mysterious voice of God speaking'; the whole assembled people has heard God's covenant recited, and knows full well that God is speaking peace to his people, and to those under his covenant (חסידיו). But the covenant contains warnings as well as promises: 'Take heed to thyself lest thou make a covenant with the inhabitants of the land . . . thou shalt worship no other אל . . . Thou shalt make no molten gods . . .' (Exod. 34:12-17). Israel is not to repeat its apostasy in the desert; so the priest adds, 'But let them not turn again to folly.' In Jer. 10:8 the root כסל is associated with idolatry. The speaker announces his faith in the אל Yahweh, with his covenant of blessing and his warnings against backsliding; no other אל for him, or for those on whose behalf he speaks (cf. 44:20f).

85:9 Surely his salvation is nigh them that fear him;
  That glory may dwell in our land.

 10 Mercy and truth are met together;
  Righteousness and peace have kissed each other.

 11 Truth springeth out of the earth;
  And righteousness hath looked down from heaven.

 12 Yea, the LORD shall give that which is good;
  And our land shall yield her increase.

 13 Righteousness shall go before him;
  And shall set his steps in the way (לדרך פמיו).

Those who fear Yahweh are his people from v. 8, and his recited covenant is their guarantee ('Surely') of blessing, both generally (v. 9) and in particular upon the harvest (vv. 11 f). His glory is a symbol of his active presence not only in the post-exilic period, with the texts referred to above from Ezekiel, II- and III-Isaiah and Haggai, but from earliest times. In Exod. 33:18, 22, in the passage which I have taken to be the recital underlying 85, Yahweh causes his glory to pass by Moses, and this could account for its presence in v. 9. More generally, God's glory was believed to 'dwell' in the Temple (I Kgs. 8:10), and earlier in the Ark (I Sam. 4:22), and later in the shrine at Bethel (Hos. 10:5). From there it radiated blessing over the land, and with the capture of the Ark there was no more glory. The 'nearness' of salvation and glory is thus suited to a cultic pilgrimage-feast, in which the ephod is about to be carried up into the shrine; and the absolute 'glory,' without 'God's,' 'his,' etc., suggests an early date (cf. I Sam. 4:21f).

It is clear that Mercy (חסד) and Truth (אמת), Righteousness (צדק) and Peace (שלום), are pairs of supernatural powers, sometimes spoken of as angels, or, more rashly, as hypostases of Yahweh. Their function remains obscure, and v. 13 a prey to emendation, unless we see the force of there being four of them. We have a similar tetrad at 96:6, 'Honour (הוד) and majesty (הדר) are before him: Strength (עז) and beauty (תפארת) are in his sanctuary'; and another at 89:14, 'Righteousness (צדק) and judgement (משפט) are the foundation (מכון) of thy throne: Mercy (חסד) and truth (אמת) go before thy face.' It is noticeable that in both 96 and 89 the tetrads are thought of as being in the sanctuary, or (even more directly) as being the foundation of Yahweh's throne; and 89:14a is repeated at 97:2, 'Righteousness and judgement are the foundation of his throne.' While the four 'powers'

are differently named in the Jerusalem psalm 96, three of the four—Righteousness, Mercy and Truth—are in common between 85 and the northern 89A, and Mercy and Truth form a pair in both, as they do in Exod. 34:6.

As we lack any description of the ephod at Dan, we have no direct means of imagining the process of its carrying up to the shrine. It is not at all likely, however, that it was carried in the priest's hands, as Abiathar took it to David. The Joseph psalm 80 addresses God as 'Thou that sittest upon the cherubim (ישב הכרובים)' (v. 1), and 47:8 speaks of him taking his seat upon his holy throne; so it is clear that in the shrine the ephod was set on a throne decorated with cherubim at Bethel, and probably at Dan as well. The phrase, 'that sitteth upon the cherubim' is used of Yahweh with respect to the ark also (I Sam. 4:4; II Sam. 6:2; II Kgs. 19:15), and it is likely that the ark and ephod alike were carried on pedestals with symbolic cherubs. I Sam. 4 and II Sam. 6 both describe the ark in procession; on the latter occasion it is being carried on a cart drawn by oxen, and we should probably think of something similar with the ephod. As for the detail, Ezekiel's Chariot visions in Ezek. 1 and 10 envisage Yahweh's throne as on four multiple wheels, each with four faces of a man, a lion, an ox (or cherub) and an eagle, and the cherubim draw the chariot. There is a somewhat similar description in I Kgs. 7:27ff of ten bases (מכונות) of brass in the Temple, with panels on which were lions, oxen and cherubs; every base had four brazen wheels, like the work of a chariot wheel.

The identification of the four 'virtues' or 'powers' with the foundation of Yahweh's throne, in the northern 89A as well as the Jerusalem 96, suggests that in both communities the cherubs were named as the virtues; indeed this process was to be carried much further in later centuries, in mediaeval Qabbalistic meditation on the Merkabah,[30] and in early Christian gnosticism.[31] The four powers also reappear in the intertestamental literature as the four angels of the presence, Gabriel, Michael, Uriel and Raphael. All this sheds new light on the last verses of 85, which are more than a succession of beautiful images (Gunkel).

The glory which is to dwell in our land (v. 9) is symbolised, then, by the arrival of the ephod at the shrine at Dan. The ephod is not merely a silver breast-plate of the kind envisaged in ch.3, but is borne on a throne, corresponding to the Jerusalem Ark with its throne-symbolism. The ephod-throne has four cherub 'foundations' (89:14; 97:2), which are thought of as angelic extensions of Elohim's glorious presence.

Their names here are Mercy and Truth, Righteousness and Peace. We have evidence in names like Melchisedek and Abishalom that Righteousness and Peace were the names of Canaanite gods,[32] who will then have been absorbed into Israel's God as cherubic extensions of his being; we have no evidence of Mercy and Truth being similar divinities, and they probably owe their position here to their place as attributes of Yahweh in traditional recitation of the revelation of his Name in Exod. 34:6, 'The LORD, the LORD . . .plenteous in mercy and truth.' If the cherubs were gilded winged bulls, we should have an explanation for the revulsion of Amos and Hosea, and the later travesties of the Deuteronomists in Jg. 17f and I Kgs. 12.

The two pairs of powers are seen as ranging out from the divine presence, bringing fruitfulness as they go. Mercy and Truth meet; Righteousness and Peace kiss in salutation (v. 10). Truth—Yahweh's truth to his covenant—is anticipated as poking her head through the soil with the first shoots of the new crop; Righteousness as the sun looks down from heaven upon man's works (v. 10). צדק was a solar god to the Canaanites, and has carried this aspect of Yahweh's all-seeing eye into Israelite faith.[33] The result of such an effusion of the divine presence is 'that which is good' / the increase of the land (v. 12). Yahweh's blessing upon the crops (יבול) is especially celebrated in the eighth month in which the autumn festival was held, the month of produce, Bul. The final entry of Yahweh on his throne into the sanctuary (and thence invisibly, throughout the land) is looked forward to in v. 13, which makes good sense unemended. The parallelism shows that the 'him' in v. 13a, i.e. Yahweh from v. 12a, is the same as the 'his' in v. 13b. Righteousness, then, is one of the two front cherubs which go before Yahweh on his throne up to the sanctuary; he acts as the leader of an earthly royal procession acts, setting his king's footsteps on the proper road. The earthly king does not actually walk, he rides on his mule, but his 'footsteps' are guided none the less; and so are Yahweh's as he rides his chariot-throne. The liturgical context once more makes sense of the text as it stands, and renders unnecessary the field of competing emendations.

One last question must detain us on the eve of the festival. Did the ephod spend the whole year at Dan, being brought out immediately before the feast so as to be carried in again? Or was it carried round to different shrines, like some of the Mesopotamian gods who moved from city to city by boat[34]? The exalted language of vv. 9-13 seems rather forced if the former answer is right, and I should prefer the latter one. It is a noticeable feature of Israelite holy places that on occasion they are mentioned in *threes*. 'Samuel judged Israel all the days of his life. And he went on a circuit, year by year to Bethel, Gilgal and Mizpah' (I Sam. 7:15f); 'seek not Bethel, nor enter into Gilgal, and pass not to Beersheba' (Amos 5:4); 'They that swear by the sin of Samaria, and say, As thy God, O Dan, liveth; and, As the way of Beersheba liveth' (Amos 8:14). When Amos and Hosea mention two shrines together, they are usually Bethel and Gilgal (Amos 4:4; 5:4b; Hos. 4:15; 9:15-10:8); Hos. 4:15, 'come not ye to Gilgal, neither go ye up to Beth-aven, nor swear (תשבעו), As the LORD liveth,' may in fact reflect three sanctuaries, with Beersheba, the Well of Swearing (Gen. 21:31; 26:31-33), as the third. This would correspond with Amos 5:4, with an oath similar to the Beersheba oath in Amos 8:14. A number of other holy places feature in these two prophets: Dan in Amos (8:14), in Hosea Mizpah and Tabor (5:1), perhaps Gilead and Ramah (5:8), Gilead (6:8; 12:11), Shechem (6:9).

It has long been a problem how so many sanctuaries could have flourished. The traditions of centralised worship in Deut. 12ff are now widely believed to have come from the north; and the unimpartial record of the D-historian imputes only two golden calves to Jeroboam, in Dan and Bethel, with none at Gilgal, or any other centre. Further, there is the troubling inclusion of Beersheba in the list of sanctuaries, a shrine forty miles into the territory of Judah. How is one to account for such a complex web of evidence? The following is a speculative answer, consonant with, but not indispensable to, the interpretation which I am proposing for the Korah psalms.

First, it is to be observed that the number of shrines is far fewer in Amos than in Hosea. An easy explanation of this would be that Amos reflects the real situation, while Hosea is using some rhetorical exaggeration. There were perhaps in fact three sanctuaries in use in the last years of the Northern Kingdom, Bethel, Gilgal and Beersheba (Amos 5:5; Hos. 4:15). Dan had been in use until the devastation of the provinces of Naphtali and Gilead around 730 (II Kings 15:29), and so is mentioned at Amos 8:14. 'The sin of Samaria' mentioned in the same verse is not likely to imply a sanctuary at Samaria itself, but to refer to the national 'idol'; as in Hos. 10:5, 'The inhabitants of Samaria shall be afraid for the calves of Beth-aven,' the Samaritan (i.e. Northern) calves (i.e. cherubs on the divine throne) being at Beth-aven (i.e. Bethel). So Amos will be criticising the Northern religious life as it was actually lived. Hosea, on the other hand, will be using a device common to religious controversialists down the ages, and found for example in early nineteenth century anti-Papalist cartoons: all the abominations of previous generations and centuries, and many which only ever existed in imagination, are lampooned as if they were present reality. There had been local shrines like Mizpah and Ramah, and they may or may not still have had a residual local following; but they were not national sanctuaries in the eighth century, and it is Bethel first and Gilgal second against which Hosea's polemic is directed. The rest are included (with the partial exception of Tabor, as I shall indicate), to tar Northern worship with the stigma of revering a multitude of local holy places, as opposed to Southern reverence for Jerusalem alone.

Second, of the three sanctuaries thus isolated, and also of the three sanctuaries on Samuel's circuit, Gilgal appears to have a connection with the Exodus and Entry traditions, and to be associated with the feast of Passover. 'The children of Israel encamped at Gilgal; and they kept the passover on the fourteenth day of the month at even in the plains of Jericho. And they did eat of the corn of the land on the morrow after the passover, unleavened cakes and parched corn, in the self-same day' (Josh. 5:10f). It was at Gilgal that Israel crossed the Jordan (Josh. 4:19); the circle of stones which give it its name was understood by the Israelites as a memorial of the sanctuary's foundation by Joshua (Josh. 4:1-10). It was from Gilgal that the conquest was undertaken (Josh. 7:6; 9:6); it was here that the manna was thought of as ceasing (Josh. 5:12)—that is, the period of the desert wanderings was over. But the passover/unleavened bread connection with Gilgal is not concerned only with the beginning of the occupation. It has influenced the assimilation of the Entry and Exodus stories, so that in both the Israelites cross the waters dryshod, and so that Joshua, like Moses, is commanded, 'Put off thy shoe from off thy foot; for the place whereon thou standest is holy' (Josh. 5:15). The parallel is made explicit at Josh. 4:22f, 'Ye shall let your children know, saying, Israel came over this Jordan on dry land. For the LORD your God dried up the waters of Jordan from before you, until ye were passed over, as the LORD your God did to the Red Sea, which he dried up from before us, until we were passed over.' The same connection between Entry and Exodus is made in Ps. 114, 'When Israel came out of Egypt . . . The sea saw it, and fled; Jordan was driven back' (vv. 1-3).

The association of Gilgal with the spring festival is so close that Kraus has proposed an attractive cultic theory of Josh. 1-6.[35] These chapters provide a series of dates and shrines where Israel encamped, which can be credibly understood as the aetiologies of an annual spring celebration. The altar by Jordan in Gilead, which is justified in Josh. 22, had associations with 'the iniquity of Peor' (v. 17), and is likely to have been at Shittim (Num. 25:1; Josh. 2:1; 3:1) by the Jordan in Gilead, where the whoring after Baal-Peor took place (Num. 25:1ff). Here Israel will have assembled each year in the first week of Nisan, three days before ritually crossing Jordan: 'for within three days ye are to pass over this Jordan' (Josh. 1:11); 'And Joshua rose up early in the morning, and they removed from Shittim, and came to Jordan . . . And it came to pass after three days . . .' (3:1f) that they crossed the river. This will have been on 7th Nisan, for the crossing took place on the 10th: 'And the people came out of Jordan on the tenth day of the first month, and encamped at Gilgal, on the east side of Jericho' (Josh. 4:19). Here each year passover was eaten on the 14th (Josh. 5:10) and unleavened bread on the 15th (5:11), after the circumcision of any new members of the community (5:2-9). There was then a week of ritual celebration of the Conquest (ch. 6), with the daily procession of the people round the long-ruined site of Jericho. While such a reconstruction is speculative, it does make sense of the careful mention of the succession of days in Nisan, and of the evidence for Jericho's destruction long before the Israelite invasion.[36]

The weakness of Kraus' theory is that he makes Gilgal, like other shrines, *the* central Israelite sanctuary for a limited period, and is therefore committed to an implausibly high turnover of central sanctuaries: Shechem, Bethel, Gilgal, Shiloh, Dan and perhaps Beersheba, Tabor and Mizpah, several of them returning to primacy after an intermission.[37] He wisely does not attempt a full account of the dates and historical reasons for this vacillation. But if we reject such a reconstruction, we are still faced with the evidence that there was an uncomfortably large number of *national* sanctuaries right down to the eighth century; and a helpful hypothesis might be that the three pilgrim-feasts were celebrated at different national centres. We should then be able to accommodate three national sanctuaries as in use in Israel (Jerusalem apart) at any one time; and since the Gilgal traditions are all associated with the spring festival we could credibly suppose that 'all Israel' went to Gilgal year by year to celebrate Passover and Unleavened Bread, somewhat in the way that Kraus has indicated. In favour of this would be the apparent connection of the root חגג with circular motion. In the preponderance of cases it is used of going to a pilgrim-feast, but it is also found in Ps. 107:27, 'They reel to and fro (יחוגו) and stagger like a drunken man,' in I Sam. 30:16, 'They were spread abroad over all the land, eating and drinking and dancing' (חגגים, RSV), and in Isa. 19:17, 'And the land of Judah shall become a terror (חגא) to Egypt.' The thing that seems to be in common between these various uses of going on festival, reeling and dancing is movement *round*, and this would then be in line with Samuel's going on circuit (סבב) year by year, if that is related to the annual cycle of worship.

But if Gilgal were the centre for the spring festival, what about the summer festival, שבעות? The first indication that we have of a non-agricultural association with the Feast of Weeks is in II Chron. 15, where Asa institutes a reform, and summons the people:[38] 'So they gathered themselves together at Jerusalem in the third month, in the fifteenth year of the reign of Asa. And they sacrificed unto the Lord ... seven hundred oxen and seven thousand sheep. And they entered into the covenant to seek the LORD ... And they sware (וישבעו) unto the LORD with a loud voice, and with shouting, and with trumpets, and with cornets. And all Judah rejoiced at the oath (שבועה): for they had sworn (נשבעו) with all their heart . . .' (vv. 10-15).

The coincidence of the stress upon oaths (שבועות), and sevens (שבע, שבעת), with the third month, in which the feast of Weeks (שבעות) falls, has led to the supposition that during the OT period Weeks, the wheat harvest, was developed into a feast of Oaths, declaring loyalty to the covenant; and this would then lead on naturally to the tradition in Exod. 19 that Israel first accepted the covenant at Sinai in the third month.[39] If this is so, it is not a long step to suggest that the early celebration of the festival could have been at Beersheba, the Well of Swearing (Gen. 21:22-23; 26:23-33), or Well of Seven (Gen. 21:31).

Two considerations seem to bear out this proposal. One is the perseverance of Beersheba as a national sanctuary from the Judges' period to the last days of the Northern Kingdom. As soon as we have heard that 'Samuel judged Israel all the days of his life. And he went from year to year in circuit to Beth-el, and Gilgal, and Mizpah; and he judged Israel in all those places' (I Sam. 7:15f), we learn that when he was old he made his sons judges over Israel, Joel and Abijah—'they were judges in Beersheba' (8:1f). The impression given is that Samuel limited himself to a small circuit in Benjamin, perhaps because of the general chaos of the settlement period, but that in his old age

Beersheba was included, his sons taking responsibility because of the distance. If so, Gilgal could have been the locus for Passover/Unleavened Bread at even so early a period, and Beersheba the locus of Weeks/Oaths by virtue of its name. We should then have an explanation for the otherwise extraordinary fact revealed by Amos that two centuries after the division of the monarchy there was an established pilgrimage from northern Israel forty miles into the territory of Judah to Beersheba: 'Seek not Bethel, nor enter into Gilgal, and pass not to Beersheba' (Amos 5:5). People swore too by 'the way of Beersheba' (8:14). It is hard to think that in Amos' time the pilgrimage is an innovation, and the triple sanctuary grouping invites comparison with the three festivals—Bethel in the autumn, Gilgal in the spring, Beersheba in the summer. Hos. 4:15, 'come not ye to Gilgal, neither go ye to Beth-aven, nor swear (תשבעו), As the LORD liveth,' seems to confirm this picture: the sentence is addressed to Judah, not Israel, and there seems no reason why Judah should not swear by Yahweh— unless the Oaths were associated with a third semi-pagan sanctuary, Oath-well.

The second link of Beersheba with the covenant tradition is a somewhat attenuated one from I Kgs. 19. Here Elijah, fleeing from Jezebel, is on his way to 'Horeb the mount of God,' where he receives a theophany echoing that of Moses at the same mountain on the occasion of the establishment of the covenant; on his way he rests at Beersheba (v. 3), where he receives encouragement and strength for the journey (vv. 4-7). Since Horeb is not an Israelite sanctuary, the suggestion is that here a tradition about Horeb has been preserved at Beersheba; and as Beersheba is the Israelite sanctuary closest to Horeb, it may be that all the early Horeb (as opposed to Sinai) traditions were preserved there. While not a strong point on its own, this link tends to confirm the argument hitherto: Beersheba was the locus for the celebration of the covenant given by God to Moses on Horeb, a celebration in the third month which ultimately developed into Pentecost as a law-festival.

All in all, then, the evidence seems to fit best with the hypothesis of an annual cycle of feasts in which the ephod was carried round to three different sanctuaries. It always went to Gilgal and the holy places nearby in the spring, for the celebration of the Exodus and Entry at Passover and Unleavened Bread. Except in the worst days of the Philistine conflict it went to Beersheba for the celebration of the covenant and law-giving at Pentecost. For the autumn festival, which gradually, as the most important agricultural feast, took over all the nation's religious themes, it had a less continuous centre. Shechem was perhaps its first locus, and then Shiloh, both centres being temporarily lost to the Philistines; then Dan in the high days of the Northern Kingdom; and finally Bethel, first when Dan was lost in Baasha's time, and again as Assyrian pressure mounted. This seems to account for the multiplicity of national centres of worship, for their occurrence in threes, for the 'circular motion' meaning of חגג, for the concentration of spring themes at Gilgal and covenant/oath themes at Beersheba, and for the connection of Dan and Bethel with 'the feast in the eighth month' in I Kgs. 12. It also lends point to the 'going up' of God into his shrine in Ps. 47, and 'the setting of his steps in the way' in Ps. 85; and makes the annual festal cycle with its three pilgrimages a far less repetitive and dreary exercise than has commonly been supposed.

THE FIRST DAYS OF THE FEAST (Psalms 45, 46)

42-43 and 84, I have argued, were pilgrimage-psalms for the autumn-festival at Dan, chanted as the national procession approached the sanctuary. 44 and 85 were national laments to be used in the same context following a day of contrition preceding the feast, on 14th Bul. We can hardly fail to ask ourselves whether the phenomenon of order does not run on. 45, 46, 47 and 48 are psalms presupposing a national setting, with extensive rituals: are these perhaps the rituals of the successive days of the festival? Eaton has reconstructed an outline of the festival,[1] beginning with the journey (including 84) and the penitential observances (including 85); he names, as the principal themes, the dramatic assertion of Yahweh's supremacy, with his enthronement (47), his pronouncement of judgement, his promise of growth, his choice of Zion (mentioning 47 and 87), and the dawn of a new age and the blessing of the king (including 89). It is an attractive conjecture that the Korah psalms provide us with evidence not just for the existence of these themes, but for the order in which they were celebrated. 45 could follow a day of ritual blessing of the king, culminating in a new marriage, on 15th Bul; 46 the celebration of Yahweh's victory over the waters, and over earthly enemies, on 16th; 47 his enthronement on 17th; and 48 a procession round the holy city on the 18th. In this way we should have a fulfilment of the promise of 42:8, 'the LORD will command his lovingkindness in the day-time, And in the night his song shall be with me.' As the processions and other rites take place, Yahweh is understood to command his covenanted grace to Israel, and the psalms follow in the evening. 45, 46 and 48 are Songs (שׁיר); 47 is a מזמור. 45 is certainly an evening psalm, as its second half is a prothalamium.

Hitherto the hypothesis of an order has been suggested by the parallel between the two Korah sequences: both the main and the supplementary groups began with a pilgrimage psalm, followed by a national lament. This parallel now gives out. There are fewer psalms in the supplement than in the main sequence, and 87, the next supplement psalm, is a pair to 48. We are driven therefore to look for support in Book IV, which, as we have seen, opens with a national lament, 90. Eaton interprets both 91 and 92 as royal psalms, blessings on the king.[2] It is the king who sits enthroned, or dwells, in God's temple, under the shadow of his wings; it is he who can say, 'My God,' and who can be guaranteed special protection from sickness and enemy arrows, though ten thousand fall beside him; he is borne in a royal palanquin, his feet protected by angels, like those at the foot of Yahweh's throne; his prayer will be answered, he will be delivered, and granted long life (91). It is the king, similarly, who speaks in 92; who triumphs over the wicked, Yahweh's enemies; whose horn is exalted, and who is moist with the new oil, being anointed to fresh vitality; whose strength is extended into the whole community of the righteous (92). Such a view has much to commend it in comparison with the 'democratised' interpretation, which is widespread, and, in the case of 91, so disgusting.[3] The parallels with 45 are evident: the king's triumph over his enemies (45:4f; 91:8; 92:4-11), his enthronement (45:6; 91:1) and establishment of righteousness (45:6f; 92:12ff), his anointing (45:6f; 92:10), 'thy God'/'my God' (45:7; 91:2, 14). What is missing in 91-92 is the marriage; but the essence of the rite is the king's reconsecration. Probably in early times this included a new wife every year, but polygamy on this scale fell into desuetude, especially in Judah. The argument for a common order between the Korah psalms and Book IV is a cumulative one, and we shall return to it repeatedly.[4]

I shall imagine, then, that 45 holds its place in the main Korah series by virtue of its suitability for the annual ritual of 15th Bul. It does not follow from this, however, that it was composed for just any year. It in fact contains a number of concrete details which make it possible to conjecture its original context with some probability. The context is controversial, as is the nature of the underlying ritual, but it will be best to consider these questions in the course of expounding the text.

> 45 For the Chief Musician; by (על) Lilies; (a Psalm) of the sons
>   of Korah. Maschil. A Song of Beloved Ones (ידידת).
> 1 My heart overfloweth with a happy event (דבר טוב):
>   I speak; my work is for a king:
>   My tongue is the pen of a ready writer.

The psalmist is, as almost throughout the series (not in [43], 48 or 87), 'the chief musician,' that is, the priest-poet of Dan; only this time he draws the curtain aside for a moment on his feeling of inspiration. The advent of the 'happy event,' the national festival with its royal marriage, stirs his heart like a cauldron, seething (רחש) and over- flowing with the divine inbreathing. The measured 4:4:4 rhythm tells him God's spirit has taken hold of him, and that it is inspiration; like the skilled scribe whose pen moves deftly back and forth with a power not its own. The oracular force bubbles forth into speech at the thought of the royal occasion at which the verses[5] are delivered.

The title gives three further notes. The traditional translation of the first, 'set to Lilies,' has little to commend it: there is no evidence that psalms in ancient Israel could be sung to alternative chants, like modern hymns 'to Cwm Rhondda.' I suggested a locative translation of על in the heading of 84, 'at the Gittite settlement,' and the same is required here. If the Korah psalms were used year by year in the ceremonies at Dan, they must have been chanted at some location. Most of them would have been sung at the bamah, where the main rites took place, and all could see, albeit from a distance; so no note of location would be required. But 45 was not sung at the bamah. It was used in conjunction with rites of enthronement: the king is pictured seated on his throne (v. 7), with the new queen standing on his right, and the rich among the people coming to offer presents to her (v. 12). The throne is not in a hall, but in an open space—no doubt with a view to the participation of onlookers. Music is said to come 'out of ivory palaces' (v. 8), and when the queen goes to change into her night attire, she is 'within' (v. 13). This throne-site was called Lilies.

We are fortunate that the actual site has been excavated by Professor Biran,[6] and that the details uncovered are sufficient to give us even an explanation for the name. The processional highway led westwards into Dan under the south walls of the city; through an outer gate into a courtyard 60ft × 30ft (19.5 × 9.4m), and on through a complex inner gate with guardrooms on either side. Biran's plan is reproduced on p.xiv. The highway led on westwards briefly before turning north into the city; the last stretch involved an incline of 28 degrees to cross the ancient rampart. The courtyard between the two gates was called the רחוב in Biblical times, and here, backing on to the wall of the inner gate and facing the outer gate, Biran found 'an unusual structure ... built of hewn limestone, [which] may have supported a king's throne or a cult statue. Four decorated bases or capitals (one of which is missing) were probably of columns that supported a canopy.'[7] Photographs are also reproduced as Pls.II, III. The cult statue is an unlikely conjecture: if such had existed in Israel, they

would hardly be set in the city gateway. The structure is for the king's
throne, the throne that was 'for ever and ever' (v. 6). There were four
pillars supporting a canopy over the throne, and the decorated bases
on which they stood seem to be shaped like pomegranates. Now we
have in I Kgs. 7:15ff a description of the two enormous pillars erected
for the Jerusalem temple, and although the text is somewhat corrupt
and obscure it is evident that they included pomegranate represen-
tations, probably a sequence of two hundred pomegranates round the
base capital. The pomegranate shape was suited to be a single base
capital, as at Dan; but would be out of proportion on a pillar of
eighteen feet circumference. But the lintels 'that were upon the top of
the pillars in the porch were of lily work, four cubits . . . And upon the
top of the pillars was lily work' (vv. 19, 22). The lintels (see Pl. V) were
carved with lilies; and perhaps the top of the pillars also was shaped
like lilies, as the top of a Corinthian pillar is shaped like acanthus
leaves; and we may take it that as Corinthian (and Doric, and Ionic)
pillars are of standard design, so were the pillars of the tenth and ninth
centuries in Israel, with pomegranates at the base and lilies at the top.
Hence the throne-site at Dan came to be called שׁשנים, Lilies,[8] after
its most distinctive architectural feature. The building on the north
side of the רחוב will have been the royal palace, sited so as to keep an
eye on all that went on in the gate. The wall will have been pierced by a
high window for the purpose (and for dropping stones on invaders *in
extremis*); on this happier occasion all that issues is joyful music (v. 8).
From such a palace window looking on to a city gateway Jezebel was
later to meet her death at Jezreel (II Kgs. 9:30f).[9]

For Maschil see above on pp.88-91, and below on v. 7.

The translation of the third note, ידידת, is in doubt. The easiest
Hebrew and the best sense is given by rendering 'a song of beloved
ones' (i.e. brides). On the theory that I am proposing, 45 was used
every year at the Dan festal sequence, and every year, I suggest, the
king either took a new bride or reconsecrated the established queen, at
least in the early period. In fact it is difficult to account for the
preservation of the psalm in the Psalter on any other hypothesis; the
common attribution of its preservation to messianic interpretation
does not account for the vital first centuries when messianic doctrines
were unknown. The translation 'love song' (Aquila, RSV) takes ידירת
as a collateral form of ידירת (Delitzsch); otherwise the ת ending can
be taken as a neuter plural with RV, 'A Song of loves.' With the former
the grammar is dubious, with the latter the meaning. It is natural

however to take the word as a straightforward feminine plural, with the same meaning as יקרות in v. 9, the king's 'treasures.' The *waw* will have been offensive to later monogamist scribes and omitted so as to give Aquila's meaning; the phrase has been further spiritualised by LXX with ὑπὲρ τοῦ ἀγαπητοῦ.

In the tenth century the kings of Judah had large harems, Solomon being credited with a fabulous number of wives and concubines; the Chronicler says that Rehoboam had eighteen of the former and sixty of the latter (II Chron. 11:21), and that Abijah had fourteen wives (13:21). The kings of Israel, with far greater resources than Rehoboam and Abijah, must have had similar seraglios, and this seems to be implied by the law from the old northern tradition in Deut. 17:17, 'Neither shall he multiply wives to himself, that his heart turn not away: neither shall he greatly multiply to himself silver and gold.' The sexual potency of the king was not a matter of private concern, but was felt to be of importance for the well-being of the whole people. David's failure to mate even with the very fair damsel Abishag was a signal that the time was ripe for a new king; hence Adonijah's usurpation, and the enthronement of Solomon (I Kgs. 1). The royal women were of two categories, wives and concubines. It is difficult to make a distinction between them except on a ceremonial basis: concubines were simply brought in to the harem from their homes, like Abishag (cf. Est. 2:8f), while wives enjoyed a formal marriage (cf. Est. 2:17f). In time no doubt harems became smaller, especially in Judah, but king Josiah still had at least two wives, Hamutal and Zebidah (II Kgs. 23:31, 36; 24:18).

The only liturgical text that we have of a royal marriage is our present psalm, which I shall argue to be from Israel in the ninth century. The extensive ceremonial implied shows that it is no personal affair of the king, and that the psalm is no prothalamium in a straightforward sense. The first part of the ritual mentioned is only distantly related to matrimony, and includes prayers that the king's sharpened arrows may fall in the heart of his enemies; the second includes an anointing and enthronement of the bridegroom in expectation that his rule will exemplify righteousness, meekness and truth. Eaton comments with characteristic diffidence, 'it is possible that the marriage was celebrated as a sequel to the annual re-enthronement of the king in the autumn festival.' The tone overall is too political, nationalistic and bloodthirsty to be suited to a marriage *tout court*. The only marriage quite like this is the wedding of the Lamb in Rev. 19-21, where the Word of God rides forth on a white horse to smite the nations, and is enthroned, crowned and acclaimed. Although the original setting of the psalm might have been a king's (original) enthronement *combined* with a marriage, we are better without hypothetical coincidences: the preservation of the psalm in a group of psalms recurrently used, some of them at the festival, suggests that Eaton is right, and further that 45 came to be used in the same way. The controversy over whether an annual enthronement ritual ever existed in Israel arises, as is well known, from the absence of evidence outside the Psalter. But the common description of 45 as 'a royal marriage psalm' does not do justice to the eight opening verses, where marriage is neither hinted at nor implied. The case for an annual setting, with procession, enthronement, anointing and finally the taking of a new wife, is much strengthened once we take seriously the sequence in which it is placed, and the interpretation provided by the plural heading, 'Song of Beloved Ones.' The serial setting also adds point to the phrase דבר טוב. Hitherto the psalmist has been the leader, and perhaps the composer, of laments, like 84 at the close of the pilgrimage and 85 on the eve of the feast; now he is called to sing of 'a goodly matter,' of God's blessing on the king in war, government and marriage.

45:2 Thou art fairer than the children of men;
  Grace is poured upon thy lips:
  Therefore God hath blessed thee for ever.
 3 Gird thy sword upon thy thigh, O mighty one,
  Thy glory and thy majesty.
 4 And in thy majesty ride on to triumph (צלח),
  In behalf of truth and meekness (and) righteousness:
  And let thy right hand teach thee terrible things.
 5 Thine arrows are sharp;
  The peoples (are) under thee;
  They fall in the heart of the king's enemies [RV amended].

The psalmist's mind runs in imagination through the whole ritual of the occasion, which cannot be thought of as taking less than a full day: first a procession in which the king rides out in full armour for the symbolic destruction of his enemies (vv. 2-5); then his enthronement, amid perfumes and music (vv. 6-8), whence the thought moves to his new bride (vv. 9-12); finally the bride retires to change into her ceremonial nightwear, and is escorted by her bridesmaids to the palace for the marriage's consummation (vv. 13-16).

Kings should be tall and good-looking, as were Saul (I Sam. 10:23), David (I Sam. 16:12) and Absalom (II Sam. 14:25); they should also be wise in judgement, like Solomon. For the latter as the meaning of 'Grace is poured on thy lips,' cf. Eccles. 10:12, 'The words of a wise man's mouth are gracious,' or Lk. 4:22. Although such expressions are common in ancient courts, the psalmist is speaking sincerely, at least in part, or he could not draw the inference with such enthusiasm, 'Therefore God hath blessed thee for ever.' As in v. 7, God's blessing is given in consequence of the king's virtue; there his goodness of character, here his physical goodness. The address, 'O mighty one,' in the following verse, similarly, can hardly be mere flattery. The king is a fine figure of a man, and the thought wells up in the psalmist that this means high hopes for the nation's future, not only now but for generations to come, 'for ever' (cf. v. 17). His ritual arming and riding in procession are a powerful symbol of his forthcoming victory in war. He is seen belting his sheathed sword on to his thigh (the personal suffix is omitted, as often with parts of the body), his glittering helmet and breastplate—his 'glory' and 'majesty'—and his quiver. His war-procession is the first step in his riding on to triumph; the repeated 'And (as to) thy majesty' is in no need of amendment, but reinforces the point—it is this divinely blessed shining splendour that will carry all before it. The power of God in his right hand will amaze him at his success, and will strike him with awe at his accomplishments. I have followed Eaton in v. 5, taking יפלו of the arrows rather than the peoples; this retains the 4:4 rhythm, with the first two phrases in chiastic balance, and reduces the harshness of the change of subject. The arrows in the king's quiver are sharpened to irresistibility. The peoples are prostrate on the ground as he drives his chariot over them, the arrows through their hearts. So will all hostile forces be deprived of the power to spoil the 'truth' and 'righteousness' that there should be in Israel; God will give the victory, while the people observe their side of the covenant with faithfulness, meekness and obedience. The missing second 'and' seems to be characteristic of the poet, coming in v. 8 also. עֶנְוָה is a unique form of the term for 'meekness,' which is elsewhere עֲנָוָה, and this, with the defective plural מני in v. 8 and שֵׁגַל for 'queen' in v. 9, seemed to Delitzsch possible indications of a northern psalm.

A procession with the king mounted was the first part of an Israelite enthronement ceremony. David made Solomon ride on his mule in I Kgs. 1:33 to the spring at Gihon, and in Zechariah's vision the king comes to the acclaiming crowds meek (עני, as in v. 4b) and riding upon an ass. A contrast is often drawn between the mule and ass as peaceful beasts and the horse as a war animal, but this requires caution: Absalom rode to battle on a mule in II Sam. 18, and so encompassed his own death. So in I Kgs. 1 Solomon rides on the royal mule, but escorted by Cherethites and Pelethites, and Adonijah had a military guard likewise (I Kgs. 1:5); and we find the same combination in the ideal king's procession in Zech. 9:9ff. There the king comes to Zion, 'his cause won, his victory gained' (NEB, צדיק ונושע), meek and riding on an ass. The chariot, horse and battlebow of invading foreigners will be cut off from Jerusalem, and the king will dictate peace to the nations, extending his dominion from the Sea to the River. The prisoners will be released, and in the coming final battle Judah will become God's bow, Ephraim his arrows and Zion his sword. The scene is by no means a pacifist's pipe-dream. Peace in the ancient world had to be imposed, and the king is a warrior who has already won victories (even if 9:1-8 is not taken as part of the same oracle), and whose greatest victory still lies ahead of him.[10] It is unthinkable that any enthronement procession of this kind should have been without military overtones in ancient Israel; even today, on so peaceful an occasion as the Queen's Silver Jubilee, her carriage is escorted by the Household cavalry, and Prince Charles wears military uniform on a horse. In Ps. 45 the manner of riding is not specified. It is conceivable that the king rode in a chariot,[11] or on a horse like the Word of God in Rev. 19—such being the tradition in (northern) Israel. But the coincidence of his riding for 'righteousness' and 'meekness' with Zech. 9:9 must incline us to think that he rode on an ass; the animal symbolising the peace that is to mark his reign, and the sword, armour and quiver the force by which that peace is to be imposed.

Since both the anointings in I Kgs. 1 took place at springs near Jerusalem, En-rogel and Gihon, and since there is mention of the king 'drinking of the brook in the way' in the enthronement psalm 110[12] (before striking through kings in many countries), it seems likely that the procession in this case was from the palace at Dan to the springs of the Jordan nearby. The king will perhaps have drunk ceremonially from waters that 'make glad the city of God,' and 'lifted up his head' (110:7) amid acclamation. But baptismal ceremonies, symbolising the king's new birth (110:3; 2:7) are also a possibility.

45:6 Thy throne, O divine one (אלהים), is for ever and ever:
A sceptre of equity is the sceptre of thy kingdom.

7 Thou hast loved righteousness and hated wickedness:
Therefore God, thy God, hath anointed thee
With the oil of gladness above thy fellows.

8 All thy garments (smell of) myrrh, and aloes, (and) cassia;
Out of ivory palaces stringed instruments have made thee
glad.

At the coronation of Solomon, the procession to Gihon was followed by the king's anointing there, and later by his enthronement in the palace: 'Take with you the servants of your lord'—viz. the Cherethites and Pelethites—'and cause Solomon my son to ride upon mine own mule, and bring him down to Gihon: and let Zadok the priest and Nathan the prophet anoint him there king over Israel: and blow ye with the trumpet, and say, God save king Solomon. Then shall ye come up after him, and he shall come and sit upon my throne' (I Kgs. 1:33ff). The D-historian does not relate that Adonijah was anointed by Abiathar, for obvious reasons; but he stresses the volume of sacrifices, and of food and drink consumed (vv. 9, 19, 25, 41), and no doubt a mass banquet at the king's expense was a standard part of the 'gladness' of the occasion. At the coronation of Joash (II Kgs. 11), there was no procession to the spring, because of the necessity of secrecy from Athaliah, if for no other reason, and the ceremony described consists of crowning, anointing and acclamation: 'Then (Jehoiada) brought out the king's son, and put upon him the crown and the testimony; and they made him king, and anointed him; and they clapped their hands, and said, God save the king' (v. 12). The occasion was then interrupted by Athaliah, and after she had been put to death, Jehoiada 'made a covenant between the LORD and the king and the people, that they should be the LORD's people' (v. 17). This was of special significance in Joash's case because of the reversal of Athaliah's pro-Baal policy, but it was probably a regular feature of so religious an occasion as a coronation.

The presence in Ps.45 of a riding ritual followed by an anointing of the king, with references to his throne and sceptre, and his anticipated reign of righteousness, forms so close a sequence with the enthronement scenes in I Kgs. 1 and II Kgs. 11 that it is difficult not to read the first half of the psalm as an enthronement hymn. In particular the anointing is an anointing to the kingship, and not in preparation for the wedding: God has anointed him (משחך) in virtue of his love of righteousness, above his fellows, to a throne and a sceptre. Only thereafter does the thought run on to the marriage following, for which the perfumes and the music make an apt preparation. We should probably think of the anointing as taking place together with the water-ceremonies at the river, on the analogy of I Kgs. 1,[13] with the enthronement to follow as the cortege returns to the city gate.

The translation of v. 6a is controversial, but it seems best to follow the natural sense of the Hebrew boldly. The throne of Israel is the place from which God rules his people, and the king is his viceroy. Earlier, litigants going before judges were said to go before God (אלהים, Exod. 21:6; 22:7ff; and especially I Sam. 2:25), and Isaiah can speak of the king as אל (9:6). Elsewhere in the Psalter he is spoken of as God's son (2:7; 89:26f), so it does not seem too unnatural a hyperbole if he is here addressed as אלהים, divine one.[14] This would concur with the phrase 'God, thy God' in v. 7b: as the king is אלהים to the people, so is God אלהים to him (cf. 42:3, 6, 10, 11; 43:4, 5; 84:3, 10; etc.). The stress upon his equity and righteousness will then correspond with the covenant which Jehoiada made between king Joash and Yahweh. The coronation involves a vow by the king to rule in Yahweh's name, according to his law; and the perfects, 'Thou hast loved . . . thou hast hated . . .,' imply that he has already been ruling with righteousness and equity. It is in view of this ('Therefore . . .') that the anointing has taken place, and the ceremony is likely to be a re-consecration and re-enthronement, in which God undertakes to continue his blessing. The same conclusion seems to follow from the marriage implied by the second half of the psalm. It is difficult to suppose a combined marriage and (first) coronation; whereas an annual ceremony at which the king was reconsecrated, and at which he might take a new wife, is quite easy to imagine. Solomon's crowning 'in the day of his espousals' is specifically mentioned in Cant. 3:11.

An attempt is often made to infer a Jerusalem context from the permanency claimed for the throne in v. 6a, by comparing the permanency promised to the house of David in II Sam. 7. This seems naive, though, for surely the court poets will have spoken like this of all ancient monarchies, regardless of historical probability. Loyal Englishmen sang, 'Long to reign over us,' of Queen Victoria at eighty; and it will have seemed much less absurd than that if the Danite priest looked forward to the permanency of the house of Omri when Ahab was in his prime, and there had been peace in Israel for twenty-five years. A Jerusalem background also does not fit the phrase מחבריך.

God has anointed the king with the oil of gladness 'from' his fellows. חבר elsewhere means a fellow-tribe, fellow-worshipper, fellow-soldier, etc., and it is not natural to take it as a fellow-king, since Israelite kings were not thought of as one of a class. All Israelites, however, were brothers and fellow-worshippers of Yahweh, and as far as a (northern) Israelite was concerned, there had been five dynasties on the throne in a hundred years (those of David, Jeroboam, Baasha, Zimri and Omri), so that a king like Ahab could quite fairly be thought of as being anointed from among his fellow-Israelites. In Jerusalem, however, it was axiomatic that the house of David was God's elect, and the thought that a king of Judah had been anointed from among, or above, his fellow-Israelites, seems inapposite.

The same is true of the ivory palaces in v. 8b. היכלי שׁן, halls inlaid with ivory, were striking innovations made by King Ahab: 'Now the rest of the acts of Ahab, and all that he did, and the ivory house which he built, and all the cities that he built, are they not written in the book of the chronicles of the kings of Israel?' (I Kgs. 22:39). They were still regarded as symbols of godless luxury by Amos, inveighing against Samaria and Bethel a century later: 'And I will smite the winter house with the summer house; and the houses of ivory shall perish, and many houses shall have an end, saith the LORD' (Amos 3:15). It is replied that Solomon imported ivory, and made his throne of it (I Kgs. 10:18, 22); but this is not the point. Solomon's palace was panelled with cedar (I Kgs. 7:3), not ivory, and it was the northern ivories which so impressed the D-historian, and so scandalised the prophet. When, on several occasions, accounts are given of the treasures which were taken from the Jerusalem palace to buy off foreign invaders, ivories are never mentioned (II Kgs. 14:14; 18:15; 24:13; 25:13-17). It is in northern towns like Megiddo that ivories of the Hebrew classical period have been excavated. All the evidence that we have would therefore incline us to suppose that the psalm comes from northern Israel, and from the time of Ahab or after.

But is the king perhaps Ahab himself? H. Schmidt suggested that there was a play upon the king's name in v. 7a, which opens with the word אָהַבְתָּ. The play, if so, is not a very exact one, since the king's name is spelt אַחְאָב, with *ḥet* instead of *he*, and (usually) an additional *'aleph*; but Hebrew is not too demanding in plays upon names, and the change of a consonant for one similar is not infrequent.[15] If this is so, then we should have an explanation for the heading Maschil, which in each of the other Korah/Ethan psalms can be interpreted as including a play on the king's name—Hoshea in 42, 44 and 88, Jehoiachin in 89. As Schmidt observes, the poet undertakes to make the king's name to be remembered in all generations (v. 17), which he could hardly do without referring to it.

The enthronement ceremonies now lead the psalmist's mind on to the evening ritual. The richly perfumed oils so impregnate the king's robes that they seem to be made of them, and send forth a fitting aroma for the coming marriage (cf. Cant. 1:3, 12f; etc.). There is no authority for omitting the cassia, and it should be retained despite its weakening of the rhythm; the 'and' is lacking as in v. 4b. The orchestra, from within the panelled hall above the north side of the רחוב provides a background of festivity and delight, as the day moves to its climax.

> 45:9 Kings' daughters are among thy treasures (יקרותיך):
>   At thy right hand doth stand the queen in gold of Ophir.
> 10 Hearken, O daughter, and consider, and incline thine ear:
>   Forget also thine own people, and thy father's house;
> 11 So shall the king desire thy beauty; for he is thy lord.
> 12 And do thou homage to him, daughter of Tyre
>   (והשתחוי־לו בת־צר):
>   With a gift (במנחה) the rich among the people intreat thy
>   favour (יחלו).

The mounted procession and the enthronement ceremony being complete, the third part of the day's rites is now celebrated; and here the psalm is sung. The anointing (v. 7) was in the perfect, the bridal procession (vv. 14f) is in the future, the queen stands (v. 9) in the present. The king has a large household of women, his jewels or precious ones, whom he has no doubt left back at Samaria; for he would have no use for them here. Maybe there were princesses among them already, but more likely the plural is poetic exaggeration, as is suggested by the rhythm, with נצבה in the first colon of v. 10:

>   Kings' daughters are among thy treasures: there stands
>   The queen at thy right hand in gold of Ophir.

The psalmist rejoices that there will be a princess among them from today, a testimony to the king's and Israel's power.

The marriage scene must be offensive to a twentieth century feminist. The court poet makes open reference to the king's seraglio; the bride must stand while the royal groom is seated; she is advised to blot out of her mind her life hitherto, that she may be a worthy object for the king's desires. But Israelite queens were not so sensitive. As a princess, she will have precedence over the lesser women in the harem, like Vashti in the Book of Esther. She is the שֵׁגָל,[16] a title given to the queen of Persia in Neh. 2:6, and with her connections, her looks (v. 11a) and her wits, can expect to hold her place. The gold of Ophir is probably her crown (Est. 2:17), a further symbol of the nation's wealth, since gold must be imported from distant lands, we know not where.[17] Her foreign origin is made clear in v. 10b, for although her 'own people' might linguistically be an Israelite clan (II Kgs. 4:13), there would be no point in bidding her to forget her father's house if this were so. Her happiness, and that of the realm, depend upon her accepting Israelite ways, and especially religious ways. She is to settle happily to her new calling of honour in Israel, and the king will desire her beauty and sire children from her. First comes her own act of homage, as she bows to the ground before him. Again royal majesty is taken as an extension of divinity. RV spells 'lord' with a capital, and translates הִשְׁתַּחֲוִי as 'worship'; and this only slightly exaggerates the sense of the words. In front of the throne-base in the city-gate at Tel Dan are three smooth stones laid together for just such a ceremony (see Pl. II).

If the bride is a foreign princess, a northern situation is still more probable, as Gunkel notes. The D-historian tells us the names of the mothers of all the kings of Judah except Joram and Ahaz, and in each case they are Israelite women, apart from Rehoboam, whose mother was from Ammon. So the likelihood is that the kings of Judah regularly married within Israel—indeed within Judah, for where the queens' homes are mentioned they are normally in Jerusalem or the towns around; and a religious reason is to hand for this practice, especially after the reign of Athaliah. Perhaps Joram's and Ahaz's mothers were omitted from the D-history because they were foreigners, but that would still limit the Jerusalem possibilities to Solomon, Jehoshaphat and Jotham, so far as our evidence goes. Northern kings were more wealthy and powerful, and are more likely to have married princesses from abroad.

The last verse presents us with a crux. The MT opens the line, as I have in the translation, with הִשְׁתַּחֲוִי־לֹו, but construes the phrase with v. 11 as in RV, 'For he is thy Lord; and worship thou him.' All the MSS but one then begin v. 12 וּבַת־צֹר, which must then be a nominative, though the syntax is defective. RV renders, 'And the daughter of Tyre (shall be there) with a gift.' It does not seem very likely that the Tyrians would have sent an embassy led by their princess, so the phrase is usually taken as equivalent to 'the people of Tyre,' e.g. by Anderson, comparing 9:14, 'daughter of Zion,' 137:8, 'daughter of Babylon.' But this is not satisfactory. Peoples are symbolised by their women folk ('daughters') in the Bible only when that is appropriate—in Ps. 137:8 because the Babylonian mothers are to watch their children dashed against the rocks; generally because of the women's place in national rejoicing, when they could crow over defeated enemy men, or in national disgrace, when their own men could no longer protect them. No instances of 'daughter' = people without such special appropriateness are cited, and there is nothing at all appropriate about women in an embassy. Nor is this the end of troubles. There are not enough words for the rhythm; hence solutions like that of the RSV, 'The people of Tyre will sue your favour with gifts, the richest of the people with all kinds of wealth.' The plural verb with 'daughter of Tyre' is harsh, and the phrase has been borrowed (and emended) from v. 13 to give 'with all kinds of wealth.' Furthermore many (beginning with the Targumists) have felt that the Tyrians could not properly share a main verb with the wealthy Israelites, and that עמים should be read for עם.

There is a simple way out of this complex of problems. One Hebrew MS omits the ו before בת, and this enables us to begin the line where the MT does and to take 'daughter of Tyre' as a vocative, with NEB. This reading is commended by BHS. V. 12 then runs on smoothly from v. 10: 'Hearken, O daughter . . . And do thou homage to him, daughter of Tyre . . .,' and the same word 'daughter' within three verses refers to the same person. The rhythm approximates to the 4:4:4 that is normal for the psalm, with 4:4:5 in vv. 10f and 4:4 in v. 12; 'with a gift' can be taken with the second half of the line as נצבה is in v. 9. The sense is exemplary. First the new queen makes her obeisance to the king; then the Israelite nobles[18] come forward and 'smoothe her face' with a gift, a corporate gift, it seems, probably of jewelry. No emendation is required.

Such a solution carries with it a probable corollary: that Hitzig was right, and that 45 was the marriage psalm for the wedding of Ahab to Jezebel, daughter of Ittobaal, king of Tyre. Perhaps, as Kraus says, many kings of Israel and Judah married 'daughters of Tyre'; but Jezebel is the one we know of, and the coincidence with the ivory palaces and the possible pun on Ahab's name combine to make her the favourite candidate. Kraus's objection is overstated, too; it is hardly possible that any kings of Judah after Rehoboam married Tyrian princesses, and Jezebel's own history must have made later kings of Israel think twice before taking Phoenician brides. The thought adds frisson to the occasion. Well may the nobles bring their present: this is a queen whose favour is worth having. There on the bench which Biran has excavated, alongside the throne to its left, sits Obadiah, Ahab's general. Somewhere among the cheering crowd are Naboth of Jezreel and Jehu ben-Nimshi and Elijah of Tishbeh. We are watching the curtain rise on one of the great tragedies of history.

But, it is often replied, how could we account for the persevering use of Jezebel's marriage hymn in view of the later abhorrence in which she was universally held? The answer seems to me to lie in the *waw* found in all the manuscripts but one at the beginning of v. 12. While Ahab lived, Jezebel was no doubt his queen year after year; when he died, Ahaziah succeeded him, and there was a new queen crowned at Dan on 15th Bul. Jezebel's splendid hymn had been in use long enough to become part of the festal liturgy; and it could be retained by prefacing an 'and' to v. 12, thus making 'the daughter of Tyre' into a nominative—Jezebel, as queen mother like the גבירה in Judah, is the principal subject in the land, and presents her gift to her daughter-in-law before the nobles. It was thirteen further years till Ahaziah and Joram were dead, and Jezebel murdered and execrated; during which time 45 had become the established marriage-hymn of the king and queen of Israel, and the 'daughter of Tyre' a harmless giver of homage. So we can make sense both of the original meaning of the phrase in the vocative, and of the Hebrew tradition of exegesis of a nominative; and both readings.

45:13 The king's daughter within (פנימה) is all glorious:
   Her clothing is inwrought with gold.
   14 She shall be brought (תובל) unto the king upon embroidered work:
   The virgins her companions that follow her
   Shall be led (מובאות) unto thee.
   15 With gladness and rejoicing shall they be brought (תובלנה):
   They shall enter the king's palace.
   16 Instead of thy fathers shall be thy children,
   Whom thou shalt make princes in all the earth.
   17 I will make thy name to be remembered in all generations:
   Therefore shall the peoples confess thee (יהודך) for ever and ever.

The day's ceremonial now moves into its fourth and final phase. The new queen has made her homage to the king, and has received the loyal presentation from her new country's leaders. She leaves 'the Lilies,' where these formalities have been conducted, and goes with her escort 'inside' (פנימה) to divest herself. The king's women had a separate building to themselves (I Kgs. 7:8; 9:24), because of the peril of female uncleanness (II Chron. 8:11) as well as more practical reasons; the arrangements in Israel were probably not very different from those described in Esther 2. She lays aside her crown and day-robes, to put on the still more splendid night-attire. The text distinguishes her clothing (לבושה) with its gold thread or buttons, which glint in the torchlight, making her 'all glorious,' from the 'broidered work' (רקמות) upon (ל) which she is carried to the king's palace. In later times Jewish brides were carried in sedan chairs from their fathers' to their husbands' homes,[19] and the רקמות, which are always textiles elsewhere, will be the damasks with which the sedan is decked. The hophʻal of יבל normally means 'to be borne,' and this is preferable to RV/RSV's 'be led,' both as giving the best sense to the preposition ל, and as giving a greater dignity, agreeing with later custom. The party of unmarried girls who have come from Tyre to be the queen's bridesmaids, and to live with her in Israel, are escorted to the palace, no doubt by eunuchs, some of whom are carrying the sedan. The party crosses the open ground from the women's house to the king's, and the people who have been waiting burst into prolonged cheering, 'joy and gladness,' felt perhaps less keenly by the bride and her retinue, to whose sophisticated upbringing the rowdy Israelites may have seemed barbarians of a strange tongue. Whereas vv. 10-12 were addressed to the queen, vv. 13ff are spoken to the king, as the earlier verses were. The bridal party is brought to him (v. 14), and in the place of his dead fathers his new wife will bear him many sons. The national aspect of the occasion is dominant to the end. The peoples of v. 5 who are prostrated before the king, over whom he has ridden in triumph, can thus be supplied with rulers who are scions of Israel's royal stock, as Alexander would have wished to supply for his later conquests 'in all the earth.' They are seen in v. 17 'in all generations' to come 'for ever and ever,' giving honour to the great house of Ahab under which they are governed in peace and righteousness. The poet forms an inclusio, ending the psalm as he began it with his own contribution. His Maschil, with its play on Ahab's name, will 'make thy name to be remembered . . . Therefore shall the peoples confess thee,' and remember him with gratitude.

15th Bul, the first day of the festival, was a full day, and king and people went to bed happy. Yahweh had indeed commanded his lovingkindness in the day-time, and in the night his song, the Song of Beloved Ones, had been with them.

Earlier commentators saw 46 as a thanksgiving for some great national deliverance, as in the days of Jehoshaphat (Delitzsch) or Hezekiah (Kirkpatrick); Gunkel took it to be an eschatological Song of Zion; but more recent exegetes have increasingly seen it as a cultic hymn, a part of the autumn festival at Jerusalem (Kraus and Anderson, as well as Mowinckel,[20] Schmidt, Weiser and Eaton). Many features of the psalm make this view likely: God's making himself found as Israel's refuge (v. 1), with his 'voice' (v. 6) in the autumn thunderstorms; the rebellion of the waters (vv. 2f) and their allies the nations (v. 6); God's making firm the earth and the mountains, and keeping inviolable his city and its river (vv. 4f); his establishment of peace (vv. 8ff). The association of the city with Jerusalem ('zweifellos,' Kraus), is unevidenced, however.[21] Kraus himself points to the absence of the ark motif, to the unsuitability of the Kidron for the river whose streams make glad God's city, and the similarity of the mountains to the mountain in the north in 48:2. He concludes that the psalm incorporates ancient Canaanite ideas; but a simpler hypothesis would be that it was not originally written for Jerusalem at all, but for a shrine with no ark, and a real river, and a real mountain in the north. All of these points suggest Dan, at the source of the biggest river in the country, standing on the spur of Hermon, its most impressive mountain, on its northern frontier. 'The city of God' was of course understood to be Jerusalem when the psalm came to be used there after 722, but such a phrase was inevitably used for a national shrine—indeed for any city where there was an important sanctuary.[22]

I have noted above the links between 46 and the ritual hymns alongside it: 45, 47 and 48. But it is not merely that 46 seems to be a liturgical hymn in a corpus of similar Korah psalms, that is significant for our own purpose. It is that its place in the main Korah sequence is paralleled in the Fourth Book by 93-94, and in the same way that 44 was by 90, and 45 by 91-92; and so we have an indication that its place in the sequence is not an accident, but a hint of the use of 46 on the day following 45, and before 47 and 48.

93 is a hymn on Yahweh's defeat of the waters. In 93:1, 'The world also is stablished, that it cannot be moved'; cf. 'Therefore will we not

fear though the earth do sway . . . God is in the midst of her; she shall not be moved' (46:2, 5). 'The floods have lifted up, O LORD, The floods have lifted up their voice; The floods lift up their roaring. Above the voices of many waters, The mighty breakers of the sea, The LORD on high is mighty' (93:3f); cf. 'though the mountains be moved in the heart of the seas. The waters thereof roar and are troubled' (46:2f). 'Holiness becometh thine house, O LORD, for evermore' (93:5); cf. 'The holy place of the dwellings of the Most High' (46:4). 94 is a prayer for Yahweh to judge the nations, the proud and wicked ones; he will not cast off his people (v. 14), or have fellowship with the throne of wickedness (v. 20). He is Yahweh, the God of Jacob (v. 7), my high tower and the rock of my refuge (v. 22). In the second half of 46 the psalmist turns from the waters to their earthly allies, the nations; they will be brought to a halt by God's voice, and their armaments destroyed. In 46:1 he began, 'God is our refuge'; at v. 7 and v. 11 he sounds the refrain, 'Yahweh of hosts is with us; the God of Jacob is our high tower.'

These parallels are significant. 46 is the only Korah psalm in which the waters threaten the world's stability, and are thwarted by the power of God; and the principal example of the same theme elsewhere in the Psalter is 93. 'The God of Jacob' is a rare expression in the psalms, and the combination with 'refuge' and 'high tower' in 94 is neat. But what is now increasingly impressive is the sequential parallel between the main Korah series and Book IV:

42-43	Pilgrimage Psalms	(No royal pilgrimage to Zion)
44	National Lament	90 National Lament
45	Royal Procession, Anointing, Marriage	91 Royal Blessing and Procession 92 Anointing, enemies destroyed
46	God stills waters and Israel's enemies	93 Yahweh stills waters 94 Yahweh to judge enemies

As before, the Korah series is taken as a sequence of evening psalms (42:8), while Book IV comprises evening and morning psalms (92:2); cf. below, p.268. The parallel begins to look a little more than coincidental, and so to require an explanation; and one explanation is that offered at the beginning of the chapter. Just as 44 was a lament for the people preceding the feast on the 14th of the month at Dan, so was 90 at Jerusalem; just as the 15th was occupied with ceremonies reconsecrating the king at Dan, culminating in 45, so was it with 91 and 92 at Jerusalem; and both communities celebrated the divine victory over their enemies, infernal and foreign, on 16th, with 46 at Dan and 93 and 94 at Jerusalem. An explanation of the significance of these rites and their order is attempted in ch.9.

46   For the Chief Musician; (a Psalm) of the sons of Korah; by
     (ל) Alamoth. A Song.

1 God is our refuge and strength,
   He has made himself found indeed (נמצא מאד) as a help in
   trouble.
2 Therefore will we not fear though the earth do sway (המיר),
   And though the mountains be moved in the heart of the
   seas.
3 The waters thereof roar and are troubled (imperfects);
   The mountains shake with the pride thereof.   [Selah

The ritual of 15th had been a blessing on the king, on his wars, his government and his marriage. The parallel sequences just outlined suggest that the rites of the 16th celebrate God's victory over the waters, and there is an immediate hint of this in the heading note, על עלמות. LXX translated this ὑπὲρ τῶν κρυφιῶν, cf. Vg. *pro occultis*, linking the expression with the root עלם, I, to conceal; and this would hardly have been possible if the Chronicler's interpretation (I Chron. 15:20, 'with psalteries set to Alamoth . . . with harps set to the Sheminith') went back to an unbroken tradition of a musical meaning. The latter is in any case obscure, since עלמות would mean 'young women' (Ps. 68:26), and translations such as 'soprano' or 'virginals' (Delitzsch) are guesswork. We do best to take על in the locative sense as before; just as 45 was sung 'by the Lilies' in the city gateway, so was 46 sung 'at the Deeps,' the mysterious depths from which the waters of Jordan flooded forth, 'a stream about twelve feet broad by three deep . . . from the bowels of the earth.'[23] This enables us to give על the same meaning in each case, and to supply a likely location for the psalm, which is plainly concerned with the waters, both as a menace (vv. 2f) and as a blessing (v. 4). The ritual underlying vv. 8f also requires, as we shall see, a site away from the bamah, and this is true of 45 and 88 also, which have similar heading-notes with על. In this way we could account for the confusion in later interpretation, once the psalm was transferred to Jerusalem, and the locative note no longer applied. The Chronicler then supposed some musical direction to be intended, and put it in parallel with Sheminith ('the Eighth'); LXX retained the original root without understanding it, and Symmachus, with ὑπὲρ τῶν αἰωνίων, conjectured a link with עולם.

46 has a final heading note, שיר, a Song. The Songs in the Korah series are 45, 46, 48, 87 and 88, of which all but the last are hymns of triumph; 47 is described as מזמור, and this is the only other triumphal psalm in the series—the heading is easily understood from the repeated זמרו in 47:6, 7. Perhaps שיר originally had a triumphal association, a thanksgiving for God's lovingkindness (42:8); cf. Isa. 30:29, 'Ye shall have a song as in the night when a feast is hallowed; and gladness of heart...' For 88 as an exception, cf. below, Chapter 7.

The 'Chief Musician,' the Danite priest-poet, begins with a confident confession. The niph'al in v. 1b should be taken in a reflexive rather than a passive sense (Duhm, Eaton), and the perfect needs to be translated in contrast with the imperfects in v. 3: 'He has made himself to be found indeed,' 'he has plainly shown himself.' The imagery is drawn from the impregnability of the city, which 'shall not be moved' (v. 5): behind the walls and towers of Dan (48:12f) stands the God who is our ultimate refuge and strength,[24] and who is to be hailed as 'our high tower' (vv. 7, 11). Before the community's eyes is the awesome spectacle of the cascades of water thundering forth down the mountainside, deep calling to deep at the voice of God's cataracts (42:7). Here is visible evidence of the subterranean ocean on which the world is founded (24:1f), and of the deep about the roots of the mountains (Jon. 2:6). It overflows with formidable force, up from invisible springs and down the hillside, roaring and turbulent, threatening the stability of God's world in its pride. But Israel will not fear even if the earth sway ('change')—perhaps in earthquakes—and the mountains totter on their storm-tossed foundations ('in the heart of the seas'). In v. 2 RV's 'though' translates the Hebrew ב + infinitive, and is correct; but in v. 3 the Hebrew verbs are imperfects, and further concessive clauses are unsuitable. A liturgical interpretation enables us to take them as English presents. The people stands in awe before the waters of Sheol ('it,' cp. v. 3, 'the seas') thundering and raging, and before the mountains, viz. the peaks of Hermon (68:15), which seem to shudder at their rebellious impact. But they are not anxious: God is the ultimate lord of all powers, and he is Israel's defence.[25]

But how has God 'made himself found indeed' as Israel's help in trouble? The removal of the historical hypothesis seems to leave a vacuum. The triumphant tone of the psalm was easily understood if

Sennacherib had just withdrawn from Jerusalem; take that away, and you need to say in what way God has plainly shown himself. Weiser speaks of 'God's epiphany in the festival cult,' and Eaton of the 'coming' of God, who 'has drawn near, letting himself be found, making his presence exceedingly felt in salvation.' Epiphanies and theophanies are often mentioned in the commentaries, and it is difficult to know what is meant by such expressions, especially when they occur annually at festivals; I find it hard to imagine the whole host of Israel 'feeling God's presence in salvation' without some outward sign. Most commentators prefer a broad historical reference, e.g. Anderson and Kraus; but then no explanation is to hand for the tone of triumph, and for the realism of vv. 8f. Weiser, in addition to his epiphany view, says, 'Having heard the testimony of God's deeds and providential rule, as transmitted in the books of the *Heilsgeschichte . . .*'; and although this seems rather bookish and unmanageable with a festal assembly, it is on the right lines. Each of the three sections of 46 closes with a Selah, and we thus have three opportunities (cf. p.102ff) for a recital of the national tradition. The wording is too vague to give us any confidence as to what parts of the tradition might have been recited, but I make a tentative suggestion below. I should not wish to rule out the possibility of a dramatic event of national salvation being the occasion of the psalm's original composition, but the Selahs provide a means of anchoring the psalm's mood of strong thanksgiving in the realities of Israel's history.

46:4   (RV There is) A river, the streams whereof make glad the city of God,
(Is) the holy place of the dwellings (משכני) of the Most High.
5   God is in the midst of her; she shall not be moved:
God shall help her at the dawn of morning.
6   The nations raged, the kingdoms were moved:
He uttered his voice, the earth melts (תמוג).
7   The LORD of hosts is with us;
The God of Jacob is our high tower.   [Selah

The Hebrew has no verb with the river, and the usual translation, 'There is' (RV, RSV, NEB), deprives the sentence of any connection with what goes before. But it is likely that the waters of vv. 2f are related to the river of v. 4. The marvel is that these waters, whose pride bid fair to threaten the order of creation, have been tamed by God to become a fruitful river, whose sources, outside (and within) Dan and away at Baneas, form a confluence beneath the city. They provide the moisture which crowns the area with lofty trees, and which waters the meadows nearby,[26] so making glad the environs the whole year round. It is not necessary to stress how much more natural these expressions are for Dan than for Jerusalem.

The Hebrew of v. 4b is difficult, and many commentators prefer the LXX text, which read קִדֵּשׁ מִשְׁכָּנוֹ, 'the Most High has sanctified his dwelling-place.' But then, as usual, we are left to account for the Hebrew tradition making sense into nonsense; and מִשְׁכַּן, being masculine, is followed awkwardly by 'her' in v. 5. But sense can be made of the Hebrew on the assumption that the river is thought of as sacred, and as indwelt by God. It is to be noted that elsewhere in the Korah psalms the 'dwelling-places' of God, i.e. the sanctuary, are spoken of as מִשְׁכָּנוֹת; but here the form is מִשְׁכְּנֵי. We must resist the temptation to emend the text every time it surprises us. Perhaps there is a reason for the difference: perhaps God dwells in the river, but it is not his 'tabernacles.' It would not be very surprising, moreover, if the river were thought of in this way. Springs were regarded as holy all over the ancient world, and the abode of divinities. The name Baneas, Panias, derives from the source of the Jordan being sacred to Pan in Hellenistic times. The possibility that the Israelites thought of it in a similar way is shown by 87:7, 'All *my* fountains are in thee': the springs at Dan are the springs of God; cf. also 42:7, 'All *thy* waves and *thy* billows.' But God was not thought to have his holy dwelling-place in the source of the Jordan once northern Israel was lost; hence the difficulty of the text, and the LXX pointing and emendation, and the modern aporia.

God is spoken of as אֶלְיוֹן, the Most High, and this is sometimes regarded as a link with Jerusalem. The connection is weak, however; for El 'Elyon was the God of Salem (Gen. 18:19, 22), and it is by no means clear that Salem is to be identified with Jerusalem.[27] There is moreover an association of 'Elyon with the mountain of the north in Isa. 14:13f: 'I will sit upon the mount of congregation, in the uttermost parts of the north . . . I will be like the Most High.' No doubt there are echoes here of Baal on Mt Zaphon near Ugarit, but to an Israelite in the prophetic tradition the northern mountain is likely to have been Hermon. The title recurs at 47:2 and 87:5, in both of which Yahweh is thought of as supreme over the peoples; and it is likely that it is used here to emphasise his supremacy over the waters. Naturally the city and river were eventually understood to be Jerusalem and its little river, the Kidron, and the northern mountain was taken—in alterations to Ps. 48—to be Zion. But the splendid divine river of Ezek. 47, Joel 3:18 and Zech. 14:8, which issues from the temple in Jerusalem in marvellous fruitfulness, is not just an extension of the Kidron in the prophetic imagination; it is the transference of the real river, the Jordan, whose waters roar and are troubled and shake mount Hermon, whose streams make glad the city of Dan with real fruitfulness. This is likely to have taken place in large part through the adoption in Jerusalem of the 46th Psalm.

Israel can now look back on centuries during which Dan has been an Israelite shrine, and generations during which it has been the centre for the annual national pilgrimage. It seems an inviolable stronghold, guaranteed by the presence of God not merely in its sacred springs but also sacramentally 'in its midst,' in the form of his ephod. Perhaps the memory of the fall of the city in the days of Baasha is still latent, and could account for the stress of these verses. The mountains may move, but the city will not move for ever; the powers of chaos cannot shake her, nor the nations. Again we have an indication that the psalm was intended to be chanted in the evening: 'God shall help her לפות בקר, at the dawn of morning.' The constant attempts to interpret such phrases 'poetically' (RV text, RSV, 'right early')[28] are to be resisted. 44 looked back on a day of self-abasement 'all the day long'; 45 celebrated the carrying of the new queen to her marriage-bed; 42:8 ran, 'And in the night his song shall be with me'—we should take the words literally. The psalm, like its predecessors, is sung in the evening, after the day's ceremonies. Tomorrow's rites, echoed in 47 to be sung tomorrow evening, consist of God 'going up' to sit upon his holy throne, and to subdue the peoples under Israel and the nations under their feet. Then indeed God will 'help' his own. To us there is an uncomfortable tension in this thought: God *is* in the midst of the city, he *will* help at dawn. We feel the discomfort the more powerfully because looking over the Israelite's shoulder is the Canaanite, to whom Baal was dead in the long summer, and resumed his reign in renewed life with the gathering of the autumn thunder-clouds. Israel's God was never dead, nor thought of as not helping his people; but in the cultic actuality of the festival it seemed as if God's help was to be looked for afresh, as perhaps it may seem also to a Christian congregation at Easter. The disappointments and failures of the last year are behind us. God, under the symbol of his ephod, is already within the city; in the morning he will go in procession up to his sanctuary, and establish his dominion, and his people's, in perpetuity.

Each year the whole of Israel's adult male force mobilised in the autumn at Dan; and each year, we must suppose, the whole adult male force of Israel's neighbours mobilised at their national centres at the same time. It was the turn of the year, when the kings go forth to war (II Sam. 11:1),[29] when the harvest is gathered in at home, and the enemies' harvest is there for the picking (Jg. 6:11), when the pruning-hooks can be beaten into spears, and the fifties and hundreds can be marshalled and exhorted to the holy war, abroad as at home. Autumn therefore was the season when enemy invasions were to be looked for or pre-empted, and the nations are imagined as 'raging' and being 'moved,' stirring in rebellion like the powers in the waters of Sheol, of whom the same verbs are used in v. 2 and v. 3, and whose puppets they are felt to be. They shake the mountains above, and they shake the kingdoms about; but both of these restless endeavours are vain in face of the transcending power of God. At any time now the first thunderstorms will break, and show who is the world's true master. For the thunder is his 'voice' (cf. 29), and when he has spoken (perfect), the earth will dissolve (imperfect) beneath his lightning. As for the enemy armies, there is nothing to fear, for Yahweh of hosts is with us. Whatever the origin of this difficult phrase,[30] the context makes it look as if the psalmist understood it to have a military meaning (which however is not clear in the several uses in 84). The heathen may rage and lift up their hand against God and his people, but Yahweh of hosts is with us, either as God of celestial armies (68:17), or of Israel's earthly ones. In the harder times ahead God would be reproached, '(Thou) goest not forth with our hosts' (44:9). The same military context is not far away in the passages about the ark of the covenant of Yahweh of hosts in I Sam. 4, or in Ps. 48:8.

For the Selah, see below on v. 11.

> 46:8 Come, behold the works of the LORD,
> Who hath made desolations in the earth.
> 9 He maketh wars to cease unto the end of the earth;
> He breaketh the bow, and cutteth the spear in sunder;
> He burneth the waggons (עגלות) in the fire.
> 10 Desist (הרפו), and know that I am God:
> I will be exalted among the nations, I will be exalted in the earth.

11 The LORD of hosts is with us;
   The God of Jacob is our high tower.   [Selah

The imperatives are addressed by Israel ('us,' vv. 7, 11) to the nations of v. 6, and they are intended concretely and not figuratively. Some of their representatives are actually present at the rites: 'the princes of the peoples are gathered together as the people of the God of Abraham' (47:9). The rest could suitably learn the same lesson. Nor are the 'desolations' merely to be seen in the mind's eye, as having taken place on some far-off battlefield, during the year: the peoples are to 'come' and 'behold.' The burning of the captured enemy weapons and waggons is the highlight of the ritual of the 16th, and the putting of them to the torch is a powerful symbol of the vanity of any rebellion such princes might be contemplating. The עגלות are waggons,[31] which is always the meaning elsewhere, never chariots; Kirkpatrick compares the laager of waggons in I Sam. 17:20; 26:7. We now have a second reason for the day's ritual being held at 'Alamoth: such captured armaments would have to be stored—and burned—well away from the bamah. A 'cast up' stone avenue, up which the Israelites once processed to the occasion, is still to be seen along the east bank of the river. Behind the pool from which wells the Jordan is the mound where for two hundred years their God's victories were symbolised in fire and smoke; and where a deposit of wood-ash some feet in depth must still await the archaeologist's spade.

Joshua houghed the enemy horses and burned their chariots with fire after the battle of Merom (Josh. 11:6, 9); and Ezekiel foresaw that after the final battle with Magog, Israel would 'make fires of the weapons and burn them, both the shields and the bucklers, the bows and the arrows, and the handstaves and the spears,' fires lasting seven years (Ezek. 39:9f). The ceremonial burning of enemy war-material at the autumn festival seems to be implied in a passage in Isaiah. 'Behold, the name of the LORD cometh from far, burning with his anger, and in thick rising smoke . . . Ye shall have a song as in the night when a feast is hallowed . . . And the LORD shall cause his glorious voice to be heard . . . and the flame of the devouring fire . . . For through the voice of the LORD shall the Assyrian be broken in pieces. For a Topheth is prepared of old; yea, for the king it is made ready; he hath made it deep and large: the pile thereof is fire and much wood; and the breath of the LORD, like a stream of brimstone, doth kindle it' (Isa. 30:27-33). Isa. 30 has much in common with Ps. 46: the song in the night when the feast is hallowed, Yahweh's voice overwhelming the enemy, the pyre which he lights. Perhaps 46 is even the 'song' to which Isaiah refers. At any event it would seem that the Tophet, referred to a number of times in II Kings 23 and Jer. 7:19, was a massive bonfire used for ceremonial purposes, and abused for the sacrifice of children, in the Valley of the son of Hinnom outside Jerusalem; and it would make the best sense of Isa. 30 if this bonfire were built up each year in the weeks before the Feast (חג, v. 29), 'prepared of old,' and then set light to 'by Yahweh' in the same way that divine power kindles the light of Christ each Easter night in the Church. The time of year is identified by the references to 'the voice of Yahweh,' which is heard soon after Tabernacles. On this occasion the steady repetition of the Tophet ritual is to be fulfilled in a real victory of Yahweh, who will break the power of Assyria in pieces, and burn their king's arms in a supernatural conflagration.

A second passage from Isaiah should perhaps be interpreted in the light of this: 'Thou hast multiplied the nation, thou hast increased their joy: they joy before thee according to the joy in harvest, as men rejoice when they divide the spoil ... For every boot of the booted warrior in the tumult, and the garments rolled in blood, shall be even for burning, for fuel of fire. For unto us a child is born ...' (Isa. 9:3-6). Israel's joy is 'according to the joy in harvest': 'Thou shalt keep the feast of booths seven days, after that thou hast gathered in ... and thou shalt rejoice in thy feast' (Deut. 16:13f). Isaiah prophesies a real victory, with the division of the spoil and the burning of the enemy's remainders after the battle, as a preliminary to the coming reign of peace. But the mention of the Tophet in Isa. 30 leads us to think that the joy in harvest was in part a rejoicing at Yahweh's provision of military blessing, celebrated in a national bonfire at the Festival, where captured items larger than boots and garments could be put to the flames.

Such a feature at Jerusalem makes plausible a ritual context for Ps. 46 at Dan. Just as the Tophet was built in the Valley of the Son of Hinnom, away to the south of Jerusalem, not far from En-Rogel and other sources of the Kidron, so was the pyre of captured waggons and weapons fired at 'Alamoth, in the valley west of Dan near the source of the Jordan. Only so do we get real force from the verbs 'come' and 'behold,' and a continuous thread of thought running through the psalm from beginning to end. The waters threaten God's city, but he turns them to a fructifying river, and his presence keeps the city impregnable; the nations, their allies, threatened God's city, but his

Copyright: Tel Dan Excavations

Pl. I

THE END OF THE 'HIGHWAY' (מסלה) TO DAN

View of the מסלה looking westwards through the inner city gates. Threshold-stones are visible towards the top of the picture: compare the plan in Fig. 3. The labour involved in 'casting up' the stones for a road paved like this for a hundred miles from Samaria must have been enormous, and testifies to the regular requirement of such a way for very large numbers of pilgrims.

Pl. II

THE THRONE-BASE IN THE DAN COURTYARD

Two of the pillar base-capitals are visible to the left.

Pl. III

A PUMPKIN-SHAPED BASE CAPITAL

One of the pumpkin-shaped base-capitals for the throne canopy.

Pl. IV

ORNAMENTAL STEPS LEADING TO THE BAMAH

Ahab's steps lie beneath these, which are from the time of Jeroboam II.

Pl. V

A PROTO-AEOLIC CAPITAL FROM HAZOR

This capital was excavated by Yigael Yadin at Hazor; see his 'Excavations at Hazor,' *IEJ* 9 (1959), pl. 9B. Yadin dates the capital to the ninth century, probably to the reign of Ahab (p. 79). W.B. Dinsmoor traces the Proto-Aeolic (= Proto-Ionic) design back to Egyptian fleur-de-lys patterns, and associates the Israelite instances with the 'lily-work' in I Kgs. 7 (*The Architecture of Ancient Greece*, pp. 59ff). Other examples survive from Samaria, Megiddo and (with pendant leaves below the volutes) Ramath Rahel. The lily, with stylised stamen, is still identifiable here. For another view see Y. Shiloh, *The Proto-Aeolic Capital and Israelite Ashlar Masonry*, pp. 26ff, who takes the design to represent a palm-tree. Thirty-four such capitals have been discovered, some with the design on both sides, all from the same period, and in association with splendid royal courts (Shiloh, p. 7).

thunder above and his armies beneath have made a bonfire of their munitions. Water and fire alike are the evidence of his invincibility.

The sequence of thought in 46 is close to that in 2. The nations assemble tumultuously and their kings take counsel together against God and his anointed one (2:1-3; 46:6a); God speaks to them in his wrath (2:4-6; 46:6b); he breaks them in pieces to the uttermost part of the earth (2:7-9; 46:8f); and the psalmist finally turns to deliver a warning to them to submit, 'Now therefore, be wise, O ye kings: be instructed, ye judges of the earth, Serve the LORD with fear...' (2:10ff). In the same way 46 closes with a warning, 'Desist (הרפו), and know that I am God...' (v. 10). The normal meaning of the hiph'il of רפה is abandon, let go, and no parallel is available for the RV/RSV translation 'Be still,' which is an attempt to keep the words as an address to Israel (Anderson). Kraus and Weiser are surely right in seeing them as an address to the nations, like 'Come, behold' in v. 8; they are to 'be wise' and desist from their imagining of vain things.

The problem here is to account for the sudden transition into the divine first person singular, usually explained as a *Heilsorakel*; the difficulty is emphasised by the fact that this is the only 'strong confessional formula with אנכי in the OT.'[32] I have before noted the difficulty of this type of explanation in the discussion of 85:8; and suggested there that the combination of promise and warning was not to be derived from the prophet's unguided inspiration, but that the terms of both promise and warning could be traced in the passage of tradition (Exod. 32-34) which seemed to underlie the whole psalm. A similar possibility is open to us in the present case. Included in the refrain verse in vv. 7, 11 is the innocent-looking phrase, 'the God of Jacob'; and in the last verse of the following psalm, 47:9, is the similar phrase, 'the God of Abraham.' The northern traditions of Jacob and Abraham are likely to have been preserved by recitation in public worship at the autumn festival (Deut. 31:10; Neh. 9:7ff); could it be that the Selahs in 46 marked intervals for the recital of sections of the Jacob saga? In this way we should have an explanation for the absence of the refrain verse after the first section of the psalm, since it is not apposite to sing, 'The God of Jacob is our high tower' until after the Jacob story has been told; and the 'raging' of the nations would be in context, since the 'nations' in the ninth century were primarily the Aramaeans, whose ancestor Laban Jacob had worsted in Aram-Naharaim.

But does the text give any support to such a speculation? In the best-known of all the Jacob traditions, God appears to him at Bethel with the words, 'I (אני) am the LORD, the God of Abraham thy father, and the God of Isaac: the land whereon thou liest, to thee will I give it, and to thy seed . . . and in thee and in thy seed shall all the families of the earth bless themselves. And, behold, I (אנכי) am with thee . . .' (Gen. 28:13-15). The recitation of such a passage in the course of the psalm would go far to explain the psalmist's boldness. His 'Desist and know . . .' stands on his own authority, like Ps. 2's 'Be wise . . . ' But the content of the confession ('know') is then in inverted commas, a partial quotation from the tradition just recited. God had told Jacob that he was the God of his fathers; that all the families of the earth would pray to Jacob's God; and that he would be with him. Both of the psalmist's opening words, אנכי אלהים, occur in the verses in Genesis, and the sense of them is Yahweh's opening phrase. His 'I will be exalted among the nations, I will be exalted in the earth' is a paraphrase of 'in thee shall all the families of the earth bless themselves.' His 'the LORD of hosts is with us' corresponds to 'I am the LORD . . . I am with thee.' His 'the God of Jacob' corresponds to 'the God of Abraham thy father, and the God of Isaac.' His 'hosts' could even correspond to the angels on the ladder.

It is no objection to this proposal that the Jacob legend in question belongs to Bethel and not Dan; for Dan was a national shrine, and those traditions from other shrines which had become part of the nation's tradition would have been used at the national sanctuaries, or they would have perished. It is an objection to say that the proposed recital is a speculation. But the fit with the Genesis text is quite neat, and once we have seen that recitals are more than possibilities behind the Selahs of 44, 48 and 85, the speculation has become a hypothesis. It is a hypothesis for which we shall have further use; and in judging it we have always to remember the fact that the *Heilsorakel* theory is a speculation also. We have all to live in glass houses; but the recital hypothesis is a glass house that ripens many grapes.

One final reflection cannot fail to strike us from the examination of 45 and 46 in the light of the present hypothesis: how rich and how real was life in the high days of Israel's nationhood! On the king's success in war, on his faithfulness and wisdom in government, on his sexual potency, hung the well-being of the people. His reconsecration and his new marriage were cause for real 'joy and gladness' as the ordinary Israelite could look forward to peace and empire. The rumbling menace of the infernal powers could be seen as overwhelmed and domesticated as the life-giving water streamed from the side of Hermon; and the ever-renewed threat of the Syrians and other more formidable armies could be seen for what they were worth as the battle-waggons went up in a tornado of flame and smoke. The modern reader, liberated alike from a naive theology of providence, and of the need to walk a hundred miles for his holiday, or to consort with sixty thousand of his fellow-citizens, puts his trust in Water Boards and in America's powers of nuclear retaliation. His closest experience to Israel's pyre of triumph is Guy Fawkes' Night, and to the annual wedding of their new queen the crowning of Miss World on the television. We can hardly dispute that his life is more comfortable.

THE MIDDLE OF THE FEAST (Psalms 47, 48, 87)

It was seen even in the last century that 47 was a national ritual psalm. Then it was thought to be a national ritual of thanksgiving after some great deliverance, as under Jehoshaphat (Delitzsch, II Chron. 20:28), or Hezekiah (Kirkpatrick); Lipiński has shown the absurdity of such proposals by fully cataloguing them.[1] In this century, under the influence of Gunkel and Mowinckel, opinion has swung towards a regular annual ritual divorced from any particular historical occasion, though the nature of this ritual has been sharply contested. Gunkel, followed by Oesterley, sees the psalm as an eschatological enthronement of Yahweh: led by the influence of Deutero-Isaiah, the psalmist sees Yahweh's ultimate enthronement as if it had already happened, and calls on the peoples to acclaim him. Mowinckel,[2] with Weiser and Eaton, sees the enthronement as sacramental: each year includes, as the high point of the national festival, a ceremonial procession in which Yahweh 'goes up' to his Temple, 'becomes king' and 'takes up his throne' anew. Others, like Kraus, Johnson,[3] Anderson, and Rogerson and McKay, think of the psalm as a celebration of Yahweh's kingship, with a procession, perhaps, and an act of homage before the Ark, but not an enthronement. The distinctions are rather fine between the second and third groups; Gunkel's eschatological view does not seem to account satisfactorily for the psalm's tone of present enthusiasm.

It is often noted that 47 is continuous with 46:10, 'I will be exalted among the nations, I will be exalted in the earth.' More generally, as we have seen, 47 belongs with 46 and 48; but for evidence for their continuity as psalms for the ritual of succeeding days of the feast, we must turn again to the parallel we have established with Book IV:

National Lamentation	44	90
Royal Blessing, Anointing (and Wedding)	45	91, 92
Yahweh's Victory over Waters and Enemies	46	93, 94

Now 47, like 46, is a psalm of distinctive character. It calls upon all peoples to shout and sing praises to God, for he is the great king over all

the earth; he is gone up with acclamation, and reigns over the nations
on his holy throne, and they are to join in his worship. Yahweh's
kingship is the theme of a number of psalms in the 90's, but 95 and 96
are not the least of them, and 96 dramatically stresses the worship of
the nations. 95:1, 'O come let us sing (נרננה) unto the LORD; let us
make a joyful noise (נריע), echoes 47:1, 'Shout (הריעו) unto God with
the voice of triumph (רנה).' There is to be singing of praises (זמר) in
95:2 and 47:6f, and more cultic cries (תרועה) in 95:2 and 47:5. 'For the
LORD is a great God, And a great King above all gods' (95:3); 'For
great is the LORD . . . He is to be feared (נורא)' above all gods (96:4):
'For the LORD is most high and terrible (נורא); He is the great King
over all the earth' (47:2). 'Declare his glory among the nations, His
marvellous works among all the peoples . . . Give unto the LORD, ye
kindreds of the peoples, Give unto the LORD glory and strength . . .
Tremble before him all the earth. Say among the nations, The LORD
reigneth' (96:3, 7, 9f): 'O clap your hands, all ye peoples . . . God
reigneth over the nations: God sitteth upon his holy throne. The
princes of the peoples are gathered together' (47:1, 8f). We may also
note the act of worship before Yahweh's throne in 95:6, 96:9, shared by
Israel and the nations—which is probably also implied in 47:8.

The combination of Yahweh's kingship and his acceptance by the
heathen in 47 and 95-96 is quite striking, for it would be difficult to
think of other psalms, even 97-99, where both these themes occur; and
the fact that they follow directly on the even more striking parallel
46//93-94 can hardly be accidental. A plausible reason for the parallels
must be the continuation of the Korah psalms as celebrations of the
ritual of succeeding days in the Dan festival. 46 celebrated God's
victory over the waters and over his terrestrial enemies, with the
burning of a pyre of captured arms and waggons, on the evening of
16th Bul; 47 celebrates God's kingship over the whole world, with a
procession of the ephod to the temple, on 17th Bul. The same outline of
a festival will have been operative in Jerusalem when Book IV became
the established psalmody—except that the festal month was Tishri
(Ethanim), the seventh, not the eighth month. The same triumph over
the waters, over his enemies, over the whole world, with the
submission of the nations, can be predicated in 93, 94, 95 and 96. But
the differences between the Korah psalms and Book IV are also only
too obvious. 47 triumphs in the inheritance Yahweh has chosen for
Jacob, and foresees the nations under their feet. The peoples (in their
representatives) are present at Israel's feast at Dan: 'The princes of the

peoples are gathered together as the people of the God of Abraham' (v. 9). But no foreign dignitaries attended the Jerusalem Tabernacles in the days of Judah's weakness; 96 must content itself with, 'Declare his glory among the nations... Say among the nations, The LORD reigneth' (vv. 3, 10). In place of joy in Israel's inheritance, 95 offers a sombre warning on their fathers' disobedience, who could not enter God's rest. The distinctions are politically but not theologically significant.

The extended series of parallels which we have been examining enables us to lay to rest an anxiety which troubles many readers of the 'liturgical' type of commentary. Eaton writes of the enthronement of God as 'the high moment' of the festival, and others speak of it as its climax. But then much other ritual is understood to lie behind the psalms—the blessing and anointing of the king (20, 21, 45, 91, etc.), a bonfire (46), a procession round the walls of the city (48), through the gates (24, 118), a sham fight (88), besides sacrifices, the taking of omens, the slaughter of prisoners and other excitements. The reader begins to wonder, how was so much fitted in? The week seems to have several climaxes. But the serial hypothesis I am proposing removes this disquiet by taking it seriously. If it is right, then we have a different ritual for every day, and underlying each psalm in turn: the pilgrimage behind 42-43, the preliminary lamentation behind 44, the royal blessing, anointing and wedding behind 45, the bonfire behind 46, the procession of the ephod to the temple behind 47, the march around the city behind 48, and more to come. Indeed, it must seem probable that the festival week should have had a traditional structure, like the Babylonian New Year, with a regularly repeated ritual for each day. It is just that hitherto we seemed to have no basis for being more than vague, since the late biblical reforms abolished most of the northern ritual, and left nothing more interesting than a differentiated number of sacrifices for each day of the feast (Num. 29:12-28).

47 For the Chief Musician; a Psalm of the sons of Korah.
 1 O clap your hands, all ye peoples:
   Shout unto God with the voice of triumph.
 2 For the LORD is most high, to be feared (נורא);
   He is a great King over all the earth.
 3 He subdueth the peoples under us,
   And the nations under our feet.
 4 He chooseth our inheritance for us,
   The excellency of Jacob which he loved (אשר אהב). [Selah

None of the Korah psalms preceding 47 is said to be a מזמור. 42, 43, 44, 45, 46 all lack this heading; while all the psalms following, 47, 48, 49, 84, 85, 87, 88, have it. Although we may be distrustful of the accuracy of preservation of the headings, this is mildly impressive, and we can hardly fail to relate it to 47:6f, where the זמר root is used five times: זמרו אלהים זמרו זמרו למלכנו זמרו. . זמרו משכיל. The meaning of זמר is not clear. Kraus thinks that it means 'sing,' following the Akkadian, and that a מזמור is identical with a שיר, except that the former is accompanied by music (I, 15f); BDB, followed by RSV, took it to mean playing musical instruments, 'make melody,' as at 33:2; 71:22; 98:5; 147:7; 149:3. But the Greek ψαλμός means a song accompanied by strings, and supports Kraus. The marked distribution in our collection suggests that in the opening phase of the festival there was no musical accompaniment to the singing, while from the fourth day, a high point in the feast, stringed instruments were introduced to dignify the entry of Yahweh with his ephod into the shrine. In support of this, the Chronicler stresses the provision of musical accompaniment for the ark's entry into Jerusalem (I Chron. 15). Against it, 84 and 85 are headed מזמור; but this could have been added, like על־הגתית to 84, when they came to be used in the south. זמר will then mean 'to sing praises to an accompaniment,' and מזמור 'a hymn sung to music.'

The festal week accordingly moves into top gear. Now is the moment when Yahweh will come into his temple and make his kingship effective. In the cultic ecstasy the defeats and losses of the past are no more. In the thunder of the rhythmical clapping of hands of sixty thousand Israelite men of war, followed by the awesome united cry of the תרועה, the cultic shout which in the fable brought down the walls of Jericho, nothing seems impossible. The scene is strongly reminiscent of the enthronement of an earthly king, for there was hand-clapping at Joash's coming to the throne (II Kgs. 11:12), and shouting when Saul became king (I Sam. 10:24). All peoples are bidden to join in the exultation at Yahweh's dominion, and this is no imaginative conceit, for their leaders are in some cases present (v. 9), testifying to the political prestige enjoyed by ninth century Israel. There is no earlier psalm in the supplement which 47 has ousted, so, like 45 and 46, it is probably from the halcyon days of the nation.

The reason for the acclamation (כי) is Yahweh's supremacy: he is עליון, the supreme God, the awesome one. There is no direct reference to other gods in the Korah psalms, except at 44:20, but Yahweh's kingship probably implies a pantheon of 'sons of God' (89:6), to whom he is 'very terrible' (89:7; 96:4). His kingship includes the whole world, and he subdues[4] the peoples to Israel—some of them since the Conquest, others in the battles to be fought in the coming year. The imperfects in vv. 3f, contrasted with the perfect in v. 5, stand for the continuity of the divine action. Duhm saw an absurdity in the nations being called to rejoice (v. 1) in their enslavement (v. 3), but in most cases there would be no tension. Israel might speak in high-flown terms of their subjugation of peoples like the Hittites and Jebusites, but in fact these peoples were absorbed into Israel with little pain, and 'foreigners' like Uriah and Zadok could take a leading part in Israelite life.

The sense of continuity runs on into God's choosing of the land as Israel's inheritance: 'for us' is surprising and emphatic, since elsewhere God chooses 'for himself.' The 'inheritance' seems plainly to be the land, as normally: but what is the גאון יעקב? The phrase means 'the pride of Jacob/Israel' in a hostile sense in the prophets (Amos 6:8; 8:7; etc.), but a positive sense is intended here. Gunkel takes 'Jacob's pride' as 'fair Canaan,' but R.E. Clements thinks it means the (Jerusalem) Temple.[5] Nor is it clear whether אשר־אהב means that God loves his people Jacob, or their 'pride'; Mal. 1:2 would support the first, and Ps. 87:1 the second.

These verses recall the mighty acts of God in giving the land to his people, and the mention of 'the God of Abraham' in v. 9, together with the gathering of the nations as his people, has suggested to many commentators—Delitzsch (citing Theodoret), Duhm and Gunkel, for example—that passages from the Abraham saga were in the writer's mind. The promise in Gen. 12:3, 'in thee shall all the families of the earth be blessed,' and the explanation of the name Abraham in 17:4 as 'father of a multitude of nations,' have most often been cited. Anderson remarks that the festal ceremony 'probably included a re-presentation of the major events of the salvation history'; and once more we find a Selah at the end of v. 4, following the praise of Yahweh for subduing the nations and choosing our inheritance. It would seem that we have here a further confirmation for the view of Selah as a break for the recital of the national tradition (cf. pp.102ff). 44 gave space for the Joshua-Conquest traditions to be recited, 85 for the Moses-Levite stories, 46 for the Jacob saga (in three parts), and now 47 is the occasion of the Abraham complex.

Can we be any more specific about the stories in use in Dan? Gen. 17 is not a very promising suggestion, as in its present form the chapter is the work of P, a later southern source; and although the call of Abram in 12:3 could be a part of the tradition used, it is only said there that the nations will be blessed (נברכו) in Abram. A more positive text is Gen. 22:17f, 'thy seed shall possess the gate of his enemies; and in thy seed shall all the nations of the earth bless themselves (התברכו)' (cf. 18:18). We are closer to Ps. 47 here, with the conquest of the nations, and their worship of Abraham's God. It is also possible that Gen. 22, which is set in the otherwise unknown 'land of the Moriah (המריה),' was originally set in Dan; and that the name of the northern sanctuary was later removed for respectability.[6]

47:5 God is gone up with a shout,
      The LORD with the sound of the trumpet.
  6 Sing praises to God, sing praises:
      Sing praises unto our king, sing praises.
  7 For God is the King of all the earth:
      Sing ye praises in a skilful psalm.
  8 God has taken up his reign (מלך) over the nations:
      He has taken his seat (ישב) upon his holy throne.

The scene recalls the induction of the ark by David into Jerusalem: 'So David and all the house of Israel brought up (מעלים) the ark of the LORD with shouting (תרועה), and with the sound of the trumpet (שופר)' (II Sam. 6:15). So here the king and all Israel have escorted the ephod through the city with rhythmical cultic cries and blasts on the horn; Yahweh is present mysteriously in the national symbol, and ascends the 'cast up' road, borne no doubt as in the ark on a plinth by priests. The procession goes up to the high place on the north side of the city, and so into the shrine, now partially excavated; in the דביר, the holy place at its rear, the priests will have set their sacred burden (cf. I Sam. 21:9). Then, the ceremonial over, the host is called upon to sing praises to God, their newly-enthroned King. The music strikes up and the chanting begins. God's universal kingship calls for a psalm of specially skilled composition, a Maschil. I have suggested above that such psalms included a play on the name of the earthly king, his vicegerent. If this is so, we have a second psalm written in the reign of king Ahab, for just as 'Thou hast loved (אהבת) righteousness' in 45:7 seemed to be an indication of the king's name, so here 'the pride of Jacob which he loved (אהב)' would carry the same purpose.

The language seems to bear out the theory of Volz and Mowinckel that the underlying ritual is an enthronement of Yahweh; and in particular עלה, מלך and ישב. The clapping and shouting and the trumpets, and the repeated use of the word 'king,' all recall the enthronement of an earthly king; but the perfects (as Kraus allows) are particularly suggestive of an enthronement of God. He 'has gone up'; that is, he has entered his temple at the head of his people. He 'has taken up his reign'; Kraus translates 'has become king,' like Mowinckel, but J. Ulrichsen has argued forcefully that the stress is on the action rather than its inception.[7] It seems natural then to translate ישב 'he has taken his seat.' This Kraus will not allow, for, as he says, Yahweh is thought of as enthroned invisibly on the ark, and all interpretation must begin from that. He suggests that either pre-Israelite or Mesopotamian enthronement ideas had influenced the Jerusalem psalmists, or that the language used at the enthronement of earthly kings, or in Isa. 52:7, had been taken on metaphorically and used of Yahweh's kingship. But we do not need these resorts once a northern setting has been understood for the Korah psalms; the Jerusalem-ark interpretation is sheer supposition, without any evidence. It is not the ark which is being carried, but the ephod, that is God's robe and not his throne, and the three perfects can be taken in the same sense.

Of course the way in which God can be thought of as having taken up his throne is in a manner metaphorical. No Israelite thought that Yahweh spent the dry summer in the underworld, like Baal slain by Mot. But the enthronement nonetheless speaks to the nation's heart with cultic actuality: 'God is gone up with a shout' is used by the Church at Ascensiontide with equal fervour and renewed reality. This does not mean, however, that Kraus is not right in part, for when 47 came to be used in Jerusalem, the metaphorical understanding had to be extended.

> 47:9　The princes of the peoples are gathered together
> 　　　　As [RV mg diff.] the people of the God of Abraham:
> 　　　　For the shields of the earth belong unto God;
> 　　　　He greatly exalts himself (נעלה).

In the high tide of Israel's prosperity, perhaps during the reign of Ahab as I have suggested, client princes attended the national festival, partly no doubt from force majeure to present their tribute, and partly also from the desire to have a voice in the war policy to which they would be expected to contribute. 'Shield' is used in parallel to 'anointed one' at 84:9, and to 'king' at 89:18, so that the inclination is to understand the 'shields' as client kings; though the word is probably used for 'nobles' in Hos. 4:18, and this may be what is implied.[8] Tyrian and Philistine leaders were at the festival according to 87:4 (see below). A concrete instance of such attendance is the visit of King Jehoshaphat of Judah to Ahab's court in I Kgs. 22, although this takes place at Samaria and not at Dan. But it is probable that the king of Israel would have to go to Dan with his mind made up on peace or war, since it was there that his army would mobilise, and he would be in a position to make his previously decided policy effective. Client kings, especially those from the south, would then find it convenient to arrive at Samaria early and 'go up' with the official procession. I Kgs. 22 gives us a dramatic insight into the way decisions were taken. Ahab's mind is in fact already made up on a campaign to recover the frontier town of Ramoth-Gilead from Syria; and a spurious divine authorization is lent to the decision by the 'prophesying' of the court prophets. Jehoshaphat is nominally given equal honour to Ahab, with a throne alongside the latter; but his request for a second opinion is sabotaged (v. 13), and when Micaiah gives a hostile prophecy it is not heeded. So the Judaean army is committed to a distant and perilous battle in whose success it could have no interest. Client kings, in other words, had little influence. They belonged to God, Yahweh the God of Israel; their armies were part of Israel's army, and their peoples were, for the moment, the people of the God of Abraham. It was in this way that tribes became peoples, and peoples became, briefly, empires; neither by conquest nor by marriage, but by adherence. The expansion of his national influence and army is a certain sign of the activity of Yahweh; he is greatly exalting himself (taking the niph'al reflexively, with Eaton). The same root dominates the psalm: Yahweh is the עליון, the Most High (v. 2), who has gone up, עלה (v. 5), and is greatly exalting himself (נעלה, v. 9).

There is some embarrassment over the syntax of v. 9ab. RVmg translates 'are gathered together Unto the people,' but there is no Hebrew preposition representing 'unto,' and this is generally disallowed (Delitzsch, Kirkpatrick). Kraus and others suppose haplography, for עם could have been written once for both עָם, 'people,' and עִם 'with.' It is this kind of ingenious proposal which could be convincing with a sheerly literary text, but hardly with a liturgical one; surely 47 was preserved because it was used in worship, regularly at Dan, and in time at Jerusalem.[9] The suggestion that עם should be taken as a nominative of effect, however, as I have translated it—'are gathered together As the people . . .'—has often seemed rather bold (though it is adopted by

Delitzsch and Kirkpatrick); can we really think that the Israelite poet could have spoken of foreign princes as being the people of the God of Abraham? The difficulty is materially eased by the Selah hypothesis we are following: if the Abraham saga has been recited after v. 4, with its repeated promise, 'In thee shall all the nations of the earth bless themselves' (Gen. 18:18; 22:18), then it would be entirely natural to see the words fulfilled in the royalty of the neighbouring lands who have come to join in Israel's festival. They too are the people of the God of Abraham.

The third psalm celebrating Yahweh's lordship over the nations is 48, and the particular theme of this psalm is the impregnability of his city. As it stands, 48 is a hymn of Zion. Mount Zion is referred to in v. 2 and v. 11, and Israel is told to 'walk about Zion' in v. 12; 'the daughters of Judah,' that is probably the villages around Jerusalem, are to rejoice in v. 11. But Kraus notes a number of features which show an earlier history going back to pre-Israelite times, such as the contest with the powers of chaos, or the mountain in the north. I shall try to show, however, that there is an intermediate stage between the primitive myths and their echo in a hymn on the impregnability of Jerusalem; for neither the syntax nor the rhythm runs smoothly in v. 2b, and the references to the mountain are not properly applicable to Zion. Moreover v. 11 (which is also different in rhythm) recurs almost verbatim in 97:8. 48 is therefore much better suited to have been originally a hymn of Dan, which is really the frontiers of the north, and stands really on a mountain fair in height, Hermon. The psalm will have formed part of the Dan autumn festal sequence, like the other psalms of the sons of Korah. Since it has a 'pair' in the second Korah sequence, 87, we should probably think of it as an eighth century hymn, which has ousted its more confident predecessor. Perhaps because of express mentions of Dan or Hermon, it has then been amended so as to take its place in the seventh century liturgy at Jerusalem. Already by the time of Lamentations it could be said of Jerusalem, 'Is this the city that men called . . . The joy of the whole earth?' (Lam. 2:15, citing 48:2).

In the exposition of the preceding psalms, I have noted the serial parallels between the two Korah sequences and Book IV—the national laments of 44-85 and 90, the royal blessing and anointing of 45 and 91-92, the establishment of Yahweh's rule over the waters and his enemies in 46 and 93-94, his kingship over the nations in 47 and 95-96.

A continuation of such a sequence of parallels is noticeable, even if less strikingly, between 48 and 97-98. First there is Yahweh's kingship again, in which the whole world is to rejoice. 48:1f: 'Great is the LORD . . . in his holy mountain . . . , the joy of the whole earth; the city of the great King'; 48:10: 'As is thy name, O God, So is thy praise unto the ends of the earth.' 97:1: 'The LORD reigneth; let the earth rejoice; Let the multitude of the isles be glad.' 98:4, 6: 'Make a joyful noise unto the LORD, all the earth . . . Make a joyful noise before the King, the LORD.' Second, God confounds the rebel kings, and displays his power. 48:4ff: 'For lo, the kings . . . saw it, then were they amazed; they were dismayed'; 48:3: 'God has made himself known as a high tower.' 97:4-7: 'the earth saw, and trembled . . . all the peoples have seen his glory. Ashamed be all they that serve graven images.' 98:2: 'The LORD hath made known his salvation: His righteousness hath he openly shewed in the sight of the nations.' Then third, in the final version of 48 as in 97, follows the triumph of Jerusalem. 48:11: 'Let mount Zion be glad, Let the daughters of Judah rejoice, Because of thy judgements.' 97:8: 'Zion heard and was glad, And the daughters of Judah rejoiced, Because of thy judgements, O LORD.' The kingship/joy themes are common to the whole of both sequences 47-48 and 95-99, and are not particularly significant; but the nations' seeing and being confounded, and the close verbal links between 48:11 and 97:8 are something special, and provide some further confirmation of our liturgical hypothesis. The Korah psalms and Book IV follow the same sequence of themes, both of them being series of psalms for the autumn feast. The Korah series will be night-time psalms at Dan, as heretofore (42:8); the Fourth Book will be psalms for morning and evening worship at Jerusalem (92:2). Psalm 48 will have been the psalm for the 18th Bul, and will reflect the ritual for that day, to wit a ceremonial procession round the sacred city. In view of the numbers involved, such a procession must have taken the greater part of a day.

48   A Song; A Psalm of the sons of Korah.
1 Great is the LORD, and highly to be praised,
     In the city of our God, in his holy mountain.
2 Fair in height (יפה נוף), the joy of the whole earth,
     Is mount Zion, (on) the frontiers (ירכתי) of the north,
     The city of the great King.
3 God hath made himself known in her citadels (ארמנותיה)
     for a high tower.

48 continues the series of triumphal Songs begun with 45, and of those accompanied by music (מִזְמוֹר) begun with 47; no special place needs to be named, as the congress of the people begins and ends at the high place for the circumambulation of the walls (vv. 12f). It begins and ends with the praise of Yahweh, on whom the impregnability of his city depends. It is meet and right to praise him at all times and in all places, but especially in his city of Dan, where Israel masses year by year for the Feast.

Three features of the present text betray the existence of an earlier version, of which this is a clumsy amendment. First, the rhythm is, as Anderson notes, unsatisfactory, and RSV is to be preferred:

> Great is the LORD and greatly to be praised in the city of our God!
> His holy mountain, beautiful in elevation, is the joy of all the earth.

This approximates to the 3:2 rhythm which dominates the psalm; and there is a trace of it in the MT, where 'his holy mountain' is written on the same line as 'beautiful . . . earth,' but with a stop following the first phrase. Second, the MT syntax is not so smooth. There are three phrases standing in apparent apposition where apposition does not seem suitable. In v. 1b 'his holy mountain' follows 'In the city of our God' without RV's second 'in'; but a city is not a mountain, and a second בְ would seem natural as in 87:1. In v. 2bc similarly, 'mount Zion' is followed by both 'the sides of the north' (RV) and 'The city of the great King' without preposition; at least the former would seem to require a בְ as in Isa. 14:13, 'upon the mountain of congregation, *in* the uttermost part (יַרְכְּתֵי) of the north.' This roughness of syntax has resulted in the transposition of the cola by Gunkel, and in various conjectural translations: 'in our divine city is his holy mountain' (Anderson), 'Zion, the heights of Zaphon' (Johnson, *SKAI*, 77), 'the angle of the north' (Delitzsch), 'Mount Zion is the heart of Zaphon' (Dahood), 'far in the north' (Kraus), '"the extreme north"' (Weiser), 'like the farthest reaches of the north' (NEB).

Perhaps neither of these objections is insuperable, but they are reinforced by the unsuitability of the language used to Zion and Jerusalem. נוֹף is connected with the Arabic root *nafa*, meaning 'to overtop,' and means 'height' (cf. נָפָה, Josh. 11:2; 12:23; I Kgs. 4:11). יָפֶה normally means 'beautiful' in Hebrew, but 'also goes back upon the root *y-p* . . . which means 'to tower forth, be high' (Delitzsch); it is used of the size of Pharaoh's cows (Gen. 41:2) and of the branches of a cedar (Ezek. 31:3). But whether we translate 'Fair in height,' as I have suggested, or 'Outstanding in height,' the stress is upon the *height*, and height is a matter in which Zion does not excel.[10] The hills stand about Jerusalem (125:2), and Zion is less high than several neighbouring hills, including the Mount of Olives. In the latter days the mountain of Yahweh's house would be established high over the hills (Isa. 2:2), but for the present age it was very unremarkable, and an expression such as 'fair in height' looks foolish—hence RV/RSV's pussyfooting 'beautiful in elevation.' By contrast the mountain on which Dan is built, Hermon, outsoars the highest other mountain in Israel by three times, and the expression could have been made for it.

The same is true of the phrase ירכתי צפון in v. 2b. It occurs four times elsewhere in the OT: three times in Ezekiel's last battle (Ezek. 38:6, 15; 39:2), and once in Isa. 14:13. In the Ezekiel passages the reference is to the 'uttermost parts of the north' geographically, the north coast of modern Turkey, whence the hordes of Gomer and Togarmah will make their incursion against Israel. In Isaiah it is to the king of Babylon, whose ambition it has been to exalt his throne above the stars of God, and to 'sit upon the mount of congregation, in the uttermost parts of the north'—that is upon the mountain of the gods, whose position in the north derives ultimately, according to Gunkel, from Mount Ararat to the north of the Mesopotamian plain, or according to many modern commentators, to the ancient Canaanite mountain of Baal, Mount Zaphon or Casius, rising steeply to 5,300 ft twenty-five miles NE of Ugarit.[11] Now neither of these uses is at all suitable to Zion. Geographically, so far from being in the uttermost parts of the north, Zion is not even in the extreme north of the kingdom of Judah, which claimed most of the territory of Benjamin. Theologically, the point about Isaiah's mountain of the gods is that it is a very *high* mountain, where the king will sit on his throne above the stars of God. We do not need to suppose that Isaiah thought of the mountain as on an unknown promontory three hundred miles away, but it is plain that he did not identify it with Zion. Hermon however is, to an Israelite, an extremely high mountain, and it does happen to lie on the farthest northern frontier of Israel, a meaning testified for ירכתים (Gen. 49:13). So there is a second expression which does not suit Zion, but is apt for Hermon.[12]

I would suggest therefore that the original text in Dan was as follows:

> Great is the LORD, and highly to be praised: in the city of our God.

His holy mountain is fair in height: the joy of the whole
earth.

In Hermon, the frontiers of the north: is the city of the great
King.

We should thus have a metre approximating to the rest of the psalm, as
in RSV. The second verse would coincide with the Hebrew line, and
would give good sense, since Hermon is 'fair in height.' In the third line
we can do no more than conjecture what was the original for which the
Jerusalem version הר־ציון was substituted. It could have been הר־חרמון
or even הר־מועד as in Isa. 14:13. The line makes better sense with an
initial ב, which could have dropped out by assimilation to the כ in the
preceding line. ארמון in v. 3 means a citadel,[13] in this case a tower
projecting from the walls of Dan. Standing on its steep mound,
surmounted by formidable stonework defences, and overshadowed by
the enormous bulk of Hermon soaring into the northern sky, the city
has not been taken for more than a century, far beyond living memory.
No, says the voice of faith, nor ever will; it is God who has displayed his
invincible power in its unscalable fastness.

48:4 For, lo, the kings assembled themselves,
 They passed the border (עברו) together.
 5 They saw it, then were they amazed;
 They were dismayed, they were stricken with terror.
 6 Trembling took hold of them there;
 Pain, as of a woman in travail.
 7 With the east wind [RV text] thou breakest
 The ships of Tarshish.

Interpreters divide over 48 in the same way that we have seen them do
over 46 and 47. Older commentators favour a historical situation, such
as in the invasions defeated by Jehoshaphat (Delitzsch) or Sennacherib
(Kirkpatrick, and more recently Krinetzki[14] and Jacquet). Gunkel
thinks of the invasion as an eschatological event seen in the mind of the
poet, and the procession that follows is then made in imitation of the
custom of marching round one's city after raising of a siege. To
Dahood the kings are literary foils, and Kraus sees them similarly as
introduced in the mind of a single visionary, who is then answered by
the response of the community in vv. 8f. They are the historical form of
the attack on Yahweh's foundation mountain by the powers of chaos,
and the mention of them precedes an act of worship of the God whom
they cannot defy with impunity. Rogerson and Mackay take this a step

further with the procession also as a mental tour. Anderson follows Mowinckel, Weiser and Eaton in setting the psalm in the Jerusalem autumn festival.

I would prefer to see the psalm as a part of the autumn festival at Dan, while still allowing for the possibility of a real origin in history. 48 has been substituted for 87 in the festal sequence, and this will not be for no reason; the element in 48 which is missing from 87 is the invasion and flight of the kings, while in the latter even Egypt and Babylon are enrolled among Yahweh's worshippers. Thus 48 is still confident, but it is not so confident as 87. We may think of the troubled times around 800; or more likely of 732, when the Assyrians took 'Ijon and Abel-Beth-Maacah, and Janoah, and Kedesh, and Hazor, and Gilead, and Galilee, all the land of Naphtali'—but Dan is not mentioned (II Kgs. 15:29). Tiglath-Pileser, the great king, the king of Assyria (II Kgs. 18:19, 28), boasted, 'Are not my princes all of them kings?' (Isa. 10:8). It has sometimes been thought (e.g. by Gunkel) that Yahweh's title, 'the great king' (v. 2), owes something to the extravagance of the Assyrian monarch.[15] The Assyrians brought client-kings and their detachments with them too: 'Assyria also is joined with them; They have been an arm to the children of Lot' (83:6-8).

עבר is used of crossing a frontier in Jg. 11:29 and II Kgs. 8:21, and that is no doubt intended here: the kings have trespassed on God's land. Their discomfiture is described in a crescendo of amazement, dismay and terror, which no doubt owes everything to pious rhetoric. It takes place before Dan: 'Trembling took hold of them there,' that is at the holy city which has dominated the first verses of the psalm, and which is the last place mentioned. The raising of sieges was a not uncommon feature of ancient warfare—compare the siege of Samaria in II Kgs. 7, or of Jerusalem in II Kgs. 19—when the feeding of large armies over long periods might be a problem, and coups at home a threat; but the sudden, unexplained withdrawal of an undefeated invader must seem to the besieged a patent proof of the action of their God. The turning-point is described in the laconic phrase, 'They saw' (without object in the Hebrew). Many commentators, like Gunkel and Kraus, suppose that a 'theophany' is intended, citing as parallel 77:16, 'The waters saw thee, O God; the waters saw thee, they were in pain.' Another text might be 97:4ff, which we have seen to have special links with 48 by virtue of its position in the series of psalms in Book IV: 'The earth saw and trembled . . . all the people have seen his glory.' Such passages suggest God's display of himself in the storm. In 77 we have to do with the Exodus: 'Thou hast with thine arm redeemed thy people, The sons of Jacob and Joseph' (v. 15). The waters 'see' God because of the rain (v. 17a), thunder (v. 17b), lightning (v. 17c, 18b) and whirlwind (v. 18a), and divide to let Israel through (v. 20). In 97 similarly there is storm-cloud (v. 2), lightning (vv. 3f) and thunder (vv. 5-6a). But there is no sign of any such action of God in 48. Rather, the kings are understood to have been seized with panic 'there,' before Dan, overwhelmed by the majestic power of God evinced by his formidable city on its mighty mountain. 97 is likely to be a later counterpart to 48, with a thunder-storm added as something for earth and the nations to see. We need to beware of the assumption (especially as it is so fashionable and widespread) that all conflicts such as that described in vv. 4-6 are 'mythological,' and that enquiry into possible settings is out of date. Mythological battles and deliverances were exemplified in real life situations, and the language and lively spirit of thankfulness in 48 are best explained by the raising of a real historical siege.

It is easier to see the general sense of v. 7 than to be sure of its particular point. Yahweh's power is shown alike in confounding invading kings and in wrecking the ocean-going argosies which proudly ride his waves. Ships of Tarshish are symbols of pride in Isa. 2:16 and Ezek. 27:25, and the east wind is the sirocco, Yahweh's instrument of destruction, in Ezek. 27:26; Isa. 27:8; etc. Perhaps the change of tense to the imperfect in v. 7 signifies that such shipwrecks occur frequently. The Ezekiel references associate the east wind and the ships of Tarshish with Tyre, and Hermon is due east of Tyre; so the connection of thought could be that Yahweh will turn back the invaders on the one side as easily as he wrecks the arrogant shipmen on the other. But it may also be that a particular dramatic storm is in mind, and here one can only speculate. Perhaps the Assyrians impressed one or other of the Phoenician cities to transport soldiers and supplies by sea; and the hostile fleet, as at Artemisium, was destroyed in a storm. Such a proposal can only be a guess, but has the merit of setting v. 7 in the military context of vv. 4-6, 8-10.[16]

48:8 As we have heard, so have we seen
       In the city of the LORD of hosts, in the city of our God:
       God will establish it for ever.   [Selah

9 We have ratified (רמינו) thy lovingkindness, O God,
    In the midst of thy temple.
10 As is thy name, O God,
    So is thy praise unto the ends of the earth:
    Thy right hand is full of righteousness.

The difficulty of these verses is the verb רמינו. דמה pi'el has two meanings, according to BDB: to liken, i.e. to consider to be like, compare (Isa. 40:18, 25; 46:5; Cant. 1:9; Lam. 2:13); and to imagine, form an idea, devise, think, intend (Num. 33:56; Jg. 20:5; II Sam. 21:5; Isa. 10:7; 14:24; Ps. 50:21; Est. 4:13). Neither meaning seems *prima facie* to make good sense, and most translators have opted either for a minimising version (e.g. RV, RSV, 'thought on,' JB 'reflect upon'), or for a bold liturgical extension of meaning (e.g. NEB 'we re-enact the story'). The former is philologically weak, since the notion of forming images, which is central to דמה, is almost lost, and it is contextually feeble if silent, internal, individual meditation is suggested. But Mowinckel's proposal, that the 'contemplation' took the form of a drama of fighting games,[17] seems worse; Jacquet is right that there is no parallel for such a translation, and no evidence of any fighting dramatic representation. Gunkel is surely right, therefore, in going back to the primary meaning of the word, 'to compare.' Both v. 8 and v. 10 offer comparisons, and v. 9 says so. In v. 8 the comparison is between what the community has heard and what it has seen; in v. 10 between God's name, i.e. his reputation, and his world-wide acclaim. Gunkel's only weakness is that he has to postulate a connection in thought with the oracles of the prophets, which are not mentioned.

It is here that again the view proposed of the significance of the Selah (pp. 102ff) comes to the rescue. Just as in earlier psalms Selah seemed to coincide with the need for recital of a section of national tradition, to which reference is implied, so here. Year after year the community has 'heard' the sacred stories publicly recited (cf. 44:1), and it has 'seen' God's promises in those stories come true. Here stands the holy city of Dan unviolated on its holy mountain, and inviolable for ever. What the kings 'saw' and fled before, we have seen, and know our faith to be justified. The promise is stated immediately before the Selah: 'God will establish it for ever.' Exactly the same promise in the same recital is implied in 48's counterpart and predecessor, 87: 'Glorious things are spoken of thee, O city of God . . . the Most High himself shall establish her' (vv. 3, 5). We have *hieroi logoi* preserved for us in the Bible for Jerusalem, and for

Shechem, Bethel and other ancient shrines. The hostility of the Deuteronomists has caricatured the foundation legend of Dan (Jg. 17f), and the guarantee of Yahweh that must once have been part of it, but it was not suppressed altogether. It is this story, and the original oracle of Yahweh that was its climax, that constituted the 'glorious things' spoken of Dan, its permanent establishment as God's dwelling-place; and it is this which was 'heard' each year.

When the tradition has been recited (Selah), the psalmist comments on it, taking up from v. 8 the thread of seeing fulfilled what we have heard. God's guarantee of his city is part of his חסר, his covenant-love (v. 9), which Israel had looked forward to his 'commanding' day by day as the pilgrims approached the end of their march (42:8). The community has compared fact with promise, and knows the latter to be true, because the centre and focus of the whole celebration is the Dan shrine, the temple, which is standing there before their eyes. The shrine, like all ancient temples, is a comparatively small building, into which only a very few people could go. Perhaps the king and his council went in and heard the story recited by the priest, while other sons of Korah told it to the thronged people on the hillside. היכל naturally means the temple building, not the courts, the bamah; and בקרב means inside. Since the whole people could not go inside the temple (or for that matter inside the bamah), they compare, or ratify, God's lovingkindness in person of their representatives. The thought is continued in v. 10. God's name, his reputation as a God of salvation, which has been laid on the line in his guarantee, answers to his praise throughout the world. Invading armies, now turned back, exalt him with awe. He is full of righteousness—that is, he is as good as his promise.

> 48:11 Let mount Zion be glad,
>   Let the daughters of Judah rejoice,
>   Because of thy judgements.
> 12 Walk about Zion, and go round about her:
>   Tell the towers thereof.
> 13 Mark ye well her bulwarks,
>   Traverse her citadels (ארמנותיה),
>   That ye may tell (it to) the generation following,
> 14 That this is God [RSV].
>   Our God (is) for ever and ever:
>   He will be our guide over (על) death.

97:8 runs, 'Zion heard and was glad, And the daughters of Judah rejoiced; Because of thy judgements, O LORD'; and some MSS and versions make 48:11 even closer, with an 'And' and 'O LORD.' If we accept an original setting for 48 in Dan, we can account for the similarity in two ways. Either 48 was written in its present form, only that 'Hermon' and 'Jacob' stood for 'Zion' and 'Judah' in v. 11, and 'Dan' for 'Zion' in v. 12; the amendments were then made when the psalm was adapted for Jerusalem worship, and 97:8 was written to take up the theme. Or 48 had an original shorter text:

10c-11a Thy right hand is full of righteousness: Let Hermon be glad.
    12 Walk about Dan, and go round about her: Tell the towers thereof.

V. 11bc will then have been incorporated from 97:8, on the strength of the similarity of 'Let Zion be glad' / 'Zion heard and was glad.' The second option is preferable: the present rhythm breaks the dominant 3:2 pattern, which is preserved if v. 10c is coupled with v. 11a (Gunkel, Anderson).

For the various features of the defensive structure of an Israelite fortress see de Vaux, 232-5. The 'towers' and 'citadels' are probably synonymous, and the bulwarks (חילה) are the connected wall between them.[18] Biran estimates that the walls rose to a height of twelve metres above the plain;[19] that is 40ft, an impressive height. These fortifications, together with an inexhaustible water supply, enabled Dan, alone of north Israelite cities, to survive the onslaught of Tiglath-Pileser's invasion in 732 (II Kgs. 15:29). Since it was after this disaster that 42-43 were substituted for 84, and 44 for 85 (see above, pp.87f), we have to reckon seriously with the possibility that 48 was substituted for 87 at the same time. Liturgies tend to be conservative, and it takes a major upheaval to change them; 732 was upheaval enough to introduce 42-44, and we do not want to postulate another. Besides, 732 fits the situation very well: it gives an occasion when the kings gathered and crossed the frontier together, and eventually withdrew without apparent human cause; and it provides an admirable reason for celebrating the strength of the city's walls, and for believing them to be impregnable through divine 'righteousness.'

Eaton thinks that the psalm will have been sung before the procession, but this is not necessary. 45, for example, was clearly sung in the evening (Chapter 5), but it opens with imperatives that must refer to ceremonies earlier in the day: 'Gird thy sword . . . ride on . . .' It seems easier to think that Yahweh commanded his lovingkindness in the daytime, with a suitable ritual for each day, and that in the night his song was with Israel (42:8). The circumambulation has received widely different interpretations. Gunkel thinks that it was a thanksgiving, Kraus that it was a celebration of the city's impregnability, Kissane that it was an inspection, Eaton that it was a carrying of the blessing of the temple into the fields. The only parallels in Israelite liturgy are the sevenfold procession round Jericho, and the procession round Jerusalem in two halves from south to north under Nehemiah (Neh. 12:31-43). The Jericho procession, as the story stands, is magic; Nehemiah's procession was understood by the Chronicler as a thanksgiving. A 732 setting would settle the matter. Like Nehemiah, Hoshea is leading a thanksgiving for divine deliverance, the miraculous preservation of God's city in face of overwhelming human enemies. He has come mourning to Dan through the ruins of once populous Naphtali (42-43), and has lamented his armies' defeat (44). But Dan never fell, her fortifications were too much even for the self-styled Great King of Assyria; and in place of the old celebration of God's covenant for the city, a new thanksgiving hymn is composed, with a reference to the day's thanksgiving march.[20]

The 732 setting is confirmed by the last lines of the psalm, which, like vv. 1f and vv. 10f, show signs of dislocation. They run, with the RV translation of the MT arrangement:

> 48:14 That ye may tell it to the generation following. 15 For this God
>
> Is our God for ever and ever: He will be our guide
> (Even) unto death.

The last phrase עַל־מוּת is difficult, and has been extruded from the rhythmical sequence. LXX(A) read עוֹלָמוֹת, which is followed by RSV, NEB and many commentators. The position of the phrase has suggested to others that it should be taken with the heading of 49, and read עַל־עֲלָמוֹת, as in the heading of 46 (or cf. the heading of 9). LXX(B) suppresses the whole phrase. The Jewish tradition (j Meg. ii.4) hesitated between the LXX(A) interpretation, and the options 'in youthfulness' and 'like virgins.' Mowinckel,[21] Johnson,[22] Eaton and others have seen a reference to Mot, the Canaanite god of the underworld, who was overcome by Baal each autumn, though so explicit a taking over of the Canaanite polytheistic myth would be unique. But if the psalm were written in the aftermath of 732 these embarrassments do not arise. Israel may indeed rejoice that her sacred city has proved impregnable, and each man needs to lay her massive defences to heart; so will he be able to tell his children at home that this is God (RSV, retaining the Hebrew line) who has saved us. But more than this is necessary after the disasters of the Assyrian invasion, in which God 'covered us with the shadow of death' (44:19) and we were 'killed all the day long' (44:22). Dan's deliverance assures us that God is there permanently, and that he will lead our armies next year to victory over death: 'Our God is for ever and ever: He will be our guide over death.' נהג is used of leading armies in I Chron. 20:1; II Chron. 25:11. Delitzsch approved the translation 'over death,' but thought the idea of surviving personal death too surprising in a pre-exilic psalm. But personal eternal life is not the question; the death over which the psalmist hopes to be led is death in—and after—battle.

There is more textual interference in 48 than in most of the psalms we have considered hitherto, but the traces of the dislocation are there in the MSS, and the Dan hypothesis provides a motivation for the changes; indeed, in vv. 1f it is not possible to give a sensible meaning to the text as it stands without some such theory. The words of the psalm give us again a clear indication of the central rite of the day, the procession round the city, and add substance to the general theory I am proposing: that the circumambulation was the rite of 18th Bul, the fourth day of a festival whose psalmody survives in its 732 order. That date provides an explanation for the kings' invasion and retreat, for the joy and triumph in the city's impregnability, for the reference to God as the great King, and for his leading his people over death; and it accounts for the ousting of an older *Danslied*, 87, to which we now turn.

87 is a pair to 48 as a hymn of God's city, in the same way that 42-3 and 84 were pilgrimage psalms, and 44 and 85 were national laments; there is no other psalm in the main Korah sequence so close to 87, not even 46, where the theme of God's city is confined to vv. 4f. The עיר אלהים (v. 3) is the theme of the whole of 87, as עיר אלהינו (vv. 1, 8) is of 48. Both psalms open with a reference to its standing on the holy mountain(s); both mention the divine oracle which has been spoken (87:3)/heard (48:8) of the city; and both specify this oracle as 'the Most High shall establish her' (87:5)/'God will establish it for ever' (48:8).

87 has other links with other psalms in the main sequence. Its welcome of foreign nations as among those who know Yahweh recalls the princes of the peoples who are gathered as the people of the God of Abraham in 47:9. But this similarity is to be accounted for as belonging

to the same period of composition, as the differences from 48 are to be accounted for by the difference of political fortunes. In the middle of the ninth century Israel was a powerful country, and Solomon's empire was still remembered; foreign nations were welcome at its festal worship as tributaries, and to honour its king. But the subject-matter of 87 is the same as that of 48, and its place in the supplement is no doubt due to the crisis that supervened in the late 730's. After that it seemed less pertinent to expect Egypt and Babylon with their tribute; more to the point to thank God for the recent miraculous deliverance. So 48 was composed, and used in the last year(s) of Dan's greatness; and in its adapted form could be used to express the same feelings after the raising of the siege of Jerusalem in 701. 87 was relegated to the supplement.

Eusebius described 87 as 'extremely enigmatic and darkly uttered,' and the commentaries are a testimony to this. Of the more restrained, Weiser permits himself two transpositions of half-verses and a repointing; Dahood four repointings; Jacquet three versional readings, a repointing, three words emended and a half-verse transposed. But since the last century it has been thought proper to go much further than this, and to shuffle the verses like a pack of cards. Gunkel, for instance, follows Hugo Gressmann with the order 1a, 2, 1b, 5c, 7, 3, 6, 4c, 4ab, 5ab, and we find similar (but different) rearrangements in Kraus, Wanke, and NEB. But such drastic measures still do not resolve the problems of the text; NEB is driven to conjecture six further 'probable readings,' one of which is partly justified by G, and five of which require alterations to the consonants. Emendations on this scale need to be justified by some hypothesis as to how they have come about, and Gunkel solves the matter by positing 'a sleeping copyist.'[23] If we have to reckon with sleeping copyists, expositors certainly have to expect nightmares.

I do not see how such violence can be called exegesis. It has to be conceded that our present text raises problems which cannot be solved on the supposition that it is what the psalmist originally wrote; but the reader can only have confidence in the exposition if proposed changes account for the state of the present more difficult text. This can in fact be achieved on the same hypothesis that I have been suggesting for 48. 87, like 48, was originally a *Danslied*, which in time was taken south and amended to become a *Zionslied*, which it now is. This involved the (rather clumsy) addition of three phrases, 'the gates of Zion,' 'with Ethiopia' and 'Yea, of Zion,' and the repointing of two verbs to give grammatical (but not substantial) sense; one repeated verb has been dropped from v. 7 in consequence of these changes, and both the rhythm and the meaning have suffered. Such a theory is plausible in itself, and it enables us to reconstruct the original form of the psalm without the 'heavy heart' which Gunkel owns to; it is possible to see both the writer and the adapter as intelligent and reasonable people, and also awake. It is not surprising that it is with 48 and 87 that we have suddenly for the first time had to suppose alteration of the text; they were the two Dan hymns on the city of God, and so required alteration if they were to be used at Jerusalem. It is not necessary to propose transpositions, which are draconian remedies.

87   A Psalm of the sons of Korah; a Song.
  1   His foundation in the holy mountains the LORD loveth,
      [even the gates of Zion]
  2   More than all the dwellings of Jacob.
  3   Glorious things are spoken of thee, O city of God. [Selah

87 is a Song, that is a triumphal hymn, such as the Danite priest looked forward to singing each night of the feast (42:8); and Isaiah spoke of such Songs as a nightly feature of the festival (30:29). It is also a מזמור, that is, it is accompanied by much strumming upon stringed instruments, like 47 and 48. The music is implied in the body of the psalm by חללים in v. 7, which is usually interpreted as 'dancing' (Delitzsch, Gunkel, et al.), but by G and RVmg as 'the players on instruments' (G 'flutes'); in either case there will be music, though the former rendering is better, and suits the strings. It is noticeable that the customary 'For the Chief Musician' is missing both here and in the heading of 48, and it would be a remarkable coincidence for this to have happened to the two Dan hymns, and them only, by accident. I suppose that they were composed and sung at Dan just like the other Korah psalms, but lost the heading in view of their adaptation by other hands at Jerusalem; 89, which has been much more extensively adapted, also lacks it. There is no note of location for the same reason as in 48: the *Tanzprozession* (v. 7, Gunkel) began and ended at the normal place, the bamah. It passed through the city, round the walls, and came back through the gates to its starting point.

As the text stands, the first verse consists of the words 'His-foundation (is) on-mountains-of-holiness,' followed by a stop. This involves a severe strain both on the rhythm and the grammar. V. 2, in its present form, has a 4:3 rhythm, and the present arrangement leaves v. 1 marooned as a two-stress half-verse. Further, if v. 1 is a sentence on its own, there is no referent for 'His'—hence the beginning of NEB's emendations. RVmg and many commentators opt accordingly to move the stop, thus resolving in part both the rhythmical and the syntactical difficulty: 'His-foundation on-mountains-of-holiness Yahweh loves.' The psalm then opens with a half-verse of four stresses, and the prefixed object is syntactically normal. I have no doubt that this solution is correct, but it is important to notice that it involves three further difficulties. First, we have now obtained four stresses in the first half-verse at the price of five in the second: 'the-gates-of Zion more-than-all the-dwellings-of Jacob.' Second, the phrase 'the gates of Zion' is nowhere evidenced as a periphrasis for Jerusalem *tout court*. Jacquet says it is synecdoche, the part for the whole, and gives parallel references: but some of these involve the expression 'within the/thy gates' (Deut. 5:14; Ps. 122:2), some 'possess the gates of your enemies' (Gen. 22:19; 24:60), and others judging (Deut. 16:18) or praising God (Ps. 9:14) in the gates. In none of these cases is 'gates' the same as 'city.' A city is within its gates, and the gates are a significant part of the city, in that he who possesses the gates controls it, and public activities like lawsuits (Ruth 4:1ff; Job 29:7) and religious gatherings (Neh. 8:1) took place there. But in 87:1 'the gates of Zion' means the city itself. Third, we are obliged to suggest some reason why Jewish tradition, in the versions as well as the Hebrew, should have misplaced the stop.

An answer to these problems (and to others later in the psalm) is provided by the suggestion that 87, like the other Korah psalms, originated in Dan, and was domesticated in later centuries in Jerusalem. The phrase 'the gates of Zion' was not in the Dan version, and the opening verse had a 4:3 rhythm of unexceptionable meaning: Yahweh loves his foundation on the sacred mountains more than all the sanctuaries in Israel—Dan on Hermon is the great national shrine. After 722 the meaning was not quite so unexceptionable, especially in view of the give-away plural 'mountains,' which does not sound like Zion;[24] so a gloss was added to give respectability. 'City of Zion' was too close to 'city of God' in v. 2, so the clumsy 'the gates of Zion,' familiar from the common phrase 'in/within the/thy gates' was inserted instead. But this now made an overloaded verse, so a second maladroit change was made, moving the stop back so as to start the sentence with אהב.

Such a proposal not only explains the state of the text; it also accounts for the 'mythological' motifs noted by Kraus and others— only instead of assuming their importation from pre-Israelite ideas, we have the smoother hypothesis of their adoption from an earlier Israelite psalm from another sanctuary. The 'sacred mountains' can then be the Hermon range, which is often found in the plural—'the Hermons' (42:6), 'the mountains' (46:2f), 'the mountain of summits . . . the mountain of Bashan' (68:15); and 'his foundation' will be the same, since it is Hermon, three times the height of the other Palestinian mountains, which alone answers to the Hebrew concept of the massive pile on which the world is built, washed about by the infernal ocean. Later on such ideas could be transferred to Zion in view of its divine election; but it is to Hermon, and to Dan, the shrine on Hermon, that they naturally belong. It is in view of this majestic height (48:2) that Yahweh clearly gives preference to Dan over all the other משכנות of Jacob, all the other shrines where it is allowed that he dwells (שכן) in the land. The same root is used in 43, 46 and 84 of the sanctuary at Dan itself, and must certainly refer to other approved shrines:[25] and this itself makes an early date plain, before centralisation became an issue.

I have argued above (pp.102ff) that v. 3, 'Glorious things are spoken of thee, O city of God. [Selah' should be understood as an introduction to the recital (Selah) of the sanctuary legend at Dan. The statements that God loves Dan the best, and later, that he will establish her for ever, do not rest upon vacuous optimism; they are implied by the shining destiny of the city which has been spoken by God himself, and is now to be heard by the whole community (48:8). Just as there were sanctuary-legends for Jerusalem and other shrines, so there must have been for Dan, and v. 3 and 48:8, each followed by Selah, are open evidence of its recital on 18th Bul. We have to reconstruct the outline of the Dan legend from Jg. 17f, in the way that I have proposed in Chapter 3. No doubt it told of Jonathan, Moses' grandson, of the Korahite Levites, of the migration from Bethlehem, and of the silver ephod; but the 'glorious things' have been carefully suppressed by the Deuteronomistic revisers. They have to be inferred from the text of the two psalms, and must have included at least the guarantee of permanent establishment, since this is stated alike in 48:8c and 87:5b. From parallel legends like that at Ophrah in Jg. 6, or at Jerusalem in II

Sam. 7, we might suppose that such a promise was made in a theophany to Jonathan. This seems a much easier interpretation of 'glorious things' than the view of Anderson and others that they refer to the 'oracle' of v. 4; in which case the city's greatness, described in vv. 1-3, is known before the oracle is given. The נכברות are thought of as a single promise, and are followed by the singular verb מדבר (cf. Gen. 27:29; Isa. 16:8).

87:4 I will declare (אזכיר) Egypt and Babylon as among them
      that know me:
      Behold, Philistia and Tyre, [with Ethiopia]
      This one was born there.
   5 [Yea, of Zion] Each man shall say (יאֱמֶר אִישׁ וְאִישׁ), He was
      born in her;
      And the Most High himself shall establish her.
   6 The LORD shall declare (יִסְפֹּר) when he writeth down
      (כתוב) the peoples,
      This one was born there.   [Selah

Almost all the commentators, following the text, draw a picture of Yahweh making a register of the peoples, and declaring them to be born in Zion. RV has no comma after 'Behold' in v. 4b. Philistia, etc. are thus in the accusative, and 'This one' refers to these peoples, one by one (not without some strain on the syntax). This enables the same meaning to be given to the last phrase as in v. 5a and v. 6b. In the Hebrew of v. 5a the verb is pointed יֵאָמֵר and אִישׁ וְאִישׁ is the subject of 'was born': 'Yea, of Zion it shall be said, This one and that one was born in her.' Often, e.g. by Gunkel, Kraus, Anderson, Jacquet and NEB, recourse is had to the Greek to strengthen and clarify this view of v. 5a. G opens the verse Μητὴρ Σιων and it is supposed that אם has dropped out of the Hebrew; indeed, Jacquet calls it the 'terme-clef' of the psalm, and Kraus heads the psalm, 'Zion nenne ich Mutter,' although this phrase does not occur in the Greek, let alone in the Hebrew. In v. 6a MT points יִסְפֹּר, 'he shall count': Yahweh is making a register of the peoples born in Zion. This is supported by a variant in both Hebrew and other traditions, בְּכְתָב, ἐν γραφῇ; there is the register actually mentioned.

We cannot but agree with Eusebius: 'very enigmatic and darkly spoken.' There is no parallel in the OT for the thought of heathen nations being born in Zion, and the interpretation of this expression as their becoming proselytes is far from obvious. The attempt of Gunkel,

Kraus and others to escape this by making Rahab mean the Israelites domiciled in Egypt, etc., is a manifest forcing of the words. It is not clear how one can enumerate five peoples in v. 4ab and then understand זֶה in v. 4c to refer to each of them in turn. V. 5a is overladen with five stresses; and it presents a further exegetical problem, for (according to the commentators) זֶה in v. 4b and v. 6b refers to the *peoples* as being born in Zion, while v. 5a says that אִישׁ וְאִישׁ was born in her. Kirkpatrick and others take the context to be determinative, and compel the latter phrase to mean 'each and every nation'; for Kraus and others it is the countries which have been compelled to mean the Israelite diaspora, and אִישׁ וְאִישׁ can mean all righteous Israelites. Furthermore G is a broken reed with which to shore up this rickety structure. The rendering of v. 7 shows the translator to have been of limited intelligence and knowledge of Hebrew. He twice supplies 'and' in v. 4b to cover his misunderstandings, and in v. 4c and v. 6b he gives 'interpretations' which do not respect the Hebrew words. He seems to have changed מַעְיָנַי in v. 7 to מָעוֹן, κατοικία. So it looks as if the γραφή and Mother Zion may be part of the interpretative exercise also.[26]

It seems to me that there is not likely to be any satisfactory way out of so many impasses, and I should like therefore to propose what is, so far as I know, a new solution. The puzzling state of the text in v. 1 led us to the conclusion that 87 was a psalm written for worship at Dan, and afterwards adopted and adapted for worship at Jerusalem; we can only expect, then, that such a setting in life will have resulted in further adaptations in vv. 4-6. In v. 4 the Danite priest hails the coming time when all the world will come to join in the national worship, as he did in 46:8-10 and 47:9. He makes Yahweh speak, as at 46:10; and since we suspected there that the source of the oracle was the recital of part of the Jacob tradition in the Selah before 46:8, so may we think here that the first person is due to Yahweh's promise in the Dan-legend Selah immediately preceding. Yahweh will declare (make public mention of, the normal meaning of הַזְכִּיר) the world's major powers, Egypt and Babylon, to be among those who 'know,' i.e. acknowledge him. Babylon was the great power of the Tigris-Euphrates valley from early times (Gen. 11); its mention makes an early date likely, since Assyria became increasingly the dominant and all too familiar Mesopotamian power from the mid-ninth century until after the fall of Samaria.[27] Philistia and Tyre are lesser powers, lying respectively to the south-west and north-west of (northern) Israel (cf. Am. 1:6, 9); if the psalm had originated in Jerusalem, we might have expected Edom, Ammon or Moab rather than Tyre, which had no frontier with Judah (cf. the list of peoples in Zeph. 2). 'With Cush' comes in as an afterthought.[28] It is additional to the natural run of the words—Rahab and Babylon/Philistia and Tyre, with Cush—and turns the geographical balance southwards. It will be a Jerusalem addition, perhaps from the time of Zephaniah, who twice mentions the people (2:12; 3:10).

If we were interpreting v. 4 on its own, without regard to vv. 5f, it would never occur to us to take 'This one' as one of the peoples just mentioned. Who then might the 'This one' be? A crucial feature in the well-being of all peoples till modern times has been the birth of a prince to continue the royal dynasty. If this was greeted with such joy by the English people in the days of Henry VIII, how much more in ancient Israel, where civil war had been an even more constant experience in the tenth and early ninth centuries. In famous oracles Isaiah greets the birth of a Jerusalem prince: 'Thou hast increased their joy: they joy before thee according to the joy in harvest, as men rejoice when they divide the spoil . . . For unto us a child is born (ילד), unto us a son is given . . . Of the increase of his government and of peace there shall be no end' (9:3-7). There is national rejoicing at the birth of a prince who will rule Judah and extend his dominion indefinitely. 'Behold, the maiden is with child, and beareth a son . . .' (7:14); the prince's birth will itself be the sign of Judah's victory over her two powerful enemies. We have seen the same hope of the birth of princes in our own psalms at 45:16. How natural then if ילד means 'was born' in a straightforward literal sense, and if it refers to the birth of a first-born son to the Queen of Israel! The threefold 'He was born' would certainly express the joy of which Isaiah speaks.

But the stress is not on the birth alone, but on the fact that it has occurred 'there,' 'in her,' 'there.' Is it likely that the pregnant queen would have come to Dan for the birth, rather than staying comfortably in Samaria or Jezreel? It is very likely that she came to Dan each year, since 45's position in the Korah sequence should mean its regular festal use, and so the reconsecration of the king's marriage as well as of his reign in general, and I have argued the case for this above. Nor would her pregnancy be an objection, since she would presumably be carried in a state litter; and she might well conceive three months after her wedding, and so be delivered after a twelvemonth. This would not happen often; but then we are not supposing that it happened often. The psalmist's joy arises precisely from the rarity of the occasion, and so the good omen. זֶה, this new baby cradled in the queen's arms, has been born in the sacred city of Dan. Look, you Philistine and Tyrian nobles, he was born there! Of the increase of his government and of peace there shall be no end; even the mighty Egyptian and Babylonian empires will come to acknowledge Yahweh, and lay their tribute at the feet of his new-born anointed one. It is not an accident that the peoples mentioned in v. 4 are ordered as they are. God will declare Egypt and Babylon one day soon as among those who acknowledge him, but the neighbouring peoples of Tyre and Philistia are present now. Philistine leaders had been a part of David's entourage, and we have seen Tyrians present at the Israelite festival in 45; Tyre and Philistia were Israel's smaller and nearer neighbours, and they are the most likely of all peoples, with Ammon, to send their princes to be gathered as the people of the God of Abraham in the days of Israel's greatness. So they are in the vocative, 'Behold, Philistia and Tyre, This one was born there.'[29]

It would be no surprise if the Dan foundation-legend contained references to the king and his subjugation of the world, as well as to the permanence of the sanctuary. In the Jerusalem legend Solomon was to build a house for Yahweh's name, and Yahweh would establish the throne of his kingdom for ever; David's line would be God's sons (II Sam. 7:13f). In Ps. 2 Yahweh has set his king upon his holy hill of Zion with the decree, 'Thou art my son'; he will give him the nations for his inheritance, and the uttermost parts of the earth for his possession (vv. 6ff). We might be tempted by the parallel between 'He was born' and 'This day have I begotten thee (יְלִדְתִּיךָ),' but there is no echo of *divine* birth in 87. 'Born' should mean 'born,' and not anointed and enthroned.

We can avoid the overweight v. 5a and the problems outlined above on the same hypothesis: וּלְצִיּוֹן is a Jerusalem gloss, and the verb was originally pointed יֹאמַר. We then have אִישׁ וְאִישׁ as the subject of the main clause, 'Each man shall say, He was born in her,' yielding the same general sense as in v. 4 and v. 6, and a fine crescendo. First the visiting princes are bidden to behold; then everyone will confess it; finally Yahweh himself shall declare it, as he enters his worshippers of all lands in the book of life: his anointed was born in this, his beloved city. We have a similar crescendo in 48:5, 'amazed . . . dismayed . . . hasted away.' But in each case it is the city, not the king, which is the focus of attention, as it was in vv. 1-3 and will be in v. 7. The royal birth is the confirmation that 'the Most High himself shall establish her' (v. 5b); as at Jerusalem the divine choice of king and sanctuary go hand in hand.

In this way it seems that good sense can be made of a text very close to the obscure one we have; and equally important, the process of adaptation can be understood. It was natural for a Danite poet to glory in the birth of the crown prince in the sacred city, and this fact would be a cause for pride and rejoicing throughout the latter's life. But the psalm would be less apt after his death, and was later replaced by 48. Its strong tones of joy and confidence ensured its preservation in Jerusalem; but what meaning now could be attached to its middle verses? We see a process of interpretation and glossing begun then in the Hebrew and extended in the Greek. 'With Cush' was added to v. 4 so as to redress the balance geographically, and 'This one' was now understood to refer to one of the peoples mentioned; cf. G οὗτοι ἐγενήθησαν. In v. 5 a similar meaning is obtained by pointing יֵאָמֵר, 'Each man was born in her,' and this was prefaced with 'Yea, of Zion,' so as to clarify what 'in her' referred to. G again takes the interpreting a step further with 'Mother Zion.' So we have a picture of the peoples being born at Zion, and it seems natural to take יִסְפֹּר in the qal instead of the pi'el: Yahweh counts them instead of declaring to them that his prince was born in Dan. So finally, if he is counting them, he will need a כְּתָב, γραφή, instead of just writing them down.

> 87:7 And singing as well as dancing they ⟨shall declare⟩ [RV differs],
>   All my fountains are in thee.

The verse is defective in both Hebrew and versions: not only has the first colon only two stresses but it lacks a verb. Our theory of an adapted Dan hymn seems to resolve the problem of the text, and the often felt puzzlement over the fountains, more easily than others variously advanced.

If the Danite version included the verb יִסְפֹּרוּ, we should have both sense and a reason for its omission. The psalmist, with his taste for repetition, might well answer Yahweh's declaration in v. 6 with the people's declaration in v. 7. The peoples mentioned in v. 4, and again in v. 6, are now written down in Yahweh's book as acknowledging him, while he declares to them their prince's birth in Dan; and they in their turn respond by declaring that it is in Dan also that the waters rise that fructify their countries. This makes good sense because Dan is visibly the main source of the Jordan which waters the lands to the south of

Hermon; westwards flows the Litanus to Tyre, and eastward Abana and Pharpar, the rivers of Damascus, all from the same massif; and northwards the Orontes. Perhaps, indeed, Hermon is thought of as the holy mountain in the North from which all the world's waters flow (cf. Gen. 2:10; Ezek. 31:4). This suggestion also makes good sense of the *waw* with which the verse begins, and which is omitted by many translators, including RV, RSV and NEB: Yahweh makes his declaration to them, *and* they make theirs to him. It also gives the best sense to the participles, which should, as Delitzsch says, indicate 'not what those confessing are, but how they bear themselves when confessing.' It is not specialist Israelite singers and dancers who speak the words, but the now registered nations, singing as well as dancing. Each of those present (אִישׁ וְאִישׁ) declares, 'All *my* fountains . . .,' speaking for his nation. They sing their praise as well as dancing in the great procession round the town walls (48:12f).

But what is the Jerusalem adapter to make of this? His Yahweh has been counting the peoples, not declaring anything, and it is hardly to be thought—at least before Ezek. 47 was written—that the nations would ever associate Jerusalem with abundant water. The Hebrew accordingly omits יְסַפֵּר, leaving the verb to be understood from שָׁרִים, and letting the rhythm go hang; after which chaos prevails, some MSS with the Greek and Syriac interpreting the last as שָׂרִים, princes, while the latter versions amend 'fountains' to 'dwelling-place.'

The Jerusalem authorities made a burlesque of the foundation-legend of Dan; but the 48th and (especially) the 87th psalms enable us to make some conjecture of how it originally ran. The two Selahs in 87 suggest that it was told in two parts. The verse, 'Glorious things are spoken of thee, O city of God' precedes the first, and I have suggested above that this would be followed by an account of a theophany to Jonathan the grandson of Moses, Yahweh's acceptance of sacrifice at Dan, his guarantee of its 'establishment' and promise of universal worship there. The second is followed by the nations' praise of Dan for its gift of universal water, and here we may imagine a further oracle in which Yahweh promised an unfailing supply of spring-water for all nations from his holy mountain, issuing forth beside his shrine. We have later versions of just such an oracle in Zech. 14:8 and Ezek. 47:1-12, but transferred to arid Jerusalem and to the prophetic future.

THE NADIR OF THE FEAST (Psalms 49, 88)

There is a very widespread consensus about the general interpretation of Ps. 49. It is, in this view, a Wisdom Poem; that is, unlike the prayers, laments and hymns which we have been considering, it is a didactic piece addressed not to God but to men, in which the moralist warns the wealthy of the emptiness of their values, and reassures himself and God's faithful poor, who are his fellows. They may be oppressed by the rich at the present time, but death is the great leveller, and ultimately will reveal the vanity of wealth. The poor, however, has put his trust elsewhere, and God will preserve him. In this way, the riddle of life's apparent unfairness can be resolved; comparison is often made with the parables of the Rich Fool, and of Dives and Lazarus, in St Luke's Gospel. Up to this point there is (with—I think—the lone exception of Peters) unanimity among modern interpreters, and I shall refer to this understanding of the psalm as the consensus view.

It is not in the nature of things for consensus to last long, and unanimity breaks down over a crucial dilemma. What does the psalmist mean by 'But God will redeem my soul from the hand of Sheol: For he shall receive me'? The majority view, represented by Delitzsch, Duhm, Schmidt, Kraus, Weiser, J. van der Ploeg,[1] von Rad,[2] Eaton, Anderson, Rogerson and McKay, and Jacquet, take this to be a first groping statement of the survival of death. Without this claim the words can only be a reassurance that the poor will not die a premature death. But this is not said, and if it is intended it is banal, 'trivial,' and 'very unsatisfying.' Furthermore it is untrue because the poor commonly do die prematurely, a fact familiar to the Israelites from the teachings of Jeremiah and Job, as well as from observation; and also to the author of the psalm, who himself notes that 'wise men die, The fool and the brutish together perish' (v. 10)—presumably the 'wise' are the same as the God-fearing. There is also some discomfort over the contrast between the weighty proem and such an interpretation of the positive message. Even Mowinckel (who supports it) owns to 'a certain disproportion between this pretentious introduction and the conventionality of the solution of the "riddle".[3] The majority therefore understand redemption from Sheol as eternal life with God. Bolder spirits, like Delitzsch, take 'receive me' (קחני) to mean God's 'taking' the psalmist direct to heaven, like Enoch and Elijah; contemporary commentators usually prefer to leave the precise thought here vague—should we not expect vagueness when so great an assertion is first being attempted?

Although this 'eternal life' option has been canvassed for a long time, there has been a persevering minority view that rejects it, including the formidable names of Kirkpatrick, Gunkel and Mowinckel.[4] They observe that almost the same phraseology as 49:15 is to be found in Hos. 13:14, 'shall I *ransom* them (אפדם) *from the hand of Sheol?* Shall I redeem them (אגאלם) from death? O Death, where are your plagues?' (RSV); where the meaning is clearly concerned with preservation from ordinary, this-worldly death. Furthermore, the same or similar expressions are used in the first half of 49 itself with this meaning: 'None (of them) can by any means *redeem* (יפדה) his brother, Nor give to God a ransom for him (כפרו): For *the redemption of their soul* is costly (פדיון נפשם)' (vv. 7f). The hope of such redemption was 'That he should still live alway, That he should not see the pit' (v. 9). The eternal life interpretation thus involves taking the words in one sense in vv. 7ff and another in v. 15. Nor is this in any way required by 'For he shall receive me,' for Kirkpatrick points to a parallel use in 18:16 where the meaning is 'He shall deliver me (from earthly perils)'; and Gunkel cites parallels for translating 'For he shall take me from the hand of Sheol.' In any case the main theme of the psalm is not concerned with the writer's future hopes but with his present fears (vv. 5, 16), and Gunkel and others have thought v. 15 to be an interpolation. It does not matter that the psalm's solution to the great riddle is so flat, or the proem so grandiloquent; the books of Job and Ecclesiastes are full of similarly impressive truisms.

A corollary of the Wisdom Poem view, for most representatives of both views of v. 15, is a late date. Wisdom literature (despite some recent hesitations[5]) is usually taken to be post-exilic, and that is where Job and Ecclesiastes seem to belong. The poor, as a faithful, oppressed class, belong naturally between Trito-Isaiah and Luke, and it was difficult in this period to be wealthy and godly. If we take the eternal life option, a late date is obvious, because other hints of an escape from death, like Daniel and Isa. 26, are late. If we refuse it, then, as Mowinckel says, the stress is on the death of the powerful, not the salvation of the speaker, who becomes 'that most reflective and rationalistic author of the "wisdom" and problem psalm 49';[6] and rationalism is a late bloom. The late date is, however, dependent upon the consensus view, and is not evidenced by Aramaisms in the text, as there are in the Songs of Ascents, or by external evidence, as with Ps. 1.

It is difficult not to feel the force of the negative arguments on both sides of the controversy over v. 15. Gunkel and Mowinckel seem entirely justified in their claim that the text gives the frailest support to the eternal life view; but then it gives very little support to their own view either, quite apart from its character of *ridiculus mus*. The psalmist does not say that he is poor, and it is doubtful whether he says that he is oppressed—the evidence for this is limited to the difficult, often emended, text of v. 5. But this is but the beginning of pangs. Von Rad says that 49 contains 'enormous textual difficulties,'[7] and Gunkel that the text is 'stark verderbt.' *BHS* gives fifteen lines of *variae lectiones* and proposals for emendation. NEB confesses to fifteen emendations, almost all of consonants, and to transposing a line, as well as following G and other MSS on four occasions. (Not all of these changes are noted in the footnotes to the English translation.) Kraus accepts four variant readings, changes the vowels twice and makes seven conjectures with the consonants, as well as despairing completely of v. 14. I cite NEB and Kraus because the former is the work of a committee of respected scholars, some of whom had conservative tendencies, and the latter is a careful exegete who cannot be accused of wildness with the text. It would be easy to mention others who have gone to work with a hatchet. Now the point is that a considerable number of the proposed changes to the MT (including some in the versions) are proposed solely to make sense of the psalm on the consensus theory. A critical example is v. 7, 'None will by any means redeem his brother,' which is discussed below. This and other verses simply have to be changed if the Wisdom Poem theory is to stand. There are conservative exegetes like Delitzsch, and Rogerson and McKay, who desert the MT only with the greatest reluctance; but then proposals of emendation on this scale are made only because the interpretation demands it, and the price of faithfulness to the MT is straining the Hebrew. The fact is that no one, neither commentator nor reader, can feel any confidence in the exegesis when resort to conjecture and to *lectiones faciliores* approaches an average of one change per verse.

It is a bold thing to challenge a consensus; but a consensus is not worth much which contains an unresolved dilemma over v. 15, and which so uncomfortably fits the textual facts. I should like to suggest in its stead an interpretation which avoids the dilemma and which accepts the Massoretic text without change; and which sites the psalm, like the other Korah psalms, at Dan in the eighth century, in the evening worship of 19th Bul.

> 49 For the Chief Musician: a Psalm of the sons of Korah.
> 1 Hear this, all ye peoples;
>   Give ear, all ye inhabitants of the world:
> 2 Yea, ye sons of Adam, yea, ye sons of men
>   (גַּם־בְּנֵי אָדָם גַּם־בְּנֵי־אִישׁ),
>   Rich and poor together.
> 3 My mouth shall speak wisdom;
>   And the meditation of my heart shall be of understanding.
> 4 I will incline mine ear to a parable:
>   I will open my dark saying upon the harp.

The speaker is again the Danite priest; but this time the musical aspect of his oracle is stressed, not only by his psalm being a מִזְמוֹר, but by the mention of his harp (?zither) in v. 4. This psalm is not a joyful שִׁיר, but a word of warning addressed to 'all ye peoples,' 'all ye inhabitants of the world.' It is a mistake to draw a line between 49 and the earlier Korah psalms on the basis of this universal address; 46 closed with four verses of warning to the nations (v. 6), bidding them come, behold the destruction Yahweh has wrought of their armaments, and desist; and 47 opened with the identical address to 49, 'O clap your hands, *all ye peoples*.' In 47 the princes of the peoples were gathered at Israel's festival (v. 9), and it is easy to read 49:1 in the light of this. Micaiah ben Imlah similarly addressed his words before Ahab and his client-allies, 'Hear, ye peoples, all of you' (I Kgs. 22:28). The tone of 49 is darker than 46 or 47, but this is explicable in terms of the political situation, and does not require a Wisdom background. It is true that the author of Wisdom addresses his poetry, 'ye kings . . . ye judges of the ends of the earth' (6:1), in a vapid manner, but this is a continuation of an earlier way of speaking when kings and leaders of other countries really were present to hear the oracles of Israel's poets.

Traditionally בְּנֵי אָדָם and בְּנֵי־אִישׁ in v. 2 have been understood as a contrast, 'Both low and high' (RV). However, van der Ploeg has carefully examined the use of both phrases in the OT, and concludes that they are used interchangeably in normal contrast with God.[8] He does not support the understanding of בני־איש to mean 'men of high estate' in 4:3 or 62:9, and points to the double use of גם in Jg. 5:4 and Isa. 48:8 with a meaning 'Yea,' rather than 'Both ... and.' The contrast is not needed by the sense here: 'all the inhabitants of the world' are still taken together in v. 2a, their frailty being stressed beside the power of God to send them to Sheol (vv. 7ff). In v. 2b they are subdivided into the wealthy leaders and the poor commoners who follow them (v. 13). As in 46 and 47, and in 2:10ff, the speaker is thinking beyond the foreign delegations present to the really wealthy and powerful kings who are not present at Israel's celebration, and whose absence is a threat. It is to be noted that the rich and the poor addressed are world-wide, and are not the wealthy oppressors and the poor oppressed within Israel, who are the subject of the poem in the consensus theory.

As in 45, where the heart of the מנצח bubbled over with inspiration at the significance of the king's anointing and marriage, so here he feels the divine force behind his words. The strumming of the zither and the parallelism of the phrases tell him that he is transcending himself, divine truth making itself heard as when the minstrel played to Elisha (II Kgs. 3:15).[9] Both 'wisdom' and 'understanding' are in the plural, intensive plurals, for this is the many-sided wisdom of God (cf. Prov. 24:7; Isa. 27:11; 42:10; etc.), the understanding of Yahweh which searches to the end. His heart 'murmurs' (הגות) the profound message which comes to him from beyond, which he 'inclines his ear' to hear, and reveals ('opens') as the rhythm draws him on. This message is described as a 'parable' or 'dark saying,' neither of which has any more specific meaning than 'oracle.' They are used in combination in Ezek. 17:1, where they refer to the allegory of the eagle and cedar; in Hab. 2:6, of taunts; in Prov. 1:6, of proverbs; and in Ps. 78:2, of the tale of Israel's rebellions. The parable and dark saying of Hab. 2:6 are especially relevant, as they are words against a foreign aggressor, Assyria, in guise of a wealthy creditor who 'increaseth that which is not his' and 'ladeth himself with pledges.' The psalmist is not undertaking to solve a theological riddle, but simply to declare a word of God; and the introduction with its measured parallelism helps him to get into his stride.

49:5 Wherefore should I fear in the days of evil,
       When the iniquity of them that would supplant me com-
       passeth me about,

6 Even of them that trust in their power (חילם),
   And boast themselves in the multitude of their riches?
7 None (of them) shall by any means ransom (יפדה) his
   brother,
   Nor give to God a price for him (כפרו):
8 (For the ransom of their life (פדיון נפשם) is costly,
   And must be let alone for ever.)
9 That he should still live alway,
   That he should not see the pit.
10 Yea, he shall see it: wise men die,
   The fool and the brutish together perish,
   And leave their power (חילם) to others.

The divine message which all peoples have been called upon to hear is
the warning not to attempt to overthrow the Israelite monarchy and
state; for any such attempt will end in their death. The RVmg
translation is almost exemplary, and I have changed it only in small
details to bring out the force of the words. The speaker is the court
priest, and speaks for the king. Perhaps 49, like 42-44 and 48, belongs
to the last decade of the kingdom in Samaria, when the days were evil,
and the iniquity (as it seemed) of foreigners compassed Hoshea round
about, with intent to supplant him. We have no parallel psalm in the
supplement to bear this out, and there were evil days and supplanters
for a hundred years before; but the unvarying use of אלהים is probably
an indication of an eighth century date. עקב is a participial noun from
עקב to supplant, or perhaps, less specifically, to take advantage of; and
these plotters surround Israel, as in 83:2-8, where Edom, Ammon,
Moab, Philistia and Tyre, beside other nations, take crafty counsel
against Israel, and are backed by Assyria. Nevertheless the psalmist
under inspiration knows that he need not fear; for God is more than a
match for them all.

The opponents are further specified in v. 6 as trusting in their power
(חילם) and boasting in their wealth. חַיִל, from the root חיל, חול II, to be
firm, strong, is a general word for strength, often used for the army:
Joab, for example, was captain of the חיל in II Sam. 24:2, when David
sinned by numbering, that is trusting in, his חיל. The word is also often
used for wealth, because wealth and power often went together then as
they do today. Solomon was Israel's most powerful king, able to hold
David's empire in peaceful subjugation. He exceeded all the kings of
the earth in riches and wisdom (I Kgs. 10:23), and his annual income
was 666 talents of gold (v. 14). Power meant tribute, and tribute meant

power. The Deuteronomic school had an ambivalent attitude to
Solomon's wealth. They were proud of it as the symbol of Yahweh's
blessing (I Kgs. 10), but they legislated against it (Deut. 17:16f): kings
should not greatly multiply to themselves silver and gold, because then
they would 'boast themselves in the multitude of their riches.' That the
psalmist is thinking of foreign kings trusting in their power and wealth,
and planning to supplant Israel, is confirmed by their calling the lands
after their own names in v. 11.

Vv. 5f are understood in the standard hypothesis to refer to powerful
wealthy Israelites oppressing (? evicting) their poor brethren. This is
not easy, because, as Gunkel says, עקב does not mean an enemy or
oppressor; Kirkpatrick cites Jer. 9:4, but the context is dissimilar. Nor,
as is remarked, do we expect a moralist to announce the solution to a
riddle and then continue by asking why he should be frightened. But
such difficulties are trivial beside the problems of vv. 7ff: 'Up to this
point,' says Delitzsch optimistically, 'everything is clear; but now the
difficulties accumulate.' The MT gives אָח לֹא־פָרֹה יִפְדֶּה אִישׁ, 'a
brother will a man by no means ransom,' and the versions are similar;
but the standard theory requires the sense to be 'a man can by no
means ransom himself' (from God's judgement), and it also requires a
'but'—they trust in their wealth, *but* they cannot escape God's
judgement. The following ways out of the impasse have been
proposed. (i) 'One man cannot redeem another; God alone can redeem
man' (Delitzsch, van der Ploeg, Eaton). This does not seem to answer
the question why the idea of one man redeeming another from death
should have been introduced, since no one has ever thought of
attempting it, to our knowledge. (ii) אָח can be translated 'Alas,' as at
Ezek. 6:11; 21:20, and יפדה repointed יִפָּדֶה to mean 'redeem himself'
(Dahood, NEB). But the death of the wealthy is not a cause of sadness
to the writer, but of comfort! Ironic alas's seem anachronistic. (iii)
Eight Hebrew MSS read אַךְ for אָח, and with the same repointing as in
(ii) one can translate, 'Truly no man can ransom himself' (RSV), or
'However . . .' (Gunkel, Kraus and many commentators). But אַךְ is
the easier reading; Kraus just says it is to be read, without giving any
account of how the 'nonsense' reading אָח came into being. It is this
'easiness' which can account for the *varia lectio*: the eight MSS could
not make sense of אָח either. The history of the interpretation of the
psalm is an object lesson in the dangers of preferring convenient
readings and treating traditional vowel-points as if they were a matter
of indifference.

Our own hypothesis commends itself by making sense of the text as it stands, and without forcing the meaning. Why should Israel fear the alliance of wealthy and powerful invaders? They will be defeated, and not a man will be ransomed—all will be put to death. אחיו. . . .איש is normal Hebrew for 'one . . . another' (Gen. 9:5; etc.), and on occasion emphasis is given in similar phrases by omitting the suffix, e.g. 'Therefore fathers shall eat sons' (Ezek. 5:10; cf. 18:18; Mic. 7:6; Mal. 1:6). Here the emphasis is as strong as the language can make it, with the object first (since the brother is the one in need of ransoming), and the absolute infinitive after the negative; we might render loosely, 'By God, not one shall ransom another.' Royal captives were sometimes taken in Israel's wars, like Oreb and Zeeb, Zebah and Zalmunna, in Gideon's campaigns, or Agag by Saul. We are not told the motivation for Saul's sparing Agag, but, to judge from the rest of the chapter, it is not likely to have been kind-heartedness; no doubt kings were worth money. But such a mercenary approach did not accord with Israelite conceptions of the holy war. The captives belonged to Yahweh, and no one could pay him a price for them. Even when no חרם had been expressly declared, as at Jericho or with Agag, it was proper to kill the leading prisoners after victory, as Gideon did, or as in the triumphal procession of Ps. 68: 'Thou hast ascended on high, thou hast led (thy) captivity captive; Thou hast received sacrifices from among men (מתנות באדם), Yea, (among) the rebellious also, that Yah God might dwell' (v. 18). The rebels are a source of uncleanness, and must be killed if Yahweh is to 'dwell' (sc. in Israel); so their 'hairy scalps' are beaten in, and the victors ceremonially dip their feet in the blood (vv. 21, 23). The ransom for their life, says our psalmist grimly, is expensive, and is wanting permanently. The same phrase פדיון נפשו, the ransom for his life, occurs in Exod. 21:30, where the owner of an ox that has gored before must pay whatever the court decides to be suitable damages; חדל means to fail or be wanting in Job 19:14 and Prov. 10:19. V. 8 is a parenthesis, for the sense of v. 9 continues from v. 7 smoothly with a consecutive *waw*: not one shall ransom another *that he should* still live on. The opening כי of v. 10 then runs the meaning on adversatively. He hoped to live on and not see the pit; 'Yea, he shall see (it)' (RVmg; Delitzsch 'Nay . . .'), cf. I Kgs. 21:15. The able and the empty-headed shall go down together, and leave their power, their money and their armies behind them. The whole paragraph coheres in meaning in the context given, without any textual problem.

49:11 Their inward thought is, (that) their houses (shall continue)
　　　for ever,
　　　(And) their dwelling-places to all generations;
　　　They call [RV their] lands after their own names.

12 But man in precious metal shall not lodge a night
　　(ואדם ביקר בל־ילין)
　　He has become like (נמשל) the beasts that perish.'

קרב with a personal suffix means 'heart, inward mind' at 5:9; 64:6; Isa.
16:11; e.g. 64:6, 'And the inward thought (קרב) of every one, and the
heart, is deep.' LXX has made an easier reading by reversing the last
two consonants to form 'their graves'; this saves understanding the
verb 'to be' twice in the line, and the not very common meaning of
קרב, in favour of continuing the theme of the death of the godless (and
actually the 'wise' also). It is preferred by RSV, NEB and most
followers of the standard theory of the psalm; but it draws more
problems in its train with v. 11c, which does not continue this train of
thought at all. RSV and many commentators then supply 'though,'
NEB transposes a line, and other more desperate expedients are
resorted to.[10] But MT gives excellent sense. In their pride the invaders
think in their hearts that their dynasties (probably a double meaning of
'house' as in II Sam. 7:2, 16) and their palaces (the Korahites' favourite
משכנת) are permanencies. They have called (קראו) captured lands
after themselves, as David did at Rabbath-Ammon: Joab sent to say,
'Now therefore gather the rest of the people together, and encamp
against the city, and take it: lest I take the city, and my name be called
upon it' (II Sam. 12:28). The word for lands, אדמות, is found only here
in the plural; it often means arable land, but is used for the land of
Israel (Ezek. 11:17 and often), the land of Egypt (Gen. 47:20, 26), etc.
The use here is probably due to אדם in the following verse (cf. vv. 2,
20), as in Gen. 2:7, 'the LORD God formed the אדם of the dust of the
אדמה.' Now אדם presumes to call the אדמה of Israel, and other lands,
after himself.[11]

V. 12 is also difficult for the consensus theory, and a prey to
conjectures. RVmg translates, 'But man (being) in honour abideth
not,' but the syntax is not very comfortable. Also יקר elsewhere means
'honour' only in Esther; it means 'precious things' (collectively) in Jer.
20:5; Ezek. 22:25; Job 28:10, the standard meaning, and RSV
translates 'in his pomp.' NEB, and many, despair and emend to כבקר
'like oxen,' for the parallel with v. 12b. ילין also is not easy, for its
primary meaning is 'lodge, pass the night'; BDB cite only one other

passage where man is said to 'continue' indefinitely (Prov. 19:23), but RSV renders 'he who has it *rests* satisfied' (so NEB). Other passages cited as parallels, Ps. 25:13; Isa. 1:21; Job 19:4, seem in fact to give the meaning 'lodge, rest,' and this corresponds with the basic meaning of temporary, not permanent dwelling. This has in turn led NEB and others to conjecture יָבִין as in the almost identical v. 20, although variety is normal in psalm refrains (cf. 42:5, 11; 43:5).

Both difficulties disappear if we take the common meanings of the words, and assume the invasion context. Warriors used to deck themselves in finery for the holy activity of battle in the early period. Gideon took golden crescents and earrings from the defeated Midianites under Zebah and Zalmunna to a weight of over 1700 shekels (Jg. 8:21-26), and the women accompanying the Israelite army in Ps. 68 are seen as publishing the victory and covering their arms with captured gold and silver bangles (vv. 11-13).[12] This gives a natural meaning for יקר as the precious metal ornaments worn by enemy soldiers coming to fight against Israel.[13] ילין can then also be given its primary meaning, and can be translated as a future in contrast to the preceding perfect קראו. They have been calling conquered lands after themselves in their pride, but not a man shall spend a night on Israelite soil in his war-finery; they will be slaughtered like cattle. נמשל elsewhere means 'has become like': 28:1; 143:7; Isa. 14:10.

49:13 This is their way, folly is with them (זֶה דַרְכָּם כֵּסֶל לָמוֹ):
And their followers (אַחֲרֵיהֶם) approve their sayings. [Selah

14 They have arrayed themselves (שַׁתּוּ) as a flock for Sheol;
Death shall be their shepherd:
And the upright shall triumph over them (יִרְדּוּ) in the morning;
And their engraved work (צִירָם) shall be for Sheol to consume,
That there be no habitation for it.

15 But God will ransom my life (יִפְדֶּה נַפְשִׁי) from the hand of Sheol:
For he shall deliver me (יִקָּחֵנִי). [Selah

This passage is the final graveyard of the consensus theory. Only the most obscure sense is available to those like Delitzsch and Kirkpatrick who are faithful to the MT. Many commentators feel forced to emend freely to achieve the sense the theory requires; NEB makes six unsupported changes. Kraus thinks that a soundly based reconstruction of v. 14de is impossible, and throws in the sponge.

A hypothesis that makes sense of the MT is better than such guesswork and despair. Vv. 5-12 have been concerned with the enemy leaders who have planned to supplant Israel, who will die unransomed, who call captured lands by their names and think their dynasties are for eternity. V. 13 resumes: this is their policy, they are full of hubris (כסל means both folly and confidence), and those behind them, that is their followers, are delighted with their 'mouth,' i.e. the 'inward thought' of v. 11ab. In just the same way did the average Israelite share full-heartedly in the territorial ambitions of his king. They (the other ranks of the enemy army) have arrayed themselves (שׁתו in a reflexive and military sense, as in Ps. 3:6; Isa. 22:7; שַׁתּוּ with dagesh as in 73:9[14]) as a flock for Sheol. Only five days before the same singer had lamented, 'Yea, for thy sake are we killed all the day long; We are counted as sheep for the slaughter' (44:22); but now the tables are to be turned. Death is not uncommonly personified—'O Death, where are your plagues?' (Hos. 13:14 RSV), 'For death is come up into our windows' (Jer. 9:21); he is 'the king of terrors' (Job 18:14), and continues his demonic life into the New Testament. He makes an apt shepherd for the silly sheep.

The context in which the enemy army is to go down to Sheol under Death's crook is of course a battle; and it is this which is described in v. 14c, when 'the upright,' that is Israel, keeping God's law, will triumph over them in the morning. Ancient battles—and indeed modern ones—were fought in the morning when possible (Josh. 8:10; 10:9; I Sam. 11:11), so as to allow leisure for slaughter and spoil; but in this case there is to be no spoil, for all will be destroyed. In this way we obtain good sense for the notoriously difficult צִירָם, which is usually connected with צוּרָה in Ezek. 43:11, 'the form of the house,' and with צוּר IV, to fashion or delineate; but the usual rendering, 'their form' (RVmg) seems vague and meaningless. BDB gives two instances of the verb: Exod. 32:4, 'and he fashioned (the gold) with a graving-tool,' and I Kgs. 7:15, 'And he fashioned the two pillars of brass.' It would make good sense to suppose that צירם meant engraved work of silver and gold, i.e. jewelry, and was a virtual synonym for יקר. Their engraved ornaments, then, will go down to destruction with them. Probably (with Isa. 9:5) they would go with the enemy's boots and garments rolled in blood, 'even for burning, for fuel of fire'; in a proper חרם these things would go into Yahweh's treasury (Josh. 6:19). At all events they should not be subject to private appropriation as at the hands of Achan

(Josh. 7) or Saul (I Sam. 15), or made into an idol, as Gideon unhappily did (Jg. 8:27). In this way there would be no 'habitation' for them.

The natural contrast then follows in v. 15. Whereas the invaders are thus destined for Sheol, and any survivors will be unable to ransom their captured leaders, God will ransom 'my' life—the psalmist speaks as in v. 5 for the king and the community. There is no suggestion of payment here, as always when God ransoms in the OT; he just saves their lives—cf. Hos. 13:14, 'Shall I ransom them from the power of Sheol?' (RSV); Ps. 89:48, 'What man is he . . . That shall deliver his soul from the hand of Sheol?'; 86:13; Prov. 23:14. We have seen the same phrase, to ransom the soul, with the same meaning, to save from dying, in vv. 7-9. יקחני 'he shall take me,' means the same: Kirkpatrick cites the parallel from Ps. 18:16, 'He sent from on high, he took me,' where the same form יקחני means 'he delivered me.' It cannot but be a relief to be rid of the suggestion that the psalmist thought he would be taken, like Enoch and Elijah, direct to heaven; the whole passage makes perfect sense in line with normal Israelite concepts if we stick to the MT and assume the Danite context.

A feature of the psalm is that it has two Selahs, after v. 13 and v. 15, neither of which coincides with the refrains in v. 12 and v. 20, where we might have expected them on the old musical theory. On my proposal they will be breaks for the recital of some part of the national tradition; and although at first sight there is no very obvious reference to a particular story, we have noticed how often the text has evoked references to the Gideon saga. I think it is possible to advance a number of different arguments to support the suggestion that the Selahs here covered the recital of Gideon's victories in Jg. 7-8 over the armies of Oreb and Zeeb/Zebah and Zalmunna. (i) 'The day of Midian' (Isa. 9:4) was remembered in association with 'the joy of the harvest,' and I have argued above that this was associated with a fire of captured enemy arms at the autumn festival (pp. 145f). Isa. 10:26, 'And the LORD of hosts shall stir up against him a scourge, as in the slaughter of Midian at the rock of Oreb,' also shows that Gideon's victories were remembered and cited as a dire example of Yahweh's way with invaders. (ii) Ps. 83 is of markedly similar theme to 49—and is perhaps of similar date—with the peoples around taking crafty counsel together to cut Israel off (Assyria being the ultimate power). The psalm continues, 'Do thou unto them as unto Midian; As to Sisera, as to Jabin, at the river Kishon: which perished at En-dor; They became as dung for the earth. Make their nobles like Oreb and Zeeb;

Yea, all their princes like Zebah and Zalmunna.' (iii) The slaughter of
the Midianites was traditionally enormous, 120,000 men (Jg. 8:10),
and corresponds well both with 'He has become like the beasts that
perish' (vv. 12, 20) and with the comparison of sheep going to Sheol (v.
14). (iv) The Gideon story ends with the appropriations of the
crescents and ear-rings and pendants for his ephod (Jg. 8:21-27), and is
the only story in the tradition where this war-jewelry is a feature. Its
presence as background to 49 would make it much easier to understand
the emphasis on יקר (vv. 12, 20) and the engraved work which is to be
consumed (v. 14de). (v) The Gideon story also contains the element of
the killing of captured enemy leaders; in fact, twice over, Oreb and
Zeeb at Jg. 7:25, Zebah and Zalmunna at 8:18-21. The same theme
does come elsewhere, e.g. Josh. 10; I Sam. 15, but is not common; and
its presence in a recital would help to explain the forceful denial that
prisoners would be ransomed (vv. 7-10). (vi) Oreb and Zeeb are
mentioned as associated with two places in Israel, the Rock of Oreb
and the Winepress of Zeeb (Jg. 7:25). The story implies that the names
were given in memory of their deaths there; but it could easily be
thought that they had 'called these ארמות after their own names' (v.
11). (vii) Gideon launched his attack at midnight (Jg. 7:19ff). This
could explain the otherwise surprising ילין. The enemy shall no more
spend a night on Israelite soil than the Midianites, who were routed
while sleeping, and butchered the following morning.

It is difficult to think that any other story could fit the detail of the
psalm so well, or indeed go so far to explain the details which scholars
have found so obscure. We may note also the way in which the story
divides into two: the night-battle, pursuit, capture and death of Oreb
and Zeeb in Jg. 7; the further slaughter, the capture and death of Zebah
and Zalmunna, and the earrings, etc., in Jg. 8. We should thus have two
suitable passages for the two Selahs. The impossibility of ransom on
capture (49:7-10), the pride that will call parts of Israel after the
invaders (v. 11), and the promise that they will not lodge a night, but
will be slaughtered (v. 12), lead up to Oreb and Zeeb in a Jg. 7 recital
after v. 13. The enemies' slaughter like sheep (v. 14a-c) and the
destruction of their precious metal (v. 14de), with the preservation of
Israel's army (v. 15), continue the themes of Zebah and Zalmunna,
which then follow. The hypothesis of Selah as recital seems to be
confirmed by its regular applicability.

49:16 Be not thou afraid when one is made rich,
Or when the glory [RV text] of his house is increased:

17 For when he dieth he shall carry nothing away;
    His glory shall not descend after him.

18 Though while he lived he blessed his soul,
    And men praise thee, when thou doest well to thyself,

19 It shall go to the generation of his fathers;
    Which never more see the light.

20 Man in precious metal and without understanding
    (אדם ביקר ולא יבין)
    Has become like (נמשל) the beasts that perish.

The psalm ends straightforwardly, for the context we are supposing. 'Wherefore should I fear . . . ?,' the priest-poet asked rhetorically in v. 5; 'Fear not . . . ,' he answers now, reassuring his king primarily, but himself also, and all Israel. The wealth of the enemy kings, and the glory of their palaces are impressive (as the Queen of Sheba found with Solomon's prosperity, I Kgs. 10:7, and 'the house that he had built,' 10:4); but when they are dead, they cannot take them with them. 'House' is a normal word for a palace, and כבוד, which we should translate 'glory' as in v. 17, is an extremely strong word to use of a normal wealthy man's home (as is required by the standard hypothesis);[15] it is used of the former and the latter houses, the first and second Temples, in Hag. 2:8, and is much better suited to a palace. The empty-handedness of a dead tyrant is a theme taken up at length in Isa. 14—'Art thou also become weak as we?' (v. 10).

Blessing one's soul is characteristic of the arrogant: 'when he heareth the words of this curse . . . he (shall) bless himself (התברך) in his heart (בלבבו) saying, I shall have peace, though I walk in the stubbornness of mine heart' (Deut. 29:19). God's blessing is nothing to him. The poet then turns to him in a prophetic apostrophe: 'Though while *he* lived *he* blessed his soul, And men praise *thee*, when *thou* doest well to *thy*self'—cf. Isa. 10:1-4; 8:6-8. He imagines the scene of self-glorification, as the over-wealthy enemy monarch presides over enormous banquets amid the sycophancy of his followers (cf. I Kgs. 10:5ff; Est. 1). But all that is gone; as Mr Chamberlain put it so memorably, he has missed the bus this time. The soul that he has blessed, and which he might have hoped should be ransomed (vv. 7f), shall go down to be with his fathers in the land of perpetual darkness; the feminine subject to תבוא is the נפש of the previous verse, cf. 16:10, 'Thou wilt not leave my soul to Sheol.' No change is desirable, let alone necessary. The last verse forms a refrain, echoing v. 12, but with the slight difference of ולא יבין for בל-ילין. The Gideon context is over now, and the psalmist recapitulates his threat. The man who marches into Israel in his war-finery is a godless man lacking true understanding (יבין); he shall be like cattle for the slaughter.

With the previous psalms of the Korah sequence, we have traced a series of parallels with Book IV: 44 with 90, 45 with 91-92 and so on to 48 with 97-98. So it will be natural for us to enquire whether the message of menace to Israel's enemies is found also in 99-100. 99 begins, 'The LORD reigneth; let the peoples tremble; He sitteth upon the cherubim; Let the earth be moved. The LORD is great in Zion; And he is high above all the peoples. Let them praise thy great and terrible name: Holy is he' (vv. 1-3). While less pugnacious, 100 also invites all the earth to make a joyful noise to Yahweh, to serve him, come before him, acknowledge him as God, and bring sacrifice into his courts. Both psalms require submission of the nations, 99 with menaces, 100 without.

So 49 is not a wisdom poem about the problems of the oppressed poor and their hope of immortality at all; nor is its author rationalistic in the least. It is a red-blooded warning to 'all ye peoples,' and it carries the same message as 45, where the king's arrows are very sharp in the heart of his enemies; as 46, where the nations are to come and behold the fire God makes of their waggons; as 47, where all peoples are to clap their hands as Yahweh subdues the nations under Israel's feet; and as 48, where the kings assembled, crossed the frontier, and were dismayed and stricken with terror. To invade Israel is to sign their own death warrant. Both sequences, the Korah psalms 45-49 and the Book IV psalms 91-100, proclaim the kingship of Yahweh over the world, and call upon the nations to recognise the fact; and both are psalms for the first five days of the autumn festival, from 15th to 19th of the month. There is a difference in tone between 49 and the rest, and the reason for that is political: 45-47 come from the high days of the ninth century, and 48 is written in the light of the miraculous raising of the siege of Dan in 732. But 49 was written in 'the days of evil,' when the peril of being 'supplanted' was real. 'Fear' of Tiglath-Pileser is only too well based. It is the Israelite court which understands not, and is destined to slaughter like the beasts.

There is almost as much consensus over Ps. 88 as there is with 49. It is not quite consensus, for the ancient view, both in the Targums and in Kimhi on the Jewish side, and in the Syriac version, Theodore and Theodoret in the Church, saw the psalm as a national lament for Israel in exile; and this has been followed in modern times by Wellhausen and Briggs. But the overwhelming majority of interpreters, including all those whom I have been listing, has seen it as an individual's lament, usually for his physical sickness (primarily at least, often taken as leprosy), but also for his spiritual distress, loneliness, and terrifying experiences unspecified. Perhaps, as Kraus says, he is dying. A second dissenting voice is that of Geo Widengren,[16] who suggested that the Canaanite pattern of belief in a dying and rising God persevered in Israel, and that 88 was a liturgical psalm spoken by the king during rituals reflecting this belief; and E. Jones has also suggested a liturgical setting in piatory rites.[17]

But although the individual lament view has been so popular, it is not without its problems. It is easy to see the attraction of the hypothesis that the speaker is a leper, for he is separated (v. 5, if that is the meaning of חפשי), and his friends and family are kept away from him (vv. 8, 18); and King Uzziah dwelt in 'a several house' (בית החפשית, II Kgs. 15:5) when he became a leper. We know of no other affliction in which the sufferer was isolated from the community. On the other hand, as Kraus says, there is no mention of any physical symptoms of leprosy, which are very distressing. Besides, there is no suggestion that Uzziah was confined to his 'several house,' and lepers elsewhere in the Bible seem to roam at large (II Kgs. 5; 7; Lk. 5:12ff; 17:11ff); but the speaker in 88 says that he is shut up (כלא) and cannot come forth (v. 8). Nor is it easy to see how the lament of a leper, outcast from Israel's common life and worship, could come to be embodied in the canon. But whether we take the leprosy option or suppose the man to be on his death-bed with a long wasting disease, we have further difficulties. The main body of the psalm speaks of the sufferer repeatedly as in the realm of death (vv. 3-7, 10-12), and it is this which has evoked the leprosy and death-bed theories. How then are we to account for v. 13, 'But unto thee, O LORD, have I cried, And in the morning shall my prayer come before thee'[18]? After a lifetime of disease (v. 15) this does sound like unbelievably vacuous optimism. Again, as with 49, there are problems with the text, though on nothing like the same scale. Almost everybody wishes to emend v. 1b, 'the day of my crying by night before thee,' beginning with the Targum and versions; many change v. 18b 'And mine acquaintance are darkness'; and there are numerous less unanimous proposals. A more general disquiet is the extent to which the language has to be taken as figurative. Elsewhere in the Korah psalms it has seemed that metaphorical language is rooted in real experience—in 42 the speaker has been really panting and thirsting, and the waves and cataracts I argued to be real waves and cataracts. But the sickness hypothesis makes almost all the language of 88 *merely* figurative—the lowest pit, the dark places, the deeps, the waves, the darkness, etc. I cannot say that this is wrong, but only that it does not accord well with the concrete use of language we have encountered hitherto.

But if we are sceptical about the sickness theory, what alternative have we? The exile theory is even more figurative, and is hard to support. Widengren notes parallels in Sumerian laments for Tammuz, and we have to remember that such practices took place in the Jerusalem Temple also, and scandalised Ezekiel (8:14). But it has proved difficult to find sufficient evidence to support any claims that Yahweh was ever thought to be a dying and rising God. It would seem possible, however, to accept a hint from Widengren that early Israelite ritual included the practice of banning a representative of the people, not necessarily the king, to act as intercessor for the day. Jones, similarly, takes the psalm as part of an atonement ritual, but thinks in terms of a personal expiation. Anderson objects that we should then expect some confession of sins, but this would not be so if it were a national representative speaking; cf. 44:17, 'All this is come upon us; yet we have not forgotten thee, Neither have we dealt falsely in thy covenant.'

Such an interpretation is suggested by two features of the psalm which have proved difficult to the standard view. V. 1b יום־צעקתי בלילה נגדך can be made sense of if we translate the opening verses, 'O LORD, the God of my salvation, In the day when I cried through the night before thee, Let my prayer enter into thy presence . . .' I will defend this translation below, merely noting here that it seems to be confirmed by v. 13, 'But unto thee, O LORD, have I cried, And in the morning shall my prayer come before thee.' In both cases the speaker has spent the night in a vigil of prayer, and expects his crying to be heard with the dawn. Again, he says that he has called upon Yahweh בכל־יום in v. 9 and that the terrors came about him כל־היום in v. 17. It is likely that both these phrases mean the same thing, 'all the day long.' He has been praying over a set twenty-four hour spell which will end with the sunrise; and this implies a liturgical situation, and not one from a lifetime of sickness.

A second expression which we have seen to cause difficulty is v. 8c, 'I am shut up, and I cannot come forth.' Now there are similar, slightly mysterious, expressions twice elsewhere in the Bible, both with a suspected ritual context. In Jer. 36:5 the prophet says, 'I am shut up; I cannot go into the house of the LORD.' In Neh. 6:10 the author goes to the house of one Shemaiah 'who was shut up.' In the two latter cases the Hebrew is עצור and in 88:8 it is כלא; but the two participles are used interchangeably in Jer. 32:2 (כלוא), 33:1; 39:15 (עצור) with reference to imprisonment. There is no unanimity on the interpretation of either of these texts. Jer. 36:5 is often taken to refer to ritual defilement, which would then prevent the prophet from entering the Temple;[19] or to some political bar.[20] Neh. 6:10, however, cannot refer to ritual uncleanness, for Shemaiah proposes that Nehemiah meet him in the Temple, and Rudolph suggests that it was some (secular) encumbrance too trivial to mention.[21] It would be more satisfying if we could find a single explanation for all three texts, rather than three different ones, especially in view of the similarity of 88:8 to Jer. 36:5; and I would suggest that being 'shut up' refers to a spiritual banning of a priest or other cultic official. Prayer, fasting and mourning were ways in which priests and others could put pressure on God to spare his people (e.g. Joel 2:17), without at all incurring defilement; and a ban, or temporary limitation on the priest's freedom, could be a similar rite—as when a modern priest 'goes on retreat.' With time the rite will have become less fierce in its application, as the Nazirite vows and other rites did. In early times at Dan, an integral part of the festal rites was (I suggest) the exclusion of a representative of the people to 'cry' to Yahweh through the sixth day of the feast. He was taken outside the city and let down into a 'pit,' so that his prayers might be uttered with the force of the greatest affliction. Later the affliction was not so great, but priests like Jeremiah and cultic prophets like Shemaiah must take their turn in praying and denying themselves, including the denial of freedom of movement. Jeremiah is a priest, but not of the Zadokite line which operates in the Temple, so he is 'shut up' in his home in Anathoth; Shemaiah is an officiant in the Temple, so he is free to meet the Governor in the temple as well as his house. Some retreats take place in village churches and some in cathedrals; and the first retreat was an altogether tougher affair of forty days in the wilderness of Jordan.

One advantage of this proposal is that it makes sense of the repeated references to the dead, and to water, and to the absence of friends, and to darkness. 'The pit,' בור, is both the word for a literal pit, such as that into which Joseph was cast, and a synonym for Sheol, the abode of the dead. If one is at the bottom of a pit, one's life is indeed drawing nigh unto Sheol (v. 3), one is counted with them that go down into the pit (v. 4), cast away among the dead, like the slain that lie in the grave (v. 5), etc. At the same time, pits had water in them. Even in Jerusalem, in the summer of 588, 'in the dungeon (הבור) there was no water, but mire' (Jer. 38:6); in Dan there would be water in the pits all the year round. So it would be natural for the psalmist to say that he had been set in the deeps, been afflicted with all Yahweh's waves, while his terrors came about him like water. A deep pit is similarly virtually dark—even by day if the entrance is narrow and angled (or covered over)—so he may well say that he is in dark places, and even, as he looks up in vain for human support, that his 'acquaintances' are darkness. In their stead he is beset by the nightmare-like Rephaim, and it is little wonder if he speaks of being surrounded by terrors and being distracted. There is nothing so concentrates the mind of a man of prayer as a night in pitch blackness alone, surrounded by ghosts and horrors, up to the waist in icy water.

The text then seems amply to support such a view; but what is there to imply that 88 was originally the successor to 49, and so the psalm for 20th Bul? We have two indications that this is so; as heretofore, one in Book II, the other in Book IV. Book II consists of the week's Korah psalms, not as they were in use at Dan in the period around 730, but as they were adapted in Jerusalem in the centuries following. In the south the ancient ritual which had accompanied 88 no doubt seemed strange and barbarous by the time of the return from exile; and Jerusalem already possessed a cycle of psalms, believed to describe the tribulations of King David and his ultimate triumph, that were established (perhaps from early times) as the liturgy for the final twenty-four hours of the southern festival. These psalms purported to cover the period from David's murder of Uriah (51) to the accession of Solomon (72), the period also described in what modern scholars call the Succession Narrative (II Sam. 10—I Kgs. 2). There were twenty-two of them by this time (51-72), enough to be sung hourly from (second) evening, sundown, on 20th Ethanim to (first) evening on 21st, 'evening and morning and noonday' (55:17). Their exposition must await another occasion, but the reader may note for himself that they run the same gamut from humiliation to triumph that we find in 88-89. In this way we have an explanation for the headings of Book II. The Korah psalms, 42-49, were the old Dan psalms of 730, for the pilgrimage and 14th-19th of the festal month. The David psalms, 51-72, were the old

Jerusalem psalms for the vigil and day 20th-21st. They were reintroduced in the post-exilic adaptation, and 88 and 89 were demoted to the supplement. At the same time an eighth day was added to the feast, and 50, an Asaph psalm, was imported and prefixed to the complex of the final day; it was selected as the psalm most like to 51.

With time Tabernacles came to be a festival of undifferentiated joy; the element of 'affliction' was generalised to everyone, and transferred to Yom Kippur—'ye shall afflict yourselves: in the ninth day of the month at even, from even unto even' (Lev. 23:32). But we find exactly the same sharp change of tone in Book IV as in the Dan psalms. Both sequences begin with pre-festal lamentation, 42-44 and 90. In both this is followed by five days celebrating the kingship of Yahweh in heaven and of his viceroy on earth, 45-49 and 91-100. Then Book IV is marked by a sudden drop in tone, as the minor key is introduced. In 101 the king makes a humble vow of loyalty to Yahweh; 102 is 'A Prayer of the afflicted, when he fainteth, and poureth out his complaint before the LORD.' They may even be, respectively, a morning and an evening psalm: 101:8, 'Morning by morning will I destroy all the wicked of the land'; 102:11, 'My days are like a shadow that is stretched out.' Now 102 is markedly similar to 88. It is headed, 'A Prayer of the afflicted (לְעָנִי), as 88 is headed 'For affliction (לְעַנּוֹת).' The openings of the two psalms are very close:

<table>
<tr><td align="center">88</td><td align="center">102</td></tr>
<tr><td>O LORD, the God of my salvation,</td><td>Hear *my prayer, O LORD,*</td></tr>
<tr><td>On the day of my crying by night before thee;</td><td>*And let my* cry *come* unto *thee.*</td></tr>
<tr><td>Let my prayer enter into thy presence;</td><td>Hide not *thy face* from me in *the day* of my distress:</td></tr>
<tr><td>Incline thine ear unto my cry . . .</td><td>*Incline thine ear* unto me; In *the day* when I call answer me speedily.</td></tr>
</table>

The speaker of 102 seems to have fasted (vv. 3-6), kept vigil (v. 7) and suffered reproach 'all the day' (v. 8); God's wrath is upon him (v. 10), and he feels close to death (v. 11). He is an individual in destitution (v. 17), pleading to God to have mercy on Zion. The greater length enables a clearer picture of the speaker's condition to emerge than in 88, and that picture is strikingly like the interpretation I have suggested for the latter. So it would seem that Book IV presupposes a sixth day of ritual humiliation and intercession just like the Korah sequence; and the two evening psalms, 88 and 102, are as close a pair as 46 and 93, or any that we have found.

But if this is so, the reader may feel, is it not likely that the representative of the people would be none other than the king? This was the view of Ivan Engnell,[22] and Widengren, and more recently Eaton;[23] and one of Eaton's points, that David's tribulations were remembered as part of the ritual of atonement, is given piquancy by the suggestion above on Pss. 51-72. It is certainly likely that David himself played an important part in the atonement rites in early times (cf. Ps. 22). It may however be questioned whether great kings like Solomon and Ahab are likely to have submitted to the kind of ordeal implied by 88, and it may seem more plausible that these duties were deputed, along with other priestly tasks, to lesser mortals. We seem to have an indication of this in the headings of 101 and 102. 101, which is clearly a royal vow, is headed 'A Psalm of David'; 102, with its fasting, mourning and vigil, is headed 'A Prayer of the afflicted.' In Book IV only 101 and 103, the thanksgiving for forgiveness, are headed with David's name; it looks as if the Jerusalem king still made the vow and the thanksgiving, but handed over the 'affliction' to a more suitable person, no doubt a priest. Similarly 88 is headed מנצח, like all the other Korah psalms but 48 and 87; the מנצח cannot be the king in 45 and 84, and is likely to be the priest here also.

> 88 A Song, a Psalm of the sons of Korah; for the Chief Musician; by (על) Mahalath, on affliction (לענות). Maschil of Heman the Ezrahite.
> 1 O LORD, the God of my salvation,
> On the day of my crying through the night before thee (יום־צעקתי בלילה נגדך),
> 2 Let my prayer enter into thy presence;
> Incline thine ear unto my cry:
> 3 For my soul is full of troubles,
> And my life has drawn nigh (הגעו) unto Sheol [RV text].

Elsewhere in the sequence 'Songs' have been joyful (45, 46, 48, 87), and this is implied by Isa. 30:29; nor is there any other psalm with this heading at all like the tone of 88. Either, therefore, we shall have to suspect the word of being added to bring the title into line with 87 (as the last phrase may have been assimilated to 89); or we may think it possible that the perfects in the psalm refer to an experience just past, and that the work of atonement is now complete, so a note of peace and joy is not inapposite. The psalmist speaks of his crying through the night as over (v. 1, cf. vv. 9, 13, 17), so the most likely moment for the chanting of the psalm will be before the sun comes up (v. 13).

Like 45 and 46, 88 has an עַל phrase in the heading. The other psalms were sung at the high place, but 45 was chanted in the city gateway beside the Lilies for the royal ceremonies, and 46 at Alamoth, the Depths, for the burning of the waggons; so now 88 is sung at Mahalath, which will again be a place-name. The construct ending may be an abbreviation for Mahalath-Dan, but the derivation of the name is not easy. Aquila and Symmachus related it to חול, to dance, and a modern suggestion has been חלה II, to appease, mollify; but the former is unsuitable, and the latter seems too abstract. A more likely origin might be חלל I, to pierce, from which we have מחלות, holes, apertures, in Isa. 2:19. Now a singular feature of the waters at Dan is that the lesser stream disappears underground for a distance outside the south-west corner of the ramparts, a site known today as Ballûʻāh or Mabbûʻāh (see map), and it is not inconceivable that this is in fact the ancient Meḥillath-Dan. In favour of the identification is the mention of waves, breakers (מִשְׁבָּרֶיךָ) in v. 7. The water which is so pervasive an element in the speaker's surroundings (vv. 6f, 17), is not static but moving water, and this must make an ordinary pit unsuitable. But in the מחלה the water is running fast, and the same panic might seize the ancient priest as is experienced by many people in the darkness and constrictions of pot-holing. The stream goes underground because the soft limestone has been eroded, and an inky chamber has been worn away in which there is space and air for a terrified human; the water cascades around him like the wrath of God (v. 7), and he must spend the hours thus in the deeps (v. 6), in the underworld, with ghosts and ghouls for companions, soaked to the skin, his teeth chattering with cold and terror. Perhaps not every such priest-victim survived the ordeal.

If such was in fact the origin of the name, it would not be surprising if the consonants caused puzzlement in later times, when the connection with, and topography of Dan were forgotten. The thrust of the psalm, however, might continue to be apparent in the Jerusalem community, and the pointing מַחֲלַת, 'Appeasement,' seem the best available interpretation of the consonants. This was followed by a phrase of explanation, לְעַנּוֹת. עַנּוֹת here means 'afflicting,' the piʻel inf., as is shown by עִנִּיתָ (v. 7), עָנִי (v. 9), עָנִי (v. 15), and לְ means 'with regard to' (BDB ad voc., 7(b), p. 517). The psalm gives expression to the rite of affliction just ended.

The long heading is completed by the phrase 'Maschil of Heman the Ezrahite,' which is extremely like the title of 89, 'Maschil of Ethan the Ezrahite.' 89 is indeed a maschil (cf. pp.90, 218f), and probably comes from Tabor (89:12); whether or not its author was named Ethan, he is called an Ezrahite because that is the description of the first of Solomon's wise men (I Kgs. 4:31), and the psalm thus gains a respectable background. Heman was the second of Solomon's wise men, but not said to be an Ezrahite in the verse cited. The three guilds of singers in Jerusalem known to the Chronicler were those of Heman, Asaph and Ethan (I Chron. 15:19), of whom Heman's ancestry goes back to Korah (I Chron. 6:33-38). The most likely explanation of the two phrases is that 89A came to be adopted as the last psalm of the Korah series ('Tabor and Hermon . . .,' v. 12), and that in Jerusalem the name Ethan kept it distinct. It became a maschil with the addition of the new Jehoiachin matter, but its heading now attested no link with the Korah psalms; and in time this was supplied by the last phrase of the heading of 88, Heman being reckoned as the colleague of Ethan, and the leading Korahite, by the fourth century. If the last phrase were old, like the main part of the heading, we should have to take 'maschil' seriously, and again date the psalm in the reign of Hoshea, in view of its opening line, 'O LORD, the God of my *salvation* (ישועתי)'; but the persistent use of Yahweh, and the absence of Elohim, as in 85, suggests a ninth, or even a tenth century date.

Stress has often been laid on the bleakness of 88. Kirkpatrick begins, 'This is the saddest psalm in the whole Psalter. It is a pathetic cry of hopeless despair . . . the last word is *darkness*.' This seems to me an error. God is from the start 'the God of my salvation'; his lovingkindness, faithfulness, wonders and righteousness are presupposed as valid in vv. 11f, and there is a firm expectation that 'in the morning shall my prayer come before thee' (v. 13). 'In the morning' is no more to be set in inverted commas and so reduced to a metaphor (Kraus) than in the earlier Korah passages where the morning has been mentioned. After a day of ritualised anguish, the priest offers his prayer in the presence of the whole community before the dawn; in the morning will come joy, with the last, triumphant day of the feast, celebrated by 89. It is the absence of this context which makes the Hebrew of v. 1b seem 'abrupt' (Eaton), and has led RSV, NEB and many commentators to emend; the Targum and Versions also seem to make minor interpretative glosses (יוֹמָם, καὶ ἐν νυκτί). But the ritual context makes good sense of the MT. יוֹם means 'on the day when,' as in 56:3, 'What time (יוֹם) I am afraid, I will put my trust in thee,' or in 78:42. The normal בְּ has been dropped (cp. 102:2, 'In the day (בְּיוֹם) when I call, answer me speedily') because of the following בְּלַיְלָה, which is not in parallel. The maqqeph has been inserted to show that this is the sense, as was already seen by Delitzsch. The half-verse is thus a clause whose main sentence follows in v. 2: 'in the day that I have cried through the night before thee, Let my prayer enter . . .' The crying (צָעַק) is not a dignified prayer, but protracted wailing (cf. Isa. 33:7; 65:14). Now that it is done (perfect), priest and community ask that it may be effective (v. 2). He has been sated with troubles, he has spent the night on the doorstep of the underworld (v. 3); now he trusts the God of his salvation (*his*, cf. 42:6, 9; etc.) to grant his prayer.

> 88:4 I have been counted (נֶחְשַׁבְתִּי) with them that go down into
>   the pit;
>   I have been (הָיִיתִי) as a man that hath no strength (אֵין־אֱיָל):
> 5 Cast away among the dead,
>   Like the slain that lie in the grave,
>   Whom thou rememberest no more;
>   And they are cut off from thy hand.
> 6 Thou didst set me (שַׁתַּנִי) in the lowest pit,
>   In dark places, in the deeps.
> 7 Thy wrath lay hard (סָמְכָה) upon me,
>   And thou hast afflicted me with all thy waves.   [Selah

The concentration of the themes of death and water suggests the appropriateness of the literal, liturgical interpretation. The speaker has been set (שִׁית), not laid (RV), in the pit of the abyss (בְּבוֹר תַּחְתִּיּוֹת); he has been counted with them that go down into the pit; his life has drawn near to Sheol, among the dead, in the dark places. It seems very natural that we should think of him as actually in a deep 'pit,' the Mᵉḥillah. The 'deeps' (מְצֹלוֹת) are always elsewhere in a watery context; waves elsewhere are always real waves (93:4; Jon. 2:4 of the sea; Ps. 42:7 of the Jordan at Dan; II Sam. 22:5 of the infernal ocean), and imply running water. Although, as Christoph Barth says,[24] the Hebrews viewed sickness as 'the sphere of death,' it is noticeable that the psalmist draws a line between himself and death: he has *drawn near* to Sheol, has been *counted with* the dead, cast away *among* them, *as* a man without strength, *like* the slain. But the expressions in vv. 6f do not draw this line: he has been set in the lowest pit, the dark places, the deeps, afflicted with waves.

The affliction is partly the water, and partly the sense of the presence of the dead; but this is by no means all. He is חפשי. The normal meaning of the word is 'free,' as when a slave goes free (Exod. 21:5; etc.), and a man may be made free of taxes; the only negative association is in the noun, when Uzziah becomes a leper, and dwells in a house החפשית, of separation (II Kgs. 15:5). So here the speaker is separated among the dead, adrift (BDB), cut loose from the community of the living into whose society he has been so happily bound hitherto. In a strikingly similar phrase the Ugaritic tablets describe the underworld as 'the house of seclusion.'[25] This separation is not only from Israel but also, so nearly, from Yahweh, who forgets the dead, and they are cut off from his power; von Rad cites 139:8 and Amos 9:2 to suggest that Yahweh was believed to rule in Sheol too,[26] but these are the thoughts of later times. Furthermore, the priest is like the 'pierced' that lie in the grave. The suspicion must cross our minds that there is a literal reference here too, for in the similar Ps. 22 we should probably read the traditional 'They pierced my hands and my feet'; and the prophets of Baal gashed themselves with knives as they called upon their god. So perhaps the intercessor's prayers have been made more potent by slashing his limbs. Surely, he feels, Yahweh's wrath lay heavily upon him; עלי is given first position in the sentence—it is he who has suffered for his people.

Even closer than Ps. 22 is the Third Lamentation, which seems to imply a similar ritual. The speaker begins, 'I am the man that hath seen *affliction* by the rod of his wrath.' He too is in a *pit*: 'They have cut off my life בבור, and have cast a stone upon me' (v. 53). Indeed, it is *the lowest pit*: 'I called upon thy name, O LORD, out of the בור תחתיות' (v. 55); and v. 53b should be interpreted with NEB, 'they closed it over me with a stone' (וידו־אבן בי). There is running water: 'Waters flowed over mine head' (v. 54). It is dark: 'He hath led me and caused me to walk without light' (v. 2), 'to dwell *in dark places*, as those that have been long *dead*' (v. 6). He is shut in: 'he hath fenced me about that *I cannot go forth*' (v. 7); 'I said, I am *cut off*' (v. 54). His ordeal lasts *all the day* (vv. 3, 14). He has prayed, but God is angry: 'Yea, when I cry and *call* for help, he shutteth out *my prayer*' (v. 8); 'Thou hast covered thyself with anger' (v. 43). He weeps: '*Mine eye* poureth down ... affecteth my soul' (vv. 49, 51). So far the description is the same, and often the words; but Lam. 3 adds many other details—he has been beaten (v. 1), his bones (v. 4) and teeth (v. 16) broken, his cheeks hit (v. 30), he has been chained (v. 7) and taunted (v. 14). Only with the greatest strain can all this be taken metaphorically, and much the same is likely to be the background, even if not expressed, in 88.

The paragraph closes with a Selah, but this time the wording of the psalm can give us no confidence as to what passage of Israel's tradition might have been recited. Job is a book often suggested as a parallel to 88, but we can hardly think that an account of Job's sufferings was available in so early a period. Perhaps the opening section of the Joseph saga would be more likely. We have had no reference to Joseph throughout the Korah sequence, and the north Israelite kings, the core of whose people came from the two great Joseph tribes, could scarcely have led an annual festival without any reference to their eponymous ancestor. If the Joseph saga was not recited in such a context, when was it recited? The opening section of the story tells how Joseph was put by his brothers in a *pit*, and left there apparently to die; he is counted with them that go down into the deeper pit of Sheol, like the slain; his companions shun him, and he is an abomination to them; he is shut in and cannot escape; Yahweh's covenanted love and faithfulness were his only hope, and did not let him down. It is possible to read the whole of 88 as a prayer of Joseph in the pit; and especially the verses 6-8 before and after the Selah might suggest such a context.

> 88:8 Thou hast put my companions (מידעי) far from me;
>   Thou hast made me an abomination unto them -
>   Shut up, that I could not come forth (כלא ולא אצא).
>   9 Mine eye wasted away (ראבה) by reason of affliction:
>   I have called all day (בכל־יום) upon thee, O LORD,
>   I have spread forth my hands unto thee.
>   10 Wilt thou shew wonders to the dead?
>   Shall the shades arise and praise thee?   [Selah
>   11 Shall thy lovingkindness be declared in the grave?
>   Or thy faithfulness in Abaddon?
>   12 Shall thy wonders be known in the dark?
>   And thy righteousness in the land of forgetfulness?

The speaker's family and close friends (מידעים, cf. γνωστοί, Lk. 23:49) are not only kept physically away from him; they actively abhor him, like the chanting crowd of Lam. 3:14. He is the community's sin-bearer, shut up (participle) and unable to climb out; perhaps there is a stone over his 'pit' also, or the sides may be precipitate. He has spent the day (v. 9, cf. v. 17) weeping and praying with hands outstretched in view of the treatment he has received. The chain of words for the realm of death—the dead, the shades, the grave, Abaddon, the dark, the land of forgetfulness—testify to his nearness to it, buried as he is in a living tomb.

But his cries are not for himself alone, but for his people. Yahweh's חסד was not normally 'lovingkindness' to each individual Israelite, though it could be this (Ruth 1:8; 2:20). His צדקה was usually a righteousness to his covenant with Israel, and to that he would be true in his faithfulness (אמונה). His 'wonders,' collective פלא, is the standard word for his mighty action in the Exodus (Exod. 15:11; etc.; Ps. 77:11; 78:12; 89:5), his marvellous redemption of his people. The series of rhetorical questions in vv. 10f has in mind the ironic contrast with the scenes of festal rejoicing so familiar from the previous days of the festival. ספר is the standard word for the public recital of the tradition: of 'what work Yahweh did in the days of old' (44:1), of 'all his works' (73:28), of the matters 'which our fathers have told us' (78:3), of 'the praises of Yahweh' told to 'the generation to come' (78:4), of his 'praise' (79:13). Israel has heard such recitals, and stood up from the dust (44:25; 119:62), and shouted 'Hallelujah' (44:8). There will be no such recitals (יְסֻפַּר) in the grave, in Abaddon, nor will the Rephaim rise to their feet, uttering confessions (יוֹדוּךָ, no 'and'). These wonders have been made known to the living in the light of the national festival, not in the dark, in the land of forgetfulness.

We have noticed the way in which in earlier psalms the Selah has often been accompanied by some reference to a recital in the text: 'Glorious things *are spoken* of thee, O city of God. Selah' (87:2), 'As *we have heard* so have we seen . . . Selah' (48:8); cf. 44:1, 8. So again here: the second Selah stands between the shades arising to praise Yahweh, and his lovingkindness being recited in the grave. How suitable if a real recital followed by praise filled the gap between v. 10 and v. 11! The Joseph tradition might conveniently be taken in two sections for the two Selahs: that covering the story of his being thrown in the pit by his brothers, now in Gen. 37, and that covering his slavery and imprisonment in Egypt, now in Gen. 39. The happy ending would not be apt for the present occasion, but could be told at the happy ending of the feast.

88:13 But unto thee, O LORD, have I cried,
And in the morning shall my prayer come before thee.

14 LORD, why castest thou off my soul?
   Why hidest thou thy face from me?

15 I am afflicted and expiring from my youthful strength
   (ונוע מנער):
   I have suffered (נשאתי) thy terrors, I am distracted.

16 Thy fierce wrath is gone over me;
   Thy terrors have cut me off.

17 They came round about me like water all the day long;
   They compassed me about together.

18 Lover and friend hast thou put far from me,
   And my companions (מידעי) were darkness.

The difference of tenses in v. 13 presents the sickness theory with an impasse. The speaker *has* cried, and he expects that his prayer *will* be heard in the morning. RSV ignores this with ' ... (I) cry unto thee; in the morning my prayer comes before thee,' and NEB similarly. Anderson says that the morning is 'a conventional and opportune time for prayer,' and Kirkpatrick that 'in spite of all discouragement (he) will not cease to pray'; but v. 13b does not say that he will pray again in the morning, but that his prayer will be answered then—cf. v. 2, 'Let my prayer *enter into thy presence*: Incline thine ear unto my cry,' 102:1, 'Hear my prayer, O LORD, And let my cry *come unto thee*.' This expectation of imminent deliverance cannot be reconciled with the sickness theory, where the psalm is 'a pathetic cry of hopeless despair in the midst of unrelieved suffering,' with 'the gloom deepest at the close' (Kirkpatrick). Other commentators see that vv. 1f imply some hope, but whether the man is understood to be a leper, or to be dying, or to have been suffering 'from his youth up' (as v. 15 is often translated), the expectation of *imminent* deliverance, 'in the morning,' has to be denied.

The ritual interpretation resolves the difficulty. 'But I (ואני),' says the priest, unlike the dead, have been praying through this day of my affliction; and at dawn my trials will be rewarded, and the people exulting in anticipation that my prayers have been accepted. In the meanwhile he puts his appeal for the last time. Why does Yahweh hide his face from him and from Israel? Cf. 102 again, 'Hide not thy face from me in the day of my distress' (v. 2). There is a word-play at the beginning of v. 15 (עָנִי, אֲנִי), like the play on the king's name in 45 (אָהַבְתָּ, אֶחְאָב), and for the rest of the line I have accepted Eaton's translation. נער comes twice elsewhere in the OT: at Prov. 29:31 it means 'youth,' at Job 33:25 'youthful vigour' (BDB). גוע means 'expire, perish, die,' and as one can hardly have been expiring from one's youth, the second rendering is to be preferred. The difference in tenses in v. 15b requires translation, though אפונה is a root found only here. Delitzsch offers an Arabic parallel *afina* which justifies RV's 'distracted'; he accounts for the cohortative by reference to the Hebrew willingness to lay hold of emotion.[27] The terrors of vv. 15-17 which have reduced the speaker to distraction are the ghosts whom he knows to inhabit this grim underworld, and whom he senses with every movement of the water. They milled about him invisibly in the blackness, like the water that chilled him below. His isolation was unbearable; he looked up for some human support, but for friends all he had was the dark. The last phrase, 'The darkness was my companions,' is bold, but gives sense in the context, and should be retained.

Ritual interpretations of this kind cannot be proved. There is no direct description of such rites in the Bible, and external evidence from neighbouring countries may not be relevant. All we can say is that they make the best sense of not just 88, where standard theories emend the text, and are left still with unresolved dilemmas, but also of other passages. Of these the closest and clearest is Lam. 3, but there are other psalms, like 102 and 22; and there is the much controverted Isa. 53. Whatever view we take of this chapter, it seems to be evidence of Israelite belief in the effectiveness of the sufferings of the innocent for the sins of the community, and in many ways it recalls 88: 'Surely he hath borne (נשא) our sicknesses, and carried our sorrows: yet did we esteem him (חשבנהו) stricken, smitten of God and afflicted (מענה). He was wounded (מחלל) for our transgressions, he was bruised for our iniquities: the chastisement of our peace was upon him (עליו); and with his stripes we are healed' (vv. 4f). It is possible to read the two passages together as descriptions, or perhaps echoes, of the same rite, the one through the eyes of the community, the other through those of the sufferer. In that case we should see more of the significance of our own text. The priest is making himself an offering, a guilt-offering; he is bearing the sins of many, and making intercession for the transgressors, indeed for 'us,' for Israel. So after his bruising and wounding and his being put in his 'grave,'[28] he prolongs his days, and sees and is satisfied with the travail of his hand; and the community rewards him with a portion among the great, and a share of the spoil with the strong. We cannot but feel that he has deserved it.

To us ritual of this kind is a survival of the superstition of our barbaric forebears—better then the still more barbaric rites that preceded it, that included castration and death, worse than the spiritualised memorial of the tribulations of David that replaced it. But it behoves us to remember that such rituals still find place in grimmer form in the divided and alienated societies in which we live: in police stations and prisons in Russia, South Africa and South America, and not there only. The ritual and pathetic prayer of 88 is prophetic in the deepest sense of the word: it speaks of the necessity of the redemptive suffering of the innocent to heal the sin of society. It is not for nothing that the Church has selected it as one of the psalms for Good Friday, when one held to be God's son was afflicted with scourges and crucifixion on the sixth day of the week, and was counted with them that go down into the pit; and whose prayer came before the God of his salvation in the morning.

VIII

THE CLIMAX OF THE FEAST, AND ITS TRANSFER SOUTH
(Psalm 89)

89 is not a psalm of the sons of Korah: its heading is 'Maskil of Ethan the Ezrahite.' It differs from the Korah psalms not only in its great length and stress on the Davidic covenant (which I shall argue to be adventitious), but in such matters as the mention of Rahab, creation, Mt Tabor, the divine council and the other gods, who get only an indirect reference in 44:20 of all the psalms we have examined. On the other hand, 89 is in a special relationship to the Korah psalms. It is placed at the end of Book III following a (broken) sequence of Korah psalms, 84; 85; 87; 88. Its heading is closely similar to the last part of the heading of 88, 'Maskil of Heman the Ezrahite,' Heman being associated with Ethan (I Kgs. 4:31; I Chron. 6:33-47; 15:19), and the word Ezrahite occurring only here in the Psalter. More important, there seems to be a verbal relationship between the appeals of 88 and the opening verses of 89. 88:11f asks, 'Shall *thy lovingkindness* be declared in the grave? Or *thy faithfulness* in Abaddon? Shall *thy wonders be known* in the dark? And *thy righteousness* in the land of forgetfulness?' 89:1, 2, 5 seem to echo this cry: 'I will sing of the *lovingkindness* of the LORD for ever: With my mouth will I make *known thy faithfulness* to all generations. For I have said, *Lovingkindness* shall be built up for ever; *Thy faithfulness* shalt thou establish in the very heavens . . . And the heavens shall praise *thy wonders*, O LORD; *Thy faithfulness* also in the assembly of the holy ones.' Yahweh's faithfulness recurs in v. 8, and his righteousness in v. 16. There is also some community of thought with other Korah psalms such as 85, where Mercy and Truth, Righteousness and Peace are semi-subsistent virtues associated with God's throne (see above, p.112), and Righteousness goes before him. In 89:14, 'Righteousness and judgement are the foundation of thy throne: Mercy and truth go before thy face.'[1] The problem therefore is first to account for both the distinctions from, and the links with, the Korah psalter, and in particular with 88.

   This initial puzzle is rendered more complex by the problem of the unity of the psalm, which is defended by Mowinckel, G.W. Ahlström,[2] Weiser, Dahood and Eaton among the moderns, and disputed by Gunkel, Schmidt, Kraus and Jacquet in varying degrees of starkness. The difficulties facing the view that the psalm was composed as a unity are fivefold. (i) The *metre* is strikingly regular for the greater part of the psalm, two different metres dominating. In vv. 1f, 5-15, 48-51, 4:4 predominates; in vv. 3f, 17-45, 3:3 is the norm.[3] (ii) This division by metre is close to coinciding with a division by *subject*. vv. 1f, 5-18 is a hymn concerned with Yahweh's lordship over the gods, his subjugation of the waters and foundation of the world, ending with a reference to his care of Israel and its king. vv. 3f, 19-51 is concerned with the Davidic covenant, and its apparent disregard by Yahweh. (iii) The same division as in (ii) is found in the *forms* of the psalm. Vv. 1-18 is a hymn (with the exception of vv. 3f); vv. 19-37 and vv. 3f are citations of the Davidic covenant; vv. 38-45 is a lament, followed by an appeal in vv. 46-51; v. 52 is a doxology, probably intended for the whole of Book III. (iv) The apparent disruption in the opening verses caused by vv. 3f is reinforced by the *syntax*. In vv. 1f 'I' is the speaker of the psalm, Yahweh is addressed: 'I will sing . . . I have said . . . thy faithfulness.' In vv. 3f 'I' abruptly becomes Yahweh, and David is spoken of, and then addressed: 'I have made a covenant with my chosen, I have sworn unto David my servant; Thy seed will I establish . . . thy throne . . .' In vv. 5ff, equally abruptly, Yahweh is addressed again: 'And the heavens shall praise thy wonders, O LORD, Thy faithfulness'; and this continues to the end, apart from Yahweh's properly introduced speech of vv. 19b-37. It is difficult to resist the smoothness of sequence that would obtain, by contrast, if v. 5 followed v. 2, 'For I have said, Mercy shall be built up for ever; Thy faithfulness shalt thou establish in the very heavens. (5) And the heavens shall praise thy wonders, O LORD; Thy faithfulness also in the assembly of the holy ones.' (v) There is a noticeable difference of *tone* between the confidence that runs through vv. 1f, 5-18, and the disasters described in vv. 3f, 19-51, which issue in an appeal that is little short of desperate. Parallels can be urged of psalms like 22 whose unity is not in question, where there are similar swings of mood; but added to the other features just named, the change of attitude seems to be significant.[4]

   Metrical and form divisions on their own are an inadequate basis on which to subdivide a psalm; but their coincidence with distinctions in subject, syntax and mood seems to make a convincing cumulative case. Anderson follows RSV in transferring 'I have said' from v. 2 to v. 3; and also in changing it to the second person, as is done in the versions. This would save the syntactical problem in v. 3 at the cost of an easier reading and an unsupported transposition: not a very comfortable solution.[5] It seems better to think with Kraus that the singer has elaborated his psalm on the basis of older, northern elements. At least vv. 1f, 5-18, on that view, and perhaps parts of vv. 46-51, were originally a northern hymn, predominantly in 4:4 metre, celebrating Yahweh's founding the earth, overwhelming the waters, and establishing Israel in face of other gods. This psalm will have been taken south and expanded in the light of the Davidic covenant, and the disasters of the period at the end of the monarchy; v. 51 is evidence that the Jerusalem king is the speaker of the whole expanded psalm. The interpolation of vv. 3f has been done rather clumsily, but the appeal to God's long promise to David fits quite neatly on to the words about 'our shield . . . our king' in v. 18.

Kraus's solution opens the way to solving my own introductory puzzle. If the original hymn was approximately vv. 1f, 5-18 (hereafter called 89A), it contained no reference to David, and very likely came from the north. This is so partly because of the links I have already traced with the Korah psalter, and other smaller details to come; but it also seems more probable because the mountains mentioned in v. 12 as 'rejoicing in thy name' do not include Zion, but are Tabor and Hermon, in that order. This constitutes a surprise which has divided commentators. (i) It has been held that Tabor and Hermon are mentioned as particularly impressive mountains. Kirkpatrick, for example, suggests that they are 'the grandest and most conspicuous natural features of Palestine,' and cites Jer. 46:18, in which Carmel and Tabor seem to stand as symbols of pre-eminence. Eaton calls them lofty mountains. But it is difficult to justify these claims in the case of Tabor. Hermon, at 9,100 ft, truly is enormous, but Tabor is only 1,843 ft, much lower than many hills in Palestine like Gerizim (2,849 ft) or Ebal (3,077 ft). It is true that it stands out from the valley of Jezreel, as Carmel does from the sea (Jer. 46:18), and this might justify the reference here. But we have also to remember that in the view of an eighth century prophet like Hosea Tabor was a byword for aberrant worship: he says to priests and king, 'Ye have been a snare at Mizpah, and a net spread upon Tabor' (Hos. 5:1). So we can hardly think of a southern psalmist innocently picking on the two most impressive mountains in the country, even if Tabor qualifies as such. (ii) NEB takes up a suggestion favoured by Kraus, Dahood and others that v. 12 intended to speak of four holy mountains, and should be translated, 'Thou didst create Zaphon and Amanus; Tabor and Hermon echo thy name.' Zaphon will then be Mt Casius, the holy mountain-home of Baal at Ugarit. Amanus is obtained by amending MT יָמִין to אָמָן, for which there is no support, but NEB claims it a 'probable reading.' Opinion is also divided on what Amanus is intended. Dahood and Rogerson and McKay think of a spur of the Taurus mountains in SE Turkey, while Kraus supposes that Antilibanus is in mind. On either view we should have an extremely liberal attitude to shrines of heathen gods, which are bracketed with mountain-shrines of Yahweh at Tabor and Dan (Hermon). Kraus speaks of the 'hohen Götterberge,' and suggests a very early date in consequence. But it is difficult to think of any text, however early, in which the worship of Yahweh and of heathen gods outside Israel are combined into one harmonious whole, quite apart from the arbitrary treatment of the text. (iii) Ahlström and Anderson suggest that a chiasmus is intended: the north and the south, Tabor and Hermon. Hermon is in the extreme north of Israel, and I should support them here by reference to what I have said on 48:2 (p. 162). But unless one happens to live by the Sea of Galilee, it is difficult to see how Tabor could symbolise the south. Certainly most Israelites lived further south still. Delitzsch, *per contra*, took Tabor to symbolise the west and Hermon the east, since they stand on either side of the Jordan.

None of these explanations seems completely convincing, though we might think suitably of a northern author for 89A who would be impressed by the skyline of Tabor and Hermon alike without being scandalised by the heterodox worship. We should have a far more satisfactory explanation, however, if 89A were originally composed at Tabor,[6] and the hymn were later adapted for use with the Dan psalms. Dan and Tabor were the most northerly of the main Israelite holy places, and it would be easy to understand some sharing of liturgical tradition between neighbouring shrines.[7] Perhaps the Tabor priests contributed to the psalmody of the national centre nearby, while the latter was in its heyday; or perhaps Dan ceased to be a pilgrim centre after Tiglath-Pileser's invasion of II Kgs. 15:29, and Tabor was used in some of the succeeding years. In any case, 89A must have been composed for national worship at some shrine (vv. 15-18), and the most likely candidates are the two that are actually mentioned in v. 12. If its origin was at Tabor, we should have an explanation both for the mention of the lesser centre before the greater, and also for the ambivalent relation with the Korah psalm-sequence. 89A will be like the Korah psalms because it is also of northern north Israelite origin; and it will be different because it comes from Tabor, not Dan. It is ascribed to Ethan the Ezrahite, while 88 is ascribed to Heman the Ezrahite, for the same reason—the same general background, but a different particular tradition. It will hold its place at the end of the Korah sequence because it was accepted by the Danite priests as a suitable psalm with which to close their festal series: after 88, the atonement psalm for the 20th Bul, came 89A for the final day of the festival, the 21st, the day on which Yahweh's triumph in creation and in providence was celebrated with rejoicing (vv. 12, 16a) and cultic shouting (v. 15).

Throughout the reconstruction of the series of festal themes which I have proposed, confidence has been maintained by the parallels with Book IV, where the themes of the Korah series have been followed step by step; only that the Korah psalms seemed to be sung each evening (42:8), while the Book IV psalms were taken in both evening and morning (92:2), so that a single Korah psalm corresponded to two Book IV psalms. As, therefore, 102 formed a pair with 88, as a psalm of affliction, fasting and humiliation, we should be looking to 103-104 to be a pair to 89A; and we find in fact that the same themes, of Yahweh's mercy, his establishment of his throne in heaven, his creation of the world by a victory over the waters, and his subjugation of the sea-monsters, are the themes of 103 and 104 as they are of 89A.

103 is primarily a response to the mercy of God prayed for in 102, and now experienced: 'Bless the LORD, O my soul . . . Who crowneth thee with lovingkindness and tender mercies' (vv. 1-4), 'plenteous in mercy' (v. 8), 'So great is his mercy' (v. 11), 'But the mercy of the LORD is from everlasting to everlasting' (v. 17). 89:1f, 'I will sing of the mercies of the LORD for ever . . . Mercy shall be built up for ever.' Both psalms speak of his righteousness and judgement (103:6; 89:14), and in both this rests upon the establishment of Yahweh's power in the skies: 'The LORD hath established his throne in the heavens; And his kingdom ruleth over all' (103:17), 'Thy faithfulness shalt thou establish in the very heavens' (89:2), 'Righteousness and judgement are the foundation of thy throne' (v. 14). But there is a difference in the manner of the 'ruling over all.' In 89 he rules over the assembly of the holy ones, the sons of the gods, by terrifying them (vv. 5-8); in 103 there are no other gods, but only obedient celestial beings: 'Bless the

LORD, ye angels of his, Ye mighty in strength . . .' (v. 20). 103 is a theologically (and chronologically) more advanced hymn; its monotheism is unsullied, its 'holy ones' have begun their sad progress down to the *English Hymnal*.

The same features may be noted in comparing 89A with 104. 104 opens with the praise of Yahweh's greatness, 'Bless the LORD, O my soul. O LORD my God, thou art very great' (104:1); as 89A begins, 'I will sing of the mercies of the LORD for ever . . . For who in the skies can be compared unto the LORD?' (89:1, 6). 104 grounds its praise in God's creation of everything: he stretched out the heavens like a curtain, 'he founded the earth upon her bases, That it should not be moved for ever' (vv. 2, 5). 89A similarly begins with the heavens: 'Thy faithfulness shalt thou establish in the very heavens. And the heavens shall praise thy wonders, O LORD' (vv. 2, 5). Then it moves on to the earth: 'The heavens are thine, the earth also is thine: The world and the fulness thereof thou hast founded them, The north and the south, thou hast created them' (vv. 11f). In 104 creation took place by Yahweh's rebuke of the waters: 'At thy rebuke they fled, At the voice of thy thunder they hasted away. They ascended the mountains, They went down into the valleys,[8] Unto the place which thou hadst founded for them' (vv. 7f). 89A prefaces the act of creation by two verses on the waters and monsters: 'Thou rulest the pride of the sea: When the waves thereof arise thou stillest them. Thou hast broken Rahab in pieces, as one that is slain; Thou hast scattered thine enemies with the arm of thy strength' (vv. 9f). 104 also contains reference to the sea-monster, but it is no longer Yahweh's equal, needing to be destroyed; Yahweh has no equals in 104. He is the master of everything: 'There is leviathan, whom thou hast formed to play with him' (v. 26). In general this is true of the difference between 89A and 104, which has no court of heaven with the sons of Elim terrified by Yahweh, and is able to take greater delight in creation for itself. But the community of theme is obvious, despite the advance of theology in 104, and it is underscored by the absence of this complex elsewhere in either series, with the partial exception of 46 and 93, 95.

The impressiveness of a series of parallels depends upon its comprehensiveness, and it is this which we have found throughout the Korah and Book IV sequences. It has been possible to set the two series out as the psalms for the autumn festival with the same themes running throughout in the same order:

	Korah	Book IV	
10th	42-43; 84	–	Pilgrimage psalms
14th	44; 85	90	Pre-festal lament
15th	45	91; 92	Royal blessing, anointing, procession (marriage)
16th	46	93; 94	Yahweh victorious over waters and human enemies
17th	47	95; 96	Adoration of Yahweh by Israel and nations
18th	48; 87	97; 98	City of God impregnable, nations put to shame.
19th	49	99; 100	Nations warned of Yahweh's supremacy
20th	88	101; 102	Day of humiliation for atonement
21st	89A	103; 104	Yahweh praised for creation, overcoming waters

I have already suggested the reason for the absence of pilgrimage psalms in the Book IV, Jerusalem sequence (p. 87). I have also suggested that 105 and 106 were historical psalms added to Book IV for the celebration of the *Heilsgeschichte* on the eighth day of the feast, which was added after the exile.[9] So the two collections must seem to be based on a common tradition of theme-sequences, and to be, as I have argued from the beginning, an order of psalms, not a rag-bag. It is this which justifies the hypothesis of a traditional theme-sequence at the autumn-festival, at Dan and Jerusalem, to account for the series of correspondences; I shall offer a further hypothesis in the final chapter to explain the rationale of the theme-sequence, as a development of pre-Israelite myth and liturgy.

89A, then, I take to be a psalm composed at Tabor, and adapted for use with the Korah psalms as the hymn of the final day of the festival; and as such it must have held its place in the festal liturgy before the fall of the Northern Kingdom. But what is to be said of the great expansion that has taken place at Jerusalem, trebling its length? This increase is the more remarkable because in all the Korah psalms we have found so little in the way of editorial activity—a few words in 48, 84 and 87 and not much besides.

Two views have been taken of the covenant-appeal and lament in 89: that they derive from a concrete historical situation (for which various further options have been proposed); and that they are part of an annual ritual, in which the king pleaded in humility for Yahweh to be true to his covenant with David, but without the threat of any particular national crisis. The second position is held by Johnson,[10] Ahlström[11] and Eaton[12] for example, and is usually, but not necessarily, combined with the position that the psalm is a unity. Eaton gives five arguments.[13] (i) The speaker is expressly 'thine anointed' in vv. 50f. (ii) 'It is difficult to imagine a king in such a desperate situation' (sc. as that set out in vv. 38ff) 'presenting his prayer in such an extended and stately form as we find in this psalm. He depicts himself dethroned, hunted and virtually done to death, yet he can still begin with a splendid song of royal witness and a lengthy unfolding of the Davidic covenant. Even the lament has a measured, rounded quality . . .' (iii) Comparisons with the language of dethronement used in the laments for Tammuz offered by Ahlström bear this out. (iv) The theme of life's brevity occurs in vv. 47f and also in 144:4, which is 'very probably from the rites of the king's humiliation.' (v) The covenant section even includes the promise of world-dominion (vv. 25ff), which is rather extreme in so dire a plight as that of the lament if it is envisaged literally. The first point is clearly right, and must count against Gunkel, who dated the psalm in the fifth century, when there were no kings. Not very much weight attaches to the last three points. Tammuz rituals, although evidenced in Israel (Ezek. 8:14), cannot be shown to have been an important influence, as Eaton concedes. There are other psalms where man's frailty is a theme, like 8, which Eaton does not claim as royal. The world-dominion theme plays its part in highlighting the contrast between Yahweh's promise and reality. So the issue really turns on the second argument, and must be a matter of judgement.

I should prefer to see the expansion of the psalm as motivated by a historical disaster, following Mowinckel, who speaks of the late monarchy, or Kraus who suggests one of the successors of Josiah. I should, however, like to be a little more specific, and date the psalm in the years after 597 when King Jehoiachin, also called Jeconiah and Coniah, was deported to Babylon at the age of eighteen.[14] I make this suggestion in the light of the meaning of Maskil which I have proposed above (pp. 88ff) as a 'skilful' psalm, playing upon the king's name, and which has been applicable in each of the Korah psalms so titled. For Yahweh's establishment (כּוּן) of his covenant and king are a repeated theme of the psalm: 'Thy faithfulness shalt thou establish (תָכֵן) in the very heavens' (v. 2), 'Thy seed will I establish for ever' (אָכִין, v. 4), 'With whom my hand shall be established' (תָּכּוֹן, v. 21), 'As the moon which is established for ever' (יִכּוֹן, v. 37). In fact it is this theme of establishment, which occurs in the second verse of the original northern psalm, which can be seen as provoking the insertion of the roughly fitting vv. 3f. 'Thy faithfulness shalt thou *establish* in the very heavens' (v. 2b) . . . 'I have made a covenant with my chosen, I have sworn unto David my servant; Thy seed will I *establish* for ever . . .' (vv. 3-4a). The same כוֹן root occurs in v. 21 and v. 37, at the beginning and in the last verse of the covenant section. The southern psalmist is moved by the contrast of ancient hymnody and present catastrophe. Yahweh's faithfulness was said to be established for ever in heaven—what about the establishment of the Davidic line which was covenanted in particular, and in the present case of a youthful king whose very name meant 'Yahweh will establish'? The case is strengthened by the unprecedented nature of the disaster of 597: never before had a king of Judah been deported with so many of the national nobles, and the details of the situation pictured in vv. 38ff fit what is reported of this occasion with some accuracy, as we shall see. Further, there is a passage in Jer. 22:24-30 which indicates that popular hope was entertained of 'Coniah' even after the deportation; Jeremiah feels impelled to contradict any such optimism, 'Thus saith the LORD, Write ye this man childless' (v. 30). The same is true of the last verses of II Kings, where the hope for the future turns upon the lifting up of Jehoiachin's head in the 37th year of his captivity (25:27-30); and it is true too of later times when Shealtiel and Zerubbabel, his descendants, are the focus of national hope. It may even be that the variant forms of his name arose in the attempt to stress its meaning, 'Yahweh shall establish.'

We have then, it would seem, a hymn from Tabor in 89A which was adapted for use on the last day of the Danite autumn festival in the eighth century; and which was expanded and re-cast for use at Jerusalem in the first decade of the sixth.

    89 Maskil of Ethan the Ezrahite.
      1 I will sing of the mercies of the LORD for ever:
        With my mouth will I make known thy faithfulness to all
          generations.
      2 For I have said, Mercy shall be built up for ever;
        Thy faithfulness shalt thou establish in the very heavens.
  3-4 [see below, p. 230]

5 And the heavens shall praise thy wonders, O LORD;
      Thy faithfulness also in the assembly of the holy ones.

I have said enough about the significance of משׂכיל; it is less easy to be confident about Ethan the Ezrahite. The Chronicler was familiar with three main guilds of singers, as well as some subsidiary ones (I Chron. 15:17ff): the Korahites with Heman as leader, and the guilds of Asaph and Ethan. The three are given full genealogies going back to Kohath, Gershom and Merari, the three sons of Levi, in I Chron. 6:33-47. The Korahites are usually mentioned first, although Gershom was the senior line. As one of the major proposals of this book is that the sons of Korah were in fact the old Danite priesthood, I should think it probable that Asaph and Ethan masked other old northern sanctuary priests who had been accepted in Jerusalem on condition that they kept their origin quiet and accepted second-class status. The Asaph psalms contain a number of plain references to a northern origin, especially in their use of the name Joseph[15] and in 80:1f, and should probably be associated with either Bethel as the second main northern shrine, or Shechem ('Salem,' 76:2). Ethan would then be the name for one of the other sanctuaries, and Tabor has seemed the obvious candidate. The Chronicler vacillates, however, between the forms Ethan and Jeduthun (I Chron. 16:41f; 25:1, 3), and we can only speculate about the reason for this. Perhaps Jeduthun was the name of the old Taborite priest, and has been assimilated to the famous Ethan the Ezrahite[16] of Solomon's time (I Kgs. 4:31); or perhaps Ethan was the name, which then suggested the assimilation to the famous Ezrahite, but was itself changed under the influence of the name in the headings of Pss. 39, 62 and 77.

The psalm opens on a high note of confidence and gratitude. The hideous doubts of Yahweh's wonders and faithfulness and covenant-mercy being lost in death (88:10-12, pp. 196, 206) are gone with the darkness of yesterday. In the clear light of the final and high day of the festival the nation's prayer has come before Yahweh (88:13), and it is felt with some assurance that his[17] promised mercies will never give out. For all his lifetime the priest/psalmist will be able to lead the people in his hymn, as generation after generation comes to participate in the festival. What brings this new confidence? It has been borne in on him ('For I have said . . .') that there is no danger of Yahweh's people being cut off in Sheol, because Yahweh has set his reign firm in the heavens, and with it his promise of favour to Israel. חסד will be built up and faithfulness established because Yahweh has put the fear of God into the gods, the holy ones, the sons of the 'El's: henceforth they and their protégés, Israel's enemies, will not dare to lift their heads. Yes, instead of insolence and rebellion these heavenly beings will adore Yahweh, praising his faithfulness and his marvellous overthrow of Rahab.[18] If we ask again, what has brought about this change of mood, the answer must be the ritual of the seventh day: the LORD has commanded his lovingkindness in the daytime, and in the night his song is with us. We shall see references to some of the ritual in the verses ahead.

89:6 For who in the skies can be compared unto the LORD?
   Who among the sons of the gods is like unto the LORD?
 7 A God very terrible in the council of the holy ones,
   And to be feared above all them that are round about him?
 8 O LORD God of hosts, who is a mighty one, like unto thee,
   O JAH?
   And thy faithfulness is round about thee.
 9 Thou rulest the pride of the sea:
   When the waves thereof arise, thou stillest them.
 10 Thou hast broken Rahab (RV) in pieces, as one that is slain;
   Thou hast scattered thine enemies with the arm of thy strength.

The mercies of Yahweh (v. 1) are, as in Isa. 63:7, his mighty deeds, his wonders of v. 5. But in 89A these are not connected with the Red Sea, which is not mentioned, and indeed was not referred to in the entire Korah corpus; and still less with the sure mercies of David, though these naturally were in mind when the psalm was used at Jerusalem. We are back in an earlier period of Israelite theology, when the myth of creation is Yahweh's primary wonder, achieved in battle with Rahab the sea-monster. We know this myth as a part of a common near-eastern culture, from the Babylonian Enuma Elish to the Ugaritic Baal myth, and it is from this common stock that Israel inherited it— an inheritance ultimately to be abjured and excised from the Genesis tradition.

In 89A, however, it is still in its primal form, more fully expressed than anywhere else in the OT. The presence of other divine beings alongside Yahweh in heaven is here taken for granted under a series of different expressions: the holy ones, the sons of the אלים, those round about Yahweh, the צבאות (which, given the context, unquestionably means the heavenly hosts). The first of these expressions and the last two were accepted into later Israelite religious language as referring to *inferior* heavenly beings—angels and the like, Yahweh's train of myriads of attending acolytes. בני אלים was too uncomfortably close to polytheism, and survives elsewhere only in 29:1. But there is no question that the קהל or סוד in which these beings are here assembled is a mere angelic court such as Isaiah witnessed at his call. The very rhetorical questions show clearly that other sons of the gods were nearly as mighty as Yahweh. He has no need to terrify his angelic servants, and there would be nothing to sing of, no faithfulness worth making known, if the pride of the seas and Rahab had not been a worthy enemy from whom Yahweh himself had been in peril.

What lies before us, then, is a still mythological form of the creation story, to which parallels in pre-Israelite religion are manifold. Ahlström cites a number of Sumerian and Akkadian texts in which the supremacy of the god is asserted in a series of rhetorical questions. 'The holy ones' is a frequent Ugaritic equivalent for the gods, and the phrase 'the assembly of *bn 'lm*' occurs in Baal II.iii.13. At Ugarit Baal invited the gods and goddesses to a banquet in his newly built palace, and terrified those not attending with his thunder (II.vi.44-vii). He established his hegemony by overwhelming Prince Sea (*ym*) and Judge River (IIIA), and these victories are later referred to as the smiting of *ltn* and other monsters (I*.i.1ff, 27ff).[19] The arrival of Baal, his messengers or his consort Anat is commonly a cause of terror to other gods, issuing in withdrawal, sweat and micturition (V.iii.47ff; etc.). But naturally Yahweh took over not only the virile traits of the Canaanite rain-god Baal; he is also *'El*, the king of the gods (v. 7). In our Ugaritic remains the victory of Baal is not associated with creation; but then we have a close enough parallel to this in the Enuma Elish, where, in an often cited passage, Marduk slays the sea-monster Tiamat and forms the universe from her corpse.[20]

The process by which such a myth was adapted and amended for Israelite use can only be a matter for speculation,[21] but it clearly was accepted and remained a part of popular cosmogony long after the sober accounts of Gen. 2-3 and Gen. 1 became orthodoxy. It was taken over by the Jerusalem community in Ps. 74:13f, often dated in its present form to the sixth century; and we find it from the same period in Isa. 51:9f, and reflected in Ezek. 24:5; 32:4ff. It occurs later in Job 26:12f; 9:13, and demythologised accounts are to be found in Ps. 104; Ecclus. 43:23 and Ps. Sol. 2:29f. But the myth appears here in a live form. Creation (v. 11) took place by the transfixing of Rahab the sea-monster as a human enemy is pierced by the sword (כחלל) and trampled underfoot. She and her 'helpers' (Job 9:13), Yahweh's enemies, were scattered by his strong arm (cf. Isa. 51:9). It is possible that creation took place from the cadaver, which was used for another purpose in Ps. 74:14; though such a hypothesis is unnecessary. The triumph over Rahab is linked with Yahweh's rule over the sea, which belongs both in the past as a part of the myth (74:13; Isa. 51:10) and to the ever-renewed and visible present (v. 9; Job 26:13). Each autumn the sea may be seen rearing its rebellious head in pride, as the waves are raised aloft; and then stilled. It is this victory in single combat which drives the lesser gods into such terror. To them Yahweh is נערץ רבה, greatly[22] (62:2; 78:15) to be feared. His sole ally is his 'faithfulness round about' him, thought of as an extension of his presence, like righteousness and judgement, mercy and truth in v. 14.

Some of these concepts are found also in the Korah psalms. God is terrible (נורא) in v. 7 and in 47:2; he is Yahweh (God) of hosts in v. 8, in 46:7, 11, and 84:1, 3, 8, 12; he overcomes the pride of the waters in v. 9 and 46:2f. Others are found only in the Elohistic Psalter. God is called Jah only here and at 68:4 in the psalms; the conquest of the sea-monster comes only in v. 10 and 74:13f; the terrifying of the lesser gods by Yahweh in their assembly comes only in v. 7 and 82. 89A shows every sign of being both primitive and northern.

89:11 The heavens are thine, the earth also is thine:
      The world and the fulness thereof, thou hast founded them.

12 The north and the south, thou hast created them:
      Tabor and Hermon rejoice in thy name.

13 Thou hast a mighty arm:
      Strong is thy hand, and high is thy right hand.

14 Righteousness and judgement are the foundation of thy throne:
      Mercy and truth attend thy presence (יקדמו פניך).

15 Blessed is that people that know the cultic shout (תרועה):
      They walk, O LORD, in the light of thy countenance.

16 In thy name do they rejoice all the day:
      And in thy righteousness are they exalted.

17 For thou art the glory of their strength:
      And in thy favour shall our horn be exalted.

18 For our shield belongeth unto the LORD;
      And our king to the Holy One of Israel [RV text].

The close connection between creation and the killing of Rahab is emphasized by the return to Yahweh's 'arm with might' (v. 13) after 'the arm of his strength' (v. 10). His strong hand and uplifted right hand are drawn from images of gods[23] overwhelming demonic enemies, as familiar to the Israelite of the centuries of settlement as they are to us from St Michael (George) and the Dragon, their lineal descendants. Yahweh's victory made possible his creation: the whole universe, the heavens and the earth and all that is therein, the north and the south as limits of the world, all were set up, all drew their being, by virtue of this turning point. I have discussed some of the options over Tabor and Hermon above; it seems easiest to understand their inclusion as the two holy mountains where the Ethanite and Korahite priests resided. They rejoice in Yahweh's name in v. 12b as God's people do in v. 16a: that is, as sanctuaries of Yahweh, they join with Israel in the worship and cries of Hallelujah, rejoicing in Jah's name.

After his opening song of Yahweh's mercy and faithfulness in creation and in domination of the world above, the priest/poet turns to describe what Mowinckel and Ahlström have correctly seen to be the day's ritual—what is in fact the ritual of the last day of the feast, 21st Bul. It goes on 'all the day' (v. 16), and is marked by the תרועה; the combination of the cultic shouting and blasts on the שופר impressively rocked the hillside (v. 15).[24] It is performed by the people (v. 15a), that is by 'all Israel,' by the massed adult male population that has come on the pilgrim-festival, and is ready for war if war it is to be. They 'walk,' or process (יהלכון) in their tens of thousands; the pi‘el form of the verb is often used in this formal sense (55:14; 85:13; 104:3; cf. BDB). They rejoice in his name, not by pious meditation, but in loud joyful cries (v. 16). Since the form Hallelujah is so widely testified as a form of such joyful crying of the divine name, and since Jah is actually given in v. 8 as a form in use in this community, it seems likely that massed cries of 'Hallelujah' in unison were a feature of the day's ritual. The warlike side of the whole liturgy is implied in vv. 17-18. Israel exults because Yahweh's presence 'adorns' (תפארת) its strength, that is its army. The third person is then changed significantly for the first: in his favour shall our horn be exalted,[25] that is in coming battles. For our shield, that is our king[26] as in 84:9 and 47:9 (both Korah psalms), belongs to Yahweh, our king to the Holy One of Israel. Ancient armies, like modern ones, knew that victory was dependent upon the skill of the general; they differed in seeing that skill as a function of divine blessing.

Such an interpretation of vv. 15-18 really seems inescapable, partly because of כל־היום which cannot be translated 'every day' without violence, and of the תרועה, which must imply a cultic context; and partly because so many other details combine to lend force to the view in the way I have suggested. Anderson and others minimise the impact of these features, and leave the psalm with a pious and colourless tone. But once the passage is seen as a reflection on the day's ritual, it is difficult not to follow Mowinckel,[27] Schmidt and Ahlström further (though not all the way). What is it which is the focus of the ritual march, which evokes the cultic cries, trumpetings and Hallelujah's? They are immediately preceded by a reference to Yahweh's throne: 'Righteousness and judgement are the foundation of thy throne: Mercy and truth יקדמו פניך' (v. 14). The last phrase is often translated 'go before thy face' (RV; RSV, NEB similar), but Delitzsch comments that it means rather 'coming to meet a person to present oneself to him,' citing 88:14; 95:2 and Mic. 6:6, cp. לפניו יהלך, to go before, in 85:13; cf. also Kirkpatrick, 'as angels attending in God's presence . . . rather than as couriers preceding him.' 'Angels' however is an approximation. Here, as in 85:10-13, we have the four extensions of Yahweh's presence which take the names of 'virtues,' and were, as we saw in that passage,[28] at least in part domesticated Canaanite gods. They are 'the foundation' of his throne, and were no doubt in the form of animals; Solomon's throne had two lions beside the arms (I Kgs. 10:19), and Ezekiel saw in his visions (1; 10) God's throne like a chariot borne by four living creatures. So it would seem likely that the focus of the processing and shouting in 89A is again the throne of Yahweh, supported on four 'virtues' in the form of animals—probably, as with Ezekiel, a lion, an ox, a man and an eagle. At Tabor they were Mercy and Truth before, Righteousness and Judgement behind; at Dan Righteousness and Peace, Mercy and Truth (85:10f, 13); at Jerusalem Honour and Majesty, Strength and Beauty (96:6).

Mowinckel and his followers think in terms of a procession with Yahweh's throne at the head, moving to his enthronement. If we take away the translation 'go before thy face,' however, there is no indication that Yahweh's symbol is on the move, and there is none of the language of kingship, going up, taking of reign and throne, such as we have seen in 47. We have already had a day of Enthronement ritual on 17th with 47, and this is something different. It may be that the central rite of the day is a processional march past the divine symbol: 'They walk, O LORD, in the light of thy countenance.' We cannot exclude the possibility that the symbol was carried at the head of the procession first, but this would rest on the applicability of other psalms as parallels, and this is hazardous. The psalm closest to 89A is 24, which follows 22-23 as 89A follows 88. It begins, like 89A, with the praise of Yahweh for founding the earth and establishing it over the seas; v. 6 runs, 'This is the generation of them that seek after him, That seek *thy face*, even Jacob.' It contains a statement of the purity required of those who stand in his holy place, and the portal dialogue, implying the entry of the ark into the Temple—features lacking from 89A. The question is not very important, however; if the carrying of the symbol was thought to be significant, it would have been mentioned.

Why should such a processional march issue in such an outburst of joy? I think because now for the first time the people see Yahweh's face, in a literal sense. 'When shall I come and see God?,' asked the priest at the beginning of the Korah sequence (42:2); and not him only, but 'Every one of them sees God' (84:7). All Israel came to see God at the festival, but so far the closest approximation to this experience has been the carrying of the ephod at the head of the procession into the Dan shrine; his presence has been invisible. But now they process 'in the light of his countenance.' As a general principle of interpretation, I have suggested that we ought to prefer the real to the spiritualised or metaphorical meaning throughout; thus here 'all the day' means 21st Bul, not 'continually'; 'knowing the cultic shout' means shouting it, not remembering it; 'walking' means processing, not passing one's life; 'their strength,' 'our horn,' mean Israel's army, not its generalised physical and moral well-being, and so on. What then are we to make of 'Thou hast scattered thine enemies with the arm of thy strength . . . Thou hast a mighty arm: Strong is thy hand, and high is thy right hand'? The last phrase especially has either to be taken as poetical, or as a reflection of the raised right hand of a real image. We may hesitate to think that real images of Yahweh were in use in northern Israel in the eighth century, but Ahlström claims that such an image buried in the shrine at Hazor was of Yahweh,[29] and such images seem to be implied both by the repeated imagery of the battle with the sea-monster, and also by the comments of Hosea. Yahweh was probably worshipped at Tabor under the form of an image with uplifted arm, like the bronze image of Baal from Ugarit.

For it is not only here that we have the repeated imagery, 'the arm of thy strength,' 'an arm with might,' 'strong is thy hand,' 'uplifted is thy right hand.' We have exactly the same picture in the same context in Isa. 51:9f, 'Awake, awake, put on *strength*, O *arm of the LORD . . .* Art thou not it that cut *Rahab* in pieces, that *pierced* the dragon? Art thou not it which dried up the *sea?*' The very cumbrousness of the expression shows how deep is the association of Rahab's death not just with Yahweh but with Yahweh's arm. Or again in Job 26:13, 'And by his understanding he smiteth through *Rahab*. By his spirit the heavens are beauty; *His hand* hath *pierced* the fleeing serpent.' The association seems to underlie 74:11ff also: 'Why drawest thou back *thy hand*, even *thy right hand?* (Pluck it) out of thy bosom (and) consume (them). Yet God is my King of old, Working salvation in the midst of the earth. Thou didst break up the *sea* by *thy strength*: Thou brakest the heads of *the sea-monsters* in the waters.' There is no arm or hand, but a sword implying one in Isa. 27:1, 'In that day the LORD with his sore and great and strong sword shall punish Leviathan.' In almost all the passages connected with the killing of the sea-monster, Yahweh's arm, hand or sword is mentioned, and the combined force of these references can hardly be accidental; it is likely to go back to ancient real images of Yahweh with real arms, hands and weapons.[30]

Our knowledge of conditions at Tabor is limited to a single significant passage elsewhere, Hos. 5:1ff,[31] and this seems to bear such a conclusion out. 'Hear this, O ye priests, and hearken, ye house of Israel, and give ear, O house of the king, for against you is the judgement; for ye have been a snare at Mizpah, and a net spread upon Tabor . . . now, O Ephraim, thou hast committed whoredom, Israel is defiled. They will not frame their doings to turn unto their God: for the spirit of whoredom is in the midst of them, and they know not the LORD' (vv. 1, 3f). Hosea saw northern worship as whoredom, idolatry, the worship of gods other than the LORD. It is not at all likely that this is what the worshippers saw themselves as doing, as our own text witnesses. But there must have been features of the worship at Mizpah, Tabor and elsewhere that gave colour to his belief; and it is only too credible that it arose from the presence of metal images in these centres—as he wrote elsewhere, 'And now they sin more and more, and have made them molten images of their silver, even idols according to their own understanding, all of them the work of craftsmen: they say of them, Let the sacrificers of men kiss the calves' (13:2). A silver, or a silver-plated image would enable us to give additional meaning to 'They walk in *the light of thy countenance . . .*

the *glory* of their strength.'[32] Whether in the shrine or borne aloft in procession, the glinting metal sheds, as from itself, rays of light on the marching concourse.

89:1f, 5-18 formed, in the opinion of Duhm, 'a poem rounded and complete in itself,' and we may cordially endorse his adjectives. The hymnic form, the weighty double-four rhythm, the centrality of the pre-Israelite myth, the primitive creation-doctrine, the unwavering confidence, the mention of northern shrines, the pre-monotheistic theology, the probable presence of an image, all mark 89A off from the rest of the psalm; but further, it is a rounded unity in itself, even without the possibility of further verses from the end. It runs from the praise of Yahweh's faithfulness in the heavens in the first verses to his glory and favour to the Israelite people and king in the last. Duhm's limitation was in thinking of it as a poem, as Gunkel's was in seeing it only as a hymn. A hymn it is, but a hymn to close a day, and a week of festival. Israel's weakness was carried on pilgrimage by king and people to Yahweh's shrine in 42 and 43, and lamented with eloquence in 44. Successive days' ritual marked the celebration of Yahweh's blessing from 15th Bul onwards: on his anointed in 45, on the year's battles in 46, on his kingship in 47, on his city in 48, against invaders in 49. On the 20th there had been a day of darkness, with grim atonement rites (88); and on 21st 89A provides the last hymn of the festival as the sun goes down. Israel has spent the day celebrating Yahweh's victory over Rahab, his foundation of the world, his incomparable power in heaven and the implacable certainty of triumph for his people's army and king. The disaster of 722 and the later development of this robust and confident liturgy at Jerusalem, are alike comments of irony and pathos.

The Dan and Tabor psalmodies were taken south after the catastrophe of 722, and eventually accepted, along with their bearers, the Korahite and Ethanite priesthoods, into a place in the Jerusalem establishment. Not many amendments were required to make them fit for use at the southern festivals; a few words to be omitted, changed or inserted, especially in 48, 84 and 87, where it must be made plain that Yahweh's city is Jerusalem and not Dan, and his mountain Zion and not Hermon. It is easy to think that the tradents made these changes themselves, and with good heart; the old belief in the inviolability of Dan had turned out to be an error, but through repeated crises in the eighth century Yahweh had demonstrated beyond doubt that his promise had in fact been directed to Jerusalem. The dew of Hermon had fallen upon Zion (133:3). The richness and force of the old psalm-sequence, and the prestige and antiquity of the northern exiles, now turned loyal Judahites, commended the collection as an alternative festal liturgy to the provincial southerners. No doubt it was the easier for the newcomers to be accepted as allies during the long reign of the impious Manasseh, when Yahwism was threatened and was a common cause to priesthoods from north and south alike; and the northern doctrine of a centralised cult, enshrined in the Deuteronomic tradition, was to prove an invaluable lever.

In the course of time two major changes were made to the old Korahite-Ethanite psalmody. One took place in the first decade of the sixth century, after the deportation of King Jehoiachin and many of the leading Israelites in 597, as I have indicated above. This involved a glaring unsuitability in the hymning of Yahweh's steadfastness to the covenant and promise that he had *established*, and resulted in a large-scale re-writing of 89A. The second took place over the following century, as the old ritual associated with 88 came to seem increasingly primitive and barbaric, and the exilic reforms brought in a specialised pre-festal Atonement Day on the 10th Tishri, and then an additional eighth day to Tabernacles. These reforms caused 88 and 89 to be transferred to the Korah appendix, along with 84 and 85, and their places to be taken by a sequence of David-psalms (51-72). I shall briefly describe the expansion of 89 in the remainder of this chapter.

The Davidic covenant had stood the test of four centuries in Jerusalem while dynasties came and went in northern Israel, and finally went for ever. It was already long enshrined in scripture (II Sam. 7, and passim in Samuel) and liturgy (Pss. 18 and 132 at least), and was to be the corner-stone of Israelite hope from the exile on to the present day. Small wonder then that the southern adapter of 89A feels that the old hymn to Yahweh's covenant-faithfulness is an occasion for intercession and reproach, that he may live up to his reputation and deliver his king and people from their present plight. To this end he appeals at length to David's covenant through Nathan, latching it on to the earlier psalm by taking up a number of its phrases, and also stretching the II Sam. promises slightly, in a way which is easily understood in the circumstances.[33]

The stress upon Yahweh's חסד being built up for ever, and his faithfulness as established in heaven (89A:2) provokes an immediate interpolation:

> 89:3 I have made a covenant with my chosen,
> I have sworn unto David my servant;
> 4 Thy seed will I establish for ever,
> And build up thy throne to all generations.   [Selah

'Covenant' draws on the covenant implied in חסד and faithfulness; 'will establish,' 'for ever,' 'build up' and 'to all generations' are direct echoes of the previous two verses. The reference to the Davidic covenant is thus made about as forcibly as one could imagine, and Yahweh is said to have sworn it, which is more than the text of II Sam. 7 strictly permits. The adapter's favourite 3+3's, and the harshness of the syntactical transitions, before and after the interpolation, both betray his handiwork. The move back to 89A, v. 5, is the less harsh of the two because the psalm is interrupted after v. 4 with a Selah. Following the interpretation of Selah set out above (pp. 102-6), we should expect a recital here of some suitable scripture; and there can be little doubt what recital is likely. The Davidic covenant appealed to is given in II Sam. 7:1-17; 'my servant David' comes in v. 5 and v. 8 of this chapter, 'thy seed' in v. 12, 'thy throne shall be established for ever' in v. 16. The detailed appeal to Nathan's prophecy both in vv. 3f and in vv. 19-37 makes it virtually certain that the Selah marks the recital of this passage.

After this brief interposition the adapter allows the old hymn to run its majestic course; and the final verse, with its confidence that Israel's shield and king belongs to Yahweh, provides him with the link with David and Jehoiachin once more.

> 89:19 Then thou spakest in vision to thy covenanted ones (חסידיך),
> And saidst, I have laid help upon one that is mighty;
> I have exalted one chosen out of the people.
> 20 I have found David my servant;
> With my holy oil have I anointed him:
> 21 With whom my hand shall be established;
> Mine arm also shall strengthen him.

22 The enemy shall not do him violence;
    Nor the son of wickedness afflict him.
23 And I will beat down his adversaries before him,
    And smite them that hate him.
24 But my faithfulness and my mercy shall be with him;
    And in my name shall his horn be exalted.
25 I will set his hand also on the sea,
    And his right hand on the rivers.
26 He shall cry unto me, Thou art my father,
    My God, and the rock of my salvation.
27 I will also make him (my) first-born,
    The highest of the kings of the earth.
28 My mercy will I keep for him for evermore,
    And my covenant shall be faithful with him.
29 His seed also will I make to endure for ever,
    And his throne as the days of heaven.

The firm 'then' (אָז), with which the passage begins, refers to the
making of David's covenant in vv. 3f, and makes a third harsh
transition. God actually spoke in vision to Nathan, and through
Nathan to David; but the vision was ultimately a revelation to all
God's people, his covenanted ones. The Hebrew MSS divide between
singular and plural, and the Versions favour the plural. We should
probably prefer the harder, more widely testified plural, which could
then have been changed to the more obvious singular (= Nathan).
David can hardly be in mind in view of v. 20. The appeal to the vision
has been made with great skill. It is precisely the survival of the
Davidic line which is now in question with the deportation of the king;
and the promised success of Israel in battle, which has now been so
demonstrably falsified, must seem increasingly unbelievable.

The adaptation has been made with a genuine feel for the
continuity, and phrases from the older hymn are repeatedly echoed:
might(y), exalted, my hand, my arm, established (note the slight
artificiality with which the key word is worked in), my-faithfulness-
and-my-covenanted-love, in my name, his horn shall be exalted, my
covenanted love for ever . . . faithful. It is this continuity which has
made it easy to see the whole psalm as coming from a single hand.
Otherwise the appeal is mainly to II Sam. 7, amplified by other
Davidic passages, and by the author's imagination. The revelation to
Nathan is called a vision in II Sam. 7:17, 'David my servant' comes in
vv. 5, 8, 'the son(s) of wickedness shall not afflict him (them)' in v. 10,

'(I will be his) father, (and he shall be my son)' is said of Solomon in v. 14, '(thy) seed . . . (the) throne (of) his (kingdom) for ever' in vv. 12f, 16. Texts for many of the other phrases spring to mind, and may be found in the commentaries.

Of the remainder, 'I have laid help upon' (v. 19) is a curious phrase, paralleled at 21:6; as honour and majesty were conferred on the king there, so is guaranteed divine aid here—perhaps even sacramentally, with the oil. That 'The enemy shall not בו ישׁיא' (v. 22) also is not clear, and may mean 'surprise' as in 55:15 (Kirkpatrick). The promised dominion from the sea (Mediterranean) to the river (Euphrates) (v. 25) is a biblical commonplace, and is probably taken from the (earlier) Ps. 72:8; 'the River' has become 'the rivers,' Tigris and Euphrates, and their tributaries.[34] 'First-born' (v. 27) is a verbal innovation, the word being otherwise used of Israel (Exod. 4:22; Jer. 31:9), but is only a midrashic expansion of the previous verse: if God was David's Father, David was his son, and with many successors to follow on his throne he was the first-born son. The kings of the earth are not God's sons, but are drawn in from v. 25, the hitherto rulers of the fertile crescent.

89:30 If his children forsake my law,
        And walk not in my judgements;
   31 If they profane my statutes,
        And keep not my commandments;
   32 Then I will visit their transgression with the rod,
        And their iniquity with stripes.
   33 But my mercy will I not utterly take from him,
        Nor suffer my faithfulness to fail.
   34 My covenant will I not profane,
        Nor alter the thing that is gone out of my lips.
   35 One thing have I sworn by my holiness;
        I will not lie unto David;
   36 His seed shall endure for ever,
        And his throne as the sun before me.
   37 It shall be established for ever as the moon (RV),[35]
        And (as) the faithful witness in the sky (RV).   [Selah

The point of the appeal was not so much what God had said to David for himself as what he had promised to his successors, his seed, and in particular King Jehoiachin. There is therefore a considerable expansion of II Sam. 7:14: 'if he (sc. thy seed) commit iniquity, I will chasten him with the rod of men, and with the stripes of the children of men; but my mercy shall not depart from him, as I took it from Saul, whom I put away before thee. And thy house and thy kingdom shall be made sure for ever before thee: thy throne shall be established for ever.' The thrust of this needs exposition. It was a limited punishment that had been laid down, a beating and nothing more, for the sins of coming generations (which had no doubt been committed), not a withdrawal of Yahweh's covenant. What is this then that has happened with the deportation of David's seed Jehoiachin? 'Commit iniquity' is expanded in Deuteronomic style—law, judgements, statutes, commandments; forsake, walk in, keep (vv. 30f), visit, transgression, iniquity (v. 32). The Deuteronomic background of the author is to be seen in other phrases too, such as 'gone out of my lips' (Deut. 23:23), 'as the days of heaven' (Deut. 11:21), and confirms Gunkel's view of the passage as a sixth century expansion of an already fixed II Sam. 7.[36] Faithfulness is coupled with 'mercy' as in vv. 1-4; and in place of the prosaic contrast with Saul, recourse is had to the idea of God's having sworn an oath to David, a gloss on the promise in Samuel, designed to put pressure on Yahweh and (subconsciously) to reassure both speaker and people.

The author's liking for celestial similes has already been shown in v. 29, 'And his throne as the days of heaven.' We have three further instances in vv. 36f, 'And his throne as the sun before me . . . as the moon, And the faithful witness in the sky.' It is the last phrase which is the trouble; the options range from Yahweh himself to the moon, the natural heavenly order, and the rainbow. As Yahweh has already sworn, and as Job 16:19 says 'Even now, behold, my witness is in heaven, And he that voucheth for me is on high,' we might think of Yahweh (Delitzsch, Kraus). But Job's witness is probably his angel, and there is something very surprising about Yahweh himself following 'the sun before me.' Kirkpatrick refers to Jer. 31:35f; 33:20f, 25f, as support for 'the ordinances of heaven and earth'; but the concreteness of sun and moon leads us to expect a third concrete object (and not, weakly, the moon again). This leads Ahlström to go back to Luther's suggestion of the rainbow, which was the guarantee of Yahweh's covenant in the clouds for ever (Gen. 9:8-17). It is not an important objection to this that there is no repeated *creation* (Delitzsch); but it may more forcefully be said that one would have expected a mention of the rainbow if that is what is intended. I think this may be countered, however, by noting the Selah that follows immediately. A second Selah would imply a second recital of tradition; and it is not impossible that the D-version of the Noah story was in use at this juncture. The flood is the later and more respectable equivalent of the Rahab story which underlies 89A: Yahweh stills the waters and limits them to their place (but having now first unleashed them himself); he covenants that such destruction will never again take place, and seals his word with a sign in the clouds. So as the sun, moon and stars were permanent signs at creation (vv. 36b, 37a), the rainbow is a dependable witness to the permanency of Yahweh's covenant in nature and in Israel's history (v. 37b). Once more the understanding of Selah as implying a recital could enable us to make sense of a difficult text.[37]

> 89:38 But thou hast cast off and rejected,
>   Thou hast been wroth with thine anointed.
> 39 Thou hast abhorred the covenant of thy servant:
>   Thou hast profaned his crown to the ground.
> 40 Thou hast broken down all his hedges;
>   Thou hast brought all his strongholds to ruin.
> 41 All that pass by the way spoil him:
>   He is become a reproach to his neighbours.
> 42 Thou hast exalted the right hand of his adversaries;
>   Thou hast made all his enemies to rejoice.
> 43 Yea, thou turnest back the edge of his sword,
>   And hast not made him to stand in the battle.
> 44 Thou hast made his brightness to cease,
>   And cast his throne down to the ground.
> 45 The days of his youth hast thou shortened:
>   Thou hast covered him with dishonour.   [Selah

The language is in part traditional (cf. 44:9-13; 79:4; 80:12); but it is sufficiently precise to make a situation in the 590's a probability. (i) The enemy has broken down all the Davidic king's 'hedges,' and made a ruin of his strongholds; i.e. he has taken all the fortified towns which stood siege, and 'all' must include Jerusalem. Nebuchadnezzar personally besieged Jerusalem in 597, and Jehoiachin quickly capitulated (II Kgs. 24:11ff). (ii) The consequence was not a 'beating' such as kings of Judah had had to stomach all too often before, but something far more drastic: 'Thou' (emphatic אתה), so far from being faithful to the covenant just rehearsed, hast abhorred it and rejected the Davidic king ('thine anointed') just like Saul in days of old, and in express contradiction to the promise of II Sam. 7:15. Yahweh has made his brightness[38] to cease, not just to be dimmed, and crown and throne have been profaned and overturned. Such a dire catastrophe could only properly refer to the disasters under Jehoahaz, Jehoiachin or Zedekiah at the end of Judah's history; but there is no mention of any sieges under Jehoahaz. The profaning of the crown to the ground (v. 39) and the casting of the throne to the ground (v. 44) would suit either 597 or 586. (iii) 'The days of his youth hast thou shortened' (v. 45) implies that the king was young, and 'thou hast covered him (העטית) with dishonour' should, as usual, be taken to imply a literal, not just a metaphorical clothing. Jehoiachin was eighteen at the time of the disaster (II Kgs. 24:8), and spent the next thirty-seven years in prison clothing (25:29). Zedekiah was thirty-two, which was not young for the age. (iv) V. 45a is often taken to mean 'prematurely old' (and v. 45b is sometimes emended to reinforce this view). But such an interpretation sounds rather anachronistic, and the phrase would suit a young king who had been deposed, though not killed, much better. But (as Eaton insists) there is a king conducting the lament in vv. 49ff. We should have a resolution of the difficulty if it is Jehoiachin who has been deposed and Zedekiah who is still there as Yahweh's anointed. In this way the details given in the lament confirm the suggestion of the repeated כון language in the first half of the psalm as a play on the royal name Jehoiachin. The Selah could suitably cover the recital of such matter as II Kgs. 24:8-17.

89:46 How long, O LORD, wilt thou hide thyself for ever?
(How long) shall thy wrath burn like fire?

47 O remember how short my time is:
For what vanity hast thou created all the children of men!

48 What man is he that shall live and not see death,
That shall deliver his soul from the hand of Sheol (RV)?

49 Lord, where are thy former mercies,   [Selah
Which thou swarest unto David in thy faithfulness?

50 Remember, Lord, the reproach of thy servants;
How I do bear in my bosom (the reproach of) all the many peoples;

51 Wherewith thine enemies have reproached thee, O LORD,
Wherewith they have reproached the footsteps of thine anointed.

52 Blessed be the LORD for evermore.
Amen, and Amen.

We have noted sharp transitions at vv. 3, 5 and 19, where the southern adapter of 89A moved in and out of the older hymn; and we have another transition at v. 46. Vv. 3-4, 19-45 were an almost unbroken succession of 3+3's; we now have a 4+3, and double fours to the end (v. 51). God is addressed twice as אדני, a form which has not occurred throughout the psalm hitherto. There is a sharp break in the train of thought: vv. 20-45 have been exclusively devoted to the Davidic covenant as a means of moving God to action, and the thought returns to this at v. 49; but vv. 47f depend upon quite a different plea, the transitoriness and pathos of the life of all men. Further, the first person singular occurs in v. 47 and v. 50, referring now to the king. While such considerations do not force us to postulate a new hand, it may well be that the court poet had been responsible for the main adaptation, and that the king himself, Zedekiah, was expected to add a few lines of his own at the end. V. 49 is a short restatement of the theme of the whole earlier piece, and it is clearly the Davidic king who is the speaker, so there is no question of an addition from a later generation. There is a similar mention of Yahweh's חסד to his anointed, the seed of David, in the last verse of 18, which could similarly be the contribution of the royal speaker himself.

V. 46 is in fact traditional wording, cf. 79:5; 13:1. The Hebrew of v. 47a is not very easy, 'Remember I what span!,' but the sense is clear, and the text best left alone. A much more pressing problem is why the train of argument has been momentarily diverted into this much more general (and less cogent) line. Once more it seems to me that the answer is given by the Selah following v. 48. 89A had been a *creation*-psalm: it celebrated the founding of the world and the fulness thereof, and the creating of the north and the south (vv. 11f). The story of creation in the bad old Tabor days had been the heathen myth of the conquest of Rahab; now was the opportunity to tell the tale of Yahweh's creation in the far more respectable, monotheistic form which has come down to us in Gen. 2-3. The language of the JE story is echoed in the words create (Gen. 2:4), man (2:7, etc.), live (immortally, 3:22, etc.), death (2:17, etc.) and soul (2:7); but the story itself underlies the meaning of both verses. Man has a limited span on earth by God's judgement of Adam; he will not live or deliver his soul from Sheol, for dust he is and to dust he shall return. All the sons of Adam were created for vanity, tilling the cursed ground in sorrow. So it would seem that the fourth Selah of the psalm provides the final recital of the week, and takes Israel's plea for Yahweh's mercy beyond his promise to David, the son of Adam whom he made strong for himself (80:17), to Adam himself whose pathetic fate lay àlso under the all-merciful word of the creator.

Not only have the Selahs in the psalms we have studied regularly coincided with indications in the near-by text of suitable traditions to be recited; we have also found indications of similar traditions in parallel psalms, e.g. in the two 'city of God' psalms, 48 and 87, whose foundation-legends are indicated in 48:8 and 87:2, both preceding a Selah. The parallel psalm to 89 we have seen to be 104, and 104 is a hymn of thanksgiving for creation which closely follows the Gen. *1* sequence: the light (vv. 1f), the waters above and below (vv. 2-9), the springs and produce of the ground (vv. 10-18), the sun and moon (vv. 19-23), the animals and fish and creeping things (vv. 24-30), the singer himself(vv. 31-35). There is no Selah in 104; the psalm has most likely provided the inspiration for the Gen. 1 account of creation,[39] and 105-106 then complete the salvation history. We have here the kernel of the tradition which has persevered into modern synagogue practice, of reading Gen. 1 on Simhath Torah, the last day of the feast of Tabernacles (now a nine-day feast). What began as the climax of the old northern festival, the celebration of creation in Yahweh's conquest of Rahab in 89A, was adapted in the days before the exile to the Gen. 2-3 story echoed in 89:47-48, and survives in the 'P' creation story to this day. The liturgical placing of the celebration has remained virtually unchanged.

With the last verses the king returns to the main theme. The former mercies sworn to David in Yahweh's faithfulness (v. 49) have been the topic of the main expansion. The reproach of the peoples is a standard gambit with which to stir him to action (44:13ff; 74:10, 18, 22; 79:4, 10). Judah had for four centuries maintained its existence in the face of single enemy peoples and alliances (Isa. 7:2). Things were different now with the arrival on the scene of empires which could draw on the military strength of 'all the many peoples'; how can Israel's leader carry so much on his heart? Kirkpatrick suggests plausibly that Yahweh's anointed in v. 51 is different from the speaker, and that the reproaches of the former's footsteps were insults hurled at Jehoiachin by the victorious Babylonian soldiers as he was led into captivity. All such insults were insults to Yahweh, which surely he would avenge. But the heavens were as brass, and there was neither voice nor answer. The son of David was to spend most of the remainder of his days in misery and iron; the speaker was to witness the killing of his children, the last thing he would see before being blinded. But such disappointment and such anguish do not extinguish religious faith. The

community which knew all this has closed the psalm and the sequence
with the defiant words, 'Blessed be the LORD for evermore. Amen,
and Amen.'

IX

FROM CANAAN TO ISRAEL

Our exegetical method, which began by respecting the psalm-
headings, the Massoretic text and the traditional order of the psalms,
has resulted in a reconstruction of the autumn festal ritual at Dan in
the ninth and eighth centuries. We have found ourselves with a
credible series of themes expressed in rites and psalms for the entire
week, to correspond with 42:8, 'The LORD will command his
lovingkindness in the daytime, And in the night his song shall be with
me.' We have the following sequence:

14th Bul	Lamentation	44, 85
15th	Royal procession, anointing, marriage	45
16th	Victory over the waters	46
17th	Yahweh goes up to reign	47
18th	The City of God	48, 87
19th	Invaders, beware!	49
20th	Atonement	88
21st	Yahweh's Triumph	89

What we do not have, at the moment, is an explanation for this
succession of themes. But it is not at all likely that so rich a series of
themes and rituals should simply have arisen by accident, especially
when we have been able to trace the same sequence of ideas through
Book IV. If we are to claim that the Dan festival had this shape, we can
hardly avoid looking for some reason behind it.

Where are we to look? Israelite religion developed out of the
dialectic between the experiences of the Exodus, desert and conquest
on the one hand, and the established traditions of the Canaanite
inhabitants on the other. A pan-Israelite explanation is not a
promising option, because we have already noted references to Israel's
sacred history in the psalms, and they are in nothing approaching the
Biblical order. Furthermore, in the earliest calendars we have, in
Exod. 23 and 34, the autumn festival is an agricultural occasion,
Ingathering; so a Canaanite hypothesis seems more hopeful. Dan, too,

was a sacred site to the Canaanites before the Israelites took it over. So our best recourse is to a possible Canaanite origin; and since we have so little evidence from southern Canaan, that is Palestine, our attention is forced to northern Canaan, or Syria—and in practice that means Ugarit.

Inferences drawn from the Ugaritic literature to conditions and ways of thought in Palestine after the conquest are not without peril. Ugarit was a port on the coastline of ancient Syria, and the greater part of its literary remains can be dated to the 14th century BC. There is thus a distance of some 150 miles in space between Ugarit and Dan, and of some five hundred years in time. Nonetheless few Ugaritic scholars have doubted that there is a more or less close relationship between the Canaanite traditions found at Ugarit, and those presupposed by the Bible. Thus Baal is the rain-god at Ugarit, who in practice exercises sway over the lesser gods, and is responsible for the fertility of the earth, features only too familiar to us from the prophetic books. But there are also aspects of Baal which are transferred to Yahweh: for example, his domination of the lesser gods in the divine council (Pss. 82; 89:6ff), or his residence in the recesses of Mount Zaphon (Isa. 14:13), or his slaying of *Ltn* the slippery serpent and (? Shaliyat) the wriggling serpent (Isa. 27:1, 'leviathan'). Baal-Zaphon is the name of a village as far south as the frontier of Egypt, and the names of Ugaritic gods like Anat and Shapash (Heb. *shemesh*) occur in Palestinian place-names. In particular there are a number of apparent echoes with phrases which have come in our psalms. For example:

> The hinds (*'aylt*) make for the spring.   Baal I*.i.17
> As the hind (*'ayyāl*) panteth after the water brooks.   Ps. 42:1
> Go down to the house of separation (*ḥpṭt*),
> Be counted with them that go down into the earth.   Baal I*.v.15f
> I am counted with them that go down into the pit . . .
> Cut off (*ḥopšî*) among the dead . . .   Ps. 88:4f
> . . . amid the assembly of the sons of the gods (*bn 'elm*)
>   Baal II.iii.13
> Who among the sons of the gods (*bᵉnê 'ēlîm*) is like unto Yahweh?
>   Ps. 89:6

It seems reasonable therefore to accept some relationship between the Ugaritic traditions and the Canaanite traditions which were current at Dan in the days of the conquest.

The Ugaritic remains were discovered in 1929 and the years following; and in the course of the half century since, great progress has been made towards the understanding of the tablets, beginning with the deciphering of the script, which is Semitic cuneiform. The most important unit is a sequence of tablets setting out the myth of Baal, and it is these which are our concern. Four of these tablets are in good, or at least fair condition, and there is virtual unanimity among contemporary scholars on the relative order in which they are to be taken, though many minor, and some major matters are still disputed. The remaining (two or three) tablets are much less well preserved, and there is not enough material on them for there to be agreement on the order (if any) in which they originally stood, although the general subjects covered are evident.

The tablets have been given various numbers, but those first given, by the French scholar Charles Virolleaud, are still the most widely used, and are followed here. The four better preserved tablets are numbered by him V, II, I* and I (in the main alternative numbering, CTA 3, 4, 5, 6). All four have text on both sides, divided into columns: six columns apiece in V, I* and I, eight in II. The original tablets measured roughly 30 × 20 cm, with about 65 lines of writing per column. About 60% of V survives, about 80% of II, about 40% of I* and about 60% of I. As the story is often repetitive—a message being given to envoys, for example, who then repeat it verbatim—a confident reconstruction can frequently be made even when the text is fairly fragmentary. The sequence can be established both on grounds of the general run of the story, and by details linking the end of one tablet with the beginning of another. Thus at the end of V an embassy is despatched to Kothar/Khasis, the craftsman god(s), and at the beginning of II Kothar/Khasis is apparently being addressed by the same embassy (although more than twenty lines are missing both at the end of V and at the beginning of II). At the end of II Baal sends an embassy to Mot, god of the underworld, and the latter seems to have begun his reply in the final missing lines, for he is speaking in the opening verses of I*, which are preserved. We have both the end of I* and the beginning of I, and they tell continuously of the lament of Anat for the dead Baal. The end of I is far from presenting a clear end to the story of V-II-I*-I, although it does close with a colophon: 'Written by Ilumilku the Shubanite . . .'[1] The general run of the story agrees with these detailed links between the tablets. In V Baal complains that he has no palace, and Anat assists him; in II Baal's palace is built; in I*

Baal is killed by Mot; in I Mot is killed by Anat, and Baal is brought to life again.

Not only is the order of the tablets thus far clear; it is also agreed that the myth is related to the agricultural cycle on which the welfare of the people depended. Baal-Hadad, 'who rides on the clouds,' is the rain-god, and the permission of El that his palace be built, is the recognition of his reign. (El is the old, enfeebled, but ultimate king of the pantheon.) In this way there will be rain for 'the people of Dagon's son' (i.e. the people of Ugarit). While a number of scholars have interpreted Mot as being the corn-god,[2] the more general view is that the long summer drought is accounted for by the myth that Baal has been swallowed by Mot; hence the dryness of the earth, and the absence of clouds and rain. However the forces of life survive the summer in the form of the goddess Anat, who probably represents the springs, and perhaps also the wine.[3] With autumn, clouds return to the mountain, and the rains begin again; plainly Anat has put Mot to death, and Baal has come to life once more. The majority opinion is that an annual cycle is in view, though others have seen certain texts as implying a seven-year cycle;[4] but that the myth represents a heavenly contest underlying the alternations of the climate is not in doubt.

Although the order V-II-I*-I is now generally accepted for the better preserved tablets, there is no such broad agreement over the more fragmentary ones. Some of these, like Baal and the Locusts (if that is the correct interpretation), are usually thought not to belong with the main myth; but the real debate is over the tablets numbered VI, III and IV (CTA 1, 2 and 10-11). VI is fragmentary, but appears to describe a petition by Yam, the sea god, and Nahar, the river-god, to El for a palace, a petition which El seems to grant. We have nearly half of III, in two fragments, and can descry the plot more confidently: Yam/Nahar have sent to El to demand the surrender of Baal, and El capitulates; later, however, perhaps at Yam's court, Baal is supplied with two magic clubs, with which he first wounds and finally lays low the two water powers. IV is in a different hand from the other six tablets, all of which were inscribed by Ilumilku; and it also differs in being written on one side only. It describes Baal's repeated sexual union with a heifer, which is either Anat, or is under Anat's care; the tablet ends with the birth of a son to Baal.

In (the small remains of) Baal and the Locusts, Baal is the only divine character to appear, so that it is plausible to think of it as a separate poem. But in IV we have the familiar alliance of Baal and

Anat, and in VI and III come El, Baal, Anat, Yam/Nahar and Kothar/Khasis, the craftman-god(s), all of whom recur in the main myth. It will be a more satisfying solution to the problem the more tablets we can fit into the myth; and in consequence there has been a tension between scholarly caution and scholarly desire to be as inclusive as possible. The most cautious position, limiting the myth to the four best preserved tablets, is represented by John Gray,[5] who takes VI and III to belong to a separate myth concerned with divine providence. More boldly, the recent edition of the French scholars, André Caquot, Maurice Sznycer and Andrée Herdner, *Textes Ougaritiques* (1974), prefaces III to the main sequence, while keeping VI and IV as separate units. Herdner herself, however, in the standard text, *Corpus des tablettes alphabétiques* (1963), included VI at the beginning of the sequence, giving VI-III-V-II-I*-I as the whole poem. J.C. de Moor, in his brilliant *The Seasonal Pattern in the Ugaritic Myth* (1971), accepts the same six tablets, but argues for inserting the two Yam/Nahar tablets between V and II; so according to him the sequence would be V-VI-III-II-I*-I. Others again, like Sir Godfrey Driver, *Canaanite Myths and Legends* (1956), have the same order as Herdner, but include IV at the end.[6]

It is not for me to maintain opinions here on so controversial a matter, though I may make the general point that the more there is of a tablet the more learned thinking seems to find it possible to include it in the sequence. Nor do the alleged difficulties over III seem to be insuperable.[7] For our purposes it is enough to take the rather cautious position of Caquot, though I should be happy to include all seven tablets. Regardless of whether de Moor is right over the order, there would seem to be so close a correspondence between the myth and the Syrian cycle of seasons that we can claim to have understood the matter in outline.

The climatic cycle in Syria does not differ greatly from that in Palestine. Following the summer drought come light rains in autumn, followed by heavy rain in November-January. At the same time the wind blows more strongly, and there are storms. The rain, which has been so much welcomed, pours down the wadis in Palestine; in Syria it falls on the majestic ranges of Libanus and Antilibanus, and the rivers swell and flood destructively, especially in places near the sea like Ugarit. Thus there are two seasons of peril for such a community. In the first half of the year (beginning there, as in Israel, with the autumn festival[8]) there is the peril of the waters: the storm-tossed sea lifting its breakers on the one side, and the flooding rivers threatening houses and crops on the other. In the second half of the year there is the peril of no water. The rain ceases, the rivers become trickles and in many cases dry up. It may even be thought inevitable that such communities should evolve a myth, both to explain such a danger-laden cycle, and to encompass its survival.

In this way we can account for the two phases of the Ugaritic myth. Baal is twice in the power of hostile gods. First El delivers him to Yam/Nahar, 'prince Sea and judge River,' and he overcomes them with the magic maces. Then he succumbs to Mot, and is restored to life thanks to the lamentations of El and Anat. The two phases of the story cover the two phases of the climatic year. It is not important whether we include VI or not, or even whether VI-III come first, or follow V.

In III, Baal is found threatening Yam, whom he will drive from his royal throne with the aid of the maces. Yam/Nahar send an embassy to El's court, demanding unceremoniously the surrender of Baal. The gods cringe before these messengers, and although Baal bids them withstand Yam's arrogance, El capitulates and promises that Baal will be Yam's slave and tributary. Baal trembles with rage, and is about to do violence to the messengers, but is restrained by Anat and Athtart, El's consort. Then, after an intermission concerned with the claims of Athtar, god of the desert, Baal is found in Yam's court (?) meditating vengeance after being handed over by El. Kothar/Khasis come to his aid, forming the maces, Yagrush and Ayyamur. Baal hurls the first, and strikes Yam/Nahar on the chest, but without damaging effect; the second, however, strikes them on the head and lays them low. Baal drags them in triumph, and Athtart salutes his victory and coming kingship.[9]

We have thus, in mythic form, the essence of the winter trial of strength between fertility and flood; by February the storms and overflowing rivers have spent their force, and order returns. The god of Dagon's people is clearly in power. It does not greatly matter, for our purposes, whether III was preceded by VI. In VI El is discovered despatching messengers to Anat: she is to make the earth fruitful, and to hasten to El. Soon afterwards El is again sending an embassy, this time to Kothar/Khasis to attend with speed after completing some work at the furnace. Later El takes a goblet in his hands, and bids proclaim the name of Yam, the beloved of El, to be Yaw, his Son; he seems then to presage a contest between Yam and Baal, and finally prepares a sacrifice. If VI in fact preceded III, then we could conjecture an explanation for these features. After the summer, Anat is to fertilise the soil once more. With the rising waters, Yam and Nahar are claiming sovereignty over the gods, to be expressed in the building of a palace; hence the message to Kothar/Khasis, who are to build it. El proclaims Yam's lordship with the throne-name Yaw, prince of the gods under himself, while fully conscious that Baal will contest this. It does not matter if VI is an unrelated poem of somewhat different interpretation, because the essence of the struggle between Yam and Baal is given in III.

A rather similar situation applies with V and II. Both are secure in the main myth, but the order is disputed, the normal (VI)-III-V-II being challenged by de Moor's V-VI-III-II. In V Baal demands a palace, and in II it is built; so that, whichever is right, the building of Baal's palace, i.e. the establishment of his reign, follows on his victory over Yam/Nahar. De Moor attempts to explain every detail in the myth in terms of the agro-climatic cycle. If he is right, then the myth is to a large extent an allegory. If he is not, then the myth is a story in its own right, but with a general relation to the seasonal fluctuations.

In V Baal is discovered ordering a feast on his mountain-home, Zaphon, and looking at his daughters, Pidray, daughter of the light(-ning), and Talay, daughter of the showers, for whom he desires a palace. He sends his servants to Anat, who has in the meantime been engaged in slaughter and in self-adornment: he has a secret message for her, and she is to come at once. She wonders what new enemy has arisen against Baal, but hastens to Zaphon, where she is told of his plan to build a palace. She undertakes to gain El's permission for the palace, by violence if necessary. She proceeds to El's court, and after a menacing introduction pleads Baal's case. El replies[10] that Baal's hegemony is by no means established, as Mot is making the skies faint; and Anat determines to get round him by bribing Athtart, his consort. She accordingly despatches Athtart's servants to Kothar/Khasis, with instructions to make jewelry with which to persuade Athtart to change her mind.

The meaning of all this is not entirely clear; but if V follows from VI-III, then we should have no problem explaining Baal's feast and aspiration to sovereignty. With the spring he seems to have all at his feet; but his supremacy is not in fact secure, being menaced by the sun and the drought. However, such perils are still in the distance, and his claim goes forward. Other features are incidental to the story, and still others, like Anat's slaughter, remain a problem. For de Moor, Baal claims his kingship in the autumn, before his battle with Yam, and his feast is a means of getting the story on the road.

II opens with the messengers delivering their request to Kothar/-Khasis, who go to work and forge numerous gold pieces of furniture for Athtart. The latter is nervous at the approach of Baal and Anat, but is soon delighted with the precious metal gifts. She accedes to their wish, and sets forth to petition El, who, after some dry remarks, agrees. The palace is to be truly sumptuous, and Anat and Baal rejoice in turn. Kothar/Khasis are summoned, and assemble the best cedars and precious metals. In a week the building has been completed; Baal invites the gods to a celebration banquet and they come. He takes possession of the earth, occupying the cities and causing the mountains to tremble as he thunders; but he still has enemies, notably Mot, who has not attended his banquet, and he sends to challenge the latter.

The general sense of this is not hard to follow. Baal is worshipped as prince of the gods at Ugarit, with a splendid temple now excavated, and lavish sacrifices; these are the counterparts to his palace and banquets on Zaphon. He is responsible for the city's crops, most of which are harvested in the early summer; and he presides over their armies' victories, and occupation of enemy cities also. The thunder, however, is primarily a winter phenomenon, and an instance of the general run of the story taking precedence over the climatic parallel. Other features remain a mystery, especially the ominous window, which at first Baal refused to have built into the palace, but later acceded to; and which is often taken to have been the cause of his downfall.[11]

I* describes the fall of Baal to Mot, though much of the tablet is missing, and the details lack clarity. After what seems to be a dinner for Mot in Baal's palace, the latter makes a return trip with his family to dine with Mot in the underworld. He pauses en route to mate with a heifer, and a calf is born. He is then swallowed by Mot, and messengers go to El to announce his death. First El and then Anat proceed to mourn for him, both in word and action, gashing themselves and grieving for the fate of his people, now deprived of the source of fertility. So the summer drought finds its counterpart in the action of the gods; the power of death seems for the moment triumphant, and the source of rain and blessing gone for ever. However, calves in Syria need to be born in time to grow strong on the winter grass,[12] and their conception in summer is a sign that there is hope for the future.

The myth continues directly into I. Anat continues her mourning, and then goes with Shapash, the sun-goddess, to bury Baal on Zaphon. Athtar, the desert god, tries to take Baal's throne, but is too small. Anat then revisits Mot, cuts him open with a sword, winnows, burns, grinds him, and scatters his remains to the birds. This opens the way to better things, and El has a vision that Baal has returned to life, and bids Anat and Shapash go and find him. Baal is alive once more, and sitting on his throne. After seven years, Mot, who has also returned to life, challenges him once more, and they confront each other like wild oxen, like snakes, like chargers. Shapash warns Mot of the folly of such a duel which he cannot win, and he retires, leaving the throne to Baal. The final column closes with what seems to be a hymn to Shapash.

In some ways this looks like a suitable end to the cycle. The long hot summer is over, and Baal has come to life again with the advent of clouds and the first rain; grass and corn begin to grow once more. Baal is on his throne, and now it is Mot who is dead. Anat, the goddess of the springs which keep running through the drought, is the power of life which has destroyed death. We are back to the autumn, when the myth is likely to have been recited;[13] the next major feature of the year is the winter contest with Yam/Nahar. Two further features have persuaded most Ugaritic scholars that the cycle closes with I. One is the colophon: 'Written by Ilumilku the Shubanite . . .'; there is no similar colophon at the end of I*, the only other tablet of the cycle where we have the end of the final column. The other is the lack of continuity with the mating sequence in IV, which in any case is written by another hand.

These points, however, are not final, and other arguments have sometimes seemed decisive the other way. There is a very similar colophon written on the side of Baal II, part way through the myth; and similarly there are colophons with the same names both at the end of the Keret myth and at the end of Aqhat II, part way. Where we have the beginnings of tablets, sometimes they begin 'Of Baal' (I), and sometimes not (I*). So the colophon does not settle the matter; and there may be many reasons why a different scribe could be employed for the last tablet. Furthermore, it is not probable that a poem the length of Baal would conveniently finish at the bottom of the last column of the final tablet; we should rather have expected a less tidy finish, as would be the case if IV were the end, with only one side inscribed.

So far as content is concerned, I is an unsatisfactory conclusion in that the last section seems anticlimactic. We should have expected some sign of Baal's supremacy at the end of the myth, and what we in fact have is a hymn to Shapash, a comparatively minor character in the story. A better ending may however be provided by IV, in that the symbol of supremacy among large animals like bulls is the possession of a harem of females with whom they mate. It is here that we find the suggestion of continuity with I, for no bull can maintain such a harem without fighting off challengers, and the contest between Baal and Mot in I bears a strong resemblance to a rutting fight: 'They charge like champions. Mot withdraws, Baal withdraws; they gore like wild oxen. Mot withdraws, Baal withdraws; they bite like serpents. Mot withdraws, Baal withdraws; they leap like chargers. Mot falls, Baal falls' (I.vi.16-22). The scene recalls such a fight in two further details. First, bulls are not strong enough to make such challenges until they are fully mature, usually about seven years of age; and this passage is prefaced by the note that seven years had passed since the last incident. Second, rutting fights are never pursued to the death, for this would weaken the stock; the vanquished simply retreats. So here Baal is the victor, but he does not kill Mot, who merely withdraws on the advice of Shapash. So in many ways IV would make an excellent end to the myth-cycle. It would provide continuity with I, and a climactic end to the whole, with the birth of a calf to Baal, and his rejoicing (IV.ii.38).

The inclusion of IV in the myth-sequence is not crucial to my argument, although it may be helpful. I have set out the positive considerations because I think they are right.[14]

Now it cannot fail to strike us that much of what we have been considering under the guise of the Ugaritic myth recurs in the Korah psalms, sometimes in a semi-demythologised form, sometimes trans-ferred to human ritual (which may also have accompanied the myth at Ugarit). The victory of Yahweh over the waters, the proclamation of Yahweh's reign, the celebration of his shrine and sacred city, the threat to his power, the going down of his priest among the dead, his return to life, the national lamentation, the royal wedding, all have powerful echoes in the story of Baal.

The Israelites settled among Canaanites (we may reasonably believe) to whom this myth was still a living reality, and a part of their annual liturgy. This would be especially probable at Dan in the very north of Israel, ירכתי־צפון (48:2). The polytheistic myth Israel would not take over. Yahweh, not Baal, was the rider upon the clouds, the giver of rain and blessing; and Anat, Yam, Nahar, Mot and the rest were vanities, dumb idols. But the climatic cycle was a reality, and could be assimilated. Yahweh did not fight Yam and Nahar, but he does overcome the seas which move in the heart of the mountains (46:2), whose waters roar and are moved and swell in their pride (v. 3), taming them into the fruitful Jordan (v. 4); he utters his voice in the thunder, and the earth melts (v. 6).

Yahweh takes up his reign, he takes up his throne (47:8), he goes up to his shrine with a shout (v. 5)—not that he has ever ceased from reigning, for there are no other gods who could compete with him; but the drought followed by the floods might make it seem so, and the old ways of speaking are not quickly lost. In 47 he moves into his sanctuary, then; and in 48 is celebrated his session on Hermon, his holy mountain, and Dan, his holy city, just as the session of Baal in his palace on Zaphon above and in Ugarit below was celebrated in Canaan. Yahweh is highly to be praised in the city of our God, in his holy mountain fair in height, the city of the great King on the frontiers of the north (48:1f). When the assembled kings saw the mountain, they were dismayed and fled (vv. 4f). Recital and ritual have been performed in the midst of Yahweh's temple, in the city of Yahweh of hosts, the city of our God, which he has established in perpetuity (vv. 8f). He has made himself known as a high tower in her walls and bulwarks and bastions (vv. 3, 12f), and the ceremonial procession round the walls serves to impress his city's impregnability on one generation after another (v. 13). The same theme rings through 87, the older, alternative psalm of Yahweh's city. His foundation in the holy mountain range of Hermon he loves beyond all the dwellings of Jacob (vv. 1f). The glorious destiny of Dan, the city of God, is recited at the festival (v. 3), for the most High himself shall establish her (v. 5). There, as the nations shall confess, was God's king born to his royalty (vv. 4ff), and all the fresh springs of the great river that waters the nations' land, rise there (v. 7). Israel, like Canaan, followed the celebration of the conquest of the waters with the celebration of God's reign in his mountain, city and temple.

The triumphant tone of the Ugaritic Baal tablets III, V and II, and of Psalms 46-48, 87, is muted in the matter that follows. Even 48 ended with the ominous phrase, 'He will be our guide עַל מוּת, over death.' Mot is a god no more, but the death of high summer is a reality, and pointing מוּת has been an embarrassment. With 49 the note has become defensive. The peoples and inhabitants of the world need repeated warning not to trust in their arms and their money-bags; they will not last a night on Israelite soil, but will go to Sheol without chance of ransom. 88 reveals the transformation of the Canaanite tradition under Israelite monotheism at its clearest. It cannot be thought that Yahweh was swallowed by Mot as Baal was, for Yahweh alone is God; but the land is parched, and the rain withheld, and there are more human perils in many years besides. So the ritual is continued without the myth. Although we have no evidence of Ugaritic rituals in any detail, comparative studies would suggest that ritual to accompany myth is very general, and many Ugaritologists have supposed that there were ceremonial actions to accompany the recital of the story. We cannot know if king or priest or some other representative of the people enacted an atonement, scapegoat rite at Ugarit, but I have argued above that it is just such a rite which underlies 88 in the festal week at Dan. Sometimes even the same phrases are used, as when the Israelite priests (88:5, 4), like Baal's messengers, and later Baal himself, goes down to the house of separation and is counted with them that go down to the depths of the earth (II.viii.7-9; I*.v. 13-15). He draws nigh unto Sheol, and his union with the ghosts in Abaddon, etc., is stressed in nearly every verse. We could not ask for a better example of the transformation of Canaanite into Israelite religion. All the mythology and polytheism are gone. The power of Mot has been replaced by the anger of Yahweh (vv. 14-16). Only the ritual—probably made more humane—and the prayer for nature's, and the nation's, rebirth remain the same. Yahweh's triumphant reign and indwelling of his mountain and city, are succeeded, like Baal's, by a ritual of death and resurrection.

88 is the last of the Korah psalms; in the tradition we have, it is followed by 89, which combines many of the themes of the complete Canaanite cycle. As Baal at various points in the story subdued the different gods and terrified them with his thunder, so here Yahweh sits on his throne in the assembly of the holy ones, terrifying them that are round about him, the sons of אלים (vv. 5-7). He rules the pride of the sea, and stills the waves when they arise; he broke Rahab and scattered his enemies (vv. 9f). Both gods close their sequences in triumph, Baal enforcing his lordship with physical, Yahweh with moral violence. Again the contrast as well as the similarity is instructive. In the Korah sequence polytheism had almost been purged away; only in 44:20 is the existence of strange gods even hinted. God did not require a name,

almost, in Dan; he was Elohim, all the gods there were. Things were not so advanced at the more rural centre of Tabor, and the Canaanite 'sons of Athtart' (I.v. 1) continue a shadowy existence as Israelite 'sons of אלים.' There is the same divine court, and the same domination by a national god, and the same stress on the defeat of the waters. But Yahweh, even at Tabor, was no longer threatened as Baal was, nor had he need of Anat or Kothar/Khasis. His faithfulness is round about him, and who, it can be asked rhetorically, is a mighty one, like unto thee, O JAH? Moral authority is enough, and Yahweh's concern is to create and establish the world, not just to defeat divine enemies.

But what if the Baal sequence included IV, as I have suggested? Our psalms would not then lack a parallel, but we should have to suppose that the cycles began from a slightly different point. After Baal's death in I* there is protracted mourning, first by El, then by Anat; Baal is restored to life and Mot killed; and the myth will then end with his victory in the rutting fight, and his mating with Anat. Our Korahite parallels began with 46 as the victory over the waters, alongside (VI-) III; and we are still without opposite numbers for 44 and 45. Now 44 is a national lament (as are 42-43 if we include them), and 45 is a celebration of the king's reign and his marriage. Perhaps we should be justified in seeing 44 and 45 as the Israelite transposition of the divine mourning and mating of the heathen past. If so, the lament of 85, with its primary concern for the harvest, will be a bridge to 44, the lament whose concern is political survival, from an ancient mythical lament whose concern was the harvest also. 45 is very different from Baal IV. Gone is all crude mention of sexual organs and bestial symbolism; the whole is conducted on an earthly plane alone, and with almost Anglican dignity and restraint. But the themes remain the same: as Baal takes up his kingdom, destroys his enemies, and engenders new life, so is the Israelite king enthroned, to drive his sharp arrows into his enemies' hearts, and to marry a princess. Instead of his fathers he shall have children, whom he may make princes in all lands.

The cogency of the Ugaritic parallels consists not just in their general frequency, but in the fact that they occur in the same *order*. The sequences are as follows:

Baal (VI Yam/Nahar demand kingship)
III	Baal worsts Yam/Nahar	Ps.46	Yahweh quells the waters
V	Baal demands palace	47	Yahweh reigns in shrine
II	Baal's palace built	87/48	Yahweh king in his city
		49	Warning to Yahweh's foes

I*	Baal swallowed by Mot	88	Yahweh's priest among dead
I	Baal mourned, resurrected	85/44	National Lament
(IV	Baal mates with Anat)	45	Royal wedding

The cycle is the same; the change of point of departure is easily explained. To the Canaanites, Baal's mating is the climax of the myth, the symbol of his supremacy. To the Israelites Yahweh has no consort, and the mating has to be transferred to his earthly representative. But a feast of Yahweh cannot reach its climax in an activity of his proxy. So lamentation and wedding and the king's consecration are taken at the beginning of the sequence. Indeed, lamentation comes naturally at the beginning of the sequence, since the community is putting the drought and all its other troubles behind it, as a preliminary to a festival of joy. Nor, of course, could such a feast end on the sombre note of 88; a triumphant hymn to Yahweh's power is required to close the occasion, such as is supplied by 89.

The Ugaritic material does two things for us. First it is not really credible that the same themes should occur in the same order in two neighbouring communities by accident; so we have an explanation for the sequence of themes and rites which underlie the Korah psalms— and not the Korah psalms only. Second, they enable us to see the sons of Korah at work in a first creative period. We have been able to watch them rewriting the confident psalmody of the tenth and ninth centuries to meet the inexorable Assyrian disaster; and we have even been able to reconstruct tentatively their later achievements in Jerusalem. But the Baal myth enables us to see them domesticating Canaanite polytheism to the worship of the one, unique, transcendent Yahweh; and so to appreciate their psalms as not merely a liturgical monument *aere perennius*, but also as a theological creation. We have good reason to admire Korah and his family.

NOTES TO CHAPTER 1

1. The *Auseinandersetzung* with Mowinckel is sustained through the sections of the *Einleitung* on the Enthronement Hymns (pp.100-116) and the Individual Laments (172-265), but forms a constant undercurrent to the whole. In the *Psalmenstudien* Mowinckel was criticising Gunkel on the basis of his earlier writings, especially the article 'Psalmen' in *RGG* (1e., 1909-13) and *Ausgewählte Psalmen* (4e. 1917). His *Psalms in Israel's Worship* (ET 1967) takes in all Gunkel's writings, but is more distanced. Gunkel died in 1932.
2. So, for example, Kirkpatrick.
3. 86 can be seen by internal criteria to be distinct from the Korah psalms. It uses אדני for God seven times, for example, a term occurring only once in the whole Korah series.
4. See BDB *ad voc.* 5(b), p.513.
5. *Die Zionstheologie der Korachiten* (1966), 1-3.
6. 89:8 alone has the construct form אלהי.
7. Gunkel, *Einleitung* 449, writes, 'Ursprünglich nichtkultisch sind im Korah-Psalter nur 42.43.49.88'; but he also takes a private view of 84.
8. P.4, citing C.A. Briggs, 'careful selection,' p.LXV.
9. The figures for Elohim are for absolute uses, omitting all such phrases as 'my God,' or 'the God of my salvation.'
10. I have taken these figures from Kirkpatrick, I, lv.
11. I, lvi-lvii; see also Gunkel, *Einleitung*, 447f.
12. *Einleitung*, 451.
13. *Einleitung*, 434.
14. *Ibid.*, 4: 'Nun ist es aber ein unverbrüchliche Grundsatz der Wissenschaft, dass nichts ohne seine Zusammenhang verstanden werden kann. Es wird demnach *die eigentliche Aufgabe der Psalmenforschung sein, die Verbindungen zwischen den einzelnen Liedern wieder auszufinden.*'
15. P.1.
16. J. Dahse, *Das Rätsel des Psalters gelöst* (1927), suggested that the 150 psalms corresponded to the fifty sabbaths of a three-year period, in line with the triennial cycle of reading the Torah, which is testified as in use in Palestine in b Meg. 29b. The idea has been taken up in a modified form by A. Arens, *Die Psalmen im Gottesdienst des Alten Bundes* (1961). But the triennial cycle is almost certainly an AD development: cf. J. Heinemann, 'The Triennial Lectionary Cycle,' *JJS* 19 (1968), 41ff, M.D. Goulder, *The Evangelists' Calendar* (1978), 56-66.
17. C. Westermann, *Lob und Klage in den Psalmen* (5e. 1977), ch.14, 195-202, suggests that an earlier Psalter ran from 1 to 119, with the first section (3-41)

mainly individual laments, the second (Elohistic Psalter, 42-83) mainly hymns in the first (Korah) group, individual laments in the second (David) group, and national laments in the third (Asaph) group etc. But there are too many exceptions to allow such a scheme to be viable.

18. m Meg. 3.4: cf. the discussion in my *The Evangelists' Calendar*, 19-66.

19. J.B. Pritchard, *Ancient Near Eastern Texts*, 331-4.

20. Pp.1-3.

21. I follow RV here; but good reasons can be given for taking the niph. reflexively, cf. Eaton, *ad loc.*

22. P.4, 'zeigen ein auffallendes Interesse an Zion-Jerusalem.'

23. Pp.59-64, 273-295, 338-352.

24. A second, and more important check is the order of the psalms in other collections, which follow the same ritual sequence even when they come from a different sanctuary: cf. below on Book IV, *passim*.

25. The historical notes in the headings of the intervening psalms are later guesses.

26. R. de Vaux, *Ancient Israel* (ET 2e. 1965), 190.

27. For other suggestions see Kraus, *Worship in Israel* (ET 1966), 63ff.

28. *Kingship and the Psalms* (1976), vii.

NOTES TO CHAPTER 2

1. So Eaton.

2. G.W. Ahlström, *Psalm 89*, pp.114f, argues that such expressions belong in the mouth of the national leader, especially the king; cf. Eaton, *KP*, 70f. For a democratised understanding of the phrase see O. Eissfeldt, '"Mein Gott" im Alten Testament,' *ZAW* 61 (1946), 3-16.

3. It is important not to pre-empt the question whether the leader is king, high priest or other leader; cf. 38, 48.

4. *Hymns of the Temple*, 43.

5. KP 70. Eaton cites Mowinckel's view here from his commentary in Norwegian on the Old Testament.

6. Kraus draws a pathetic picture—but surely not a very probable one—of the speaker as a loyal Israelite fatally ill, walking about in dust-covered penitents' clothes, pursued by the sarcastic cries of the heathen.

7. On 88:7 see below, pp. 204ff.

8. It was earlier believed, e.g. by George Adam Smith, *The Historical Geography of the Holy Land*, that the ancient Dan was at Baneas, for: (i) Baneas is the better site for the capital of a district, (ii) the ancients and the mediaevals, from Josephus on, took Baneas as the main source of the Jordan, (iii) the radicals of Miz'ar, with one justifiable change, reappear in the modern

names Za'ura, Wadi Za'arah, Khurbet Mez'ara, places near Baneas. But excavation has settled the matter.

9. Pp.472f.

10. A. Biran, 'Dan, Tel,' in M. Avi-Yonah (ed.), *Encyclopaedia of Archeological Excavations in the Holy Land*, 313ff.

11. Cf. also Gen. 49:25, 'Blessings of the deep that coucheth beneath,' cited by P. Reymond, *L'Eau, sa vie et sa signification dans l'A.T.*, 196-8.

12. Peters, 274, followed by Waddy, takes the psalm so.

13. m Taan.1.

14. R. de Vaux, *Ancient Israel*, 65ff. The pilgrims were potentially also the Israelite army, which was reduced by treaty to ten thousand in the days of Jehoahaz (II Kgs. 13:7), a figure felt to be very small.

15. BDB, על 6a, p.756a.

16. צלע is rather rare as an image for God, unlike צור; it comes four times in the Psalter.

17. N.M. Waldman, 'Some notes on Malachi 3:6, 3:13, and Psalm 42:11,' *JBL* 93 (1974), 548, argues from Akkadian and Arabic cognates that the translation should be 'with a breaking in my bones.'

18. These are described in a sequence of reports in the *Israel Exploration Journal*; see especially 24 (1974), 262-4; 26 (1976), 202-6; 27 (1977), 242-6; 28 (1978), 268-70. On high places, see also P. Vaughan, *The Meaning of 'Bāmā' in the Old Testament*. The Israelite במה was re-used in Hellenistic times, and the four top steps of the approach flight are from this period. On the masonry see Y. Shiloh, *The Proto-Aeolic Capital and Israelite Ashlar Masonry*, 51f. The excavations alone do not make clear the use of the במה, and no altar has been found other than a small incense-altar in the main shrine building to the south of the platform. On the other hand a considerable quantity of animal bones has been discovered; and the normal method of desecrating a 'heathen' sanctuary was to destroy its altar (e.g. II Kgs. 23:12, 15). So it is not very likely that the original altar(s), if any, would have survived.

M. Haran, *Temples and Temple-Service in Ancient Israel*, 30f., is sceptical to the point of absurdity: 'Though the excavators decided to label this place במה, this can at most be taken as a figurative use ... an archaeological technical term, and not ... the authentic, biblical one.' If this 'gigantic quadrilateral' is to be only a figurative במה, how shall we recognise an authentic one? It is weak too to suggest that the incense altar may have been brought from another location: whoever brought it must have used the site as a shrine—but what more holy place could there be for a shrine than the site of the previous shrine?

19. Another possibility is that the plural form was normal for a shrine/palace, as in the Ugaritic *msknt* (Aqhat II.v.32f), cf. J.H. Patton, *Canaanite Parallels in the Book of Psalms*, 45.

20. See O. Eissfeldt, *The Old Testament*, 203f.

21. Elohim predominates also in the second David collection, 51-72. I take these to be early Jerusalem psalms, and suggest that they are evidence of a

counter-tendency. Yahweh was originally God of some of the northern tribes, and in the north the drift was towards using the more comprehensive Elohim. In Judah Elohim had been used in the early period, but once Yahweh was accepted it became the norm. In the same way High Anglicans are sometimes accused of taking over practices which are in the process of being dropped by Roman Catholics.

22. The only timed journey in the Bible is the sixty stades (7.5 miles) from Jerusalem to Emmaus, which took Cleopas and his friend a day—but they made the return journey in the evening (Lk. 24:13ff).

23. Tosefta, Sanh. 2.6.

24. Ps. 81 is in use as a Psalm for New Year to this day, and this tradition goes back to later Talmudic times (TB Soph. 18).

25. Kraus, for example, does not attempt an explanation of the origin of the tenth day in *Worship in Israel*, 66-70, nor does de Vaux, 510ff. Mowinckel's suggestion, *Ps. St.* II, 22, that the days between Atonement and Tabernacles were originally intercalary days, like the epagomenal days in Egypt, does not seem likely: Israel never had intercalary *days*, but an intercalary *month*.

26. G.F. Moore, *Judaism*, II, 62f.

27. I am grateful to Dr Martin Goodman for this information.

28. So Schmidt, Kraus. E. Baumann, 'Struktur-Untersuchungen in Psalter II,' *ZAW* 62 (1950), 132-6, thinks that the birds' nestlings point to the spring; but no nestlings are mentioned. Kissane envisages the birds' nests as indicative of the Temple's ruin, and the speaker as yearning for God's courts in exile.

29. Mowinckel has argued for a royal setting in several of the Korah psalms in the 40's (46-48), and Eaton for more (42-43; 44), as well as Gunkel's 45; but Eaton's arguments for a royal *speaker* (*KP* 61, 69ff) really only justify a national leader, who might as well be priest as king. In particular it is weak to argue that 'my God' implies the king in 42-43 when it cannot be the king in 84. Current interest in the theology of kingship has blurred the importance of the earlier priesthood, whose leaders, like Samuel, prayed to the LORD for Israel (I Sam. 7:5 ,8f) before there were kings, and resented the loss of their prerogatives thereafter (I Sam. 8). I. Engnell, *Critical Essays*, 86, suggested that למנצח was a northern equivalent for לדויד; but the heading comes alongside לדויד quite often, e.g. in 20, 21, 22.

30. See further below, p. 48. Gunkel and Kraus regard the speaker as a private pilgrim; but this is hard to reconcile with the intercession for the king, and makes v. 6f rather unnatural. Kraus's suggestion that the private pilgrim dwells in Yahweh's house (v. 4) also seems forced.

31. See below, p. 41.

32. H.G. May, ed. *Oxford Bible Atlas*, 50. Safad is higher than Dan, and has a slightly higher rainfall than Dan itself; but the pilgrim-routes must have passed very close to Safad.

33. m Taan. 1.3ff.

34. *B.J.*, 3.39.

35. de Vaux, 223.

36. Delitzsch, II, 477, cites the growth of such balsam-trees in the arid valley of Mecca. It is vain to object that balsam-trees are unknown in Palestine; בכאים come in II Sam. 5:23f.

37. So F.M. Abel, *Géographie de la Palestine*, II s.v.

38. *PIW* II, 215.

39. Biran, *IEJ* 24 (1974), 262-4.

40. Biran, *ibid.*, also found a small incense altar inside the shrine building.

41. The Hebrew is not easy, but it is best left unimproved (cf. Rogerson and McKay on NEB). מורה is the word for the early rain in Joel 2:23, a passage which we have seen above to have a number of connections with 42 and 84. The hiph'il העמה means to wrap or envelop, and can take a double accusative. The conjecture 'pools' for 'blessings,' changing a vowel-point, is impossible: valleys cannot be wrapped in pools. But Jacob prayed 'blessings of heaven above,' i.e. fruitfulness from the rain, upon Joseph (Gen. 49:25), just as Isaac had blessed him, 'May God give you of the dew of heaven' (Gen. 27:28). BDB offer, rather questionably, two concrete instances of 'blessings,' Mal. 2:2 and Prov. 11:11.

42. May, *Oxford Bible Atlas*, 50f.

43. There is a much more serious sequence of mistranslations in 49, which has distorted the meaning of the whole psalm. The root of the trouble in both cases has been the quest for a 'spiritual' meaning, and the missing of the liturgical setting.

44. Kirkpatrick suggests translating 'Surely,' which is not impossible; but כי recurs at the beginning of the next verse with the meaning 'for,' and most modern commentators retain the traditional translation, leaving the connection 'obscure' (Kirkpatrick). NEB suppresses, and leaves a space between v. 9 and v. 10, which seems disingenuous.

45. Jastrow's dictionary takes טוב as a noun, BDB as an adjective. The former makes better sense, and is borne out by the use of טוב as a noun in v. 11.

46. BDB, 1053b. מן ... בחר = 'prefer ... to ...' in v. 10b, Jer. 8:3, etc.

NOTES TO CHAPTER 3

1. Biran has a general account up to 1971 in M. Avi-Yonah (ed.), *Encyclopaedia of Archaeological Excavations in the Holy Land*, 313-320, and annual reports in the *Israel Exploration Journal*, especially 24 (1974), 262-4; 26 (1976), 202-6; 27 (1977) 242-6; 28 (1978), 268-70.

2. M. Noth wrote, 'It is not very probable that the Philistines, at about the same time as they destroyed the central sanctuary at Shiloh, should also have

brought to an end the remote tribal sanctuary at Dan.' This was in 'The Background of Judges 17-18,' published in 1962; and excavation since has really tended to confirm his view.

3. The case for two independent sources is well argued by C.F. Burney, *The Book of Judges*, 408ff. He is followed more recently by A. Murtonen, 'Some Thoughts on Judges xvii sq,' *VT* I (1951), 223f, and by C.A. Simpson, *Composition of the Book of Judges*, 63-70.

4. Noth prefers a single source, *art. cit.*, 69, citing the support of three commentaries of the 1950s; cf. more recently Aelred Cody, *History of Old Testament Priesthood*.

5. 'The Background of Judges 17-18.'

6. 'Aux origines du sacerdoce Danite,' 113.

7. (I) *Könige*, 285f. The only argument offered by Noth is that the phrase 'the sons of the Levites' is un-Deuteronomic; but this is doubtful, since the context is stressing Levitical *ancestry*.

8. G. von Rad suggested that the 'graven image' was carved wood, covered with the 'molten image' overlaying it; the ephod was a 'cuirass-like case,' and the teraphim 'possibly a cultic mask' (*Old Testament Theology* I, 216n). But so close an association of the graven image and molten image would require them to be mentioned together, whereas they are divided by the ephod and teraphim at 18:17, 18. In fact the two terms were probably indistinguishable to the D-historians, and are used loosely, with or without the original ephod and teraphim, for comic and pejorative effect.

9. Noth, *art. cit.*, 73.

10. Noth, *ibid.*, 74, takes Micah to have treated the Levite generously, thus laying more odium on the latter; but ten shekels for a year does not look generous beside the eleven hundred just mentioned, and it was a third of the price of a slave (Exod. 21:32).

11. The repetition of the quietness and security of Laish in 18:7, 10, 27 indicates that the slaughter was heartless cruelty in the eyes of the writer—a view he did not take over Jericho.

12. Almost all commentators accept Moses as original. Noth, 70, thinks that v. 30b is a later addition, on the grounds that the Levite suddenly receives a name there, having been anonymous throughout. But in the Danite original surely he was not anonymous at all—who, in Noth's hypothesis of *two* hostile tradents, would add so friendly a gloss?

13. Noth, 83, discounts the eighth century date in v. 30 in favour of the eleventh century one in v. 31. But they refer to different things. Dan may have been taken by the Philistines at about the same time as Shiloh (cf. n.2), and it is from this time that we find the ephod in use in the entourage of Saul and David (I Sam. 14-30). This suggests that some of the Danite priests escaped; and no doubt returned to their shrine when the city was recovered. Noth's theory constantly causes him to prefer the tendentious I Kgs. 12 account to details in Jg. 17f which are embarrassing to the D-theology, and therefore likely to be

historical.

14. Ephod originally meant a robe: Baal's robe in the Ugaritic tablet I*.i.5 is called *'epd*, and priests wore a linen ephod. But the ephods made by Micah and Gideon are of precious metal; an ephod was 'carried before Yahweh' (I Sam. 2:28; cf. 14:3), stood upright in the shrine at Nob (21:9), and could be transported (23:6), and brought out (23:9; 30:7) by the priests who had charge of it, for the purpose of divination. Isa. 30:22 uses אפדה of the gold-plate covering of a molten image. It seems best therefore to think of the ephod as a breastplate with a pocket (חשׁן) from which lots were drawn; and that the high-priest's ephod (Exod. 28:6-14; 39:2-7), with its pocket and its gold thread, was a compromise between this and the linen priestly garment. For a discussion of various proposals, cf. de Vaux, 349-352; K. Elliger, 'Ephod und Choschen,' *VT* 8 (1958), 19-35.

15. Note that in Hos. 3:4 ephod and teraphim alone are linked by ו, whereas the other pairs, king and prince, sacrifice and pillar, have a repeated אין: they are inseparable. The nature of teraphim is disputed. A list of theories is given in A.R. Johnson *The Cultic Prophet in Ancient Israel*, 32f n.3; cf. J. Lindblom, 'Lot-casting in the Old Testament,' *VT* 12 (1962), 164-178.

16. In Saul's ephod (I Sam. 14, following the LXX against the MT, which has substituted the more reputable ark in v. 18), the lots were severally called Urim and Thummim, but a combined name is not given. If they had earlier been known as teraphim, and had been primitive images, the suppression of the name would be easy to understand.

17. Cf. Cody, 41-52. Moses gives God's statutes and תורה in Exod. 18 as the people come to enquire of God, and presides over the sacrifices of Exod. 24: even in P, which never calls him a priest, and suppresses his priesthood, Moses manipulates the sacrificial blood (Exod. 29; Lev. 8) and consecrates Aaron and his sons.

18. Cody, 29-38.

19. K. Möhlenbrink, 'Die Levitische Überlieferungen des Alten Testaments,' *ZAW* 52 (1934), 191-7; Cody, 34f; A.H.J. Gunneweg, *Leviten und Priester*, 55ff; de Vaux, 370. For the whole of Num. 26, cf. M. Noth, *Das System der Zwölf Stämme Israels*, 33ff, 122ff. The significance of the verse was noted by J. Wellhausen, *Die Composition des Hexateuchs*, 182f; it is denied by Wanke, 27, who calls it a secondary insertion.

20. *Ibid.*, 192f.

21. Möhlenbrink, 196, where earlier authorities are cited.

22. *Ibid.*, 194.

23. Noth, *Exodus*, 245: 'The situation rather favours the presence of a basic narrative, which has been expanded into several strata by secondary additions.' Noth thought the basic narrative was an attack by a southern author on the worship of Bethel and Dan introduced by Jeroboam; but this line of explanation always runs into the difficulty that Aaron is to a large degree the villain of the story. Noth is reduced to saying, 'Unfortunately we

can no longer ascertain the time or the circumstances of the history of these passages' (*ibid.*). The reconstructions of the history of Exod. 32 are many and complicated: cf. S. Lehming, 'Versuch zu Exod. XXXII,' *VT* 10 (1960), 16-50. For a recent account of the state of the question, see H. Valentin, *Aaron*, 14-25.

24. *Hexateuch-Synopse*, 51-3, 154*f.

25. Gunneweg, 37-44, defends the theory that 'him whom thou lovest' refers to Moses, not Levi, since Levi does not appear in connection with Massah/Meribah elsewhere. But then Moses is not said elsewhere to have killed his relations; and it cannot be a good method to iron out every aberrant detail on the grounds that it does not occur elsewhere.

26. Cp. Cody, 69f, who argues that Eli was a Levite, (a) because his sons' names are of Egyptian origin, (b) because Phinehas is an important priestly name, (c) because of the attack by the man of God in I Sam. 2:27ff. But Cody himself concedes the weakness of (a), since any Israelite might have a name of Egyptian origin; and (c) does not mention the Levites, and can be read without difficulty as an attack on the house of Eli (who were rivals to the Zadokites in the tenth and ninth centuries). For (b), Phinehas need not be exclusively Levitical, any more than Eleazar (I Sam. 7:1; II Sam. 23:9): cf. below, p. 68.

27. Cf. Burney, 477f, who assigns the verses to the Redactor. 'The ark of the covenant' is a Deuteronomistic phrase, cp. the earlier 'the ark (of Yahweh/God)'; so is 'stood before,' cf. Deut. 10:8; 18:7.

28. See Biran, esp. *IEJ* 24 (1974), 262-4.

29. 'The Background of Judges 17-18,' 82f.

30. The plural במות probably refers to the *temenos* complex, cf. the 'courts' of 84:2, 10. The same phrase occurs as a place-name on Mesha's stele: cf. de Vaux, 335. Noth deletes the את, and translates 'Höhen-Häuser,' *Könige*, 268, 285.

31. De Vaux, 334f; Debus, 46.

32. H. Cazelles, 'The History of Israel in the Pre-exilic Period,' in G.W. Anderson, ed. *T.&I.*, 306.

33. For the significance of the triad Bethel, Gilgal, Beersheba, see below, pp. 114-120.

34. See J.B. Segal, 'Intercalation and the Hebrew Calendar,' *VT* 7 (1957), 250-307; S. Talmon, 'Divergences in Calendar-Reckoning in Ephraim and Judah,' *VT* 8 (1958), 48-74; de Vaux, 499.

35. *Arbeit und Sitte in Palästina*, II, 6.

36. 499.

37. For ad hoc intercalation, cf. Tos. Sanh. 2.6: it was the only possible practice in early times, and continued through into our era. The suggestion of Segal and de Vaux that the feast was held in the eighth month for one year only, by intercalation, can hardly be right; I Kgs. 12 is accusing Jeroboam of a serious and permanent act of blasphemy, not a mistaken intercalation.

38. Cf. Noth, *Exodus*, 247: 'As the ancient Near East (in contrast to Egypt) knows no theriomorphic deities but only the association of beasts with deities

pictured in human form whose companions and bearers they are, the 'golden calves' of the royal sanctuaries of Jeroboam are also surely meant as pedestals for the God who is imagined to be standing invisibly upon them.' Cf. de Vaux, 335; Debus, 46.

39. Hosea does also speak of a 'calf' in the singular: 'he hath cast off thy calf, O Samaria . . . the calf of Samaria shall be broken in pieces' (8:5f). This is probably a reference to Bethel also; if so, it is of a pejorative kind, exalting the double cherubim into single idols, as in I Kgs. 12:32b/28f. 'Calves' recur in the plural at Hos. 13:2.

40. The LXX text is usually preferred, e.g. de Vaux, 352, but is explained as an interpretation of תָּמִים as תֻּמִּים by J. Lindblom, 'Lot-casting in the Old Testament,' *VT* 12 (1962), 164-178.

41. In I Sam. 28:6, Yahweh did not answer Saul, 'neither by dreams, nor by Urim, nor by prophets'; and Saul did not have the Urim and Thummim then, because David had them. But the story-teller may not have realised that Abiathar's taking of the ephod implies that the Urim (and Thummim) had gone too.

42. It is noted by Cody, 85, that the eighty-five persons that did wear a linen ephod at Nob, who were killed by Doeg (I Sam. 22:18), are too many to have descended from Ichabod/Ahitub alone in two generations. They must include other priests, and the fact that the ephod is there in the shrine suggests that Nob was dignified with refugee priests not only from Shiloh but also from Dan.

43. For the ephod in Exod. 28, cf. K. Elliger, 'Ephod und Choschen,' *VT* 8 (1958), 19-35.

44. *De Vit. Mos.* II.113; BDB 22a.

45. Cody, 89.

46. *Ibid.*

47. Möhlenbrink, 204; H.H. Rowley, 'Zadok and Nehushtan,' *JBL* 58 (1939), 113-141; but cf. de Vaux, 374; Cody, 88-93.

48. The oracle of the man of God in I Sam. 2:27ff prophesies the beggary of the house of Eli, and the rise of a faithful priest (Zadok) to walk before mine anointed (David) for ever (cf. I Kgs. 2:27). Cody interprets this, 66ff, 113, 136f, as anti-Levitical, but there is no evidence for the house of Eli being Levites, nor any mention of Levites in the oracle. In the tenth century the Zadokites were concerned to keep the house of Abiathar out of the Temple: the Levites had not yet arisen.

49. R. Abba, 'Priests and Levites in Deuteronomy,' *VT* 27 (1977), 257-267; cp. J.A. Emerton, 'Priests and Levites in Deuteronomy,' *VT* 12 (1962), 128-138.

50. *Exodus*, 122f; *A History of Pentateuchal Traditions* (ET 1972), 180f.

51. *Hexateuchsynopse*, 49f.

52. Cody, 41.

53. Noth, *Exodus*, 25.

54. So Johnson, *SKAI*, 114-8; Weiser, Eaton, Dahood, Anderson.

55. *JTS* 6, 169-186.

56. Cf. F.S. North, 'Aaron's Rise in Prestige,' *ZAW* 66 (1954), 191-9; S. Lehming, 'Versuch zu Exod. XXXII,' *VT* 10 (1960), 16-50; W. Beyerlin, *Origins and History of the Oldest Sinaitic Traditions*, 126-133; Gunneweg, 29-37, 88-95; Cody, 146-156; B.S. Childs, *Exodus*, 555-581; Valentin, 205-303.

57. *Exodus*, 245.

58. The Levite tradition is taken to be ancient by Eissfeldt, *Hexateuchsynopse*, 50-3, 152*-6* (who ascribes it to L); W. Rudolph, *Der Elohist von Exodus bis Josua*, 52; Gunneweg, 29-37; Childs, 561. Cody writes that it was added to the Exod. 32 complex after the latter was complete, 'as all today agree'; it is this widespread consensus which has led to the present frustration. Cody himself is an example of this, as he has to water down the strong element of anti-Aaron polemic in the story.

59. Cf. Eissfeldt, *Hexateuchsynopse*, 154*-6*, 276*; cp. Noth, *Numbers*, 91-7. Noth identifies the Ethiopian wife story as primary, and associated with Miriam only: but, as with Exod. 32, this leads him into a cul-de-sac in which 'the complex of this chapter . . . can no longer be disentangled' (93).

60. W. Rudolph, *Chronikbücher*, notes that the law prescribing universal celebration of the Passover at Jerusalem goes back only to Deut. 16, and therefore would be unknown to Hezekiah; and that the obstinate refusal of Jerusalem claims was characteristic of the Samaritans in Ephraim and Manasseh in the Chronicler's day. But the reason for suspecting that some historical substratum underlies the story is the remarkable feature of its being a second-month Passover; cf. Talmon, 59f. It was a northern tradition to take Unleavened Bread in Ziv and Ingathering in Bul, rather than in Abib and Ethanim as at Jerusalem. An influx of northern pilgrims in Ziv would need justification by the Chronicler in terms of second-month Passover rules, priestly slackness in purifying the Temple, royal initiatives, etc. Asher and Zebulun are specified because the Chronicler read in II Kgs. 15:29 that the Assyrians had devastated Galilee and Gilead, all the land of Naphtali.

61. The main northern links of the Asaph psalms are: (i) the references to God's people as Joseph in 77:15; 80:1 and 81:5, and as Ephraim, Benjamin and Manasseh in 80:2 (both descriptions are unparalleled elsewhere in the Psalter); (ii) mention of Salem in 76:2 and 'all the meeting-places of God in the land' in 74:8; (iii) the consistent preference for Elohim as the name of God, and the use of Yahweh (God) of hosts and other names of God found principally in the Korah psalms; (iv) certain historical traditions, especially in 78 and 81; (v) various points in common with Hosea, cf. M.J. Buss, 'The Psalms of Asaph and Korah,' *JBL* 82 (1963), 384ff. Several of the psalms have been rewritten in part for use at Jerusalem, noticeably 74, 76, 78 and 79.

62. Cf. v. 26, 46f. Kraus notes striking agreements between the psalm and the work of the D-historian. 'It must belong to the early post-Exilic period' (Anderson).

63. So Gunkel, who sets out the above points also.

64. Eissfeldt, *Hexateuchsynopse*, 190*, 278*; Noth *HPT* 75f, 195f; *Numbers*, 194-9. Noth thought the Phinehas legend was added very late, in the fourth century: but it is difficult to date Ps. 106 so late.

65. Eissfeldt, *Hexateuchsynopse*, 63, 173*-5*; Noth, *HPT*, 125f; *Numbers*, 118ff; S. Lehming, 'Versuch zu Num. XVI,' *ZAW*(1962), 291-321; Cody, 172f. It is easy to separate the Korah from the Dathan-Abiram story; and the secondary expansion of the Korah story in vv. 8-17, 19-22 is almost common ground.

66. Philo, *Spec. Leg.* i.51 (275); Schürer, *History* II (1979), 305.

67. J.A. Emerton, 'Priests and Levites,' *VT* 12 (1962), 129-138.

68. Emerton was arguing against a short article by G.E. Wright, 'The Levites in Deuteronomy,' *VT* 4 (1954), 325-330. Wright's case was restated by R. Abba, 'Priests and Levites in Deuteronomy,' *VT* 27 (1977), 257-267; but Abba does not come to terms with Emerton's arguments. For instance Emerton claims that where there are two phrases in Deut., and the second begins כל (as at 18:1), the second is in apposition to the first; Abba produces a list of passages which do not correspond with this specification. Emerton says that it was a priestly duty to 'stand before' Yahweh; Abba cites Num. 16:9; Ezek. 44:11 of the Levites 'standing before,' but it is before *the people.* His suggestion that the Levites carried the ark normally, and the priests on special occasions, is absurd.

69. The identity with the country priests is usually assumed; e.g. by Cody, 128; Emerton, *art. cit.*, 135; E.W. Nicholson, *Deuteronomy and Tradition*, 55, 86; but cp. G. von Rad, *Deuteronomy*, 122.

70. Von Rad, *Deuteronomy*, 122; Cody, 128.

71. W. Eichrodt, *Ezekiel* (ET), 564; Cody, 134ff.

72. P.135.

73. The in-fighting is most closely observed by Möhlenbrink, *art. cit.*, and by W. Rudolph, *Chronikbücher* and *Esra und Nehemia.*

74. Korah's father is Izhar in Exod. 6:21; Num. 3:19 and generally; but in I Chron. 6:22 this has been amended to Amminadab. The name comes from Exod. 6:23, where its bearer is father-in-law to Aaron; it no doubt represents an optimistic attempt to improve the standing of the Korahites. The descendants of only the eldest sons are given, so the implication is that Amminadab was older than Amram; but the days were past when this could be done successfully.

75. See Möhlenbrink, 202-4; Rudolph, 56-9.

76. The same is true of the line of Korah in the preceding Levite genealogy; cf. Möhlenbrink, 199ff.

77. Now spelt with an *m*, like Moses' elder son.

78. Cf. pp. 215, 220.

79. See n. 61. It is possible that the Bethel priesthood was also descended from Gershom as the Danite priesthood was; cf. p. 56, Talmon, *art. cit.*, 52. In that

case the Bethelites would be attaching themselves artificially to a different Gershom, son of Levi, perhaps in the vain hope of outflanking the Zadokites, as junior sons of Levi, via Kohath. But the Phinehas story had already settled the primacy of the Aaronid Zadokites.

80. In Num. 4:34ff they are numbered first, though Merari is the most numerous; in Num. 7:6ff they are charged with the holy things, while Gershom and Merari do the heavy work with waggons and oxen; in Num. 10:21 they bear the sanctuary. In Josh. 21:4ff they are allotted their land first, and receive the best after the priests—Ephraim, Dan and western Manasseh. (It would be convenient to think that this association of the Korahites with Dan was ancient, as some have supposed, but the arguments are too weak to rehearse.) In I Chron. 15:5 they are first with the ark under David, and in II Chron. 29:15 they are first to purify themselves at Hezekiah's reformation. But the Gershomites kept the Temple treasure (I Chron. 26:21ff) and jewels (29:8), and the Merarites were first with Josiah's reforms (II Chron. 34:12). See Möhlenbrink, 212ff.

81. Rudolph, 173.

82. See Rudolph, 173 n.3. Rudolph emends 'Asaph' to 'Abiasaph' as at 9:19, as a 'Schreibfehler' (170); but an original text for which we could see a motivated change could be, 'of the Korahites Meshelemiah the son of Kore; of the sons of Asaph Obed-Edom; from the sons of Merari Hosah.' Obed-Edom's large numbers are due to 'God's blessing' (v. 5b; 13:14), but it remains a mystery whether the whole Obed-Edom clan is a theological construction, or whether there was a fourth-century group claiming descent from him.

83. Rudolph, 87-9.

84. Rudolph, 262.

85. So also at Deut. 10:8; cf. 31:9, 25f, where bearing the ark and the associated tables of the law takes priority over ministering at the altar.

NOTES TO CHAPTER 4

1. Pp. 23-37.
2. P.11.
3. II, 74.
4. M.D. Goulder, 'The Fourth Book of the Psalter,' *JTS* 26 (1975), 269-289.
5. *Le Poème royal du Psaume LXXXIX 1-5,20-38* (1967), 11f. Lipiński's argument is forced. He confesses, for example, 'le sens "instruction" ne convient point' at 47:7, and proposes that the word once stood at the heading of 49 and was moved!
6. *PIW* II, 209.
7. P. Kahle, *The Cairo Genizah* (1959), 82ff.

8. For the northern provenance of the Korah group, see above pp.13ff; for 44 as a substitute for the earlier 85, and therefore as coming late in the northern period, cf. pp.43f. For the northern bull-symbolism of v. 5 see below. 44 shows several signs of being pre-Deuteronomic. God is still thought of as going forth with Israel's hosts (v. 9), as in Num. 10:35 and I Sam. 4; the clear-headed self-respecting protest of innocence in vv. 17-21, unparalleled in a national lament, breathes a healthier air than that induced by the stifling Deuteronomic *Vergeltungsdogma* (cp. Lamentations); no one, after the writing of I Kgs. 18, would have dared to pray, 'Awake, why sleepest thou?' (v. 23) to Yahweh. John Hyrcanus stopped the daily recital of the verse as irreligious (b Sot. 48a). There is some indication in vv. 10-16 that the adversary/enemy is different from our neighbours/them that are round about us; and this would also fit the last years of the northern kingdom, when the enemy was Assyria, and Israel's neighbours could mock her pains with impunity.

9. At Deut. 31:9 Moses delivers the law to 'the priests the sons of Levi ... and all the elders of Israel' to recite. When we consider the magnitude of the gathering, and the problem of audibility, at the full-scale festival at Dan, we can understand the need for numerous speakers who knew the tradition by heart; the text suggests that the Levites alone were not enough. Naturally elders would be preferred, so 'our fathers' is to be expected; but even a youthful Levite at Dan was 'father' to his people (Jg. 17:10), like a newly ordained Catholic priest.

10. Von Rad's *Das formgeschichtliche Problem des Hexateuchs* (1938), 9-86, opened the discussion. For a recent review, see R.E. Clements, 'Pentateuchal Problems,' in G.W. Anderson, ed., *Tradition and Interpretation* (1979), 107ff.

11. *Ibid.*. Von Rad suggested that the 'Credo' originated at Gilgal at the Feast of Weeks.

12. Cf. M. Noth, *Das Buch Josua* (2nd edn, 1953), 135ff; Clements, 108. Clements writes, 'The summary in Josh. 24:2b-13 is certainly post-exilic'; but Eissfeldt, *Introduction* (1965), 253, could still say, 'In xxiv, the farewell speech of Joshua generally agreed to be from E at least so far as its main material is concerned ...,' and thought a few points to be contributed by his ancient source L.

13. Cf. also 83:18 and 69:10 (Delitzsch).

14. The image of the horn is widely used, but נגח is not found of Judah (except in a different sense at Ezek. 34:21). The closest parallel is Mic. 4:13, where Judah is compared to an ox threshing.

15. Pritchard, *ANET*, 283b-284a.

16. The language is somewhat condensed—cf. Kirkpatrick, 'crushed us and reduced our country to a desert.' The meaning is not that Israel has been driven into the desert (Duhm), but that the cities of the northern provinces have been stripped of human inhabitants, and taken over by jackals. תַנִּים is the reading of most Hebrew MSS, and makes proper sense in the context; G's

κακώσεως, 'desolation' is more probably an interpretation of it. When the real world context was lost, the more mysterious תַּנִּין, the Dragon, was substituted.

17. G.B. Gray, *The Book of Isaiah, I-XXXIX* (ICC, Edinburgh 1912), 161; A. Alt, *Kleine Schriften II*, 206ff; O. Kaiser, *Isaiah 1-12* (ET 1972 = 2nd edn, 1963), 125; H. Wildberger, *Jesaja I*, 370f; II, 553.

18. Debus, 94, comments on this sole exception to the rule of complete hostility to the northern kings, but offers no explanation.

19. Citing H.W. Wolff, *Hosea*, 156; E. Dietrich, שׁוּב שְׁבוּת (1925). This interpretation is confirmed by the inscription on the stele of an eighth century Aramaean king, 'The gods have restored the restoration (והשׁבו שׁיבת) of the house of my father' (J. Fitzmyer, *Aramaic Inscriptions from Sefire*, 100).

20. For completeness I should refer also to the suggestion that the perfects in vv. 1-3 are 'precative perfects'; but this proposal, which has dubious grammatical justification, is now generally abandoned. Cf. Johnson, *CPIP*, 202, n.1.

21. *Ps. St.* III, 54ff.

22. *The Hebrew Book of Psalms*, 80-90. Eerdmans relates the Aramaic root to Hebrew סלה I, which, however, comes no nearer in meaning than 'break, put away.'

23. 'Die Bedeutung des Wortes Selah,' *ZAW* 58 (1940/1), 153-6.

24. 'Die Versdubletten des Psalters,' *ZAW* 57 (1939), 104ff; *ZAW* 58 (1940/1), 317f.

25. 'Selah,' *VT* 2 (1952), 43-56.

26. Something of this kind would suit the two uses of Selah in 84.

> 84:4 Blessed are they that dwell in thy house:
>   They will be continually praising thee.   [Selah

It would be appropriate at this point for the Korahite priesthood actually to 'lift up' its voice in praise. Later in the psalm,

> 84:8 O LORD God of Hosts, hear my prayer: Give ear, O God of Jacob.
>   [Selah
>   9 Behold our shield, O God, And look upon the face of thine anointed.

The formal introduction to the prayer in v. 8 seems rather overweight for the one-verse petition in v. 9. Israelites knew how to compose long prayers (I Kgs. 8:12-21,23-61; etc.). 84:8 could well be an introduction to such a prayer, which was then offered (Selah), and merely recapitulated in v. 9.

27. Moses' absence is presupposed, which must be for some reason; Aaron and Hur are in charge (Exod. 24:14); Yahweh's smiting of the people (32:35a) implies a later reconciliation. Cf. Eissfeldt, *Hexateuchsynopse*, 49ff; Beyerlin, 12ff.

28. 'Lade und Stierbild,' *ZAW* 58 (1940/1).

29. Dependence on G is, as often, a dangerous move, and requires more justification than it receives. καρδίαν implies that the translator read לב סלה and left the סלה out; he read עַל as אֵל, and took πρὸς αὐτόν we know not whence. It looks like a determined attempt to understand the line as a parallel to אל־עמו ואל־חסידיו. If it were correct, the Hebrew has made a

straightforward parallel into a difficulty; and the continuity of Hebrew use has to be forgotten. Similarly the addition of ἐν ἐμοί in v. 8a seems the easiest explanation of G, whose translator is facing the same difficulty as Mowinckel. How is God speaking? It must be a mysterious voice within.

30. The primary Qabbalistic symbol is the divine throne of Ezek. 1, pictured as ten *sefirot* in three columns, three each in the outer two, and four in the centre. The topmost symbol in the centre column, standing higher than the outer two columns, is the Crown, resting on the invisible head of God. The second symbol in the centre column, midway between the two lower symbols in the two outer columns, is Beauty (תפארת), which thus forms the seat of the Throne. Below the lowest symbols in the outer columns, beneath Beauty, is Foundation (יסוד), the foundation on which the Throne stands. Beneath that is Kingdom, God's kingdom on earth, which is his footstool. In the outer columns, level with God's head on the shoulder-points of the Throne, are Understanding and Wisdom. The mid-points, or arm-rests, are Might (גבורה) and Mercy (חסד), suited to God's arms. The bottom two symbols, or feet of the Throne, are Honour (הור) and Eternity (נצח). Thus seven of the ten symbols, all but Crown, Foundation and Kingdom, are abstracts; and three of these, Beauty, Mercy and Honour, are among the Virtues associated with the throne and sanctuary in the psalms cited. The date of these speculations is not known, but Merkabah 'mysticism' goes back to at least the first century of our era. See further G.G. Scholem, *On the Kabbalah and its Symbolism* (ET 1965), and other works.

31. Primitive Christian Gnosticism seems to have drunk of the same spring. Irenaeus describes a relatively simple Gnostical system, which has been partially confirmed by the Apocryphon of John. Between the Father/the Invisible Virginal Spirit and the rest of the pantheon stands Barbelo, from whom came the first four aeons; and these in turn produced further aeons, some of whom also fall in fours, including four luminaries and four virtues. The best explanation for Barbelo remains the nineteenth century proposal בארבע אלוה, God in tetrad; in which case the subdivision into tetrads, and later ogdoads, of aeons would be understandable, given the known contemporary meditation on Ezekiel's Chariot with its four living creatures each with four faces. Irenaeus' four virtues are Charis, Thelesis, Synesis and Phronesis, rather intellectualised virtues compared with the psalms, but in line with what we should expect from a gnostic system; and Charis remains an equivalent for חסד.

32. *Shalim* rather than *Shalom* is testified in the Ugaritic tablets.

33. R.A. Rosenberg, 'The God Sedeq,' *HUCA* 36 (1965), 161-7; cf. Dahood, who cites Joel 2:23 for a connection with rain.

34. B. Landsberger, *Der kultische Kalender der Babylonier und Assyrer*, 4, 74.

35. *Worship in Israel* (ET 1965), 152-165.

36. J. Gray, 'Recent Archaeological Discoveries,' in G.W. Anderson, ed., *Tradition and Interpretation* (1979), 78f.

268   *The Psalms of the Sons of Korah*

37. *WI*, 125-178.
38. Kraus, *WI*, 59. In the Targum the reform is specified further, from the third month to the Feast of Weeks.
39. *Ibid.*, 59f.

NOTES TO CHAPTER 5

1. 'The Psalms and Israelite Worship,' in G.W. Anderson, ed., *Tradition and Interpretation*, 264-272; id., *Kingship and the Psalms*, 102ff.
2. *KP*, 57-9.
3. During the 1941 night bombing of London, a lady wrote to the *Daily Sketch* to tell of the comfort she drew from Ps. 91, citing several verses including, 'A thousand shall fall beside thee . . .' It is difficult to see the difference between such religion and learned interpretations centring on the pious pilgrim!
4. 92:1f says that it is a good thing 'To shew forth thy lovingkindness in the morning, And thy faithfulness every night'; 96:2 exhorts to 'Shew forth his salvation from day to day.' In 'The Fourth Book of the Psalter' I have argued that these prescriptions were intended to apply to the autumn festival, whose eight days (in post-exilic Jerusalem) would provide seventeen occasions of worship, evening and morning. There are seventeen psalms in Book IV, of which 90 and perhaps 102 are evening psalms, and 95, 97 and 101 are morning psalms: even numbers for the evenings, odd numbers for the mornings. Thus 90, on this hypothesis, is for 14th Tishri, and is to be compared with 44; both 91 and 92 are for 15th, and to be compared with 45; 93 and 94 for the 16th, with 46, and so on.
5. מעשׂי is pointed plural in MT, which is followed by the versions. Gunkel, and many, emend to the singular, but we do better to leave the harder text, with NEB; perhaps the author meant 'verses' rather than 'poem.'
6. A. Biran, 'Tel Dan,' in M. Avi-Yonah, ed., *Encyclopaedia of Archaeological Excavations in the Holy Land* (1975), 313-320.
7. *Ibid.*, 320. There is an idealised picture of the throne and canopy in Cant. 3:9f, with pillars of silver, etc.; אפריון is a canopied throne, not a palanquin, cf. אפר, covering, headband, I Kgs. 20:38.
8. The headings, על־שׁושׁן עדות at 60, and אל שׁשׁנים עדות at 80 may be related. The עדות, or 'testimony,' was put on the king at his coronation (II Kgs. 11:12), being inscribed on an armband (II Sam. 1:10). In the 'democratised' form in which we seem to find reference to it in Deut. 6, it refers to the Shema‘ (6:6), which all Israelites are to 'bind for a sign upon thine hand . . . and thou shalt write them upon the doorposts of thy house' (vv. 8f). So perhaps, earlier, the posts of the royal throne had been inscribed with the Shema‘ as well as surmounted with lilies.

9. Biran thinks that the palace is to the left rather than the right of the place where the road crosses the rampart into the city proper, and has excavated large buildings there. But these may be the queen's house, mentioned in v. 13, and implied to be close (within carrying distance) of the palace. Later palaces were often built overlooking the gate from the right, e.g. Herod's palace at Jerusalem, and his main ('Western') palace at Masada. The arrangements are different at Hazor and Megiddo, but this may be explained by the fact that the king did not live there.

10. J. Lindblom, *Prophecy in Israel*, 419f, takes the passage as entirely peaceful in intention, the ideal king forming a contrast with Alexander. But this can only be done by isolating 9:9-10 from what follows, and even then Lindblom translates, like NEB, 'successful and victorious.'

11. So Mowinckel, 'Drive and/or Ride in O.T.,' *VT* 12 (1962), 278-299.

12. So Mowinckel, *Ps. St.* III, 88-93, and many subsequent commentators.

13. G. Widengren, *Sakrales Königtum im Alten Testament und in Judentum*, 48f.

14. Kraus aptly comments how ill at ease Israel felt, however, with such expressions, whose rarity testifies to the gulf between the transcendent God and his human son. J.S.M. Mulder devotes a considerable part of his *Studies in Psalm 45* (35-80) to the question. He disputes the vocative translation with its human referent, as requiring an article, and עולם = (is) permanent, as requiring a preposition; and, noting that אלהים is in the same relative position in the sentence in v. 2b and v. 7b as in v. 6a, he suggests that this implies the same translation. But there is no article in I Sam. 2:25, Isa. 9:6, nor should we expect one with a vocative; and עולם means 'is permanent' without preposition at 48:14. Mulder gives the later part of his book to a considerable list of Akkadian parallels to the psalm, and argues for a date 720-586 when Assyrian influence was strong. Many of the parallels are rather general and inexact, though.

15. Cf. Achan/Achor in Josh. 7, Levi/ילוה in Gen. 29:34, שכר/ישכר in Gen. 30:18, זבר/זבלון in Gen. 30:20, etc.; or in our own psalms עָנִי אָנִי (88:15) is usually taken to be a play on words.

16. The שגל is sometimes interpreted as the queen-mother, like the powerful queen-mothers in Judah; cf. de Vaux, 118f. But surely on her wedding-day it is the new queen who stands at the king's right hand.

17. Anderson thinks the most likely conjectures are India, Yemen and Somalia.

18. Biran uncovered a bench of stone running some 5m from the throne-base to the city wall, i.e. on the king's left hand, facing east. It will be here that the nobles sat, and from which they rose to make their presentation to the queen. The plan on p.xiv shows that there is room for the queen to stand on the king's right without being on the roadway. Her bridesmaids will have stood behind her in the embrasure on the north side of the inner gate. See *EAEHL* 320.

19. Strack-Billerbeck, I, 509f.

20. *PIW* I, 174, 181.

21. The assumption that any mention of a mountain in the Psalms implies Zion is almost universal; so, for example, Herbert Schmid, 'Jahwe und die Kulttraditionen von Jerusalem,' *ZAW* 68 (1955), 171, 'Damit kann nur der Jerusalemer Tempelberg gemeint sein.'

22. So Troy, Pylos and Thebes were 'holy cities' in Homer, and later Athens; many centres of pilgrimage were holy in the Middle Ages, and especially Rome.

23. G. Adam Smith, cited above, p. 27.

24. Gunkel, followed by NEB and others, derived עוז from √ עוז, to take refuge, so making the word equivalent to מחסה. This might be right, but God is a 'help' in v. 1b, a more active concept, closer to 'strength.'

25. The frequently conjectured addition of the refrain, 'The LORD of hosts is with us . . .' after v. 3 (*BHS* and many commentators) lacks any evidence in the Hebrew or the versions, and should be eschewed. A suggested reason for its absence is offered below.

26. G. Adam Smith, 473.

27. RVmg renders Gen. 33:18, 'And Jacob came to Shalem, a city of Shechem . . . ,' and a Salim not far away is known in NT times, John 3:23. The only indication of Jerusalem being called Salem is Ps. 76:2, where Salem amd Zion are in parallel; but 76 is an Asaph psalm of northern origin (cf. p. 262), and the first two verses have been edited for Jerusalem use. The original may have run, 'In Jacob is God known: His name is great in Israel. In Salem also is his covert, And his lair in Gerizim.' Cf. F.L. Horton, *The Melchizedek Tradition*.

28. Appeal is often made to J. Ziegler's article, 'Die Hilfe Gottes am Morgen' (1950). Ziegler offers three explanations: (1) God's help is as dependable as the coming of light to end darkness; (2) judgement in Israel begins in the morning; (3) the Egyptians were drowned in the Red Sea at dawn. These are true elements in the meaning, but such verbal symbolism is a pale thing beside ritual reality.

29. In Exod. 23:16 Ingathering (*at* Tabernacles) is said to be at the end (בצאת) of the year. While צאת could grammatically mean 'the going forth' of the year, Tabernacles is mentioned last in all the Biblical calendars, so 'the going out' or end, of the year, is clearly intended. At Exod. 34:22 Ingathering is said to be at the revolution (תקופה) of the year, which naturally has the same meaning: and the 'turn' (תשובה) of the year in II Sam. 11:1 should mean the same. This qualifies, but does not contradict, the theme of 'New Year' in the autumn festival which has been so much stressed since Volz. Tabernacles marked the revolution or turn of the year, and its last day brought in the new year—cf. below Chap. 8. The autumnal new year is determined by the climatic cycle in Israel, as is to be seen from the Gezer calendar; and the same was probably celebrated at Ugarit, cf. p. 279, n.8. It endures in Jewish practice today. A spring New Year was observed in many Mesopotamian cities, for different climatic reasons, and in consequence Babylonian kings went out to war in the

spring. During the exile the Jews adopted the Babylonian practice of counting their months from Nisan in the spring, and a compromise was eventually reached with New Year on the first day of the seventh month (Lev. 23:24). For a fuller account see my *The Evangelists' Calendar*, 21-6: for counter-arguments see D.J.A. Clines, 'The Evidence for Autumnal New Year in Pre-Exilic Israel Reconsidered,' *JBL* 93 (1974), 22-40.

At II Sam. 11:1 most Hebrew MSS have not מלכים, 'kings,' but מלאכים, 'messengers,' and the versions are divided. But the meaning is not very different. The context shows that war at this season was normal. It is likely that מלכים was original, giving the better sense, but that with no phrase 'to war,' an *'aleph* was added to align the words to the story of the embassy in II Sam. 10.

30. G. von Rad, *Old Testament Theology*, I, 18.

31. The disproportionate size of the waggons, beside the bow and spear of v. 9b, led to the conjectured repointing עֲגִלוֹת, 'round (sc. shields),' which occurs in the Targum and is supported by NEB and some commentators. G has θυρεούς which means an ear-ring in biblical Hebrew, and the meaning 'round shield' does not occur elsewhere in rabbinic writing.

32. W. Zimmerli, *Erkenntnis Gottes nach dem Buche Ezechiel*, 35, 40, cited by Kraus.

NOTES TO CHAPTER 6

1. E. Lipiński, *La Royauté de Yahwé dans la poésie et le culte de l'ancien Israël* (Brussels 1965), 21ff: 'C'est le Ps. 47 qui eut le privilège du plus grand nombre d'hypothèses.'

2. *Ps. St.* II, *PIW* I; 106-192.

3. *SKAI*, 65ff.

4. יְדַבֵּר is a somewhat surprising form, and is amended by Gunkel to יַדְבִּיר and by NEB to יִדְבָּר or יַדְבֵּר. It occurs again at 18:47, and is justified by Duhm as a poetic abbreviation of the hiph'il.

5. *God and Temple* (Oxford 1965), 55 n.1.

6. The Chronicler takes 'mount Moriah' to be Zion (II Chron. 3:1); but such an interpretation was inevitable, and carries no historical conviction (G. von Rad, *Genesis*, 235). The Syriac understood 'the Amorites'; the Samaritans, Symmachus and Jerome 'vision' (המראה).

It is singular that in a patriarchal saga where almost all the material is associated with specific sanctuaries, the greatest story of all should lack a clear connection with a shrine, and this must raise the suspicion that the original shrine is likely to have been Dan, and the original text will have read 'to the land of Hermon'; המריה with its orthodox Yahwist termination would be a suitable corruption. It is noticeable that a major function of the Abraham complex is the patriarch's journeys up and down Canaan, taking possession of the land in principle by building altars and receiving promises. 'Into the land of Canaan they came. And Abram passed through unto the place of Shechem . . . And he removed from thence unto the mountain on the east of Bethel . . . And Abram journeyed, going on still toward the South' (12:5-9). The impression is given that he was 'passing through' from north to south, that is from Dan to Beersheba, where he eventually settles. In ch.14 he leaves the oaks of Mamre in the south to rescue Lot, and pursues the kings similarly as far as Dan (14:14), before pressing on to Hobah. At 13:14 he is bidden to lift up his eyes and look, northward, southward, eastward and westward; all the land he sees is his. The same movement may be implied in ch.22 where he is told to go from Beersheba to the land of Moriah. The journey is said to have taken till the third day, but we have no idea of the speed or the number of hours travelled; and if it was originally a longer period it will have been shortened in any case to make Jerusalem possible.

7. *VT* 27 (1977), 361-374. Ulrichsen shows usefully that the word-order is not significant: both the order subject-predicate (like יהוה מלך, 93:1, etc.) and the order predicate-subject (like מלך אלהים, 47:8) are found with the ingressive meaning ('has become king'), and both are found with the durative meaning ('is king') in secular instances. In this way the articles 'Jahwäh malak' by L. Köhler in *VT* 3 (1953), 188f, and J. Ridderbos in *VT* 4 (1954), 87-89, can be answered.

8. Gunkel suggests that kings are intended but the word is deliberately not used; only Yahweh is King.

9. The same point would tell against Johnson's minimal change, 'with Him who is the God of Abraham,' and NEB's much bolder 'with the tents of Abraham.' NEB has two further emendations to the verse.

10. It is often claimed that Zion was thought of as high theologically, being the centre of the earth, etc; but 48 gives the impression of describing a real city, with its palaces and bulwarks.

11. Baal lives *bṣrrt ṣpn*, which can be rendered 'in the recesses of the north' (Driver) or 'the folds of Zaphon' ('les replis de Saphon,' Caquot).

12. The phrase is insoluble on the hypothesis that 48 was composed in Jerusalem. Delitzsch notes that the Temple stands on a hill to the north of the City of David and north-east of the Lower City, hence in an angle (ירכתי) of the north; but the phrases in v. 3b are in apposition as they stand, and no modern commentator has found this convincing. J. Morgenstern, 'Psalm 48,' *HUCA* 16 (1941), 1-95, suggested that the name Zaphon, originally applied to a mythological Akkadian mountain that was the north-west pillar of the universe, was later taken over by other peoples for their sacred mountains (e.g. at Ugarit), and so came to be used of Zion. He finds echoes of this in Isa. 14:12-15; Ezek. 28 and I Enoch 18:6-14; 24:2-25:5. But Isaiah's mountain of congregation has nothing to do with Zion, and the mountain in Ezekiel and

Enoch is in Eden, whence the tree of life will be transplanted to Zion (I Enoch 25:5). Kraus, *WI*, 201f, suggests that the notion is due to Jebusite influence; for which also no evidence is offered. A. Robinson, 'Zion and *Saphon* in Psalm xlviii.3,' *VT* 24 (1974), 118-123, follows Johnson, *SKAI* 77, 84f, in translating ירכתי as 'utmost peak,' for which there is no parallel; and he claims that Zaphon is the transcendental counterpart of Zion, although 'the city of the great king' is in apposition to it. The Danite hypothesis is the solution to an aporia.

13. Cf. de Vaux, 232-5.

14. L. Krinetzki, 'Zur Poetik und Exegese von Ps 48,' *BZ* 4 (1960), 70-97, thinks that the reference is to the preservation of Jerusalem in 701, but that the psalm was not composed till after the exile ('As we have heard . . .'). The psalm arises from the rebuilding of Jerusalem, and expresses eschatological hopes.

15. The Babylonian title is *šarru rabu*, which is closer to מלך רב in v. 2 than to מלך גדול in 47:2; but Sennacherib is המלך הגדול in II Kgs. 18.

16. NEB prefers the easier reading כרוח, with some MSS; but it is clumsier, as רוח is then the subject of the simile where כילדה was the object; and it is less pointful as God's power is no longer the issue.

17. *Ps. St.* II, 127; *PIW* I, 181.

18. NEB points with mappiq, which may be correct.

19. *EAEHL*, 320.

20. Almost all commentators (except Rogerson and McKay) assume that vv. 12f imply a formal procession, and this seems most likely to me; but it is possible that the psalmist is merely bidding the people to go informally and note the city's strength. But cf. below on 87:7.

21. *PIW* I, 182. My own solution is not so far from Mowinckel's.

22. *The Labyrinth*, 94ff.

23. 'Anstelle der Verwirrung, die ein schlafender Abschreiber angerichtet hat . . .' (p.378).

24. If the psalm were written for Jerusalem, we should have to choose between taking 'mountains' as a plural of majesty (Kraus) and a reference to the two mountains, Zion and Moriah, on which Jerusalem stands (Jacquet). There is no clear instance of a plural of majesty in the Korah psalms, and I know of no text in which Jerusalem is said to be built on two hills.

25. So Kraus, Eaton, Anderson and others, but without seeing the inference to a multiplicity of accepted shrines, and so an early date and a northern locus. Kirkpatrick, Kissane and others interpret as 'cities,' cf. Num. 24:5.

26. It is sometimes suggested that אם followed יאמר, and was omitted by the consonants being repeated (cf. NEB); but it should be noted that this is not supported by G's Μήτηρ Σιὼν ἐρεῖ ἄνθρωπος καὶ ἄνθρωπος ἐγενήθη ἐν αὐτῇ, where 'Mother' comes first, and the verb is active. It is not impossible that G preserves some correct readings—ἐρεῖ and διηγήσεται agree with my pointings—he copies correctly some words he does not understand; but the evidence of interpretations can leave us with no confidence.

27. If 87 were a Jerusalem psalm, it could also be dated between the resurgence of Babylon in the late seventh century and its fall to the Persians; but the tone is rather confident for such a low period in Judah's fortunes.

28. Cf. Jacquet, 'Pour un meilleur équilibre du stique, on transpose "avec" et "et".' But how did the original transposition arise?

29. Shalmeneser's Black Obelisk refers to twelve kings of the coast as part of the coalition he fought at Qarqar in 853, the leading powers being Syria under Hadadezer, Israel under Ahab, Hamath and Arpad. H. Cazelles takes Tyre and Sidon to be two of these ('The History of Israel in the Pre-exilic Period,' *Tradition and Interpretation*, 306), and some of the Philistine cities are likely to have been represented.

NOTES TO CHAPTER 7

1. 'Notes sur le Psaume XLIX,' *Studies on Psalms*, 137-172.

2. *Wisdom in Israel* (1970, ET London 1972), 203-6.

3. *PIW* II, 138.

4. *Ibid.*, 93f, 112ff, 138ff. This position is also taken by Kissane, and by Chr. Barth, *Die Errettung vom Tode in den individuellen Klage- und Dankliedern des Alten Testaments*, 158-161.

5. For a review see J.A. Emerton, 'Wisdom,' *Tradition and Interpretation*, ed. G.W. Anderson, 214-237.

6. *PIW* II, 94.

7. *Wisdom in Israel*, 204.

8. 141f.

9. Anderson comments, against the Wisdom Poem theory, 'nowhere else in the OT is there any reference to instruction being accompanied by musical instruments.' But Solomon's 'songs were a thousand and five' (I Kgs. 4:32).

10. Van der Ploeg, for example, suggests the meaning: (after death) they call a man's burial-field(s) by his name (cf. Gen. 3:19).

11. See also below, p. 193. K. Galling, 'Die Ausrufung des Namens als Rechtsakt in Israel,' *ThLZ* 81 (1956), col.67, is often cited in support of the standard view. But Galling's claim that II Sam. 5:9 and 12:26ff are by analogy with peaceful transactions lacks any plausible Israelite evidence.

12. See Eaton *ad loc.*

13. The root is familiar in this meaning to the Korahite poets. Kings' daughters were among Ahab's 'precious ones,' יקרותיך (45:9), and the 49th psalmist himself says the captives' ransom-price comes dear, יקר (v. 8).

14. BDB accepts the duplication, and speaks of metaplasm; NEB and others write שְׁתוּ.

15. Gunkel compares Isa. 22:24; but the meaning here is 'weight,' not

'glory'—'they shall hang on him all the weight of his father's house' (RSV), till the nail comes out of the wall.

16. *Sakrales Königtum im Alten Testament und in Judentum*, 75f, and 'Konungens vistelse i dödsriket' in *Svensk Exegetisk Aarsbok* 10 (1945), 66-81.

17. *The Cross in the Psalms*, 63f.

18. I.e., shall be heard, cf. below, pp. 203, 208.

19. See comments by J. Skinner, *Prophecy and Religion*, 237n, who leaves the question open.

20. So A. Weiser, *Das Buch Jeremia*; H. Cunliffe-Jones, *The Book of Jeremiah*, ad loc. Weiser carefully safeguards the prophet's reputation for courage.

21. *Esra und Nehemia*, 135-7.

22. *Studies in Divine Kingship in the Ancient Near East*, 176.

23. *KP*, 177-181.

24. *Die Errettung vom Tode . . .* , 82.

25. Baal II.viii.7-9, 'and go down to the house of seclusion (*ḫptt*) in the earth, be counted with them that go down into the earth (*tspr byrdm 'arṣ*).'

26. *Old Testament Theology*, I, 389.

27. Delitzsch's care in explaining the cohortative is typically impressive. The meaning, though not the tense, corresponds with G.

28. The grave will correspond to the pit of 88 and Lam. 3, and since it is only for a ritual period that he is 'buried,' we should have an explanation of his 'prolonging his days,' etc., in the following verses. His grave is with the wicked, which suggests that in Jerusalem the pit was used in which the bodies of criminals were thrown.

NOTES TO CHAPTER 8

1. The first half of the verse is duplicated in 97:2; the second is close to 85:13. For the translation 'go before thy face,' see below.

2. *Psalm 89*.

3. Gunkel marks as 4+4: 1, 2, 5-15, 47-51; as 3+3: 3, 4, 16-45, with the exception of v. 26 only, which with v. 46 he gives as 4+3.

4. Cf. Gunkel, 'nach der Hymnus Volk und Königtum in Macht und Ansehen stehen 16-19, während sie nach dem Klageliede aufs tiefste gesunken sind.'

5. It is often noted, e.g. by Ahlström, that v. 2, 'For I have said, Mercy shall be built for ever,' balances v. 1, 'I will sing of the mercies of the LORD for ever.'

6. Gunkel suggests that the author lived and worshipped on one of the two places, but did not see the force of Tabor as a preference.

7. Parallels with Jerusalem are obvious, since all the northern psalms which survive were integrated into Jerusalem worship. Probably the Asaph psalms

similarly represent a core of Shechem ('Salem,' 76:2) traditions which were taken over at Bethel; and parallels could be cited from the development of Christian uses in different areas of the mediaeval Church.

8. I have followed Eaton here against RV and RVmg.

9. 'The Fourth Book of the Psalter,' 285f.

10. *SKAI*, 97-103.

11. See especially 146f.

12. *KP*, 57, 121f.

13. *Ibid.* 121f.

14. In this way Eaton's second argument can be countered: King Jehoiachin is 'dethroned, hunted and virtually done to death,' but the speaker is his successor and uncle, Zedekiah, whose eleven-year reign allows respite for the extended, stately, rounded, etc. form of the psalm. For four hundred years the throne of David had descended in lineal succession from father to son, with the sole exception of Jehoiakim, who had been put in as king by Pharaoh instead of his brother Jehoahaz (II Kgs. 23:33f). Jehoiachin is therefore regarded as the true king, still alive in exile, and Zedekiah as his regent (II Kgs. 25:27; Jer. 22:24); like an Anglican bishop-in-exile from South Africa.

15. 77:15; 80:1; 81:5. On this hypothesis we should have to allow for considerable southern adaptations, e.g. 74:2; 76:1f; 79:1, 3, and aggressive redaction in 78:9, 67-72; but the difficulties are worse without it.

16. Ahlström, following Mowinckel, suggests that אזרחי means an aboriginal inhabitant (Exod. 12:48f), and indicates that the hymn originated in a Canaanite temple; even allowing for the primitive associations of the psalm, this seems unlikely.

17. LXX, Theodotion give the second person, 'thy mercies'; an easier reading which is to be resisted.

18. In the Ugaritic myth similarly, Baal terrifies the gods with his thunder on the completion of his temple (II.vii.29ff), and his mighty deeds in overcoming the sea-monster *ltn* are conceded even by Mot (I*.i.1ff, 27ff).

19. This point, the equivalence of Yam/Nahar with the various sea-monsters, is not entirely clear, but is the most probable interpretation of the texts. In V.iii.53ff Anat claims to have smitten Yam/Nahar and the monsters in succeeding lines; and although elsewhere it is Baal, not Anat, who does the smiting, it is probable that she was his aide in procuring the magic clubs—see below, p. 279.

20. J.B. Pritchard, *Ancient Near Eastern Texts*, 60-72.

21. See E.M. Wakeman, *God's Battle with the Monster*. I offer the following outline as my own suggestion. The Hebrews accepted a traditional geography in which the central feature was a fourfold spring in Eden, issuing in the rivers Gihon (Nile), Tigris, Euphrates and Pishon, the latter being the equivalent of the Greek Ocean. The last was the Sea, overthrown by Baal and Yahweh alike. Both Baal I*.i.1, 28 and Israelite tradition speak of a double serpent smitten by Baal/Yahweh, in almost identical terms (*ltn btn brḥ . . . btn 'qltn*; Isa.

27:1, לויתן נחש עקלתון ... לויתן נחש בריח—'leviathan the fleeing serpent, and leviathan the winding serpent'). Isa. 27 consists of two prose oracles in v. 1 and vv. 12f separated by a song. The prose oracles read, 'In that day the LORD with his sore and great and strong sword shall punish leviathan the fleeing serpent, and leviathan the winding serpent; and he shall slay the dragon that is in the sea . . . In that day from the river Euphrates to the brook of Egypt the LORD will thresh out the grain, and you will be gathered one by one, O people of Israel. And in that day a great trumpet shall be blown, and those who were lost in the land of Egypt will come and worship the LORD' (RSV). I suggest that the double serpent *ltn*/leviathan was a symbol for the double river Tigris/Euphrates, which from the point of view of a Syrian do 'flee,' i.e. flow away from him, and 'wind' in an impressive manner. In Isa. 27 the prose oracles, linked by 'in that day . . . ,' show first the river monsters of Assyria and then the sea-monster associated with Egypt being smitten by Yahweh; and then the Israelites being released from Assyria and Egypt, 'from the river Euphrates to the brook of Egypt.' The rivers that mattered in Ugarit were Tigris/Euphrates, and other names mentioned such as Shaliyat may refer to the Orontes, etc. Rahab is not mentioned, since the Nile was a long way away. Egypt was an ever-present neighbour to Israel, so a Hebrew name, Rahab (proud, insolent), was coined to symbolise the Nile monster; and eventually Israel had four monsters as counterparts to the four rivers—Rahab for the Nile (and so Egypt), the two Leviathans for Tigris/Euphrates (and so Assyria), and the 'dragon' (תנין) for the sea. *Ltn* was given a bogus Hebrew connection with לָוָה, interpreted as 'joined' (Gen. 29:34), and eventually was demythologised to be a mere real river-monster, the crocodile, in Job 41.

22. I have accepted RV here despite the difficulty of the balance of the line. Many commentators prefer to take 'great' at the beginning of the second half of the line with G; but this means reading רב or רב הוא and it then becomes difficult to see how the MT came by the harder present text.

23. Cf. J.B. Pritchard, *The Ancient Near East in Pictures*, 166ff; *The Ancient Near East: supplementary texts and pictures*, 352. The latter (no. 827) comes from Ugarit.

24. P. Humbert, *La 'terou'a.' Analyse d' un rite biblique.*

25. For the warlike significance of the horn, cf. I Kgs. 22:11; Deut. 33:17; and above pp. 94f on Ps. 44:5.

26. Johnson, *SKAI*, 100, Dahood, Anderson and others take ל to be emphatic, and translate, 'Our shield is indeed Yahweh.' Dahood offers as instances of the emphatic ל in the Psalter: 22:29; 25:14; 69:11, 23; 85:10; 101:5(sic); 109:16; 110:3; but all these passages yield good sense on other meanings of ל. The normal meaning is to be preferred here, and gives excellent sense, in line with the parallels cited.

27. *Ps. St.* III, 36ff.

28. Pp. 112-114.

29. G.W. Ahlström, 'An Israelite God Figurine from Hazor,' *Orientalia*

Suecana 19-20 (1970), 54-62, and 'An Israelite God Figurine, Once More,' *VT* 25 (1975), 106-9, replying to O. Keel, 'Das Vergraben der "Fremden Götter" in Genesis XXXV 4b,' *VT* 23 (1973), 306-336. Ahlström argues that the figure is a statue of El/Yahweh, or perhaps of Baal, buried by the Israelites under the floor of the high place.

30. Cf. also 44:3 from the Korah corpus, 'Neither did their own arm save them: But *thy right hand* and thine *arm*, and *the light of thy countenance*, Because thou hadst *favour* unto them.'

31. Deut. 33:18f merely implies that sacrifices were offered at Tabor by Zebulun, Issachar and neighbouring tribes. Kraus, *WI*, 165ff, makes extensive use of Ps. 68, but his grounds for associating the psalm with Tabor are not very convincing.

32. Ahlström's association of these texts with solar deities seems excessive.

33. Gunkel remarks with characteristic sympathy, 'verständlich aus einer Zeit, da die Erfüllung der Gottesworte den Frommen zweifelhaft zu werden begann.'

34. The Nile is often suggested, but does not make sense: Israel was to stretch from the Sea in the west to the River(s) in the east.

35. RV text is here to be preferred to the margin: II Sam. 7:16, on which the passage is based, has 'thy throne shall be established for ever.'

36. Kraus, following L. Rost, *Die Überlieferung von der Thronnachfolge Davids*, 47ff, takes 89 as a part of the tradition which has gone to make II Sam. 7. But the absence of important theological words like 'covenant' and 'swore' in the historical account make 89 look like the later version.

37. Eaton has suggested in an interesting article, 'The King as God's Witness,' *ASTI* (1970), 35f, that the reference here is to the king. I do not find the argument quite convincing: the parallels of kings with their thrones in the clouds are both cases of hybris (Isa. 14 and Ezek. 28).

38. The rhythm is defective here, and the form a hapax; but proposed emendations raise further problems,

39. Gunkel, *EP*, 92; 'The Fourth Book of the Psalter,' 288f.

NOTES TO CHAPTER 9

1. See the short discussion below, p. 247.

2. This proposal was initiated by R. Dussaud, *Les Découvertes de Ras Shamra et l'Ancien Testament*, 115f, and may be found in F. Hvidberg, *Weeping and Laughter in the Old Testament*, and elsewhere. For a discussion see A. Caquot et al., *Textes Ougaritiques*, I, 230f.

3. See Caquot, 85-92, who derives the name from '*nt*, springs. The association with wine may be inferred from the interpretation of the slaughter passage in

V.ii as the picking and pressing of the vintage.

4. The seven-year theory was proposed by C.H. Gordon in *Ugaritic Literature* (1949), 38-49, and defended in 'Sabbatical Year or Seasonal Pattern?,' *Orientalia* 22 (1953), 79-81; J.C. de Moor replies to his arguments in *The Seasonal Pattern in the Ugaritic Myth*, 32-4. There is only one passage in the myth which mentions a seven-year period, I.v. 8f.

5. 'The bulk relates to the phases in the year of the Syrian peasant' (*The Legacy of Canaan*, 11).

6. The second edition of Driver's book, edited by J.C.L. Gibson, reverses this decision.

7. In V.iii.53ff Anat refers at length to her victory over Yam, Nahar, the twisting serpent, the seven-headed monster, and other marine deities; and apparently at the beginning of V.iv Baal is included in this victory. According to I*.i.1ff, 27ff, it is Baal and not Anat who is said to have smitten Ltn, the twisting serpent and the seven-headed monster. How are these data to be reconciled with the victory of Baal over Yam and Nahar in III? Much of II is missing, and the course of the story elsewhere would suggest that Anat was responsible for persuading Kothar/Khasis to provide the magic clubs with which Baal overthrew the sea-powers. In this way III could precede V, and we should be able to combine the statements into a harmonious whole.

8. Cf. de Moor, 56-9. At Ugarit Tishri was called 'First of the Wine'; on the first day a bunch of grapes was offered to El, and during the following seven-day feast the new wine was offered to Baal, and wine was distributed among the people. The king sacrificed 'on the roof on which there are four by four dwellings of cut foliage' (*CTA* 35.50f). The parallels with Israelite Tabernacles are obvious. The year was counted from the equinox.

9. Gray, 23-9, takes Baal's victory to be the ebbing of the winter sea and river floods which threaten Ugarit. In so doing he draws close to the climatic myth. Cf. Caquot, 116.

10. I follow Caquot's interpretation here, which seems to make good sense of the sequence.

11. The window remains something of a problem. De Moor took it to symbolise the latter rains; Caquot to signify that in the thunder and rain Baal exhausts himself, and so is swallowed into the underworld.

12. Calves are in fact born in different seasons in the Levant, but those thrive most which are born in Nov.-Jan., or a little later; see Dalman I, 170; de Moor, 80, 123, 189.

13. De Moor, 56f, cites the passage about the minstrel in *CTA* 17:VI.28-33.

14. The suggestion about the rutting-fight is my own, and I hope to expound it shortly.

BIBLIOGRAPHY

Commentaries referred to throughout the book by the names of their authors are shown in capitals. Where a book is cited a number of times in the text, I have used an abbreviation of its title, which is given here in brackets following the entry. I have not thought it necessary to repeat a standard list of abbreviations.

Abba, R. 'Priests and Levites in Deuteronomy,' *VT* 27 (1977), 257-67.

Abel, F.M. *Géographie de la Palestine*, I-II (Paris, 1933-38).

Aharoni, Y. *The Land of the Bible* (2nd edn. ET London 1979).

Ahlström, G.W. *Psalm 89* (Lund 1959).

Ahlström, G.W. 'An Israelite God Figurine from Hazor,' *Orientalia Suecana* 19-20 (1970-1), 56-62.

Ahlström, G.W. 'An Israelite God Figurine, Once More,' *VT* 25 (1975) 106-9.

Alt, A. *Kleine Schriften*, II (Munich 1953).

ANDERSON, A.A. *The Book of Psalms*, I-II (New Century Bible, London 1972).

Anderson, G.W., ed. *Tradition and Interpretation* (Oxford 1979). (= *T.& I.*)

Arens, A. *Die Psalmen im Gottesdienst des Alten Bundes* (Trier 1961).

Barnes, W.E. *The Psalms*, I-II (Westminster Commentary, London 1931).

Barth, Chr. *Die Errettung vom Tode in den individuellen Klage- und Dankliedern des Alten Testaments* (Zollikon 1947).

Baumann, E. 'Struktur-Untersuchungen in Psalter II,' *ZAW* 62 (1950), 132-6.

Beyerlin, W. *Origins and History of the Oldest Sinaitic Tradition (Herkunft und Geschichte der ältesten Sinaitradition*, 1961 = ET, Oxford 1966).

Biran, A. 'Dan, Tel,' in M. Avi-Yonah ed., *Encyclopaedia of Archaeological Excavations in the Holy Land* (Oxford 1975).

Biran, A. 'Dan, Tel,' *Israel Exploration Journal* 24 (1974), 262-4; 26 (1976), 202-4; 27 (1977), 242-6; 28 (1978), 268-70.

Biran, A. 'Dan, Tel,' *Biblical Archeologist* 43.3 (1980), 168-182.

Briggs, C.A. *A critical and exegetical Commentary on the Book of Psalms*, I-II (ICC, Edinburgh 1906-7).

Brockington, C.H. *The Hebrew Text of the Old Testament, The Readings adopted by the Translators of the NEB* (Oxford & Cambridge 1973).

Brown, F., Driver, S.R. and Briggs, C.A. *Hebrew-English Lexicon of the Old Testament* (Oxford 1907, corr. 1966). (= BDB)

Burney, C.F. *The Book of Judges* (2nd edn. London 1920).

Buss, M.J. 'The Psalms of Asaph and Korah,' *JBL* 82 (1963), 381-92.

Caquot, A., Sznycer, M. and Herdner, A. *Textes Ougaritiques*, I (Paris 1974).

(= Caquot, *TO*)

Cazelles, H. 'The History of Israel in the Pre-exilic Period,' in G.W. Anderson, ed., *T.& I.*, 274-319.

Childs, B.S. *Exodus* (London 1974).

Clements, R.E. *God and Temple* (Oxford 1965).

Clements, R.E. 'Pentateuchal Problems,' in G.W. Anderson, ed., *T.& I.*, 96-104.

Clines, D.J.A., 'The Evidence for an Autumnal New Year in Pre-Exilic Israel Reconsidered,' *JBL* 93 (1974), 22-40.

Cody, A. *History of Old Testament Priesthood* (AB 35, Rome 1969).

Cunliffe-Jones, H. *The Book of Jeremiah* (London 1960).

DAHOOD, M. *Psalms*, I-III (Anchor Bible, Garden City, New York, 1965-70).

Dalman, G.H. *Arbeit und Sitte in Palästina*, I-VIII (Gütersloh 1928).

Debus, J. *Die Sünde Jerobeams* (Göttingen 1967).

DELITZSCH, F. *Biblical Commentary on the Psalms*, I-III (4th edn. = ET, Edinburgh 1887-8).

Dietrich, E.L. שוב שבות (Giessen 1925).

Dinsmoor, W.B. *The Architecture of Ancient Greece* (3rd edn. London 1950).

Driver, G.R. *Canaanite Myths and Legends* (Edinburgh 1956; 2nd edn., ed. J.C.L. Gibson, 1977).

DUHM, B. *Die Psalmen* (Freiburg 1899).

Dussaud, R. *Les Découvertes de Ras Shamra et l'Ancien Testament* (2nd edn. Paris 1941).

EATON, J.H. *Psalms* (Torch Bible, London 1967).

Eaton, J.H. 'The King as God's Witness,' *ASTI* 7 (1970), 25-40.

Eaton, J.H. *Kingship and the Psalms* (Studies in Biblical Theology, II.32, London 1976).

Eaton, J.H. 'The Psalms and Israelite Worship,' in G.W. Anderson, ed., *T.& I.*, 238-73.

Eerdmans, B.D. *The Hebrew Book of Psalms* (OTS 4, Leiden 1947).

Eichrodt, W. *Ezekiel* (*Der Prophet Hesekiel*, ATD 22,1965-6 = ET London 1970).

Eissfeldt, O. *The Old Testament, An Introduction* (3rd edn. = ET Oxford 1965).

Elliger, K. 'Ephod und Choschen,' *VT* 8 (1958), 19-35.

Emerton, J.A. 'Priests and Levites in Deuteronomy,' *VT* 12 (1962), 128-38.

Emerton, J.A. 'Wisdom,' in G.W. Anderson, ed., *T.& I.*, 214-37.

Engnell, I. *Studies in Divine Kingship in the Ancient Near East* (Uppsala 1943).

Engnell, I. *Critical essays on the Old Testament* (ET London 1970).

Ewald, G.H.A. von *Commentary on the Psalms*, I-II (1866 = ET London 1880).

Fitzmyer, J.A. *The Aramaic Inscriptions from Sefire* (Rome 1967).

Galling, K. 'Die Ausrufung des Namens als Rechtsakt in Israel,' *ThLZ* 81 (1956), 65-70.

Gordon, C.H. *Ugaritic Literature* (Rome 1949).

Gordon, C.H. 'Sabbatical Year or Seasonal Pattern,' *Orientalia* 22 (1953), 79-81.

Goulder, M.D. 'The Fourth Book of the Psalter,' *JTS* 26 (1975), 269-89.

Goulder, M.D. *The Evangelists' Calendar* (London 1978).

Gray, G.B. *The Book of Isaiah, I-XXXIX* (ICC, Edinburgh, 1912).

Gray, J. *The Legacy of Canaan* (2nd edn. Leiden 1965).

Gray, J. 'Recent Archaeological Discoveries,' in G.W. Anderson, *T.& I.*, 65-95.

Gunkel, H. 'Psalmen,' *Die Religion in Geschichte und Gegenwart* (1st edn. Tübingen 1909-1913).

Gunkel, H. *Ausgewählte Psalmen* (4th edn. Göttingen 1917).

GUNKEL, H. *Die Psalmen* (Göttinger Handkommentar zum AT, 4th edn. 1929).

Gunkel, H. and Begrich, J. *Einleitung in die Psalmen* (Göttinger Handkommentar zum AT, 1933) (= *EP*).

Gunneweg, A.H.J. *Leviten und Priester* (FRLANT 89, Göttingen 1965).

Gyllenberg, R. 'Die Bedeutung des Wortes Selah,' *ZAW* 58 (1940-1), 153-6.

Haran, M. *Temples and Temple Service in Ancient Israel* (Oxford 1978).

Hauret, Ch. 'Aux origines du sacerdoce Danite,' in *Mélanges bibliques redigés en l'honneur de André Robert* (Paris 1958).

Heinemann, J. 'The Triennial Lectionary Cycle,' *JJS* 19 (1968), 41ff.

Herdner, A. *Corpus des tablettes alphabétiques découvertes à Ras Shamra-Ugarit de 1929 à 1939* (Paris 1963).

Hitzig, F. *Die Psalmen*, I-II (Leipzig/Heidelberg 1863-5).

Horton, F.L. *The Melchizedek Tradition* (Cambridge 1976).

Humbert, P. *La 'terou'a.' Analyse d'un rite biblique* (Neuchâtel 1946).

Hvidberg, F. *Weeping and Laughter in the Old Testament* (1938 = ET Leiden 1962).

JACQUET, L. *Les Psaumes et le coeur de l'homme*, I-III (Gembloux 1975-8).

Jastrow, M. *A Dictionary of the Targumim, the Talmud Babli and Yerushalmi, and the Midrashic Literature* (1903, r.p. New York 1975).

Johnson, A.R. 'The Role of the King in the Jerusalem Cultus,' in S.H. Hooke ed., *The Labyrinth* (London 1935), 73-111.

Johnson, A.R. *The Cultic Prophet in Ancient Israel* (Cardiff 1944) (= *CPAI*).

Johnson, A.R. *Sacral Kingship in Ancient Israel* (Cardiff 1955) (= *SKAI*).

Johnson, A.R. *The Cultic Prophet in Israel's Psalmody* (Cardiff 1979) (= *CPIP*).

Jones, E. *The Cross in the Psalms* (London 1963).

Kahle, P. *The Cairo Geniza* (2nd edn. Oxford 1959).

Kaiser, O. *Isaiah 1-12* (ATD 2nd edn. 1963 = ET London 1972).

Kapelrud, A.S. *The Violent Goddess* (Oslo 1969).

Keel, O. 'Das Vergraben der "Fremden Götter" in Genesis XXXV 4b,' *VT* 23 (1973), 303-36.

Kennett, R.H. 'The Origin of the Aaronite Priesthood,' *JTS* 6 (1905), 161-186.

KIRKPATRICK, A.F. *The Book of Psalms*, I-III (The Cambridge Bible for Schools and Colleges, Cambridge 1891).

KISSANE, E.J. The Book of Psalms, I-II (Dublin 1953-4).

Köhler, L. 'Jahwäh malak,' *VT* 3 (1953), 188f.

KRAUS, H.-J. Psalmen, I-II (BKAT, 5th edn. Neukirchen-Vluyn 1978).

Kraus, H.-J. *Worship in Israel (Gottesdienst in Israel* 2nd edn. 1962 = ET Oxford 1966) (= *WI*).

Krinetzki, L. 'Zur Poetik und Exegese von Ps. 48,' *BZ* 4 (1960), 70-97.

Landsberger, B. *Der kultische Kalender der Babylonier und Assyrer* (Leipzig 1915).

Lehming, S. 'Versuch zu Exod. XXXII,' *VT* 10 (1960), 16-50.

Lehming, S. 'Versuch zu Num. XVI,' *ZAW* 74 (1962), 291-321.

Lindblom, J. 'Lot-casting in the Old Testament,' *VT* 12 (1962), 164-78.

Lindblom, J. *Prophecy in Ancient Israel* (Oxford 1962).

Lipiński, E. *La Royauté de Yahwé dans la poésie et le culte de l'ancien Israel* (Brussels 1965).

Lipiński, E. *Le Poème royal du Psaume LXXXIX 1-5, 20-38* (Cahiers de la Revue Biblique, Paris 1967).

May, H.G. *Oxford Bible Atlas* (2nd edn. Oxford 1974).

Möhlenbrink, K. 'Die levitische Ueberlieferungen des Alten Testaments,' *ZAW* 52 (1934), 184-231.

Moor, J.C. de *The Seasonal Pattern in the Ugaritic Myth of Ba'lu* (Kevelaer 1971).

Moore, G.F. *Judaism in the first centuries of the Christian era, the Age of the Tannaim* (Harvard 1927).

Morgenstern, J. 'Psalm 48,' *HUCA* 16 (1941), 1-95.

MOWINCKEL, S. *Psalmenstudien* I-VI (Kristiania 1921-4) (= *Ps. St.*).

MOWINCKEL, S. *The Psalms in Israel's Worship, I-II (Offersang og Sangoffer* rev. = ET Oxford 1962) (= *PIW*).

Mowinckel, S. 'Drive and/or Ride in the O.T.,' *VT* 12 (1962), 278-99.

Mulder, J.S.M. *Studies on Psalm 45* (Witsiers 1972).

Murtonen, A. 'Some Thoughts on Jg. xvii sq.,' *VT* 1 (1951), 232f.

North, F.S. 'Aaron's Rise in Prestige,' *ZAW* 66 (1954), 191-9.

Noth, M. *Das System der Zwölf Stämme Israels* (Stuttgart 1930).

Noth, M. *Das Buch Josua* (HAT, 2nd edn. Tübingen 1953).

Noth, M. *Exodus* (ATD 1959 = ET London 1962).

Noth, M. 'The Background of Judges 17-18,' in B.W. Anderson and W. Harrelson, eds., *Israel's Prophetic Heritage* (New York 1962).

Noth, M. *Numbers* (ATD 1966 = ET 1968).

Noth, M. *I Könige* (BKAT, Neukirchen-Vluyn 1968).

Noth, M. *A History of Pentateuchal Traditions (Ueberlieferungsgeschichte des Pentateuchs* 1948 = ET, London 1972).

Oesterley, W.O.E. *The Psalms* (London 1939).

Patton, J.H. *Canaanite Parallels in the Book of Psalms* (Baltimore 1944).

PETERS, J.P. *The Psalms as Liturgies* (London 1922).

Ploeg, J. van der 'Notes sur le Psaume XLIX,' in B. Gemser *et al.*, eds., *Studies on Psalms* (OTS, Leiden 1963).

Pritchard, J.B. *Ancient Near Eastern Texts relating to the Old Testament* (3rd edn. + Suppl., Princeton 1950) (= *ANET*).

Pritchard, J.B. *The Ancient Near East in Pictures* (Princeton 1954).

Pritchard, J.B. *The Ancient Near East: supplementary texts and pictures* (Princeton 1969).

Rad, G. von. *Das Formgeschichtliche Problem des Hexateuchs* (Stuttgart 1938).

Rad, G. von. *Genesis* (ATD 1956 = ET London 1961).

Rad, G. von. *Old Testament Theology*, I-II (2nd edn. = Edinburgh 1962).

Rad, G. von. *Deuteronomy* (ATD 1964 = ET London 1966).

Rad, G. von. *Wisdom in Israel* (1970 = ET London 1972).

Reymond, P. *L'Eau, sa vie et sa signification dans l'A.T.* (*VT* Suppl. 6, Leiden 1958).

Ridderbos, J. 'Jahwäh malak,' *VT* 4 (1954), 87-9.

Robinson, A. 'Zion and *Saphon* in Psalm xlviii 3,' *VT* 24 (1974), 118-23.

ROGERSON, J.W. and McKAY, J.W. *Psalms*, I-III (The Cambridge Bible Commentary on NEB, Cambridge 1977).

Rosenberg, R.A. 'The God Sedeq,' *HUCA* 36 (1965), 161-7.

Rost, L. *Die Ueberlieferung von der Thronnachfolge Davids* (BWANT 3, Stuttgart 1926).

Rowley, H.H. 'Zadok and Nehushtan,' *JBL* 58 (1939), 113-41.

Rudolph, W. *Der Elohist von Exodus bis Josua* (BZAW 68, Berlin 1938).

Rudolph, W. *Esra und Nehemia* (HAT, Tübingen 1949).

Rudolph, W. *Chronikbücher* (HAT, Tübingen 1955).

Schmid, H. 'Jahwe und die Kulttraditionen von Jerusalem,' *ZAW* 68 (1955), 168-197.

Schmidt, H. *Die Psalmen* (HAT, Tübingen 1934).

Scholem, G.G. *On the Kabbalah and its Symbolism* (1960 = ET New York 1965).

Schürer, E. *The History of the Jewish People in the Age of Jesus Christ*, II (revised ed., Edinburgh 1979).

Segal, J.B. 'Intercalation and the Hebrew Calendar,' *VT* 7 (1957), 250-307.

Shiloh, Y. *The Proto-Aeolic Capital and Israelite Ashlar Masonry* (Qedem 11, Jerusalem 1979).

Simpson, C.A. *Composition of the Book of Judges* (Oxford 1957).

Skinner, J. *Prophecy and Religion* (Cambridge 1922).

Smith, G. Adam. *The Historical Geography of the Holy Land* (25th edn. London 1931).

Snaith, N.H. *Hymns of the Temple* (London 1951).

Snaith, N.H. 'Selah,' *VT* 2 (1952), 43-56.

Stieb, R. 'Die Versdubletten des Psalters,' *ZAW* 57 (1939), 104ff; 58 (1940-1),

317f.

Strack, H.L. and Billerbeck, P. *Kommentar zum Neuen Testament aus Talmud und Midrash*, I (Munich 1926).

Talmon, S. 'Divergences in Calendar-Reckoning in Ephraim and Judah,' *VT* 8 (1958), 48-74.

Ulrichsen, J. '*Jhwh mālak*,' *VT* 27 (1977), 361-74.

Valentin, H. *Aaron* (OBO 18, Freiburg/Göttingen 1978).

Vaughan, P. *The Meaning of 'Bāmâ' in the Old Testament* (Cambridge 1974).

Vaux, R. de. *Ancient Israel, Its Life and Institutions* (ET 2nd edn. 1965).

Volz, P. *Das Neujahrsfest Jahwes* (Tübingen 1912).

Waddy, S. *Homes of the Psalms* (London 1928).

Wakeman, E.M. *God's Battle with the Monster* (Leiden 1973).

Waldman, N.M. 'Some Notes on Mal. 3:6, 3:13 and Psalm 42:11,' *JBL* 93 (1974), 548.

Wanke, G. *Die Zionstheologie der Korachiten* (BZAW 97, Berlin 1966).

WEISER, A. *The Psalms* (ATD 5th edn. 1959 = ET London 1962).

Weiser, A. *Das Buch Jeremia* (ATD 5th edn. Göttingen 1966).

Wellhausen, J. *Prolegomena to the History of Israel* (ET Edinburgh 1885).

Wellhausen, J. *The Book of Psalms* (Baltimore/London 1895).

Wellhausen, J. *Die Composition des Hexateuchs* (3rd edn. Berlin 1899).

Westermann, C. *Lob und Klage in den Psalmen* (= *Das Loben Gottes in den Psalmen*, rev., 5th edn. Göttingen 1977).

Widengren, G. 'Konungens vistelse i dödsriket,' *SEA* 10 (1945), 66-81.

Widengren, G. *Sakrales Königtum im Alten Testament und in Judentum* (Stuttgart 1955).

Wildberger, H. *Jesaja*, I-II (BKAT, Neukirchen-Vluyn 1972/8).

Wolff, H.W. *Hosea* (BKAT, Neukirchen-Vluyn 1961).

Wright, G.E. 'The Levïtes in Deuteronomy,' *VT* 4 (1954), 325-30.

Yadin, Y. 'Excavations at Hazor,' *IEJ* 9 (1959), 79ff.

Ziegler, J. 'Die Hilfe Gottes am Morgen,' in H. Junker, ed., *Alttestamentliche Studien F. Nötscher . . . gewidmet* (Bonn 1950).

Zimmerli, W. *Erkenntnis Gottes nach dem Buche Ezechiel* (ATANT, Zürich 1954).

INDEXES

INDEX OF PASSAGE REFERENCES

INDEX OF NAMES

* * *